The New XFree86

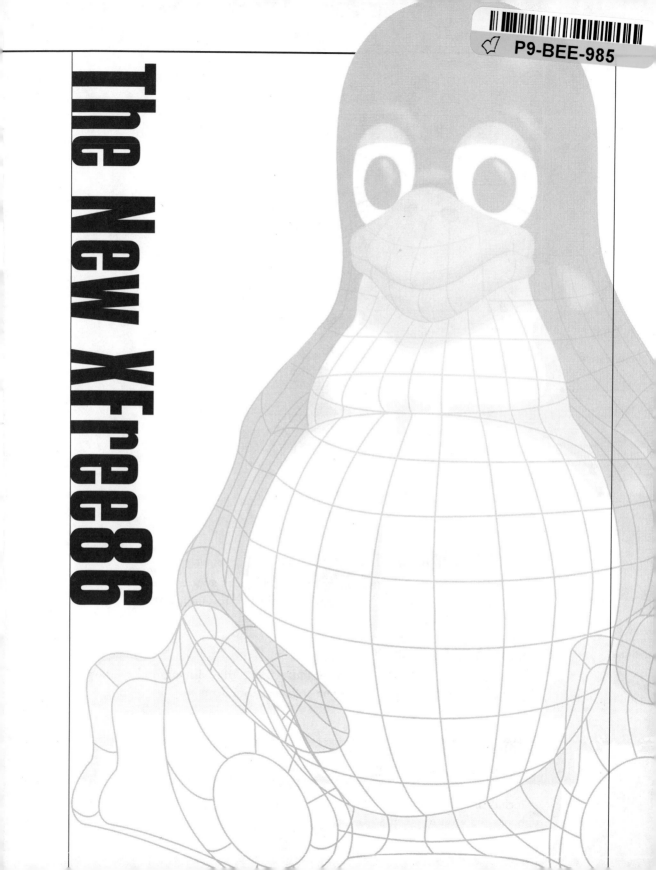

Check the Web for Updates

To check for updates or corrections relevant to this book and/or CD-ROM, visit our updates page on the Web at **http://www.prima-tech.com/updates**.

Send Us Your Comments

To comment on this book or any other PRIMA TECH title, visit our reader response page on the Web at **http://www.prima-tech.com/comments**.

How to Order

For information on quantity discounts, contact the publisher: Prima Publishing, P.O. Box 1260BK, Rocklin, CA 95677-1260; (916) 787-7000. On your letterhead, include information concerning the intended use of the books and the number of books you want to purchase.

The New XFree86

Bill Ball

PRIMA
TECH

A Division of Prima Publishing

A Division of Prima Publishing

Prima Publishing and colophon are registered trademarks of Prima Communications, Inc. PRIMA TECH is a trademark of Prima Communications, Inc., Roseville, California 95661.

XFree86™ is pending trademark registration by The XFree86 Project, Inc.

Important: Prima Publishing cannot provide software support. Please contact the appropriate software manufacturer's technical support line or Web site for assistance.

Prima Publishing and the author have attempted throughout this book to distinguish proprietary trademarks from descriptive terms by following the capitalization style used by the manufacturer.

Information contained in this book has been obtained by Prima Publishing from sources believed to be reliable. However, because of the possibility of human or mechanical error by our sources, Prima Publishing, or others, the Publisher does not guarantee the accuracy, adequacy, or completeness of any information and is not responsible for any errors or omissions or the results obtained from use of such information. Readers should be particularly aware of the fact that the Internet is an ever-changing entity. Some facts may have changed since this book went to press.

ISBN: 0-7615-3152-1
Library of Congress Catalog Card Number: 00-110450
Printed in the United States of America

00 01 02 03 04 BB 10 9 8 7 6 5 4 3 2 1

Publisher
Stacy L. Hiquet

Associate Marketing Manager
Heather Buzzingham

Managing Editor
Sandy Doell

Acquisitions Editor
Lynette Quinn

Project Editor
Elizabeth A. Agostinelli

Technical Reviewer
Brandon Palmer

Copy Editor
Andy O. Saff

Interior Layout
Marian Hartsough

Cover Design
Prima Design Team

Indexer
Katherine Stimson

Proofreader
Mitzi G. Foster

To Cathy,
who knows how to peer
into the window of my soul.

Acknowledgments

Without a doubt, this book would not have been possible without the support and assistance of my career mentor, Lynette Quinn. Many thanks to everyone at Prima, especially Andrew Ossian Saff and Elizabeth Agostinelli for their efforts to make this book the best product on the market. Many thanks to Brandon Palmer for the technical edits. Also, to those programmers, such as Jim Gettys and others of the original X and past and current XFree86 Project releases, many thanks for porting, improving, and distributing the best networking graphical interface in the world. Thanks are also due to Richard M. Stallman for his GNU GPL, and to Linus B. Torvalds for bringing Linux into the world as free software.

BILL BALL is the best-selling author of a dozen books about Linux, including such titles as *Linux for Your Laptop*. He has been a fan of Linux since kernel 0.99, and first started using XFree86 in 1994, albeit in 16 colors. He is also an active member of the Northern Virginia Linux Users Group (NOVALUG) and lives in the Shirlington area of Arlington, Virginia.

Contents at a Glance

Contents

Part II
Using the X Window System 99

Chapter 6
Starting X11 101

Chapter 7
First Steps with X11 121

Chapter 8
Using X11 Clients 137

Chapter 9
X11 on a Network 149

Chapter 10
XFree86 X11 Clients 163

Chapter 11
Popular X11 Clients 177

Chapter 12
X11 Multimedia Clients. 205

Chapter 13
Popular X11 Games 229

Part III
Managing the X Window System 257

Chapter 14
Configuring X11 Input 259

Part IV
X11 Programming 327

Chapter 17
Building X11 329

Chapter 18
Basic X11 Programming 341

Chapter 19
X11 Programming Toolkits Overview 357

Chapter 20
Using LessTif and Open Motif 371

Chapter 21
Using Qt and KDE 385

Welcome to the new XFree86! This book is for readers who want to learn more about the X Window system, a fascinating and capable networking graphic interface for UNIX, Linux, and other operating systems. This book is all about helping you, the reader. You'll better understand how the X Window system (also known as X11) and the XFree86 Project, Inc., came into being. You'll also learn how to install and configure a version for your computer, and see how to use X11, or X, more efficiently. If you take the plunge, later chapters will show you how to compile and write programs for X, starting with the basics, and then using today's high-level toolkits.

There's a growing interest today in using and programming for X. One of the reasons for this interest is the explosive growth in the installed user base of operating systems such as Linux and FreeBSD. Another is that as computer software and hardware companies search for new ways to bring more power to the desktop or embedded systems by introducing ever faster and more capable computers, they are discovering that they no longer have to be held hostage to a monopolistic software industry; there are better, faster, and royalty- and license-free solutions for crafting better, faster, and more efficient human-and-computer interfaces. One of these solutions is X. This book is about one of the most popular versions of X, XFree86 from the XFree86 Project, Inc. XFree86 is one of the reasons for this book, and this book is being written partially to celebrate the latest version of XFree86, version 4, which was two years in the making.

The main focus of this book is using XFree86 for Linux on Intel-based PCs. However, you'll find that no matter what hardware platform you use for X, the majority of techniques, tips, and tricks outlined here can apply to your environment. You'll also find coverage of other operating systems, such as BSD UNIX and its variants, OpenBSD and FreeBSD. If you're an Apple Macintosh user, you'll also learn about configuring and using X on that platform. In other words, I hope to present enough information in this book to help more than just Linux PC users.

It is important to learn about X and how to use it, for a number of reasons. One reason is to broaden your knowledge of computer operating system interfaces and networking. Another is to become aware of cheaper, faster, and more secure graphical interface and network alternatives that exist despite the current monopolistic software industry. X can be a perfect solution, as you can use it to develop commercial products and environments without the worry of royalties or paid licensing. Yet another reason to learn about X is that although it is not as mature as UNIX, its architecture is tested, stable, and proven.

What Is X?

To quote the rather modest X man page, "The X Window System is a network transparent window system which runs on a wide range of computing and graphics machines." More importantly, you should know that X is *not* X Windows! X should be referred to as *X*; *X Window system*; *X Version 11*; *X Window System, Version 11*; or *X11*. Some people also refer to X by its latest major revision number, *X11R6*.

X is a protocol that defines how programs, known as *clients,* interact with another program, known as a *server,* possibly running on a remote computer. The server handles how objects are drawn on displays by providing the specific device drivers. This relationship of device-independence allows software developers to concentrate on writing clients that will run on nearly any computer platform; moving, or *porting* an X11 client to a different workstation, such as running a client from an Intel-based PC to a Sun Microsystems SPARC workstation, can be as easy as a simple recompile of the source.

Whatever you call X, don't call it X Windows! At best, any UNIX gurus within earshot will immediately labeled you as either as a "suit" or "newbie." At the worst, you'll be termed a "luser," and if you are on a network with a BOFH (Bastard Operator from Hell), you could lose your username, home directory, or both.

A Short History

Modest definitions aside, X is a sophisticated networking graphical interface that has been in use for nearly 20 years. Maturing along with UNIX, development of X was started in 1982 as part of an effort by the Massachusetts Institute of Technology (MIT) and the Digital Equipment Corporation (DEC) to create a *Distributed Computing Environment* (DCE). The effort, named Project Athena, resulted in a capable environment that quickly grew to support more than 10,000 users on over a 1,000 workstations. Several versions followed rapidly, including X10, then X11, released in 1988. Other successful elements of the project are still in use today, such as the Kerberos authentication system.

Since 1987, X11 has gone through at least six major revisions and five minor revisions. At the time of this writing, the current X curator, the X Consortium (**http://www.x.org**), was about to introduce X11R6.5. Although you'll learn about some of the new features of X11R6.5, this book focuses on X11R6.4, which forms the base for the XFree86 Project's XFree86 X11 distribution.

What's New?

As mentioned, a new minor revision of X was introduced as this book was developed. However, it can be important to understand the lineage of features added to X over the years, as some computer manufacturers are slow to jump to the latest version of X (because the previous version works so well).

New developments include better handling of fonts, compressed audio and video data streams, internationalization, and incorporation of support for more input devices, such as keyboards, graphics tablets, and pointing devices.

Why Use X?

This section introduces general features of X, and presents some rationale for using this windowing system instead of other commercial operating systems that initially could only mimic X. Originally thought to be the high-end windowing system for premium workstations and systems, X has experienced a huge resurgence in popularity, as free software and operating systems rise in popularity with the Open Source movement. Today's users of X are more likely to be running Linux or FreeBSD on a $1,500 home PC, rather than HP/UX or Solaris on an $20,000 workstation.

General Features of X

One of X's most impressive features is the system's portability. Originally developed from research by Xerox and refined by researchers at MIT, X builds on the capabilities of its host operating system. Although best known as a graphical network interface for UNIX, X has been ported to many different computer platforms and operating systems, ranging from mainframes to personal digital assistants (PDAs).

X appeals to researchers, administrators, and users for a number of reasons. Although the ebb and flow or pendular momentum in the computer industry swings between centralized or distributed computer systems (systems that either depend on one large system or that derive power and flexibility from the combination of many systems), X has provided both! You can use X as a standalone system on a large network or launch clients from a remote server.

Taken to an extreme, this means that you can sit at one display somewhere in North America, for example, and launch clients on a workstation or server on the other side of the world. The clients may be viewed or used on either terminal. X also works over slower networks, such as dial-up lines via a serial port.

The intrinsic networking features of X have added to its appeal. Another strength could also be viewed as a weakness: X, as a standard, does not enforce graphics standards. This means that the developer is free to create clients with a variety of interfaces. As a developer, you are given the basic function calls and libraries to craft programs, but so-called "standards" of an interface are left up to you and your choice of software toolkit, window manager, or operating system.

Other features include font manipulation, use of color, use of *resources* (or configuration files for system or client-specific tweaks), example source code, many included clients, standard command-line interfaces, geometry settings (for sizing and placement of windows), and general graphics device–independence.

Another appeal of X is that, like UNIX, the system enables you to activate or update multiple windows at same time. Basic copy-and-paste operations are supported between windows and clients, and processes can also share data.

Finally, one of best reasons for the popularity of X is its licensing. A split (or *fork*) in its development was threatened in early 1998, when the then-curators of X, The Open Group (TOG), changed X's copyright and announced prohibitively expensive monetary licensing for "official" development and distribution of X. Fortunately, cooler heads prevailed, the copyright of X11R6.4 reverted to its original free version, the licensing was withdrawn, and stewardship of X was transferred to another Open Group organization, the X Consortium.

You are free to develop and distribute X11 clients without paying royalties. You are also free to develop and distribute your own version of X! The pertinent portion of the licensing (found under the `/usr/X11R6/lib/X11/doc` directory after you install XFree86's X11), is as follows:

Copyright ©1996 X Consortium

Permission is hereby granted, free of charge, to any person obtaining a copy of this software and associated documentation files (the "Software"), to deal in the Software without restriction, including without limitation the rights to use, copy, modify, merge, publish, distribute, sublicense, and/or sell copies of the Software, and to permit persons to whom the Software is furnished to do so, subject to the following conditions:

The above copyright notice and this permission notice shall be included in all copies or substantial portions of the Software.

THE SOFTWARE IS PROVIDED "AS IS", WITHOUT WARRANTY OF ANY KIND, EXPRESS OR IMPLIED, INCLUDING BUT NOT LIMITED TO THE WARRANTIES OF MERCHANTABILITY, FITNESS FOR A PARTICULAR PURPOSE AND NONINFRINGEMENT. IN NO EVENT SHALL THE X CONSORTIUM BE LIABLE FOR ANY CLAIM, DAMAGES OR OTHER LIABILITY, WHETHER IN AN ACTION OF CONTRACT, TORT OR OTHERWISE, ARISING FROM, OUT OF OR IN CONNECTION WITH THE SOFTWARE OR THE USE OR OTHER DEALINGS IN THE SOFTWARE.

Except as contained in this notice, the name of the X Consortium shall not be used in advertising or otherwise to promote the sale, use or other dealings in this Software without prior written authorization from the X Consortium.

X Window System is a trademark of X Consortium, Inc.

Feature Overview of the New XFree86

This book is about the version of X distributed by the XFree86 Project, Inc., and known as XFree86. Why XFree86? Because this collection of software provides X, is free, and is focused on Intel-based PC platforms. This does not mean that you won't find versions for computer platforms using the Motorola PowerPC or Compaq Alpha CPUs. Again, because X is distributed with source code and is written in C, it has been converted, or *ported,* to numerous different architectures. This means that you'll find a version of XFree86 that runs on your Apple Macintosh with nearly all the same features as the version for an Intel-based PC.

XFree86's version of X is exactly like X for other platforms. This means that you can write and develop clients on your PC-based system, then copy the source to another platform and rebuild your client. X is X as X is X! Besides offering compatibility, X gives you the following advantages:

- Versions for more than a dozen operating systems, and 100 versions of those operating systems
- Flexible network connections
- Use of in-memory, or *user environment variables*
- Nearly two-dozen command-line options for server operations
- Support for specialized keyboard operations, such as stopping a session or using other text-only logins (or *consoles*) under Linux

Until very recently, the XFree86 X distribution (XFree86 3.3.6) was based on X11R6.3. However, the newest and latest versions, XFree86 4.0 and now 4.0.1, are based on X11R6.4. The culmination of nearly two years' work, the new XFree86 has many new features specific to its internal architecture that will appeal to users, administrators, and computer graphics card developers and manufacturers.

This new release is the reason for writing this book. Although this author's efforts pale compared to the expertise of XFree86's developers, I hope that this book will help you share in the joy, empowerment, and satisfaction that so many users have derived from using these developers' software.

The Future

As mentioned previously, at the time of this writing, the free software and commercial computer industry is poised to receive a new revision of X, X11R6.5. The good news is that within releases of minor revisions to the X distribution, X clients and source code are generally upward-compatible. This means that you'll be able to build your favorite clients easily using the new software, and that older clients usually will still run under the new system.

Revisions to X, even minor ones, are generally few and far between. The last major revision, from X11R5 to X11R6, took place almost 10 years ago. Even so, you may find some computer systems still running X11R5 to this day.

Although specific features in future revisions are hard to predict, you can bet that X will continue to evolve to incorporate new network, communication, or input standards. These features include audio, video, multiple-displays, and support for new input devices. You can get an idea of some of the planned improvements by browsing to **http://www.x.org**.

Features of This Book

This book is for you, a user of the X Window system, in the expectation that when you are using one of X's modern day windowing environments, such as KDE or GNOME, you'll take the time to learn about the raw power and facilities offered by X. Beneath the layers of drag-and-drop and window dressing lurks a fantastic system and architecture that makes the user GUI possible. I also hope that many of the tips and tricks outlined in this book will make life easier for you at your workstation, as you're probably trying to get work done in the fast lane of the Information Super-highway.

Conventions Used in This Book

As with previous editions of my work, I'll end each chapter with a section titled "Resource Information." This section contains a list of source information, pertinent URLs, and author contact information. You can use these resources as a starting point to learn more about the topic discussed in the chapter. Experienced hands may have the pertinent printed documents on hand, but everyone can benefit from access to the latest information on the listed Web sites.

> — Bill Ball
> Writing upstairs using a client launched downstairs
> Arlington, Virginia
> September 2000

Resource Information

http://www.homepage.montana.edu/~sheehan/bookreviews/champine.html— a review of George A. Champine's *MIT Project Athena: A Model for Distributed Campus Computing*, 1991, Digital Press (ISBN: 0135853249).

http://www.xfree86.org—home page of the XFree86 Project, Inc.

http://www.x.org—home page of the curators of X, the X Consortium.

http://www.x.org/about_x.htm—a simple chart describing how X works.

PART I

Introduction to The X Window System

Chapter 1: X11, XFree86, and Linux

This chapter provides a small bit of historical background about X, XFree86, and other X distributions for Linux. The lineage of X, its various revisions, and how X was ported to Linux comprise a fascinating story of the potential of collaborative programming, the power of the Open Source movement, and the efforts of thousands of programmers around the world. Although the idea of providing a graphical interface began at Xerox's Palo Alto Research Center in the middle of 1970, many of the windowing solutions available for Linux would not be available today without the quirks of fate and history of X11 and the XFree86 Project, Inc.

The Early X11 Distributions

Development of X started in 1984 at the Massachusetts Institute of Technology (MIT) as part of Project Athena, an effort to build a portable graphical interface to enable the use of workstations in the teaching process. Based on earlier work at Stanford (on a system named W), X was originally developed by Jim Gettys of Digital Equipment Corporation (DEC) and Ron Newman and Bob Scheifler of MIT.

Commercially released in 1986 as X10.4, X quickly evolved to X11R1 (X11, revision 1) the following year, and within a year to X11R2 in 1988.

The appeal of X is due in no small part to several important features:

- **Portability**—X works with nearly every known computer graphics system capable of pixel addressing or bitmap display.
- **Standardization**—The X Window System provides a standard set of libraries and function calls that allow programmers to concentrate on developing clients instead of worrying about how to work with graphics hardware.
- **Networking**—X11 was built from the ground up to support networking, and it works over a variety of media, such as Ethernet or serial network connections.
- **Modular Architecture**—Features and support for new technologies can be added to X without major difficulty, due to the fact that X is officially distributed in source form only.

X was released under the largess of the MIT X Consortium, a nonprofit organization supported by nearly every large computer manufacturer at the time. Today, most Linux distributions use X11R6.3 or X11R6.4, although X11R6.5.1 was released late in 2000.

The Early Days

X has provided the basics for developing and running a networking graphical interface right from the start. One of the earliest releases, X10R3, worked with only six different displays. But this 7MB, source-code–only X distribution supported color, overlapping windows, and copy and paste operations, and came with a terminal emulator, a clock client, and other example clients.

The September 15, 1987 release of X11R1 was a "major redesign and enhancement of X," according to MIT's announcement document included in the distribution. Contributors included researchers at MIT, along with programmers from Apollo, DEC, HP, IBM, Sun Microsystems, and Textronix. X was now supported under four major operating systems, and comprised 19MB of source code and documentation.

The 1988 second release, X11R2, provided numerous fixes, compressed fonts, and changes to command-line arguments for servers and clients. The release included a contributor distribution of third-party software, along with additional libraries of programming functions, such as the Andrew Toolkit from IBM and Carnegie-Mellon University. These contributed toolkits provided programmers with easier ways to develop clients quickly for X. New clients were also added, including the now-classic `xlogo` and `xbiff`.

Subsequent revisions, such as X11R4, added improved handling and the creation of objects known as widgets. A *widget* is a graphical user interface item that can be created, displayed, hidden, or destroyed in or from memory. Thus, the ability to create nonrectangular window shapes was introduced. The `xdm` client became the standard login manager for X.

The August 29, 1991 release of X11R5 provided a client *resource* or customization mechanism, in which text file resources can be used to change the appearance of a client's buttons and windows, change fonts, and so on. This release also added internationalization capabilities, improved font handling, and support for Apple's monochrome and color displays. The release also added support for Video Graphics Adapter (VGA) displays for ATT's System V/386 UNIX.

In 1993, the X Consortium, a nonprofit group of companies, adopted X as the MIT Consortium dissolved. One year later, on April 21, 1994, X11R6 was released. The release improved window management, resource sharing, session management (the ability to save settings between X sessions), and numerous other features.

X11R6.1, released March 5, 1996, supported 16 different operating systems, including Linux kernel 1.2.11. The release added new clients, but not much had changed with the introduction of X11R6.

The next version was X11R6.3, released on December 23, 1996. X11R6.3 was to be the last X Consortium release before stewardship was turned over to yet another nonprofit organization named The Open Group (TOG), comprising 200 corporations and many original members of the X Consortium.

The Open Group X Project Team released the next version, X11R6.4, on January 30, 1998—but not without controversy. TOG decided that X was no longer to be free of licensing or royalty payments. The group decided that if you were making a profit from selling a version of X, you would have to pay an annual licensing fee starting at $7,500 for 50,000 units.

Faced with annual fees up to $65,000, or the need to cough up $30,000 for membership to get lower fees, many companies and programmers involved in the Open Source community threw up their hands in horror. A split in the development of the older free version and the newer fee-based revision became imminent.

Fortunately, the XFree86 Project, Inc. (discussed in the next section), a nonprofit organization comprising programmers from around the world and devoted to bringing a free X distribution to the Intel-based PC platform, vowed to continue development of the free version. In another positive development, TOG changed its mind in early September 1998 and reverted X11R6.4's license to the old MIT version.

Today, X resides with X.Org, an organization of TOG. X.Org took charge of X on May 12, 1999, and now oversees its development and evolution.

The XFree86 Project, Inc.

The XFree86 Project, Inc., formally incorporated May 19, 1994, was created partly in response to problems with funding and status for membership in the X Consortium. The project has two classes of membership: full and associate members. Original members of the board include David Wexelblat, Dirk Hohndel (now with SuSE, Inc.), Dr. Richard Murphey, Glenn G. Lai, David Dawes, Dr. Jon Tombs, and James Tsillas. Run entirely by donations, XFree86 became an honorary member of X.Org in November 1999.

Originally started in 1992 by a small band of developers, the project quickly took shape to provide an X11 implementation for Intel-based PCs. Today's XFree86 distribution, however, supports other platforms, such as Compaq's Alpha, Sun's SPARC, and Motorola's PowerPC CPU-based systems, thanks to the efforts of programmers from around the world.

XFree86 2.1, introduced March 18, 1994, was the first version of XFree86 for Linux, and was designed to work with Linux kernel version 0.99pl15h. Thus, XFree86 has supported Linux since the first usable kernel.

Updates quickly followed, with version 2.1.1 for Linux 1.0, and the next release, XFree86 3.0, which introduced support for X11R6. The XFree86 3.0-series distributions lasted more than two years, from 1998 until January 2000, and many Linux distributions still use the last version, XFree86 3.3.6.

A major watershed for XFree86 arrived on March 7, 2000. XFree86 4.0 was officially released, and incorporated nearly two years of work by the XFree86 Project. Major changes were made to the server architecture, and many new features were added. These features include the following:

- Built-in configuration features in the main server
- Improved font support
- Incorporation of X11R6.4 features, such as support for multiple monitors
- Introduction of new configuration utilities
- Support for more than 500 graphics cards and 30 types of graphics chipsets using a single server
- Use of loadable modules and drivers, instead of a single server for a type of graphics chipset

The current version of XFree86 is 4.0.1, which incorporates features found in the official X11R6.4 release from X.Org.

New Features of X11R6.5.1

The latest version of X, X11R6.5.1, was introduced on August 15, 2000. According to X.Org, the release incorporates nearly 200 updates, and provides support (via a patch) for the Euro and improved X Print Service support (which allows images to be sent to an output device such as a printer).

This new release, composed of four compressed files, has bloomed to 144MB of source code, 20 times larger than the original X10 distribution. The source includes more than 8,100 files, nearly 600 fonts, 345 man pages, 20 libraries, 70 images, and 60 clients.

System administrators, computer network analysts, and programmers will also find nearly 150 white papers, documentation, and other research included as compressed PostScript files under X11R6.5.1's xc/doc/hardcopy directory. These treatises can provide invaluable information when planning or programming. You can quickly read these documents during an X session by entering the gv client, followed by the document's name, as follows:

```
# gv xc/doc/hardcopy/Xserver/analysis.PS.gz
```

After you press Enter, the gv client automatically decompresses the PostScript document, and you can read David P. Wiggins' "Analysis of the X Protocol for Security Concerns."

Other Distributions

Since the beginning of X support under Linux, there have been commercial distributions of X as well as distributions of commercial software libraries for X, such as Motif (now at version 2.1.30), that are designed for use with Linux. A number of vendors, at one time or another, have provided proprietary X distributions (usually with special features or updated drivers) that work quite well.

One of the first companies to ship commercial software for Linux (nearly nine years ago) is Metro Link, Inc. This company has marketed an X distribution for Linux since the first stable kernel. Today, Metro Link offers four basic products for Linux:

- **Metro-X**—a general-purpose X server for Linux on the Intel and Alpha CPU platforms, with support for more than 100 different graphics chipsets, touch screens, multihead (multiple-monitor) displays, and 3D-input devices, such as a tablet stylus
- **Micro-X**—a scalable X server, for use in embedded systems (Intel, Alpha, PowerPC, and ARM CPUs), that has a very small memory footprint (according to Metro Link, as small as 600KB)
- **Metro Link Motif**—a distribution of the latest three versions of the Motif programming libraries and clients for X
- **Metro OpenGL**—3D graphics card support for Linux (this product includes Metro-X)

Another company, Xi Graphics, today provides some of the cutting-edge support for the latest graphics cards used on Intel-based PCs. These cards, which require special servers and software support libraries, give the best performance for clients requiring acceleration and 3D displays. Xi Graphics, which has been providing X for Linux since 1995, currently markets several classes of base products for X support:

- **3D Accelerated-X Display Server**—a distribution of the latest X revision
- **Laptop Accelerated-X Display Server**—X servers specifically for performance on laptop graphics chipsets
- **Multi-head Accelerated-X Display Server**—support for multiple monitors with X
- **3D Linux Graphics Drivers**—support libraries to enable use of the latest 3D graphics cards with Linux
- **OpenGL Supplement**—supplemental graphics libraries for display cards
- **DeXtop v2.1 Common Desktop Environment (CDE) for Linux**—a version of the CDE X environment and suite of clients

Other commercial software packages for Linux, now no longer distributed, were InfoMagic's MooTif Motif 1.2, Lasermoon's SWiM Motif 1.2, and TriTeal's CDE

Motif, Open Motif, or LessTif?

Until recently, Motif was a set of proprietary, binary-only, and commercially sold and distributed software libraries and clients. The Motif libraries provide X programmers with timesaving functions and standardized widgets for quickly creating clients. Built upon the X libraries, Motif, first introduced before 1993, has gone through a number of revisions and stewardships (from X/Open, to The Open Software Foundation, or OSF, and now to TOG).

LessTif is a clone set of libraries that provides compatibility with Motif version 1.2. However, on May 15, 2000, TOG released the Motif source code under a free for-personal-use license.

In response, the LessTif developers write, "Usage of the OpenGroup™'s implementation does neither match the OpenSource definition nor any more general definition of 'free' usage, it's in fact rather limited."

"In this situation there's still need for LessTif at least to have a LGPL'ed version around which can be used on the vast majority of operating systems. Once the OpenGroup™ would release their Motif under a license compatible with common OpenSource definition LessTif *might* become obsolete."

"So we encourage people still to use, test and enhance LessTif. Until the details have been worked out any code contributors shouldn't look (closely) at the OpenGroup™'s sources to avoid any possible license violation."

The caution by the LessTif team points out a potential problem for any developer attempting to provide Open Source software sporting compatibility with proprietary software: Your efforts at cloning can be tainted by looking at the source! Meanwhile, you can still buy commercial versions of Motif or register and download Open Motif (see the section "Resource Information," at the end of this chapter).

for Linux. Red Hat, Inc., marketed CDE for Linux for only 18 months, starting around 1994.

Resource Information

http://www.xfree86.org—the starting point for the latest information about X11 for Linux and other operating systems.

http://www.x.org—the current X Consortium.

http://www.cs.utexas.edu/users/kharker/linux-laptop/—the first place to go to find information about running Linux and configuring X11 your notebook.

http://userwww.sfsu.edu/~kroll/CLASSES/630/TOPICS/60-X.htm—a quick introduction, by Lawrence S. Kroll, to X11.

http://slashdot.org/askslashdot/00/05/04/1321234.shtml—"What GUIs Came Before X11?"; readers of the premiere geek site chime in with information about other pre-X11 windowing systems, such as Smalltalk-72 or Interlisp.

http://members.fortunecity.com/pcmuseum/alto.html—screenshots of the Xerox Star, circa 1981.

http://www.hp.com/workstation/support/documentation/manuals/user_guides/graphics/LGAG/Reference/X.html—Hewlett Packard's X information page.

ftp://rtfm.mit.edu/pub/usenet/comp.answers/Xt-FAQ—the *comp.windows. x.intrinsics* frequently asked questions (FAQ), containing information about the basic X programming library.

ftp://ftp.rge.com/pub/X—if you want to download and read the source to earlier versions of X, this site is the one place to get every distribution since 1986.

ftp://ftp.x.org—another place to find historic versions of X.

ftp://ftp.xfree86.org/pub/XFree86-Inc/corp_profile—history of the XFree86 Project, Inc.

http://www.x.org/press1.htm—a press release announcing and describing the stewardship role of X by TOG's X.Org.

http://www.xig.com—the home page of Xi Graphics, an X11 vendor for Linux.

http://www.metrolink.com—the home page of Metro Link, Inc., one of the first vendors of commercial X software for Linux.

http://www.infomagic.com—the home page for a Linux software and merchandise reseller.

http://www.lasermoon.co.uk—a still-functional link to a previous vendor of Motif 1.2 for Linux.

http://www.hungry.org—site of the Hungry Programmers, developers of the Motif 1.2 clone LessTif.

http://www.lesstif.org—the best place to get LessTif.

http://www.lesstif.org/future.html—the LessTif developers' view of OpenMotif and the future of LessTif.

http://www.opengroup.org/openmotif/—register and download the sources for TOG's OpenMotif at this site.

Chapter 2: Getting and Installing XFree86

This chapter discusses the XFree86 distribution for Linux, along with some initial considerations concerning your computer's display, memory requirements, and storage requirements. There are a number of ways to acquire and install XFree86. This chapter will show you how to install or update a new distribution or version of X. You'll also learn about the various components of XFree86, so that you can decide which components may be most important for your system.

Initial Considerations

Most new Linux users simply install Linux and XFree86 on an existing computer using an acquired Linux distribution on CD-ROM. The user puts little thought into any preplanning process, and simply crosses fingers and hopes for the best regarding compatibility (and in the majority of cases, ends up pleasantly surprised!). However, today's more experienced Linux users are choosing to plan installation on specific hardware, with the most savvy building systems from scratch using researched components.

Whether you're new to Linux or an experienced hand, your installation will benefit if you either develop a good understanding of your existing computer's graphics hardware or carefully choose your graphics hardware ahead of time. If you are building a Linux server, however, the type of graphics hardware in your system may not be much of a concern, as whether or not X is installed or used may not be important. (My system's graphics hardware is important to me as an author, because I run nearly all my large X clients over Ethernet from a large server in the basement, and use a desktop-replacement laptop with a high-resolution display as a writing and graphics terminal. You'll learn how to do this in Chapter 9, "Using X11 on a Network.")

Display Requirements

If you plan to buy a computer to run Linux and need a specific resolution or graphics capability, then you should definitely do a bit of research ahead of time. If you're installing Linux on an existing system, or just want to run a dual-boot system (which enables you to choose Linux or another operating system at boot time), you can also benefit from understanding the capabilities of XFree86 and your computer's hardware. By knowing the specifics, you'll be able to get the most out of what you have.

As you know, Linux works quite well in *console mode*, or text-only display. But the fact is that your personal computing experience is enriched when using a graphical interface. Older hackers may remember (although not fondly) the days of flipping

The Resolution Revolution

Most early personal computers (that is, pre-IBM PCs) used either a TV or a *monochrome*, or single-color, text-only display (usually with the standard 80 characters by 24 or 25 lines resolution). The capabilities of PC graphics cards and monitors have increased dramatically since those early days, progressing from *Video Graphics Adapter* (VGA) *resolutions*, or horizontal pixels of 320 by 200 vertical pixels, to today's resolutions of 2,048 by 1,536. Cutting-edge graphics cards now sport onboard video random access memory (RAM) that may equal or exceed that of one's PC, and also offer features such as TV, composite, and S-Video output. Performance and power are now measured by a card's *fill rate*—that is, the speed at which the card can paint the screen. This rate, in *megapixels* (or millions of pixels) can indicate the number of frames per second that a card can provide at a specified resolution and at a specific *color depth* (number of colors per pixel). Color depths, represented by the number of bits, (such as 1-bit for monochrome) can range from four bit-planes per pixel (bpp), or 16 colors, to 32 bpp, or millions of colors. Today's fast cards can provide up to 100 frames per second (fps) at 32 bpp at 1,280 by 1,024.

switches, loading paper tape, and rewinding cassettes to load programs, or modifying IBM Selectric typewriters for use as printers and swapping five-inch floppy disks. Armed with faster CPUs, high-resolution color monitors, multiple-button pointing devices, ever-increasing hard drive space, and rewritable CD-ROM drives, today's desktop sessions allow us to get to work and to accomplish work more efficiently than ever.

Unless you have older hardware, such as a laptop with limited resolution such as 800×600, try to acquire or set up your computer to display X at a minimum of 1,024 pixels wide by 768 pixels high, with a color depth of thousands of colors (16 bpp). Although you can get work done at 800×600, you'll find that you'll quickly run out of screen real estate when using a lower resolution and that some graphics display poorly when represented on a 256-color display.

Monitor Specifications

XFree86 supports nearly every monitor on the market, and comes with a database (actually, a text file named MonitorsDB) containing 1,727 model names, types, and horizontal and vertical frequency ranges. The frequency ranges are crucial bits of information needed by XFree86's server, and are used to calculate the types of resolution offered by your system's monitor and graphics card. The horizontal and vertical frequencies refer to the times per second that lines can be scanned across and up and down your display.

> For a complete description of how your monitor and graphics card work together, see Eric S. Raymond's *XFree86-Video-Timings-HOWTO*. You may find a copy under your system's /usr/doc/HOWTO directory, under the /usr/X11R6/lib/X11/doc directory with the name VideoModes.doc, or at the URL listed in the "Resources" section at the end of this chapter.

For example, if you have an NEC Multisync XV monitor, you can quickly look up your monitor's capabilities by using the fgrep command like this:

```
# fgrep 'MultiSync XV' /usr/X11R6/lib/X11/MonitorsDB
NEC Technologies; NEC MultiSync XV14; NEC37FB; 30.0-57.0; 55.0-100.0
NEC Technologies; NEC MultiSync XV15+; NEC3D5E; 31.0-65.0; 55.0-100.0
NEC Technologies; NEC MultiSync XV15; NEC3C14; 31.0-65.0; 55.0-100.0
NEC Technologies; NEC MultiSync XV17+ (-2); NEC43BD; 31.0-82.0; 55.0-100.0
```

The database, found under the /usr/X11R6/lib/X11 directory after you install XFree86, shows that an NEC XV15 monitor supports a horizontal frequency range of 31 to 65, whereas its vertical range is 55 to 100. Although it is not absolutely necessary, you should keep your monitor's manual on hand when you configure X for your system. Knowing the exact frequencies for your monitor will help ensure accurate configuration of your display, and this information is even more important if you use an off-brand display. In the recent past, before the advent of XFree86 4.0, this information was critical; using incorrect settings outside a monitor's range could damage a monitor's internal components. Fortunately, most of today's monitors have built-in circuitry to prevent problems. Better yet, the latest X server, XFree86, in XFree86 version 4.0.1, internally incorporates the *Video Electronics Standards Association* (VESA) modes for most monitors, making configuration much safer with newer equipment. This server automatically calculates the ranges during startup!

Memory Requirements

Although most computer users think in terms of a system's random access memory (RAM) when discussing memory, the amount of video RAM included with your computer's graphics card also plays a large role in determining the resolution and color depth supported by your computer. Many early, pre-PC era computers used part of the computer's system memory for graphics display. As the PC has matured, most of today's computers have separate video and system memory (although some computers on the market have motherboards that, almost like those from the earlier era, use shared system and video memory).

Video RAM on your graphics card or in your graphics chipset is used to draw pixels on your monitor. Many notebooks on the market today sport at least 2MB of graphics memory, enough to provide thousands of colors at 1,024×768. For example, if one byte of memory is needed to display one of 256 colors per pixel, then a 1,024×768 display requires 1,024*768, or 786,432 bytes of storage. If two bytes are required to display thousands of colors, then the requirement doubles to 1,572,864 bytes. However, trying to use millions of colors at that resolution would require 2,359,296 bytes and exceed the capacity. Therefore, many notebooks that can provide millions of colors do so at a resolution of 800×600 (which requires only 1,440,000 bytes). However, certain notebook chipsets, such as those from NeoMagic, sport 2.5MB of RAM, which provides enough memory for displays of millions of colors at 1,024×768.

You should also know that just having a lot of video RAM won't help provide you with a higher resolution unless your monitor supports the display. Many monitors have limited resolutions; for example, most (but not all) 15-inch monitors support resolutions of only 1,024×768.

Aside from these graphics issues, there are other important reasons for carefully assessing your system's RAM when using XFree86. Even though most computers today are equipped with a base 64MB of RAM, you may want to consider adding more (perhaps an additional 64MB) if you plan to use a number of memory-intensive clients at the same time. Although XFree86 3.3.6 will run on a system with 16MB RAM and use 4MB of swap space, these are considered minimum memory requirements for a system.

Hard Drive Requirements

The amount of hard drive storage required for a base XFree86 installation can vary, depending on whether or not you choose to install the X11 development libraries, additional support libraries, and higher-level desktop suites such as GNOME and the K Desktop Environment. If you're going to use only XFree86, the hard drive requirements are rather modest—the initial compressed distribution comprises 25 files and is about 25MB.

Even if you include many additional clients, development libraries, man pages, and window managers, a full X11 installation may require only 150MB of hard drive space. It is when hard drive space is at a premium that shoe-horning a working X install onto a tiny file system can be a problem. This is the type of obstacle faced

Windowing for Small Footprints

If you need a windowing environment for your Linux system but have extremely limited amounts of system memory and hard drive space, consider trying Torsten Scherer and Eero Tamminen's W1R4, an X11-like server and client windowing system that also runs on Atari, Sun, and Intel-based PCs. The system includes 28 clients, with other graphical applications—such as a Web browser, a text editor, audio utilities, a drafting program, and network utilities—available for the system. The W server, wserver, is only 128KB, and most clients are less than 60,000 characters. Browse to http://www.students.tut.fi/~t150315/ to download W.

today by X developers working to bring a graphical interface to Linux on *Personal Digital Assistants* (PDAs).

Choosing a Graphics Card

Many new XFree86 users install Linux on preexisting hardware, most likely an older home desktop PC or laptop. For laptop users, choosing a graphics card is moot point, as the graphics chipset is an integral part of the notebook and cannot be replaced. This is also true of some desktop PCs that may have a video subsystem installed on the PC's motherboard (although you can usually disable the video by installing a new card).

If you're not happy with your current desktop PC video and are looking to choose a new graphics card, you'll be better informed by understanding the types of cards and chipsets supported by XFree86. Understanding graphics cards is also helpful if you're looking to buy a new notebook.

The older version of XFree86, version 3.3.6, supports a formidable list of graphics cards through the use of 12 servers. Table 2.1 lists each server, along with the supported video card. This table can help ensure that you're using the correct server for your card, and help you check for compatibility with your card.

The new XFree86 4.0.1 replaces the previous architecture of the XFree86 releases, which provided a server for a particular family of graphics chipsets or video cards and included support for hundreds of cards with a single server. The new approach (due in part to work donated by Metro Link, Inc.) uses loadable code modules and a single server. This framework provides a more flexible framework for adding support for new graphics cards.

Table 2.1 XFree86 3.3.6 Distribution

XFree86 Server	Supported Video Card
XF86_3DLabs	3DLabs Oxygen GMX, AccelStar Permedia II AGP, Creative Blaster Exxtreme, Diamond Fire GL 1000, 1000 Pro, GL 3000, ELSA Gloria Synergy, Gloria-L, Gloria-L/MX, Gloria-S, Gloria-XL, Winner 2000/Office, Leadtek WinFast 2300
XF86_AGX	AGX (generic), Boca Vortex (Sierra RAMDAC), EIZO (VRAM), Hercules Graphite HG210, Graphite Power, Graphite Pro, Orchid Celsius (AT&T RAMDAC), Celsius (Sierra RAMDAC), Spider Black Widow, Black Widow Plus, XGA-1 (ISA), XGA-2 (ISA)
XF86_I128	Number Nine Imagine I-128 (2–8MB), I-128 Series 2 (2–4MB), Imagine-128-T2R, Revolution 3D AGP (4–8MB SGRAM), Revolution 3D (T2R)
XF86_Mach32	ATI Graphics Ultra Pro, Mach32, Ultra Plus
XF86_Mach64	ASUS PCI-AV264CT, PCI-V264CT, ATI 3D Pro Turbo, 3D Pro Turbo PC2TV, 3D Xpression, 3D Xpression+, 3D Xpression + PC2TV, All-in-Wonder, All-in-Wonder Pro, All-in-Wonder Pro Turbo, All-in-Wonder Pro Turbo (AT&T 20C408, ATI68860, ATI68860B, ATI68860C, ATI68875, CH8398, STG1702, STG1703, TLC34075 RAMDAC), ATI Graphics Xpression, ATI Graphics Xpression (ATI68860, ATI68860B, ATI68860C, ATI68875, AT&T 20C408, CH8398 RAMDAC), ATI Graphics Xpression (Mach64CT, STG1702, STG1703, TLC34075 RAMDAC), ATI Mach64, ATI Mach64, 3D RAGE II, 3D RAGE II+DVD, 3D RAGE IIC, 3D Rage Pro, Mach64 CT, Mach64 GT, Mach 64VT, Mach64 (AT&T 20C408, ATI68860, ATI68860B, ATI68860C, ATI68875, CH8398, IBM RGB514, Internal, STG1702, STG1703, TLC34075 RAMDAC), ATI Pro Turbo+PC2TV, Video Xpression, Video Xpression+, ATI WinBoost (AT&T 20C408, ATI68860, ATI68860B, ATI68860C, ATI68875, CH8398 RAMDAC), ATI WinCharger (AT&T 20C408, ATI68860, ATI68860B, ATI68860C, ATI68875, CH8398, STG1702, STG1703, TLC34075 RAMDAC), ATI Win Turbo (AT&T 20C408, ATI68860, ATI68860B, ATI68860C, ATI68875, CH8398, STG1702, STG1703, TLC34075 RAMDAC), ATI Xpert 98, Xpert XL, Xpert@Play PCI, AGP, Xpert@Play 98, Xpert@Work, ATI (integrated on Intel Maui MU330EX motherboard)
XF86_Mach8	ATI 8514 Ultra, ATI Graphics Ultra
XF86_Mono	All
XF86_P9000	Diamond Viper PCI 2MB, Viper VLB 2MB, Orchid P9000 VLB

Table 2.1 XFree86 3.3.6 Distribution *(continued)*

XFree86 Server	Supported Video Card
XF86_S3	2 the Max MAXColor S3 Trio64V+, 928Movie, ASUS Video Magic PCI V864, VT64, Actix GE32+ 2MB, GE32i, GE64, Ultra, Compaq Armada 7380DMT, 7730MT, Cardex Trio64, Trio64Pro, DSV3326, DataExpert DSV3365, Dell S3 805, Diamond Stealth 24, 64 DRAM SE, 64 DRAM (S3 SDAC, S3 Trio64), 64 VRAM, 64 Video VRAM (TI RAMDAC), Stealth Pro, Stealth VRAM, Stealth Video DRAM, Stealth64 Graphics 2xx0 series (864 + SDAC), 2xx0 series (Trio64), Stealth64 Video 2001, 2120, 2121, 2200, 2201, 3240, 3400 (IBM RAMDAC), 3240, 3400 (TI RAMDAC), Elsa Gloria-4, Gloria-8, Winner 1000/T2D, Winner 1000AVI (AT&T 20C408 version), 1000AVI (SDAC version), 1000ISA, 1000PRO (S3 SDAC), 1000PRO (STG1700, AT&T RAMDAC), 1000PRO/X, 1000TRIO, 1000TRIO/V, 1000TwinBus, 1000VL, 2000, 2000AVI, 2000PRO-2, 2000PRO-4, 2000PRO/X-2, 2000PRO/X-2, 2000PRO/X-4, 2000PRO/X-8, ExpertColor DSV3365, Genoa Phantom 64i (S3 SDAC), VideoBlitz IIIAV, Hercules Graphite Terminator 64, 64/DRAM, Pro 64, Terminator 64/Video, JAX 8241, LeadTek WinFast 2430, WinFast S510, Miro Crystal 10SD (GenDAC), 12SD, 16S, 20SD PCI (S3 DAC), 20SD VLB (S3 DAC), 20SD (ICD2061A, ICS2494), 20SV, 22SD, 40SV, 80SV, 8S, Miro Video 20SV, Number Nine FX Motion 221, 531, 771, FX Vision 330, GXE Level (10, 11, 12), GXE Level (14, 16), GXE64, GXE64 Pro, GXE64 (S3 Trio64), Orchid Fahrenheit 1280, Farhrenheit VA, Farenheit-1280+, S3 801/805 (ATT20c490, ICD2061A, SC11482, SC11483, SC11484, SC11485, SC11487, SC11489 RAMDAC), S3 864 (20C498, 21C498, STG1703 RAMDAC), S3 868 (ATT 20C408, 20C498, 21C498), S3 86C764, 86C765, 86C775, 86C785, 86C801, 86C805, 86C864, 86C868, 86C911, 86C924, 86C928, 86C964, 86C968, 86CM65, S3 911/924, 924 (SC1148 DAC), S3 928, 964, 968, S3 Auroa64V+, Trio32, Trio64, Trio64V+, Trio64V2, Trio64V2/DX, Trio64V2/GX, S3 Vision864, Vision868, Vision964, Vision968, SHARP 9080, SHARP 9090, SPEA Mercury 64, Mirage, SPEA/V7 Mercury, Mirage P64, Mirage P64 (S3 Trio64), STB Pegasus, STB PowerGraph 64, PowerGraph 64 Video, PowerGraph X-24, STB Velocity 64 Video, Spider Tarantula 64, VL-31, VidTech FastMax P20, VideoLogic GrafixStar 300, 400, 500, 700, WinFast S430, S510
XF86_SVGA	ALG-5434(E), ASUS 3Dexplorer, AT24, AT3D, ATI Wonder SVGA, ATred ATC-2165A, Actix ProStar, ProStar 64, Acumos AVGA3, Alliance ProMotion 6422, Ark Logic ARK1000PV, ARK1000VL, ARK2000MT, ARK2000PV, Avance Logic 2101, 2228, 2301, 2302, 2308, 2401, Binar Graphics AnyView,

Table 2.1 XFree86 3.3.6 Distribution *(continued)*

XFree86 Server	Supported Video Card
XF86_SVGA cont	California Graphics SunTracer 6000, Canopus Co. Power Window 3DV, Canopu Total-3D, Carex Cobra, Chips & Technologies CT64200, CT64300, CT65520, CT65525, CT65530, CT65535, CT65540, CT65545, CT65546, CT65548, CT65550, CT65554, CT65555, CT68554, CT69000, Cirrus Logic GD542x, GD543x, GD5446, GD544x, GD5462, GD5464, GD5465, GD5480, GD62xx (laptop), GD64xx (laptop), GD754x (laptop), Colorgraphic Dual Lightning, Creative Labs 3D Blaster PCI (Verite 1000), Blaster 3D, Blaster Eclipse, Blaster MA201, Blaster MA202, Blaster MA302, Blaster MA334, DFI-WG1000, DFI-WG5000, DFI-WG6000, DSV3325, Dell onboard Et4000, Diamond Edge 3D, Diamond Multimedia Stealth 3D 2000, 2000 Pro, Diamond SpeedStar 24, 24X (not fully supported), 64, A50, HiColor, Pro (not SE), Pro 1100, Pro SE (CL-GD5430/5434), SpeedStar64 Graphics 2000/2200, Diamond Stealth 32, 3D 2000, 3D 2000 PRO, 3D 3000, 3D 4000, Stealth II S220, Video 2500, Stealth64 Graphics 2001 series, Viper 330, 550, Viper Pro Video, ELSA ERAZOR II, ERAZOR, Victory 3D, Victory 3DX, Winner 1000 R3D, 2000AVI/3D, 3000, 3000-L-42, 3000-M-22, 3000-S, Epson CardPC (onboard), ET3000, ET4000, ET4000 W32i, W32p, ET4000/W32, ET6000, ET6100, ExpertColor DSV3325, Genoa 5400, 8500VL(-28), 8900 Phantom 32i, Hercules Dynamite, Dynamite 128/Video, Dynamite Power, Dynamite Pro, Stingray, Stingray 128 3D, Stingray 64/V with ICS5342, Stingray 64/V with ZoomDAC, Stingray Pro, Stingray Pro/V, Terminator 3D/DX, Terminator 64/3D, Thriller3D, Integral FlashPoint, Intel 5430 , Interay PMC Viper, Jaton Video-58P, Jaton Video-70P, Jazz Multimedia G-Force 128, LeadTek WinFast 3D S600, WinFast 3D S680, WinFast S200, MELCO WGP-VG4S, WGP-VX8, MSI MS-4417, Matrox Comet, Marvel II, Millennium 2/4/8MB, Millennium (MGA), Millennium G200 4/8/16MB, Millennium G200 SD 4/8/16MB, Millennium II 4/8/16MB, Millennium II AGP, Mystique, Mystique G200 4/8/16MB, Productiva G100 4/8MB, MediaGX, MediaVision Proaxcel 128, Mirage Z-128, Miro Crystal DVD, miroCRYSTAL VRX, miroMedia 3D, Miro MiroVideo 20TD, Neomagic 2200, 2160, 2097, 2093, 2090, 2070, Number Nine FX Motion 332, Number Nine Visual 9FX Reality 332, Oak 87 ISA (generic), Oak 87 VLB (generic), Oak ISA Card (generic), Ocean (octek) VL-VGA-1000, AVGA-20, Combo-26, Combo-28, VL-VGA-26, VL-VGA-28, Orchid Kelvin 64, Kelvin 64 VLB Rev A , Kelvin 64 VLB Rev B, Orchid Technology Fahrenheit Video 3D, PC-Chips M567 Mainboard, Paradise Accelerator Value, Paradise/WD 90CXX, PixelView Combo TV 3D AGP (Prolink), Combo TV Pro (Prolink),

Table 2.1 XFree86 3.3.6 Distribution *(continued)*

XFree86 Server	Supported Video Card
XF86_SVGA cont	RIVA TNT, RIVA128, Rendition Verite 1000, Rendition Verite 2x00, S3 86C260, 86C280, 86C325, 86C357, 86C375, 86C385,86C988, S3 ViRGE, ViRGE/DX, ViRGE/GX, ViRGE/GX2, ViRGE/MX, ViRGE/MX+, ViRGE/VX, SNI PC5H W32, SNI Scenic W32, SPEA/V7 Mirage VEGA Plus, SPEA/V7 ShowTime Plus, STB Horizon, Horizon Video, LightSpeed, LightSpeed 128, MVP-2, MVP-2 PCI, MVP-2X, MVP-4 PCI, MVP-4X, Nitro (64), Nitro 3D, Nitro 64 Video, STB Systems Powergraph 3D, Systems Velocity 3D, Velocity 128, nvidia 128, SiS 3D PRO AGP, 5597, 5598, 6326, SG86C201, SG86C205, SG86C215, SG86C225, Sierra Screaming 3D, Sigma Concorde, Legend, Spider VLB Plus, TechWorks Thunderbolt, Techworks Ultimate 3D, Toshiba Tecra 540CDT, Tecra 550CDT, Tecra 750CDT, Tecra 750DVD, Trident 3DImage975, 3DImage975 AGP, 3DImage985, 8900/9000, 8900D, Trident Cyber 9382, Cyber 9385, Cyber 9388, Cyber 9397, Trident TGUI9400CXi, TGUI9420DGi, TGUI9430DGi, TGUI9440, TGUI9660, TGUI9680, TGUI9682, TGUI9685, TVGA9200CXr (generic), VI720, VideoLogic GrafixStar 550, VideoLogic GrafixStar 560 (PCI/AGP), VideoLogic GrafixStar 600, ViewTop PCI, WD 90C24, WD 90C24A or 90C24A2 (laptop), Weitek P9100 (generic), WinFast 3D S600, WinFast S200
XF86_TGA	Digital 24-plane TGA (ZLXp-E2), 24-plane+3D TGA (ZLXp-E3), 8-plane TGA (UDB/Multia), 8-plane TGA (ZLXp-E1)
XF86_VGA16	Generic VGA, S3 86C365 (Trio3D), S3 86C391 (Savage3D), S3 Savage3D, S3 Trio3D, Trident TVGA 8800BR, TVGA 8800CS

Although 4.0.1 is the latest version of XFree86, you may find it more convenient (and perhaps necessary) to use the previous 3.3.6 release. This is because the new XFree86 does not support all graphics cards listed in Table 2.1. In some instances, XFree86 has dropped support for certain cards, in which case you must use the older release. Table 2.2 describes the status of driver support in the new modules for classes of cards at the time of this writing. Note that, in general, newer versions of XFree86 will add greater support for a wider variety of cards, but support for legacy cards is not assured. You should always check the XFree86 Web site for updates!

You can use Tables 2.1 and 2.2 to determine which version of XFree86 to use for your graphics card. But note that these tables list support in the XFree86 distribution only. If the tables do not list your card, it may be supported elsewhere.

Table 2.2 XFree86 4.0.1 Driver Status

Chipset	Support
3Dfx	Same support as XFree86 3.3.6
3Dlabs	Same support as XFree86 3.3.6
Alliance	AP6422 is not supported; AT25 is supported
ARK Logic	No support
ATI	All supported except Mach8, Mach32; unaccelerated support for all except Mach64, Rage, and Rage 128
Avance Logic	No support
Chips and Technologies	Same support as XFree86 3.3.6
Cirrus Logic	No support for 5420, 5422, 5424, 5426, 5428, 5429, 6205, 6215, 6225, 6235, 6410, 6412, 6420, 6440, 7541, 7542, 7543, 7548, 7555, 7556
Compaq/Digital	No Compaq AVGA support
Cyrix	No support
Epson	No support
Genoa	No support
IBM	VGA is supported; no support for 8514/A or XGA-2
IIT	No support
Intel	Same support as XFree86 3.3.6
Matrox	Same support as XFree86 3.3.6
MX	No support
NCR	No support
NeoMagic	Same support as XFree86 3.3.6
Number Nine	No support
NVIDIA	Same support as XFree86 3.3.6, except no support for NV1
Oak Technologies, Inc.	No support
Paradise/Western Digital	No support
RealTek	No support
Rendition/Micron	Same support as XFree86 3.3.6
S3	No support, except for ViRGE and Trio3D
Silicon Integrated Systems (SiS)	No support for 86C201, 86C202, 86C215, 86C225, 5597, 5598
Silicon Motion, Inc.	No support
Trident Microsystems	No support for TVGA8200LX, TVGA8800CS, TVGA8900B, TVGA8900C, TVGA8900CL, TVGA9000, TVGA9000i, TVGA9100B, TVGA9200CXr, TGUI9400CXi, TGUI9420, TGUI9430DGi
Tseng Labs	Same support, except no support for ET3000
Video 7	No support
Weitek	No support

Getting Support

If you have an older card (at least two years old), you usually can get XFree86 to work with your card using the 16-color `XF86_VGA16` or monochrome `XF86_Mono` servers. If you have a newer card, browse to your card's manufacturer Web site and look for links to support or driver downloads. The new XFree86 4.0 architecture enables card manufacturers to release binary-only drivers (loadable modules) to provide support for a new product. Although many Open Source purists will avoid purchasing a card that relies on proprietary drivers, the good news is that many more card manufacturers are releasing information to the XFree developers.

Some of the manufacturers providing support for Linux (at least in the form of FAQs, links, or other information) and X11 include ELSA, Matrox, S3, Inc., 3dfx, Interactive, Inc., and ATI Technologies, Inc. Some manufacturers provide custom X servers, whereas others will point you in the right direction.

Other sources of support include SuSE, Inc., which has a program of developing specialized servers for a variety of cards, and including support in its distributions for specialized or newer cards. In general, if you have one of the latest and greatest graphics cards, don't expect support for Linux right away. Although this situation is getting better every year, you need to:

- Understand that legacy graphics cards are generally supported, but may not be supported by the latest version of XFree86. Read the XFree86 release notes and documentation regarding chipset support.
- Keep in mind that the best support will be for the best-selling and most popular cards that have been on the market for at least 18 months. The market will demand support, and you should always let the manufacturer know about your needs for Linux support (if the manufacturer does not support Linux as a matter of policy, vote with your pocketbook).
- Realize that the latest and greatest video card may not be supported right away. Again, you may have to vote with your pocketbook, but at least let the manufacturer know about a missed sale.
- Do research ahead of time if you plan to purchase an expensive ($50 or more) graphics card for use with XFree86. Check to make sure about any return policy, and keep your receipt!
- Choose the proper card for your needs. If you plan to play graphics-intensive games, you may need to install additional support libraries and use a 3D-capable graphics card.

Choosing an Archive Source

The easiest way to install XFree86 is from a Linux distribution's CD-ROM. You'll find the XFree86 files packaged in the same format as other software packages in the distribution. For example, Red Hat, Mandrake, Yellow Dog, Caldera OpenLinux and

SuSE all use RPM (Red Hat Package Manager) files. The RPM files contain the binaries, documentation, man pages, and fonts, along with installation and deinstallation shell scripts.

For example, Table 2.3 lists the RPM archives of the XFree86 3.3.6 distribution included with Mandrake Linux 7.1.

Table 2.3 Mandrake Linux 7.1 XFree86 3.3.6 RPM Files

File	Description
`XFree86-100dpi-fonts-3.3.6-14mdk.i586.rpm`	100-dpi X fonts
`XFree86-3.3.6-14mdk.i586.rpm`	X clients, bitmaps, documentation
`XFree86-3DLabs-3.3.6-14mdk.i586.rpm`	3DLabs X server
`XFree86-75dpi-fonts-3.3.6-14mdk.i586.rpm`	75-dpi X fonts
`XFree86-8514-3.3.6-14mdk.i586.rpm`	8514 X server
`XFree86-AGX-3.3.6-14mdk.i586.rpm`	AGX X server
`XFree86-cyrillic-fonts-3.3.6-14mdk.i586.rpm`	Cyrillic X fonts
`XFree86-devel-3.3.6-14mdk.i586.rpm`	X development libraries
`XFree86-FBDev-3.3.6-14mdk.i586.rpm`	X framebuffer server
`XFree86-glide-module-4.0-6mdk.i586.rpm`	3D support libraries
`XFree86-I128-3.3.6-14mdk.i586.rpm`	I128 X server
`XFree86-ISO8859-2-1.0-12mdk.noarch.rpm`	Central European X fonts
`XFree86-ISO8859-2-100dpi-fonts-1.0-12mdk.noarch.rpm`	Central European X fonts
`XFree86-ISO8859-2-75dpi-fonts-1.0-12mdk.noarch.rpm`	Central European X fonts
`XFree86-ISO8859-2-Type1-fonts-1.0-12mdk.noarch.rpm`	Central European X fonts
`XFree86-ISO8859-9-100dpi-fonts-2.1.2-13mdk.noarch.rpm`	Turkish language fonts
`XFree86-ISO8859-9-2.1.2-13mdk.noarch.rpm`	Turkish language fonts
`XFree86-ISO8859-9-75dpi-fonts-2.1.2-13mdk.noarch.rpm`	Turkish language fonts
`XFree86-libs-3.3.6-14mdk.i586.rpm`	X support libraries
`XFree86-Mach32-3.3.6-14mdk.i586.rpm`	Mach32 X server
`XFree86-Mach64-3.3.6-14mdk.i586.rpm`	Mach64 X server
`XFree86-Mach8-3.3.6-14mdk.i586.rpm`	Mach8 X server
`XFree86-Mono-3.3.6-14mdk.i586.rpm`	Monochrome X server
`XFree86-P9000-3.3.6-14mdk.i586.rpm`	P9000 X server
`XFree86-S3-3.3.6-14mdk.i586.rpm`	S3 X server

Table 2.3 Mandrake Linux 7.1 XFree86 3.3.6 RPM Files *(continued)*

File	Description
XFree86-S3V-3.3.6-14mdk.i586.rpm	S3V X server (no longer actively supported; use the XF86_SVGA server instead)
XFree86-server-4.0-6mdk.i586.rpm	Development snapshot of the 4.0 X server
XFree86-server-common-3.3.6-14mdk.i586.rpm	Server support files
XFree86-SVGA-3.3.6-14mdk.i586.rpm	SVGA X server
XFree86-VGA16-3.3.6-14mdk.i586.rpm	VGA16 X server
XFree86-W32-3.3.6-14mdk.i586.rpm	W32 X server (being phased out; use the XF86_SVGA server instead)
XFree86-XF86Setup-3.3.6-14mdk.i586.rpm	X configuration tool
XFree86-xfs-3.3.6-14mdk.i586.rpm	X font server
XFree86-Xnest-3.3.6-14mdk.i586.rpm	X nested server (can run as a client)
XFree86-Xvfb-3.3.6-14mdk.i586.rpm	X virtual framebuffer server (used for testing purposes)

The RPM files are usually installed during an initial Linux installation, although you can install the files manually using the rpm command or a graphical RPM client such as GNOME's gnorpm or KDE's kpackage clients. The compressed file size of the XFree86 3.3.6 distribution in Table 2.3 is nearly 40MB, but not all of the fonts or X servers are installed if you configure XFree86 during a Linux install session.

Downloading Binary Archives

You can go to The XFree86 Project, Inc.'s FTP site to get the latest copy of XFree86. The software is distributed in source code form so you can build the distribution yourself, or in binary form (compressed archives). There are versions for the following operating systems:

- FreeBSD 2.2, 3.X, 4.X
- Linux (Alpha)
- Linux (Intel)
- NetBSD 1.3
- OpenBSD 2.7
- Solaris-8
- Unixware

For Linux, you have your choice of libc5, glibc20, and glibc21 distributions. The libc5 and glibc20 versions are for older Linux distributions. Most Linux users using newer distributions, such as Red Hat 6.2, Mandrake 7.1, and SuSE 7.0, should use the glibc21 distributions, as the software will match the software libraries used in the Linux distributions.

Table 2.4 lists the contents of the XFree86 4.0.1 distribution for Linux Intel-based PCs using the latest glibc21 libraries.

Table 2.4 XFree86 4.0.1 for Linux (Files Marked with an Asterisk [*] Comprise a Minimal Installation)

File	Description
BugReport	Report form for bug and test reporting
extract*	Distribution extraction utility
extract.exe	Distribution extraction utility
FILES	Complete list of files in each compressed archive
Install*	Installation instructions for XFree86 4.0.1
README	Short abstract regarding XFree86 4.0.1
RELNOTES*	Release notes and technical details of components
SUMS.md5	Checksums of each file in the distribution
SUMS.md5sum	Checksums of each file in the distribution
Xbin.tgz*	X clients, libraries, and utilities
Xdoc.tgz*	Text documentation for XFree86 4.0.1
Xetc.tgz*	Configuration files
Xf100.tgz	100-dpi fonts for X
Xfcyr.tgz	Cyrillic fonts for X
Xfenc.tgz*	Font encoding data
Xflat2.tgz	Latin fonts for X
Xfnon.tgz	Bitmap fonts for X
Xfnts.tgz*	Basic fonts for X
Xfscl.tgz	Scalable fonts for X
Xfsrv.tgz	X font server
Xhtml.tgz	Documentation in HTML format
Xinstall.bin	XFree86 installation script (same as *.bin)
Xinstall.sh*	XFree86 installation script (same as *.sh)
Xjdoc.tgz	Japanese documentation
Xlib.tgz*	Software libraries for XFree86 4.0.1
Xman.tgz*	XFree86 man pages
Xmod.tgz*	XFree86 4.0.1 driver modules
Xnest.tgz	XFree86 nested X server
Xprog.tgz	XFree86 programming support files
Xprt.tgz	XFree86 X print server
Xps.tgz	Documentation in PostScript format
Xvar.tgz*	Runtime data for XFree86
Xvfb.tgz	XFree86 virtual framebuffer X server
Xxserv.tgz*	XFree86 X server

Table 2.4 lists the components of the latest XFree86 distribution, and the files marked with an asterisk (*) are part of a minimal installation. This means that at a minimum, you must download and copy those archives to a single directory on your system prior to installing the distribution. You can extract and install the other archives later.

Before beginning the installation, you should carefully read the files `Install` and `RELNOTES`. These files contain important installation directions and technical information regarding the distribution. The entire 4.0.1 compressed distribution requires 25MB hard drive storage. Note that this distribution is much smaller than the previous version, 3.3.6. Two reasons for this smaller size are XFree86 4.0.1's new architecture and the use of loadable driver modules.

Installing the XFree86 Archives

To install the archives, log in as root, than navigate to the directory containing the XFree86 compressed archives. Do not perform the installation while running an X11 session. If you use the `startx` command to start your X session, log out or press Ctrl+Alt+Backspace to kill the current session. If you have not installed X, you can manually install the files by following directions in section 4.1 of the `Install` file.

You can ensure that you have the correct files by running the `Xinstall.sh` shell script with its `-check` option, as follows:

```
# sh Xinstall.sh -check
Checking which OS you're running...
uname reports 'Linux' version '2.2.14-15mdk', architecture 'i686'.
Object format is 'ELF'.  libc version is '6.1'.


Binary distribution name is 'Linux-ix86-glibc21'
```

This example shows that the system is running Mandrake Linux 7.0, which uses the glibc21 software libraries. If you have an existing X installation, read section 4.2 of the `Install` file for directions on how to back up and save your current X installation. If you're confident about installing 4.0.1, then just proceed with the install, as it will overwrite your current X system under the `/usr/X11R6` directory.

Start the installation by again using the `Xinstall.sh` script, as follows:

```
# sh Xinstall.sh
                Welcome to the XFree86 4.0.1 installer


You are strongly advised to backup your existing XFree86 installation
before proceeding.  This includes the /usr/X11R6 and /etc/X11
directories.  The installation process will overwrite existing files
```

```
in those directories, and this may include some configuration files
that may have been customised.
```

```
Do you wish to continue? (y/n) [n]y
```

Note that a default answer is included in brackets ([]), and in this case is *n*. This means that you can accept the default by pressing Enter or override the default by typing a different answer. Type a *y* to continue the installation. After you press Enter, you'll see the following:

```
Checking which OS you're running...
uname reports 'Linux' version '2.2.15-4mdk', architecture 'i686'.
Object format is 'ELF'.  libc version is '6.1'.


Checking for required files ...


You appear to have an existing installation of X.  Continuing will
overwrite it.  You will, however, have the option of being prompted
before most configuration files are overwritten.
Do you wish to continue? (y/n) [y]
```

Press Enter to continue the installation if you're sure you want to overwrite your existing install. You then will see the following message:

```
Removing some old directories that are no longer required...
        removing old directory /usr/X11R6/lib/X11/xkb/compiled

XFree86 now installs most customisable configuration files under
/etc/X11 instead of under /usr/X11R6/lib/X11, and has symbolic links
under /usr/X11R6/lib/X11 that point to /etc/X11.  You currently have
files under the following subdirectories of /usr/X11R6/lib/X11:

   app-defaults lbxproxy proxymngr rstart xserver

Do you want to move them to /etc/X11 and create the necessary
links? (y/n) [y]
```

The installation asks whether you'd like to create symbolic links of existing configuration files. This is acceptable, and probably a good idea, especially if you've edited the app-defaults file (which you can use to customize X clients). Press Enter to continue. You then see the following:

```
Moving /usr/X11R6/lib/X11/app-defaults to /etc/X11/app-defaults ...
./
Viewres
```

```
XCalc
XCalc-color
...
Xmh
Xvidtune
XTerm
Moving /usr/X11R6/lib/X11/lbxproxy to /etc/X11/lbxproxy ...
./
AtomControl
Moving /usr/X11R6/lib/X11/proxymngr to /etc/X11/proxymngr ...
./
pmconfig
Moving /usr/X11R6/lib/X11/rstart to /etc/X11/rstart ...
./
commands/
commands/@List
commands/ListContext
...
contexts/default
contexts/x11r6
rstartd.real
Moving /usr/X11R6/lib/X11/xserver to /etc/X11/xserver ...
./
SecurityPolicy
Extracting Xetc.tgz into a temporary location ...
== Extracting /root/xf41/Xetc.tgz ==
Do you want to overwrite the app-defaults config files? (y/n) [n]
```

The installation script then lists the files that it is moving and asks for permission to overwrite existing configuration files. You can choose to overwrite the files or retain them. If you're performing a fresh install, it is best to overwrite the files, but if your system requires specific settings, you can retain them and then edit them later. The installation then continues and extracts and installs archive components found in your download directory:

```
== Extracting /root/xf41/Xbin.tgz ==
== Extracting /root/xf41/Xlib.tgz ==
== Extracting /root/xf41/Xman.tgz ==
== Extracting /root/xf41/Xdoc.tgz ==
== Extracting /root/xf41/Xfnts.tgz ==
```

```
== Extracting /root/xf41/Xfenc.tgz ==
== Extracting /root/xf41/Xxserv.tgz ==
== Extracting /root/xf41/Xmod.tgz ==
== Extracting /root/xf41/Xvar.tgz ==
Checking for optional components to install ...
Do you want to install Xfsrv.tgz (font server)? (y/n) [y]
```

When the install detects an optional component (the X font server in this example), the program asks whether you want to install it. Choose each component as you go along (you can and probably should install the `xfsrv.tgz` file, which contains the X font server). The installation script then runs the `ldconfig` command to update the new X11 libraries, then create font directory files for any new installed fonts. You'll then see the following message:

```
You appear to have a termcap file: /etc/termcap
This should be edited manually to replace the xterm entries
with those in /usr/X11R6/lib/X11/etc/xterm.termcap

Note: the new xterm entries are required to take full advantage
of new features, but they may cause problems when used with
older versions of xterm.  A terminal type 'xterm-r6' is included
for compatibility with the standard X11R6 version of xterm.

On some platforms (e.g., Linux), the OpenGL standard requires
that the GL shared library and header files be visible from the
standard system lib and include directories (/usr/lib and
/usr/include).  This can be done by installing links in those
directories to the files that have been installed under /usr/X11R6.

NOTE: installing these links will overwrite existing files or
links.

Do you wish to have the (new) links installed (y/n)? [n]
```

Type *y* and press Enter to create these symbolic links. These links help ensure that software libraries are recognized. The install script will also find any old code modules for servers or fonts and back them up if desired. The installation is then complete.

Chapter 3, "Configuring XFree86," continues with instructions on how to configure your new 4.0.1 distribution.

Resource Information

/usr/X11R6/lib/X11/MonitorsDB—the XFree86 monitors database, containing information needed to configure and run X on your computer.

http://www.ibiblio.org/pub/Linux/docs/HOWTO/XFree86-Video-Timings-HOWTO—Eric S. Raymond's "how-to" documentation, with complete explanations of how to create custom resolutions for your computer's graphics card and monitor.

http://www.delorie.com/djgpp/doc/ug/graphics/vesa.html—a page describing VESA graphics modes, and providing C source showing how to interrogate and derive the information from a device.

http://www.neomagic.com/—home page of NeoMagic, a former notebook graphics chipset manufacturer supporting 16 notebook makers and more than 100 notebook models.

http://www.xfree86.org/cardlist.html—XFree86's video card and X server listings for XFree86 3.3.6; this is the place to look if you are using the older version of XFree86.

http://www.xfree86.org/4.0.1/Status.html—a 33-part HTML listing of graphics chipset families and support under the new XFree86, 4.0.1.

http://www.suse.de/en/support/xsuse—links to the latest versions of SuSE, Inc.'s X servers and XFree86 distribution for SuSE Linux.

http://www.elsa.com—click on the drivers link to search for Linux drivers for ELSA products.

http://www.matrox.com/mga/drivers/latest_drivers/home.htm—this page lists the latest drivers (including Linux) for a variety of Matrox products.

http://www.s3.com/—the place to start searching for products, then updated drivers.

http://Linux.3dfx.com—Linux drivers for 3dfx products.

http://support.ati.com/faq/linux.html—ATI's FAQ page regarding Linux.

http://dri.sourceforge.net—home page of the Direct Rendering Open Source Project, providing 3D Rage 128 support.

http://utah-glx.sourceforge.net—the UTAH-GLX Project for 3D Rage Pro support.

http://www.core.binghamton.edu/~insomnia/gatos—home page of the GATOS Project for ATI video support.

ftp://ftp.xfree86.org/pub/XFree86/4.0.1/—the FTP site and directory to download XFree86 4.0.1.

"Graphics: Pick a Card...Any Card," Matt Matthews, *Linux Journal* 78, pp. 152–158, Oct. 2000—article on choosing a 3D graphics card for Linux and X.

Choosing a configuration tool

Performing text-based configuration using xf86config

Performing console-based configuration using the XFree86 server

Using xf86cfg

Using Xconfigurator

Using DrakConf and Xfdrake

Using SaX

Using kvideogen

This chapter covers configuration of XFree86 for Linux. Configuring X during system installation can still be a frustrating and debilitating process even though Linux installation methods and system software install tools have vastly improved and matured over the last eight years. X configuration is now an integral part of the install process for a majority of Linux distributions. When everything goes right, an automatic and correct configuration of X for your computer's graphics card during an install is a wonderful thing. But when probing of your graphics hardware returns wrong values, or the software tools fail to return proper settings, you'll need to resort to other methods to get X working properly on your computer.

This chapter arms you with information about the arsenal of X configuration tools available in your Linux system. Until computer manufacturers realize the value of properly supporting Linux and X on desktop PCs, you'll need this information to overcome obstacles placed in your path to a working system. Commercial operating systems have the advantage of holding hardware and software developers hostage in a monopolistic industry. For this reason, Linux users, as a select group of computer users recognizing the merits of free and Open Source software, have to overcome the limitations imposed by a closed system of proprietary hardware and software.

The good news is that these efforts are succeeding; today, ever-increasing numbers of hardware and software developers are understanding the merits of open specifications, which have led to increased cross-platform compatibility, improvements in software design and execution, and widespread increases in the use of popular graphics systems. It no longer makes sense to introduce or support a product limited to a single market or platform; hardware manufacturers are beginning to realize the merits of opening up specifications, which leads to increased support, and in many cases better performance, from existing designs.

Several of the XFree86 configuration tools described in this chapter are universal among XFree86 distributions. Others, such as Xconfigurator, SaX, or XFdrake, are tools developed for a specific distribution (in these cases, Red Hat, SuSE, and Mandrake Linux, respectively).

Choosing a Configuration Tool

The choice of a configuration tool is normally a personal preference. Every XFree86 software configuration tool has one specific purpose: to generate an accurate, working XFree86 configuration file named `XF86Config`. This file is parsed when X starts and contains essential information needed to provide a proper display.

You can generate a new file during your Linux install, while running X, or from the text-based console. Some tools, such as `xf86cfg`, launch a base X server to offer graphical installation, whereas others, such as `xf86config`, are text-based.

> You should never use someone else's `XF86Config` file for your system unless you use the exact same video card and monitor combination. Linux notebook users can also share configuration files, but again, only among notebooks of the same model. You should always, as a matter of practice and to avoid damaging your equipment, generate your own `XF86Config` file. Incorrect settings can damage older computer monitors!

CAUTION

You can also manually craft your own `XF86Config` file by editing a template file named `XF86Config.eg`. This file is normally located under the `/usr/X11R6/lib/X11` directory, and contains sample sections that you can customize for your system. You'll also find example entries for popular pointing devices, and details about more advanced configurations, such as using two monitors during your X session. Use the `less` pager command as follows to read the file after you install XFree86:

```
# less /usr/X11R6/lib/X11/XF*.eg
```

If you use a simple text editor, such as `pico` (part of the `pine` email package), don't forget to disable the line-wrapping feature. Enter `pico`'s `-w` option, followed by the template file's name, as follows:

```
# pico -w /usr/X11R6/lib/X11/XF86Config.eg
```

After making your changes, you can use `pico`'s Save As feature by pressing Ctrl+o to save the file under a different directory and with the name `XF86Config`.

Manually creating your own `XF86Config` file is not recommended if you're new to XFree86. However, editing the file to make quick changes may sometimes be necessary, especially if you want to enable or disable features of X for your session or to take advantage of any special features or options available for your system's graphics driver. Seasoned experts will trim the file down to its bare minimum for full functionality, but those new to XFree86 will most likely use a configuration tool that is much easier to use.

Performing Text-based Configuration Using xf86config

The `xf86config` command is a venerable XFree86 configuration tool that has the flexibility of working at the console or through an X11 terminal window. This means that you can configure X immediately after installation or reconfigure X during a current X11 session. A companion program named `reconfig` is included with XFree86 and can be used to convert old XF86Config files (which were named Xconfig and used until the release of XFree86 3.1) into the newer format. XFree86 4.0.1 again changes the format of XF86Config, but parses older versions (from 3.1 to 3.3.6) correctly for compatibility.

Using SuperProbe to Explore Your Graphics Hardware

Before starting your configuration, you may need to get more information about your computer's graphics components. XFree86 includes the SuperProbe command, which has 10 different command-line options, and reports on hardware that the configuration tool is programmed to understand. To see the list of hardware known by your version of SuperProbe, use its -info option as follows:

```
# SuperProbe -info
SuperProbe Version 2.22 (2000 March 6)


SuperProbe can detect the following standard video hardware:
        MDA, Hercules, CGA, MCGA, EGA, VGA
SuperProbe can detect the following SVGA chipsets/vendors:
        WD, Video7, MX, Genoa, UMC, Trident, SiS, Matrox, ATI, Ahead, NCR,
        S3, AL, Cirrus54, Cirrus64, Epson, Tseng, RealTek, Rendition, Primus,
        Yamaha, Oak, Cirrus, Compaq, HMC, Weitek, ARK Logic, Alliance,
        SigmaDesigns, Intergraphics, CT,
SuperProbe can detect the following graphics coprocessors/vendors:
        ATI_Mach, 8514/A, I128, GLINT,
SuperProbe can detect the following RAMDACs:
        Generic, ALG1101, SS2410, Sierra15, Sierra16, Sierra24, MU9C4870,
        MU9C4910, ADAC1, 68830, 68860, 68875, ATIMisc, Cirrus8, Cirrus24B,
        Cirrus24, 20C490, 20C491, 20C492, 20C493, 20C497, Bt485, 20C504,
        20C505, TVP3020, TVP3025, EDSUN, 20C498, 22C498, STG1700, S3_GENDAC,
        S3_SDAC, TVP3026, RGB524, RGB514/525, RGB528, STG1703, 20C409,
        20C499, TKD8001, TGUIDAC, Integrated, MU9C1880, IMSG174, STG1702,
        CH8398, 20C408, TVP3030, ET6000, w30C516, PM642x, ICS5341, ICS5301,
        MGA1064SG, MGAG100, MGAG200, SiS,
```

If you do not see your hardware listed, don't bother running the program. But if you think SuperProbe may help provide useful information, run the command with its -verbose option and redirect its output to a text file as follows:

```
# SuperProbe -verbose >report.txt
```

You can then read the report:

```
# cat report.txt
```

SuperProbe Version 2.22 (2000 March 6)

       (c) Copyright 1993,1994 by David Wexelblat <dwex@xfree86.org>

       (c) Copyright 1994-1998 by The XFree86 Project, Inc

       This work is derived from the 'vgadoc2.zip' and

       'vgadoc3.zip' documentation packages produced by Finn

       Thoegersen, and released with all appropriate permissions

       having been obtained. Additional information obtained from

       'Programmer's Guide to the EGA and VGA, 2nd ed', by Richard

       Ferraro, and from manufacturer's data books

Bug reports are welcome, and should be sent to XFree86@XFree86.org.
In particular, reports of chipsets that this program fails to
correctly detect are appreciated.

Before submitting a report, please make sure that you have the
latest version of SuperProbe (see http://www.xfree86.org/FAQ).

BIOS Base address = 0xC0000

Doing Super-VGA Probes...

       Probing WD...

       Probing Video7...

       Probing MX...

       Probing Genoa...

       Probing UMC...

       Probing Trident...

       Probing SiS...

       Probing Matrox...

       Probing ATI...

Doing Graphics CoProcessor Probes...

       Probing ATI_Mach...

First video: Super-VGA

       Chipset: ATI 264GT3 (3D Rage Pro) (Port Probed)

       Memory: 8192 Kbytes

       RAMDAC: ATI Mach64 integrated 15/16/24/32-bit DAC w/clock

           (with 6-bit wide lookup tables (or in 6-bit mode))

           (programmable for 6/8-bit wide lookup tables)

```
            Attached graphics coprocessor:
                  Chipset: ATI Mach64
                  Memory:  8192 Kbytes
```

The information in the report can be helpful when using xf86config, as the chipset, clock and memory information for your graphics card may be needed when manually configuring X to work with your system.

Starting the Configuration

To use xf86config, log in as root, then launch the program from the command line as follows:

 # xf86config

After you press Enter, you'll see the following introductory text:

```
This program will create a basic XF86Config file, based on menu selections you
make.

The XF86Config file usually resides in /usr/X11R6/etc/X11 or /etc/X11. A sample
XF86Config file is supplied with XFree86; it is configured for a standard
VGA card and monitor with 640x480 resolution. This program will ask for a
pathname when it is ready to write the file.

You can either take the sample XF86Config as a base and edit it for your
configuration, or let this program produce a base XF86Config file for your
configuration and fine-tune it.

Before continuing with this program, make sure you know what video card
you have, and preferably also the chipset it uses and the amount of video
memory on your video card. SuperProbe may be able to help with this.

Press enter to continue, or ctrl-c to abort.
```

Press Enter to start the configuration process. The program then asks you to select your pointer's protocol:

```
First specify a mouse protocol type. Choose one from the following list:

1.  Microsoft compatible (2-button protocol)
2.  Mouse Systems (3-button protocol)
3.  Bus Mouse
```

```
4.  PS/2 Mouse

5.  Logitech Mouse (serial, old type, Logitech protocol)

6.  Logitech MouseMan (Microsoft compatible)

7.  MM Series

8.  MM HitTablet

9.  Microsoft IntelliMouse
```

```
If you have a two-button mouse, it is most likely of type 1, and if you have
a three-button mouse, it can probably support both protocol 1 and 2. There are
two main varieties of the latter type: mice with a switch to select the
protocol, and mice that default to 1 and require a button to be held at
boot-time to select protocol 2. Some mice can be convinced to do 2 by sending
a special sequence to the serial port (see the ClearDTR/ClearRTS options).
```

```
Enter a protocol number: 4
```

Most Intel-based PCs use PS/2 mouse. Type the number that matches your system's pointing device, then press Enter. The program then asks whether you want three-button emulation:

```
If your mouse has only two buttons, it is recommended that you enable
Emulate3Buttons.
```

```
Please answer the following question with either 'y' or 'n'.
Do you want to enable Emulate3Buttons?   y
```

USB on the Horizon

Newer Linux distributions now include support for Universal Serial Bus (USB) devices such as mice and keyboards. These devices are generally recognized at boot time. For specific directions on how to enable USB pointers for your system, read the file input.txt under the /usr/src/linux/ Documentation/usb directory. You may have to create a proper entry in the /dev directory and change the General Purpose Mouse (gpm) drive to use the new mouse. If you have a USB mouse and a newer Linux distribution, continue running the xf86config command, but then edit the resulting XF86Config file's Pointer section to add support under X. See the section "Pointer Issues" in Chapter 14, "Configuring X11 Input."

A three-button mouse is essential for working efficiently during an X session. The buttons—referred to as 1, 2, and 3, or left, middle, and right—are used for different actions while using X and various window managers. Three-button emulation provides for a simulated button 2, or middle-button mouse click, when the user simultaneously clicks buttons 1 and 3, the left and right buttons of a PS/2 mouse. One common use of the middle button, button 2, is to paste selected or clipboard text.

If you select a "Microsoft-compatible" protocol, the program may also ask you the following:

```
You have selected a Microsoft protocol mouse. If your mouse was made by
Logitech, you might want to enable ChordMiddle which could cause the
third button to work.


Please answer the following question with either 'y' or 'n'.
Do you want to enable ChordMiddle?
```

The ChordMiddle feature is an option that the program can enter into your configuration file and may help certain Logitech pointing devices.

> Yellowdog or PPC Linux users on the Apple iBook and other computers have a one-button Apple Desktop Bus (*ADB*) mouse. Yellowdog and PPC Linux maps function keys (such as F11 and F12) or the left-Ctrl and Opt keys as the middle and right buttons (that is, buttons 2 and 3) for X. The mapping is generally accomplished by passing kernel arguments before Linux boots, or, in the case of USB pointers, through arguments sent to the /proc directory.

Then the program asks you to choose your mouse device:

```
Now give the full device name that the mouse is connected to, for example
/dev/tty00. Just pressing enter will use the default, /dev/mouse.


Mouse device:
```

Unless you have a serial pointer, press Enter to continue. Then the program asks you to choose a keyboard:

```
Please select one of the following keyboard types that is the better
description of your keyboard. If nothing really matches,
choose 1 (Generic 101-key PC)


  1  Generic 101-key PC
```

```
 2   Generic 102-key (Intl) PC

 3   Generic 104-key PC

 4   Generic 105-key (Intl) PC

 5   Dell 101-key PC

 6   Everex STEPnote

 7   Keytronic FlexPro

 8   Microsoft Natural

 9   Northgate OmniKey 101

10   Winbook Model XP5

11   Japanese 106-key

12   PC-98xx Series


Enter a number to choose the keyboard.   1
```

Type a number for your keyboard, or just type **1** and press Enter if you're not sure. The program then asks about the language for the keyboard:

```
 1   U.S. English

 2   U.S. English w/ISO9995-3

 3   Belgian

 4   Bulgarian

 5   Canadian

 6   Czech

 7   German

 8   Swiss German

 9   Danish

10   Spanish

11   Finnish

12   French

13   Swiss French

14   United Kingdom

15   Hungarian

16   Italian

17   Japanese

18   Norwegian


Enter a number to choose the country.

Press enter for the next page

1
```

XFree86 supports 25 different keyboard languages. Type a number for your language and press Enter. The program next asks about your system's monitor, or display:

```
Now we want to set the specifications of the monitor. The two critical
parameters are the vertical refresh rate, which is the rate at which the
the whole screen is refreshed, and most importantly the horizontal sync rate,
which is the rate at which scanlines are displayed.


The valid range for horizontal sync and vertical sync should be documented
in the manual of your monitor. If in doubt, check the monitor database
/usr/X11R6/lib/X11/doc/Monitors to see if your monitor is there.


Press enter to continue, or ctrl-c to abort.


You must indicate the horizontal sync range of your monitor. You can either
select one of the predefined ranges below that correspond to industry-
standard monitor types, or give a specific range.


It is VERY IMPORTANT that you do not specify a monitor type with a horizontal
sync range that is beyond the capabilities of your monitor. If in doubt,
choose a conservative setting.


    hsync in kHz; monitor type with characteristic modes
1   31.5; Standard VGA, 640x480 @ 60 Hz

2   31.5 - 35.1; Super VGA, 800x600 @ 56 Hz

3   31.5, 35.5; 8514 Compatible, 1024x768 @ 87 Hz interlaced (no 800x600)

4   31.5, 35.15, 35.5; Super VGA, 1024x768 @ 87 Hz interlaced, 800x600 @ 56 Hz

5   31.5 - 37.9; Extended Super VGA, 800x600 @ 60 Hz, 640x480 @ 72 Hz

6   31.5 - 48.5; Non-Interlaced SVGA, 1024x768 @ 60 Hz, 800x600 @ 72 Hz

7   31.5 - 57.0; High Frequency SVGA, 1024x768 @ 70 Hz

8   31.5 - 64.3; Monitor that can do 1280x1024 @ 60 Hz

9   31.5 - 79.0; Monitor that can do 1280x1024 @ 74 Hz

10  31.5 - 82.0; Monitor that can do 1280x1024 @ 76 Hz

11  Enter your own horizontal sync range


Enter your choice (1-11): 6
```

Type a number for the range that matches the capabilities of your monitor's horizontal frequencies, then press Enter. Remember that you should not enter values that are out of range. Although the new XFree86 4.0.1 server will attempt to determine values automatically and use correct values, you should be as exact as possible. You can enter exact values by typing **11** and pressing Enter. After entering these values, you'll then be asked about your monitor's vertical sync ranges:

```
You must indicate the vertical sync range of your monitor. You can either
select one of the predefined ranges below that correspond to industry-
standard monitor types, or give a specific range. For interlaced modes,
the number that counts is the high one (e.g. 87 Hz rather than 43 Hz).


1   50-70
2   50-90
3   50-100
4   40-150
5   Enter your own vertical sync range


Enter your choice: 4
```

Again type a number for a range, or type your own range values, then press Enter. You can now enter a description of the monitor:

```
You must now enter a few identification/description strings, namely an
identifier, a vendor name, and a model name. Just pressing enter will fill
in default names.


The strings are free-form, spaces are allowed.
Enter an identifier for your monitor definition:
```

If you just press Enter, the xf86config command will use a definition of "My Monitor." This information is not critical, but can help document your settings. After you press Enter, the program asks whether you want to look at XFree86's card database:

```
Now we must configure video card specific settings. At this point you can
choose to make a selection out of a database of video card definitions.
Because there can be variation in Ramdacs and clock generators even
between cards of the same model, it is not sensible to blindly copy
the settings (e.g. a Device section). For this reason, after you make a
selection, you will still be asked about the components of the card, with
the settings from the chosen database entry presented as a strong hint.


The database entries include information about the chipset, what driver to
run, the Ramdac and ClockChip, and comments that will be included in the
Device section. However, a lot of definitions only hint about what driver
to run (based on the chipset the card uses) and are untested.
```

```
If you can't find your card in the database, there's nothing to worry about.You
should only choose a database entry that is exactly the same model asyour card;
choosing one that looks similar is just a bad idea (e.g. aGemStone Snail 64
may be as different from a GemStone Snail 64+ in terms of hardware as can be).


Do you want to look at the card database?  y
```

Type **y**, then press Enter. The card database, a file named `Cards`, found under the `/usr/X11R6/lib/X11` directory, contains descriptions and settings for more than 750 different video graphics chipsets and cards. The program asks you to select your system's card from the database:

```
 0   2 the Max MAXColor S3 Trio64V+          S3 Trio64V+
 1   2-the-Max MAXColor 6000                 ET6000
 2   3DLabs Oxygen GMX                       PERMEDIA 2
 3   928Movie                                S3 928
 4   AGX (generic)                           AGX-014/15/16
 5   ALG-5434(E)                             CL-GD5434
 6   ASUS 3Dexplorer                         RIVA128
 7   ASUS PCI-AV264CT                        ATI-Mach64
 8   ASUS PCI-V264CT                         ATI-Mach64
 9   ASUS Video Magic PCI V864               S3 864
10   ASUS Video Magic PCI VT64               S3 Trio64
11   AT25                                    Alliance AT3D
12   AT3D                                    Alliance AT3D
13   ATI 3D Pro Turbo                        ATI-Mach64
14   ATI 3D Pro Turbo PC2TV                  ATI-Mach64
15   ATI 3D Xpression                        ATI-Mach64
16   ATI 3D Xpression+                       ATI-Mach64
17   ATI 3D Xpression+ PC2TV                 ATI-Mach64
```

```
Enter a number to choose the corresponding card definition.
Press enter for the next page, q to continue configuration.
```

Scroll through the database by pressing the Enter key. When you find your card, type the number from the far-left column and press Enter. The program then prints a summary describing your select card, as in the following example:

```
Your selected card definition:


Identifier: NeoMagic (laptop/notebook)
Chipset:    MagicGraph 128 series
Driver:     vga
```

```
This card is basically UNSUPPORTED. It may only work as a generic VGA-compatible
card. If you have an XFree86 version more recent than whatthis card definition
was based on, there's a chance that it is now supported.
```

```
Press enter to continue, or ctrl-c to abort.
```

In this example, the selected card is for a laptop using a NeoMagic graphics chipset. You should know that although the **xf86config** command may report that the card is unsupported, this may not be true. You should always check the latest information regarding chipset support at the following site:

```
http://www.xfree86.org/4.0.1/Status.html
```

After you select your card and press Enter, the program may ask you to enter the amount of video memory for your card:

```
Now you must give information about your video card. This will be used for
the "Device" section of your video card in XF86Config.
```

```
You must indicate how much video memory you have. It is probably a good idea
to use the same approximate amount as that detected by the server you intend
to use. If you encounter problems that are due to the used server not
supporting the amount memory you have (e.g. ATI Mach64 is limited to 1024K
with the SVGA server), specify the maximum amount supported by the server.
How much video memory do you have on your video card:
```

```
1   256K
2   512K
3   1024K
4   2048K
5   4096K
6   Other
```

```
Enter your choice:   6
```

If you enter **6** for "Other," the program asks you to enter a value for the memory (note that this value won't be true for a NeoMagic chipset):

```
Amount of video memory in Kbytes: 8192
```

For example, if you have a video card with 8MB video RAM, the value in kilobytes (1,024 bytes) would be 1,024 times eight, or 8,192 kilobytes. Type in the number and press Enter. The program asks you again to enter information about your card:

```
You must now enter a few identification/description strings, namely an
identifier, a vendor name, and a model name. Just pressing enter will fill
in default names (possibly from a card definition).
```

```
Your card definition is ATI Mach64 3D RAGE II.


The strings are free-form, spaces are allowed.
Enter an identifier for your video card definition:
```

Again, it doesn't matter if you just press Enter, as the xf86config command will fill in the information automatically. The program then asks you to select a variety of *modes*, or resolutions and color depths for your monitor and card:

```
For each depth, a list of modes (resolutions) is defined. The default
resolution that the server will start-up with will be the first listed
mode that can be supported by the monitor and card.
Currently it is set to:
"640x480" "800x600" "1024x768" "1280x1024" for 8-bit
"640x480" "800x600" "1024x768" "1280x1024" for 16-bit
"640x480" "800x600" "1024x768" "1280x1024" for 24-bit


Modes that cannot be supported due to monitor or clock constraints will
be automatically skipped by the server.


 1  Change the modes for 8-bit (256 colors)
 2  Change the modes for 16-bit (32K/64K colors)
 3  Change the modes for 24-bit (24-bit color)
 4  The modes are OK, continue.


Enter your choice:
```

Type **1**, **2**, or **3** to change the modes, or **4** if the modes are adequate as currently set. If you type **2**, to change the modes for thousands of colors, for example, you'll see the following information:

```
Select modes from the following list:


 1  "640x400"
 2  "640x480"
 3  "800x600"
 4  "1024x768"
 5  "1280x1024"
 6  "320x200"
 7  "320x240"
 8  "400x300"
```

```
9   "1152x864"

a   "1600x1200"

b   "1800x1400"

c   "512x384"
```

```
Please type the digits corresponding to the modes that you want to select.

For example, 432 selects "1024x768" "800x600" "640x480", with a

default mode of 1024x768.
```

```
Which modes?    43
```

The program prints a list of modes, and you can then enter a set of consecutive numbers (43 in this example) to represent the modes. In this particular example, the program will build an entry for 1,024×768 as the first choice of resolution in thousands of colors, followed by 800×600 as the second choice. Press Enter to continue the configuration, and you'll then see the following:

```
You can have a virtual screen (desktop), which is screen area that is larger

than the physical screen and which is panned by moving the mouse to the edge

of the screen. If you don't want virtual desktop at a certain resolution,

you cannot have modes listed that are larger. Each color depth can have a

differently-sized virtual screen

Please answer the following question with either 'y' or 'n'.

Do you want a virtual screen that is larger than the physical screen?
```

A *virtual screen* can be handy if your monitor and graphics card are limited to 800×600, but you would like to run clients that require 1,024×768. If you'd like a virtual screen, type **y** and press Enter. The program then returns you to the previous screen and again asks whether you want to change the modes. If you are satisfied with the current modes, type **4** to continue the configuration. This time, the program asks you to select a default color depth:

```
Please specify which color depth you want to use by default:

    1   1 bit (monochrome)

    2   4 bits (16 colors)

    3   8 bits (256 colors)

    4   16 bits (65536 colors)

    5   24 bits (16 million colors)

Enter a number to choose the default depth.
```

Type a number from the far-left column. Note that most Linux clients and X sessions work well at a color depth of thousands (65536) of colors, but you can also choose to try millions (16 million colors) of colors. Press Enter to finish the configuration:

```
I am going to write the XF86Config file now. Make sure you don't accidently
overwrite a previously configured one.
Shall I write it to /etc/X11/XF86Config? y
```

This will write your XF86Config file to the /etc/X11 directory. If you answer by entering **n**, the program displays the following:

```
Please answer the following question with either 'y' or 'n'.
Shall I write it to the default location, /usr/X11R6/etc/X11/XF86Config? n

Do you want it written to the current directory as 'XF86Config'? n

Please give a filename to write to:
```

In this example, the program first gives you the choice of writing to the /usr/X11R6/etc/X11 directory, then to the current directory, and finally to any directory with any filename that you choose. This scheme can be handy to avoid overwriting an existing, working XF86Config file, or to create some test files for examination.

Performing Console-based Configuration Using the XFree86 Server

A new feature introduced with the new XFree86 architecture is the ability of the XFree86 X server to configure X from the command line of your console. To do this, log in as root, then use the XFree86 server's -configure command-line option as follows:

```
# XFree86 -configure
```

After you press Enter, the server probes your computer's hardware and generates a configuration file named XF86Config.new in the /root directory. You can then test the configuration by running the server, specifying the test configuration with the server's -xf86config command-line option and the pathname to the configuration file, as follows:

```
# XFree86 -xf86config /root/XF86Config.new
```

After you press Enter, the server starts and uses your new configuration file. If the configuration file works, you can then copy or move the file to the /etc/X11 directory with the name XF86Config.

Using xf86cfg

XFree86 4.0.1 also includes a new graphical configuration client, named `xf86cfg`, that you can use to configure X. To start the configuration, type the client's name on the command line as follows:

```
# xf86cfg
```

After you press Enter, your screen may clear, and you can start the configuration. This client may or may not work with your computer's hardware, but if it does, `xf86cfg` will use the `twm` window manager to offer a configuration window showing the results of running the XFree86 server to probe your computer's hardware, and an accessx window for configuration. The configuration window features four buttons along the top of the screen for adding additional hardware, along with a graphic representation of your computer's monitor, graphics card, keyboard, and mouse (in other words, those components that the server has recognized and found). The bottom portion of the window features a Help and Quit button, along with a Layout button to define new configurations. The Layout button is helpful if you have added new hardware, such as a second graphics card and monitor or a new keyboard or mouse.

Edit the Files Section First!

The `xf86cfg` client will generate a working `XF86Config` file, but unfortunately does not add at least one critical element: a `FontPath` entry in the Files section. Open the generated `XF86Config.new` file with your favorite text editor and look for the Files section, which should look like this:

```
Section "Files"
EndSection
```

Change this section by adding (at a minimum) a `FontPath` entry pointing to X's miscellaneous fonts:

```
Section "Files"
                    FontPath "/usr/X11R6/lib/X11/fonts/misc"
EndSection
```

You can then use the `startx` command to start a test X session, as follows:

```
# startx — -xf86config /root/XF86Config.new
```

When you're satisfied with your configuration, copy the `XF86Config.new` file to the `/etc/X11` directory with the name `XF86Config`.

The accessx window displays the numeric keypad equivalents of button presses and clicks in case the configuration tool does not recognize your mouse.

To configure a component, such as your mouse, right-click the recognized mouse; a pop-up menu appears, allowing you to configure the device, select options for the device, and enable, disable, or remove the device. Click the configure menu item to select a new mouse device or protocol, then click the Apply Changes button and the OK button to save the changes. Your changes will be saved in a file named `XF86Config.new` in the `/root` directory.

Configuration of a new graphics card involves selecting your computer's graphic card from a list. To configure your monitor, you must enter correct horizontal and vertical frequency ranges. If you right-click the computer in the graphical layout, you can enter X server options. For example, you can select the option DontZap or Dont-Zoom to enable or disable Ctrl+Alt+Backspace or Ctrl+Alt+KeyPad+/-. These key combinations enable you to change resolutions.

When you've finished configuration, click the Quit button in the Configuration window. The session quits, and you can then test your new `XF86Config.new` file.

Using Xconfigurator

Red Hat Linux includes a custom `XF86Config` file generator named `Xconfigurator`. You can invoke this command from the console or command line of an X11 terminal window. Start the command as follows:

```
# Xconfigurator
```

After you press Enter, the screen clears and you'll see the dialog box shown in Figure 3.1.

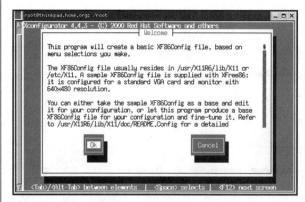

Figure 3.1 *Red Hat's* Xconfigurator *command creates an* XF86Config *file using a graphical interface.*

Use the Tab key to navigate through Xconfigurator's buttons, highlight the OK button, then press the Enter key. The command then probes your computer's hardware and reports on the type of graphics card found, as shown in Figure 3.2.

After the probe, press Enter. Xconfigurator then asks you to select your monitor, as shown in Figure 3.3.

Use your up or down cursor keys to scroll through the list of monitors. If you find your monitor, make sure that it is highlighted, then press Enter. If you do not see your monitor listed, highlight the Custom entry and press Enter. You can then press Enter again, and the program presents a list of generic ranges, as shown in Figure 3.4.

Scroll through the list of generic horizontal frequency ranges and select one that matches your computer's monitor. If you do not see a suitable range, again select Custom and press Enter. You'll see another dialog box, as shown in Figure 3.5.

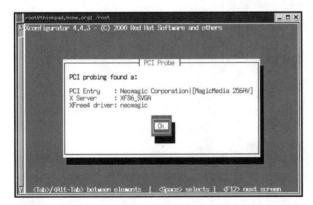

Figure 3.2 Xconfigurator *first probes your computer's graphics hardware.*

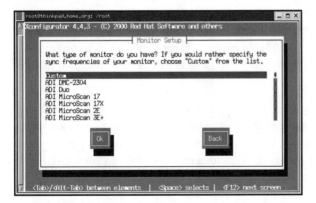

Figure 3.3 *Scroll through the list of monitors to select your monitor, or press Enter to enter custom settings.*

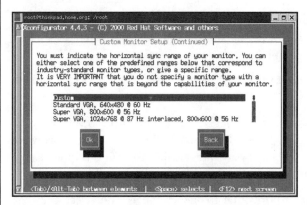

Figure 3.4 *You can select a generic range or type of monitor, or select Custom to enter specific settings.*

Figure 3.5 *Enter the horizontal and vertical frequency ranges for your computer's monitor.*

Enter the exact ranges specified in the manufacturer's manual included with your monitor. Although most recently manufactured monitors incorporate circuit protection, older monitors can be damaged through incorrect settings. When finished, press Enter. The program asks you to select the amount of video memory installed in your computer or graphics card (see Figure 3.6).

Scroll through the values, then press Enter after highlighting the correct amount of video memory. The program then asks about your graphics card's clockchip, as shown in Figure 3.7. Clockchips are used by some video cards to help determine frequency timings for horizontal and vertical modes of resolution, or how fast pixels can be drawn.

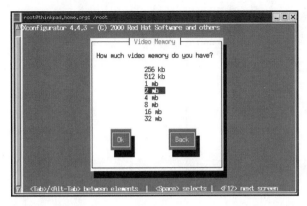

Figure 3.6 *Scroll through the list of values to pick the amount of video memory installed.*

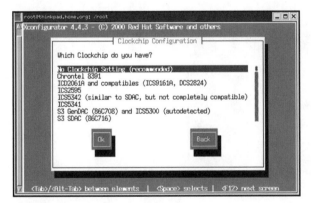

Figure 3.7 *If required, select your card's clockchip type.*

XFree86 will perform better with some cards if a clockchip setting is enabled in the configuration file. However, if Xconfigurator detects your card, or if you're not sure about your card's clockchip, go with Xconfigurator's recommendation or do not enter a clockchip setting. When finished, press Enter to continue. Xconfigurator then presents sets of video modes, or pairs of color depths and resolutions, to use with your card (see Figure 3.8).

Navigate to each desired mode, then press the spacebar to select the mode. You'll see an asterisk (*) when the mode is selected. If you can select different resolutions within each color depth, you can then use the Ctrl+Alt+numeric keyboard's plus (+) and minus (−) keys to jump to each different resolution. For example, to try to jump to a higher resolution, press and hold Ctrl+Alt, then press the plus (+) key on your

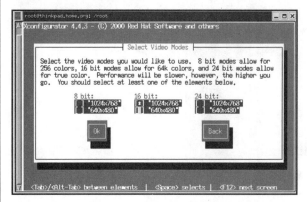

Figure 3.8 *Select desired video modes using your Tab key and spacebar.*

Figure 3.9 *You can have* Xconfigurator *test your configuration manually, or you can skip this step to check your settings manually.*

keyboard's numeric keypad. Laptop users may have to also first press and hold a special Fn key and turn on the numeric pad to accomplish the same task. When you've finished selecting the modes, tab to the OK button and press Enter.

You can choose to test your configuration, or you can skip the test by selecting the Skip Test button and pressing Enter. If the test fails, you can go back and enter new settings. If you skip the test, your new XF86Config will be saved under the /etc/X11 directory.

Using DrakConf and XFdrake

Mandrake Linux (which is similar to Red Hat's distribution, but diverging with each release, because of the addition of varying configuration tools) includes several utilities that you can use to reconfigure X. The graphical tool providing configuration options for Mandrake is the DrakConf utility. You can start this client (as root) from the command line of an X terminal window, as follows:

```
# DrakConf &
```

After you press Enter, you'll see the dialog box shown in Figure 3.10.

You can click the X Configuration button to perform a total reconfiguration of X. This approach launches the XFdrake client. This client leads you through several dialogs boxes, including the one shown in Figure 3.11, which enables you to choose a monitor type.

Click to highlight your monitor type in the dialog box, then click the OK button to continue the configuration. You can cancel the configuration by clicking the Cancel button. Using the XFdrake client is handy if you have changed the monitor or graphics card used with your computer. If you'd like to change the resolution and color depth of your X sessions, click the Xdrakres (Change X Resolution) button on DrakConf's dialog box (as shown in Figure 3.10). You'll then see the dialog box shown in Figure 3.12.

Click the drop-down menu to choose a different color depth, or click a button next to a desired resolution, then click the OK button to save your changes. The changes will take effect the next time that you start X.

Figure 3.10 *The* DrakConf *client provides two utilities,* XFdrake *and* Xdrakres, *when reconfiguring X.*

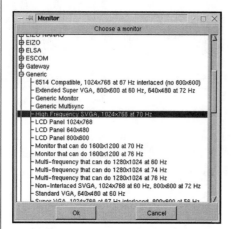

Figure 3.11 *Choosing a monitor type is the first step when you reconfigure X using the* XFdrake *client.*

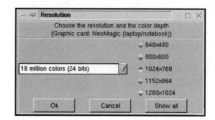

Figure 3.12 *The* Xdrakres *client allows you to change your X session resolution and color depth settings.*

Using SaX

SuSE Linux provides a graphical X configuration tool named SaX. This tool, launched from the command line following installation or at any time if X needs to be reconfigured, graphically leads you through the configuration process. Like other software tools, such as xf86config, the SaX client builds a working XF86Config file to enable X to work with your computer.

After installing SuSE Linux, type the following command:

```
# sax
```

After you press Enter, you'll see the dialog box shown in Figure 3.13.

The configuration starts by asking you to select the type of mouse used on your system. Click the drop-down menus to select the type and protocol. To change your pointer's properties, use the Properties tab at the top of the dialog box. You can also test your pointer after configuration. When finished, click the Apply button, then the OK button. The dialog box disappears, and you should then click the Next button in the bottom-right corner of the dialog box to continue the configuration of your keyboard, graphics card, monitor, resolution, and color depth settings. When finished, use the SaX File menu to save your changes.

Using kvideogen

Another client that may help you configure X is the kvideogen client. However, this client is useful mostly for configuring versions of XFree86 older than version 4.0.1.

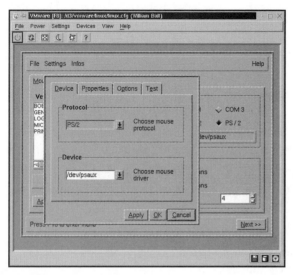

Figure 3.13 *The SuSE Linux sax client enables you to configure your X system using a graphical user interface.*

You can use kvideogen, which is included with the K Desktop Environment (KDE), to create frequency and resolution settings, known as *modelines*, for inclusion in your XF86Config file. Note that you do not need this client when using XFree86 4.0 or higher, as these versions calculate modelines automatically.

You must start the client from the command line of an X terminal during an X session, as follows:

kvideogen

After you press Enter, you'll see the dialog box shown in Figure 3.14.

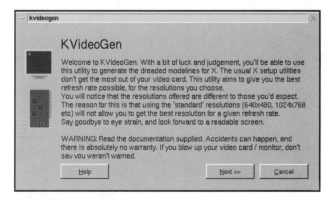

Figure 3.14 *The* kvideogen *client can help you create modelines for* XF86Config *files for XFree86 4.0 or higher.*

Begin the configuration by clicking the Next button. The client then asks you a series of questions regarding your graphics card and monitor. When finished, you can use kvideogen to save the modeline as a text file.

Resource Information

http://www.xfree86.org/4.0.1/index.html—release information for the XFree86 4.0.1 distribution, and documentation regarding support for specific chipsets.

http://www.redhat.com/support/docs/howto/XFree86-upgrade/XFree86-upgrade.html—a mini-HOWTO document from Red Hat, Inc., with information on how to upgrade XFree86 on a Red Hat Linux system.

http://www.yellowdoglinux.com/products/guide.shtml—a Web page for downloading the latest installation and XFree86 configuration guide for Yellow Dog Linux (for PowerPC CPU-based computers).

http://www.xfree86.org/4.0.1/manindex1.html—entry to a full index of the man pages for XFree86 4.0.1.

http://www.cs.utexas.edu/users/kharker/linux-laptop/—the Linux on Laptops pages, a great resource for notebooks users in search of information about Linux on specific laptop models (and a great place to get a working XF86Config file for your laptop).

http://www.suse.com/us/support/hardware/index.html—entry to the SuSE Linux hardware compatibility database, with information regarding supported monitors and graphics cards and other video hardware.

http://www.bdstoday.com/2000/July/Features242.html—an article by Ralph Krause, describing how to configure XFree86 on NetBSD-based systems.

Chapter 4: Overview of XFree86

This chapter introduces you to the features and components of XFree86 4.0.1 after installation and configuration on your system. Although you'll find the majority of XFree86's software—such as the XFree86 server, fonts, libraries, drivers, and documentation—installed under the /usr/X11R6 directory, there are other critical configuration files and essential elements of your X installation. Knowing the location of important files and understanding the role that these files play will help you when using and managing X for Linux.

The chapter begins with a discussion of the features, software components, and file system layout of the XFree86 distribution. You'll then learn about fonts, some essential files found under the /etc/X11 directory, and documentation included with XFree86.

Features

The new XFree86 (version 4.0 and 4.0.1) is the result of more than two years' effort by The XFree86 Project, Inc. Originally, these efforts were intended to redesign X for Intel-based PCs, to improve portability and produce a new, modular architecture for the distribution. Along the way, ports of XFree86 (such as FreeBSD, NetBSD, OpenBSD, and PPC Linux) have benefited from these improvements to the Intel-based distribution. The new architecture means better support for other operating systems and hardware platforms, and allows graphics chipset manufacturers to release binary-only drivers to support new video cards entering the market.

One of the most important features of the new XFree86 distribution is the design of the XFree86 X server, named XFree86. This server incorporates major changes to previous versions; support for all hardware is now incorporated into a single server instead of multiple servers. Along with this major architectural change to the distribution, other features introduced with the new server include the following:

- Reduced size of the configuration file (XF86Config)
- Improved configuration parser (although legacy 3.3.X compatibility for Keyboard and Pointer sections has been retained at least through XFree86 4.0.1)
- XINERAMA, a feature that provides multihead, multiple-screen, and multiple driver support
- Support for many additional fonts, font rasterizers, and keyboard internationalization
- Improved probing and built-in configuration support by the server

- Modular driver support with common code that all drivers can use
- Modular library support for sophisticated and complex 3D drawing
- Peripheral Component Interconnect (PCI) device identification (which aids in multihead displays)
- Incorporation of standard Video Graphics Array (VGA) timing modes
- Ability to mix color depths on different screens

The new server benefits from many other improvements, ranging from wider input device support to new configuration tools and a runtime loader (based on code donated by Metro Link, Inc.). This means that better support for newer video cards is introduced a lot faster than in the past.

Major Software Components

The components of this new architecture (and the architecture itself) are discussed in detail in the document named DESIGN, found under the `/usr/X11R6/lib/X11/doc` directory. You can also find a copy by browsing to **http://www.xfree86.org/**. What follows is a simplified overview of the new elements, with a focus on how these elements may affect you when installing, configuring, or managing XFree86.

As you know, you can install XFree86 while installing Linux, by using compressed tarballs (such as `file.tar.gz` or `file.tgz`) and an install script from The XFree86 Project, Inc., or through various other software package-management systems such as Red Hat's RPM, or front-end clients such as KDE's `kpackage` or GNOME's `gnorpm`.

The majority of the software is installed under the `/usr/X11R6` directory tree. Depending on your system and your requirements, this directory tree can include additional documentation, such as man pages; additional libraries, such as add-on toolkits like OpenMotif; additional development and programming support, such as libraries and documentation; and additional fonts and clients.

File System Layout

The majority of software, fonts, and files included with XFree86 are found under the `/usr/X11R6` directory. However, other elements, such as configuration files, are included under the `/etc/X11` directory, and some services, such as the `xfs` font server, may be started by a system initialization script under the `/etc/rc.d/init.d` directory (this scheme is especially common on Red Hat–based Linux systems). Software developers should become familiar with XFree86's layout for `#include` files and development libraries, which are essential to the process of creating new clients for X.

Table 4.1 lists the major directories and briefly explains each directory's contents.

Table 4.1 XFree86 Component Directories

Directory	Description
/etc/X11	Configuration files and directories
/usr/X11R6/bin	X clients and other programs
/usr/X11R6/include	X11 development #include files and graphics
/usr/X11R6/lib	X client support and shared libraries
/usr/X11R6/lib/X11	Configuration files, application resource files, documentation, fonts, and internationalization files
/usr/X11R6/lib/modules	Seven directories of XFree86 modules (drivers, extensions, fonts, etc.)
/usr/X11R6/man	Six directories of X man pages
/usr/X11R6/share	Shared resources for various X clients

A base installation of XFree86 for Intel-based PCs—including development software, libraries, and documentation—consists of nearly 90MB of hard drive space, 141 directories, and more than 3,700 files. This includes nearly 1,200 files of X man pages, more than 100 graphics images, and 900 font files (for nearly 6,000 fonts). You can print a graphic display of the majority of the elements of an installation by using the tree command, along with its -d (directory-only) option, as follows:

```
# tree -d /usr/X11R6
/usr/X11R6
|- bin
|- doc
|- include
|    |- X11
|    `- Xaw3d -> X11/Xaw3d
|- lib
|    |- X11
|    |    |- app-defaults
|    |    |- config
|    |    |- doc
|    |    |- etc
|    |    |- fonts
|    |    |- fs -> ../../../../../etc/X11/fs
|    |    |- fvwm2
|    |    |- lbxproxy -> ../../../../etc/X11/lbxproxy
|    |    |- locale
```

```
|    |    |— proxymngr -> ../../../../etc/X11/proxymngr
|    |    |— rstart -> ../../../../etc/X11/rstart
|    |    |— twm -> ../../../../etc/X11/twm
|    |    |— x11perfcomp
|    |    |— xdm -> ../../../../etc/X11/xdm
|    |    |— xinit -> ../../../../etc/X11/xinit
|    |    |— xkb
|    |    |— xserver -> ../../../../etc/X11/xserver
|    |    `— xsm -> ../../../../etc/X11/xsm
|    |— modules
|    |    |— codeconv
|    |    |— dri
|    |    |— drivers
|    |    |— extensions
|    |    |— fonts
|    |    |— input
|    |    `— linux
|    `— xscreensaver
|— man
|    |— man1
|    |— man3
|    |— man4
|    |— man5
|    |— man6
|    `— man7
`— share
```

Note that this output is edited (not all directories are shown) to show the major directories. Symbolic links are represented by ->. Other directories include language support files and programming extensions.

XFree86 Fonts

You can control and support fonts in a number of ways when using XFree86. You can install fonts locally or on a remote server. Most users working on a standalone Linux X workstation will have X11 fonts installed under the /usr/X11R6/lib/X11/font directory, although other fonts may be found under the /usr/share/fonts directory.

Font management utilities for X first appeared in X11R3. This release includes utilities such as the mkfontdir client, which is used to create font name databases in each font subdirectory included under the /usr/X11R6/lib/X11/font directory. Other font utilities include the xlsfonts client, which lists installed fonts; the xfontsel client, which displays individual fonts selected from various font families; and the xfd client, which displays characters in an X font.

Fonts are stored in compressed form in separate directories, sorted according to type and resolution. Compressed font support has been present in XFree86 at least since version 2.1; however, starting with version 3.3.1, XFree86 has stored fonts in the more efficient gzip format instead of the UNIX compress format.

For example, the font directories included with XFree86 4.0.1 include the following:

- 100dpi
- CID
- Speedo
- cyrillic
- latin2
- misc
- 75dpi
- PEX
- Type1
- encodings
- local

Each directory contains a fonts.alias and fonts.dir file. The fonts.dir file contains a line indicating the number of fonts, along with a list of abbreviated font filenames and names of each font. X and xfs font server use this minidatabase to find font files. Scalable font directories also contain a file named fonts.scale (generated by the ttmkfdir client). The fonts.alias file contains two columns of information: an alias name and a font name. This file is used to create new font names for existing fonts. The encodings directory contains Type1 (also known as TrueType) font encodings generated by the mkfontdir client. This information is used to scale and draw fonts for your display.

The most important configuration file entry is the FontPath entry in your system's XF86Config file in the Files section. For example, the following is the minimum entry required to use XFree86 on a standalone workstation:

```
Section "Files"
     FontPath    "/usr/X11R6/lib/X11/fonts/misc"
EndSection
```

Using the previous listing of font directories, an example set of FontPath directories might be as follows:

```
Section "Files"
     FontPath    "/usr/X11R6/lib/X11/fonts/misc"
```

```
        FontPath       "/usr/X11R6/lib/X11/fonts/100dpi:unscaled"

        FontPath       "/usr/X11R6/lib/X11/fonts/75dpi:unscaled"

        FontPath       "/usr/X11R6/lib/X11/fonts/100dpi"

        FontPath       "/usr/X11R6/lib/X11/fonts/75dpi"

        FontPath       "/usr/X11R6/lib/X11/fonts/CID"

        FontPath       "/usr/X11R6/lib/X11/fonts/PEX"

        FontPath       "/usr/X11R6/lib/X11/fonts/Speedo"

        FontPath       "/usr/X11R6/lib/X11/fonts/Type1"

        FontPath       "/usr/X11R6/lib/X11/fonts/cyrillic"

        FontPath       "/usr/X11R6/lib/X11/fonts/latin2"

        FontPath       "/usr/X11R6/lib/X11/fonts/local"
EndSection
```

You can view the current FontPath by using the xset client with its -q option, as follows:

```
# xset -q
...
Font Path:

/usr/X11R6/lib/X11/fonts/100dpi,/usr/X11R6/lib/X11/fonts/75dpi,/usr/X11R6/lib/X11/fo
nts/CID,/usr/X11R6/lib/X11/fonts/cyrillic,/usr/X11R6/lib/X11/fonts/misc
...
```

Note that the preceding example does not show all the xset output that the command would generate. Another way to see a larger list of fonts available for your X session is to use the xlsfonts client, as in the following example:

```
# xlsfonts
-adobe-courier-bold-o-normal—0-0-100-100-m-0-iso8859-1

-adobe-courier-bold-o-normal—0-0-75-75-m-0-iso8859-1

-adobe-courier-bold-o-normal—10-100-75-75-m-60-iso8859-1

-adobe-courier-bold-o-normal—11-80-100-100-m-60-iso8859-1

-adobe-courier-bold-o-normal—12-120-75-75-m-70-iso8859-1

-adobe-courier-bold-o-normal—14-100-100-100-m-90-iso8859-1

-adobe-courier-bold-o-normal—14-140-75-75-m-90-iso8859-1

-adobe-courier-bold-o-normal—17-120-100-100-m-100-iso8859-1

-adobe-courier-bold-o-normal—18-180-75-75-m-110-iso8859-1

-adobe-courier-bold-o-normal—20-140-100-100-m-110-iso8859-1

-adobe-courier-bold-o-normal—24-240-75-75-m-150-iso8859-1
...
```

Again, this example shows only part of the output of the command.

Networking Fonts

The `xfs` font server is primarily responsible for network font management, and thus provides fonts to the local or remote display server (XFree86). This means that you can use fonts installed on a remote computer, reducing the need for local storage.

The `xfs` server is managed by its configuration file, config, found under the `/etc/X11/fs` directory. This file contains a number of elements, one of the most important of which is the font catalogue. The following is an example of a font catalogue:

```
catalogue = /usr/X11R6/lib/X11/fonts/misc:unscaled,
        /usr/X11R6/lib/X11/fonts/75dpi:unscaled,
        /usr/X11R6/lib/X11/fonts/100dpi:unscaled,
        /usr/X11R6/lib/X11/fonts/misc,
        /usr/X11R6/lib/X11/fonts/Type1,
        /usr/X11R6/lib/X11/fonts/Speedo,
        /usr/X11R6/lib/X11/fonts/cyrillic,
        /usr/X11R6/lib/X11/fonts/75dpi,
        /usr/X11R6/lib/X11/fonts/100dpi,
...
```

Note that the example replicates only a portion of the catalogue entry. Table 4.2 lists the major elements of the `xfs` config file. See the `config` file for example entries.

Table 4.2 xfs config File Elements

Option	Description
alternate-servers	Provides a comma-delimited list of alternate servers
catalogue	Prints a comma-delimited list of font paths
client-limit	Specifies the maximum number of clients that can connect
clone-self	Spawns a new server when the maximum number of clients is reached
default-point-size	One-hundredths of a point (default 120 decipoints)
default-resolutions	Provides a comma-delimited list of resolutions
deferglyphs	Specifies the encoding size used for 16-bit fonts
error-file	Specifies the error logging pathname
no-listen	Turns off listening on specified type of port
port	Listens on specified port
use-syslog	Toggles logging on and off

When you use `xfs` on a standalone Linux workstation, you can replace the entire list of `FontPath` entries listed in your `XF86Config` file with a single entry:

```
FontPath    "unix/:7100"
```

This entry corresponds to the workstation hostname (`localhost` in this example, as the field is blank) and port number. Other Linux distributions may use the following entry:

```
FontPath    "unix/:-1"
```

Note that the preceding example also works for `localhost`. Typically, a system initialization script starts the `xfs` font server. Under Red Hat Linux–based systems, this is the `xfs` script under the `/etc/rc.d/init.d` directory. You can start the script as follows:

```
# /etc/rc.d/init.d/xfs start
```

If your system doesn't use an initialization script for `xfs`, you can start the font server before starting your X session as follows:

```
# xfs &
```

After you press Enter, the server begins running.

You can also access the fonts provided by a server running on a remote computer on your network. To do this, use the xset client to add fonts provided by a remote server to the current display's FontPath. For example, use xset's `+fp` `option`, along with the name of a remote server, such as **thinkpad.home.org**:

```
# xset +fp unix/thinkpad.home.org:7100
```

Essential Files

The `/etc/X11` directory contains a number of important configuration files used by XFree86 and other X software components, such as: the font server; *proxy*, or service managers; *display managers*, or X login choosers; and various window managers. Obviously, the most important file in this directory is `XF86Config`. This file may also be located under the `/usr/X11R6/lib/X11` or `/root` directories. You can also rename this file to anything you want by invoking the `-xf86config` command-line option when starting X11 (see the section "Using the `startx` Script," in Chapter 6, "Starting X11").

Many Linux distributions (and previous XFree86 distributions) also include a symbolic link named X under the /etc/X11 directory. This link points to the X server used for your X session. With XFree86 4.0.1, the link X points to the `XFree86` server under the `/usr/X11R6/bin` directory:

```
# ls -l /etc/X11/X
```

```
lrwxrwxrwx  1 root   root     22 Oct 11 11:27 /etc/X11/X -> /usr/X11R6/bin/XFree86
```

Another important file is `Xresources`. This file contains system-wide default resource information for a number of X11 clients, such as `emacs`, `xterm`, and `vim`. Resource settings use individual *identifiers*, or text strings that define default color and size. Also, in some cases, these settings toggle features on or off using Boolean (true or false) logic. Note the following example:

```
emacs*Background: DarkSlateGray

emacs*Foreground: Wheat

emacs*pointerColor: Orchid

emacs*cursorColor: Orchid

emacs*bitmapIcon: on

emacs*font: fixed

emacs.geometry: 80x25
```

In this example (a portion of `Xresources`), the `emacs*Background:` identifier is set to the value of `DarkSlateGray`. The foreground color is set to `Wheat`. This means that when any user on your system launches the `emacs` editor during an X session (unless overridden by local settings), the default editing session will use light text on a dark background.

Other directories, such as those labeled with the name of a window manager, contain system-wide default settings that define how the window manager draws and handles windows and the desktop. And the `app-defaults` directory contains default resource settings for many different X clients. Note that you can override these settings by using comparable resource files in your home directory or from the command line. You'll learn more about managing these resources and settings in Chapter 8, "Using X11 Clients."

XFree86 Documentation

Every XFree86 client has a corresponding man page, found under the `/usr/X11R6/man` directory tree. However, you'll find additional documentation installed on your system under the `/usr/X11R6/lib/X11/doc` directory. In addition, a number of X clients included with your Linux distribution (especially with Red Hat Linux) have a directory of additional documentation under the `/usr/doc` directory.

Table 4.3 describes the documentation included in the `README` and `.TXT` files for XFree86 3.3.6 and 4.0.1 under the `/usr/X11R6/lib/X11/doc` directory. There are other files you should also read under this directory, especially the file named `RELNOTES`, which contains release information about the version of XFree86 installed on your system.

Table 4.3 XFree86 3.3.6 and 4.0.1 Documentation

Filename	Description
README	Overview of XFree86 4.0.1
README.3DLabs	Information about support for 3DLabs chipsets
README.Config	(Outdated) information on configuring XFree86
README.DECtga	Information for DEC 21030 users
README.DGA	Direct graphics access (framebuffer) support information
README.DRI	Information about Precision Insight's Direct Rendering Interface (DRI)
README.DRIcomp	Directions for building DRI support
README.I128	Number Nine I128 chipset support information
README.LinkKit	Directions for building XFree86
README.Linux	Compatibility notes for Linux users on older versions of Linux and XFree86
README.LynxOS	Updated information on LynxOS support by XFree86
README.MGA	Information for Matrox chipset users
README.Mach32	Notes on using Mach32 graphics
README.Mach64	Directions for using the XFree86 3.3.6 Mach64 server
README.NVIDIA	Support for NVidia NV1, SGS-Thomson STG2000, Riva 128, Riva TNT, and TNT2 graphics cards
README.NetBSD	Directions for using XFree86 with NetBSD UNIX
README.Oak	Oak Technologies support information
README.OpenBSD	Directions for using XFree86 with OpenBSD UNIX
README.P9000	P9000 server and computer support
README.S3	S3 chipset information
README.S3V S3	Virge chipset information
README.SiS	SiS chipset information
README.Video7	Video7 driver information
README.W32	W32 and ET6000 chipset support information
README.WstDig	Western Digital chipset support
README.agx	Support information for AGX chipsets
README.apm	Alliance Promotion chipset information
README.ark	ARK Logic chipset information
README.ati	ATI chipset (Mach) support
README.chips	Chips & Technologies chipset support
README.cirrus	Cirrus Logic chipset support information

Table 4.3 XFree86 3.3.6 and 4.0.1 Documentation *(continued)*

Filename	Description
README.clkprog	Directions for using clockchip option settings in XF86Config
README.cyrix	Cyrix chipset options and support
README.epson	Epson SPC8110 chipset support information
README.fonts	Detailed font support information for XFree86 4.0.1
README.i740	Support for Intel 740–based graphics cards
README.i810	Support for Intel 810 motherboard graphics
README.isc	Support for Interactive UNIX
README.mouse	Directions for using various pointing devices with XFree86
README.neo	Information for NeoMagic chipset users
README.r128	Support for ATI Rage 128 graphics cards
README.rendition	Information for Rendition (Micron) Verité users
README.s3virge	S3 chipset information
README.trident	Trident Microsystems chipset information
README.tseng	Tseng Labs chipset information
DPMS.TXT	Directions for using Display Power Management Signaling (DPMS) with X
DPMSLib.TXT	DPMS specification for X
bigreq.TXT	Suggestions for dealing with large X protocol requests
buffer.TXT	Buffer extensions for XFree86
ctlseqs.TXT	Documentation of xterm client escape sequences
evi.TXT	Extended Visual Information protocol specification
libGL.TXT	Open/GL library specification for XFree86
mit-shm.TXT	Documentation for the MIT Shared Memory extensions for X
record.TXT	Documentation for the X Record Extension protocol
recordlib.TXT	Specification of the X Record Extension Library
shape.TXT	Directions for using arbitrary shapes (windows) with X
shapelib.TXT	Specification of the X nonrectangular shape library
tog-cup.TXT	Colormap Utilization Policy and Extension abstract
xc-misc.TXT	Documentation for the X MISC protocol
xtest.TXT	Directions for automating X server testing
xtestlib.TXT	Specifications for the testing library
xv-protocol-v2.TXT	Abstract describing X video extensions

Note that information for the new driver modules included with XFree86 4.0.1 is being moved to individual man pages. This means that whereas previous versions of XFree86, such as 3.3.6, provided documentation about a chipset in a README file (such as the README.neo file), you will now find newer information in a man page with the driver's name, such as neomagic. For example, if you look under the /usr/X11R6/lib/modules/drivers directory, you'll see the following:

```
# ls /usr/X11R6/lib/modules/drivers
apm_drv.o        fbdev_drv.o      neomagic_drv.o     tga_drv.o
ati_drv.o        glide_drv.o      nv_drv.o           trident_drv.o
chips_drv.o      glint_drv.o      r128_drv.o         tseng_drv.o
cirrus_alpine.o  i740_drv.o       rendition_drv.o    vga_drv.o
cirrus_drv.o     i810_drv.o       s3virge_drv.o
cirrus_laguna.o  linux/           sis_drv.o
cyrix_drv.o      mga_drv.o        tdfx_drv.o
```

To find information about a driver, you can then enter the man command followed by the name of the driver, as follows:

```
# man mga
MGA(4)                                                    MGA(4)


NAME
       mga - Matrox video driver

SYNOPSIS
       Section "Device"
         Identifier "devname"
         Driver "mga"
         ...
       EndSection


DESCRIPTION
       mga is an XFree86 driver for Matrox video cards. The
       driver is fully accelerated, and provides support for the
       following framebuffer depths: 8, 15, 16, 24, and an 8+24
       overlay mode. All visual types are supported for depth 8,
       and both TrueColor and DirectColor visuals are supported
       for the other depths except 8+24 mode which supports PseudoColor,
       GrayScale and TrueColor. Multi-head configurations are supported.


SUPPORTED HARDWARE
       The mga driver supports PCI and AGP video cards based  on
       the following Matrox chips:

...
```

The preceding example does not display all the output that the command generates. You may also find that some documentation is missing in the first few versions of the new XFree86 4-series. Note the following example:

```
# man neomagic
NEOMAGIC(4)                                                    NEOMAGIC(4)


NAME
       neomagic - NeoMagic video driver


SYNOPSIS
       Section "Device"
         Identifier "devname"
         Driver "neomagic"
         ...
       EndSection


DESCRIPTION
       neomagic is an XFree86 driver for NeoMagic video chips.
       THIS MAN PAGE NEEDS TO BE FILLED IN.
...
```

Perhaps subsequent releases will provide additional documentation. You should always check the XFree86 home page for the latest information regarding your chipset.

Resource Information

/usr/X11R6/lib/X11/doc/DESIGN—a draft overview of the new XFree86 server, with specific information for driver developers or programmers writing new modules using the new server architecture.

/usr/X11R6/lib/X11/doc/RELNOTES—release notes covering the XFree86 distribution, with specific information about configuration tools, compatibility, features, fonts, drivers, modules, updates, and problems; a must-read for better understanding XFree86 4.0.1.

XF86Config man page—details about each section of the X configuration file.

xfs man page—details about configuring X for local and remote font service.

ftp://ftp.xfree86.org/pub/XFree86—a site from which you can download current or legacy versions of XFree86.

Chapter 5: Choosing a Window Manager

What is a window manager?

Window manager features

An overview of window managers

An overview of desktop environments

This chapter introduces a special type of X11 client known as a window manager. You'll learn what a window manager is, what features a window manager should have, and how to choose an appropriate window manager for your system. This chapter covers window managers for XFree86; the focus is on those window managers that work with XFree86 and Linux. However, in many cases, the software works in much the same way for other operating systems that can use X, such as FreeBSD, OpenBSD, or NetBSD.

Again, this is an introduction to window managers for XFree86 and Linux. If you're new to Linux and X, you'll be quite surprised to learn about the available choices. Experienced users may already have a preferred X environment. You can find details about managing and configuring window managers in Chapter 16, "Window Manager Configuration."

What Is a Window Manager?

A *window manager* is an X client that manages X windows and the X desktop. You'll also find several desktop environments available for XFree86 and Linux. The difference between a window manager and a desktop environment is that, in general, a window manager is a single X client, whereas a desktop environment includes a specialized window manager and suite of clients that take advantage of special software libraries or other features of the specialized window manager.

Some examples of simpler window managers introduced later in this chapter include twm and fvwm. Examples of desktop environments include the Common Desktop Environment (CDE), the K Desktop Environment (KDE), and window managers using the GNOME libraries.

You don't have to use a window manager with X. If you want to run X without a window manager, first create an .xinitrc file in your home directory containing the following:

```
xterm -fg black -bg white
```

Next, save the file. This entry starts the xterm client using black text on a white background. Then you can choose to use the startx command or the xinit client to start an X session. To use the startx command, you simply enter the following:

```
# startx
```

Or, you can use the xinit client to start an X session, by entering the following:

```
# xinit
```

Figure 5.1 *An* xterm *client can run without a window manager during an X session.*

After you press Enter, you should see a display such as that shown in Figure 5.1.

The display shows the xterm window sitting at the upper-left corner of the X *root* display or main desktop. As you can see, you can run X clients without a window manager (type **exit** to quit the session, or press Ctrl+Alt+Backspace to kill the server), but some familiar and quite necessary elements are missing from the display. How many elements do you think are missing?

Window Manager Features

Window managers are an essential element for using X. The following are some of the basic tasks performed by a window manager:

- Managing new or *child* windows (and hiding, iconifying, or destroying a window)

- Managing window decorations (such as titlebars, scrollbars, and buttons)

- Managing window movement and placement (such as determining where to place a newly created window)

- Handling the resizing of windows (providing animation or redrawing of resized windows according to your pointer or keyboard input)

- Creating an icon or restoring an icon to a client window (and perhaps docking icons).
- Handling tiling, overlay, or overlapping of windows
- Handling *focus policy*, which determines how a window becomes active (such as whether a window should receive focus when your pointer is over a window) and when a window becomes active (such as whether you must click to make a window active)
- Possibly providing menus from the root desktop or on a client window
- Possibly mapping keyboard input into pointer movement or other actions (so you can, for example, use X without a pointing device)
- Possibly providing *virtual desktops*—that is, a new, blank desktop—from memory
- Handling transfer of *interclient communication*—the exchange of data between windows—such as copy and paste operations and object linking

Most window managers provide these features. And some window managers support additional features, such as dragging and dropping of icons to copy, print, delete, link, or move files. Newer window managers may also automatically draw icons of files based on the file's name or even its content.

A window manager runs in the background (in memory) during your X session. The only time you may know that one is running is when you have an active client; you'll then see how your window manager draws the client's window frame, titlebar, buttons, and scrollbars.

One of the great things about using XFree86 (and Linux) is that you have freedom of choice. This means that, unlike a commercial operating system provided by a monopolistic software industry, XFree86 lets you choose the type of window manager to use during your X session. The difference in appearance of your desktop will be more than just window dressing using a different background display. You can choose a window manager with as many or as few features as you desire. Some window managers (such as wm2 or wmx) have an extremely small memory and storage footprint, whereas other desktop environments require 100MB of hard drive space and at least 32MB of memory. And some compact and efficient window managers can mimic other operating systems, even those that run on different hardware platforms!

An Overview of Window Managers

This section introduces a number of window managers available for XFree86 and Linux. You'll find a number of these included with most Linux distributions, whereas others may be downloaded from various sites on the Internet. Although all window managers described in this section share some common features, each possesses a unique character or attribute that you may find desirable.

Unless proscribed by corporate policy or your local system administrator, choosing a window manager is usually a personal choice, dictated by aesthetics, need, or applicability. Note that you can customize nearly all of them either by using resource settings, creating systemwide defaults for consistency, or configuring each individually with settings stored in a user's home directory.

The twm Window Manager

The only window manager included with XFree86, twm (Tab Window Manager) is a legacy-type client that provides the bare minimum of features to support a productive X session. This window manager features a smaller memory footprint than others, but provides window decorations, customizable root desktop menus, icons, and other desirable features.

Most Linux distributions use twm as a fallback or *failsafe* window manager because it is included with XFree86. Its systemwide resource file, system.twmrc, is found under the /etc/X11/twm directory. You can find unique user settings in a user's home directory in a file named .twmrc.

You can launch this window manager using the startx command, if you include the following in your home directory's .xinitrc file:

```
twm
```

When your X session starts, you can build a desktop, as shown in Figure 5.2.

To access the desktop menu, left-click over a blank area of the desktop. A menu appears, from which you can select window control items or menus of applications (as defined in twm's .twmrc file).

The FVWM Window Manager

The FVWM window manager is another legacy-type client that has been popular with X power users for a number of years. Like twm, FVWM has served as a building block for many other window managers. Based on twm, FVWM incorporates additional features, one of the most important of which is the *virtual desktop*, or additional in-memory root displays. This feature enables you to assign different applications to different desktops; for example, you can devote one desktop to word processing, another to Internet browsing, and others to specific tasks. This feature can help you organize your workspace (if you have enough memory!).

This window manager also features 3D decorations, as well as a modular architecture that enables you to add features through additional code modules. The FVWM interface is very customizable. Although at one point in the recent past there were two versions, fvwm and fvwm2, there is now only one supported version, fvwm2, which derives from the previous version, fvwm2.

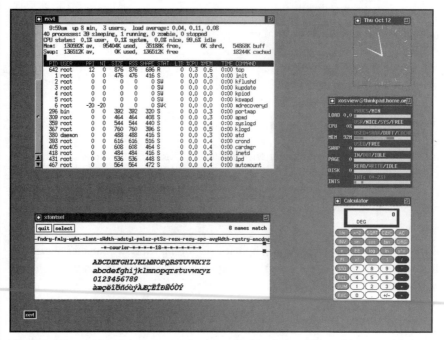

Figure 5.2 *The* twm *window manager features window decorations and icon management.*

fvvm2's systemwide resource file, system.fvwm2rc, is found under the /etc/X11/fvwm2 directory. You can find unique user settings in a user's home directory in a file named .fvwm2rc.

You can launch this window manager, like others, using the startx command, if you include the following in your home directory's .xinitrc file:

fvwm2

When your X session starts, you can build your FVWM desktop, as shown in Figure 5.3.

Note that FVWM provides an icon window list, desktop *pager*, or navigation mini-window, along with a mailbox, clock, and load client in a wharflike dock on the desktop. The pager is used to navigate between desktops. To move to a different desktop, you can click on the desktop's represented block in the pager; alternatively, if you configure FVWM to use "borderless" margins, you can simply drag your pointer to the edge of your desktop to move into an adjacent desktop.

One version of twm, vtwm, includes virtual desktop features. You can download, build, and install vtwm from **ftp://ftp.x.org/R5contrib/vtwm-5.3.tar.gz**.

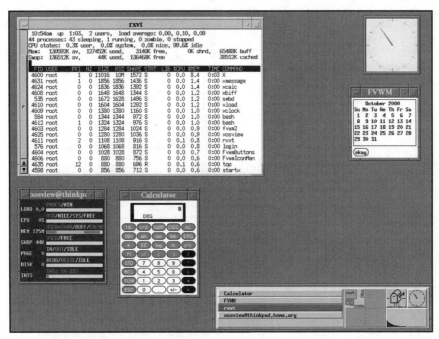

Figure 5.3 *The FVWM window manager, like* twm, *features window decorations and icon management, but also provides virtual desktops through a pager module.*

The FVWM95 Window Manager

The FVWM95 window manager builds on FVWM, but provides a look and feel similar to that of a well-known commercial operating system. Like FVWM, FVWM95 also has 3D icons, a wharf, and virtual desktops, but also includes a *taskbar*, or floating menu, along the bottom of the desktop that features a pop-up hierarchical menu.

FVMW95's systemwide resource file, `system.fvwm95rc`, is found under the `/usr/local/lib/X11/fvwm95` directory. Unique user settings may be located in a user's home directory in a file named `.fvwm95rc`.

You can launch this window manager, like others, using the `startx` command if you include the following in your home directory's `.xinitrc` file:

```
fvwm95
```

When your X session starts, you can build your FVWM95 desktop, as shown in Figure 5.4.

FVWM95 can provide a wharflike dock on the desktop, but the most interesting features are the familiar window buttons and Start menu on the desktop's taskbar.

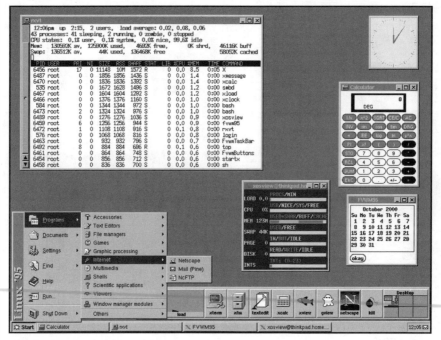

Figure 5.4 *The FVWM95 window manager features virtual desktops, but also provides a taskbar and Start menu for launching X clients and other commands.*

The AfterStep Window Manager

The AfterStep window manager, based on fvwm, provides a similar look and feel as another well known but perhaps less popular commercial operating system known as NeXTSTEP. Like each of the previous window managers with virtual desktops, AfterStep provides a pager in its root display. A windowlist, or taskbar, is placed along the top of the desktop, and a wharf is used to provide rapid access to various X clients. Among AfterStep's most notable features are its desktop menu (accessed by left-clicking the mouse over a blank area of the desktop), the number of window buttons placed in window titlebars, the use of *themes* (comprehensive look-and-feel desktop schemes), and pop-up help displays that appear when the pointer hovers over a window decoration.

AfterStep's default settings are contained in numerous files, with systemwide settings under the /usr/share/afterstep or /usr/local/share/afterstep directories. User settings are located in a user's home directory in a subdirectory named GNUstep.

You can launch this window manager, like others, using the startx command if you include the following in your home directory's .xinitrc file:

```
afterstep
```

When your X session starts, the AfterStep desktop appears, as shown in Figure 5.5.

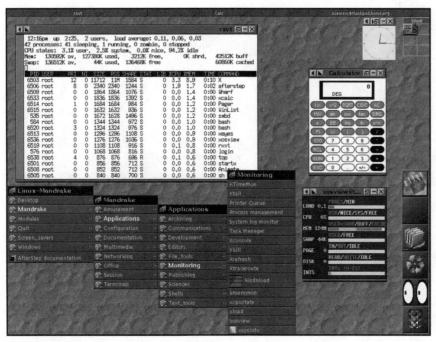

Figure 5.5 *The AfterStep window manager features complex but flexible settings derived from numerous configuration files installed on your system.*

The Enlightenment Window Manager

The Enlightenment window manager, like AfterStep, was first based on another window manager (fvwm2), but the similarity ends there. Completely revised, Enlightenment, also known as E, is one of the new breed of X window managers. Although Enlightenment is quite complex, it offers an amazing variety of features. This window manager (shown in Figure 5.6) was one of the first to take advantage of the GNOME software libraries, which provide many unique features but overall consistency in X client interfaces.

Enlightenment includes a floating desktop pager, xv. The window manager takes now-familiar features of docking, taskbars, virtual desktops, and menuing to dazzling extremes. Like AfterStep, Enlightenment keeps its default settings in numerous files, with systemwide settings under the /usr/share/enlightenment directory. User settings are located in a user's home directory in a subdirectory named .enlightenment.

You can launch this window manager, like others, using the startx command if you include the following in your home directory's .xinitrc file:

```
enlightenment
```

When your X session starts, the Enlightenment desktop appears (the desktop should look similar, but not quite the same, as shown in Figure 5.6).

Figure 5.6 *The Enlightenment window manager brings numerous new features to the X desktop, such as hosts of applets (miniclients), transparent terminals, and whimsical themes.*

This window manager, unlike the previous window managers described in this chapter, can require significant disk space. A typical systemwide configuration and support directory contains nearly 3,000 files and consumes more than 11MB of hard drive space. Cache files created in each user's .enlightenment directory can grow larger than 5MB.

Themes are one of the main attractions of this window manager. Literally thousands of different themes are available for download from various Internet sites. This means that you can make your desktop look like (or unlike) any computer. For example, Figure 5.7 shows the same Enlightenment desktop as shown in Figure 5.6, but after installation and selection of a new theme.

Themes available for system-wide use are downloaded and generally installed under the /usr/share/enlightenment/themes directory. You can also copy themes into the .enlightenment/themes directory in your home directory. After copying the theme to the directory, press the middle mouse button with the cursor over a blank area of the desktop, then select the Restart Enlightenment menu item. To select the newly installed theme, again press the middle mouse button, but click the Themes menu item, then click the new theme from the submenu. Your desktop will change to the new theme (although you may have to choose a new background).

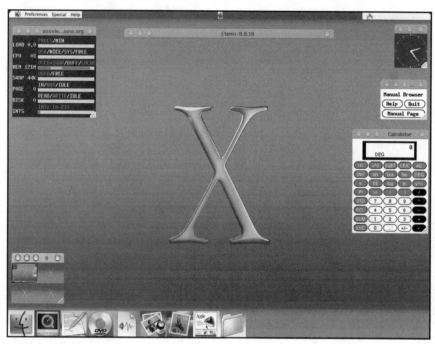

Figure 5.7 *Themes are one of the main attractions of using the Enlightenment window manager for your X sessions.*

Enlightenment is a popular window manager that also works well with the GNOME software libraries. However, according to E developers, future improvements aim for Enlightenment "to become a desktop shell." This will move Enlightenment out of the category of a window manager and into the category of a desktop environment.

The mlvwm Window Manager

The `mlvwm` window manager mimics the classic Apple Macintosh interface and provides all the necessary window management and decorations needed to handle X clients. You can access a virtual desktop by clicking the upper-right corner of the display, or launch other clients by clicking the upper-left corner of the display. No desktop root menus are available, but you can iconify windows (using a window-shade effect) by double-clicking the titlebar. `mlvwm` is a compact and efficient window manager that is only 86K in compress source code form, and which uses a single configuration file located in a user's home directory with the name `.mlvwmrc`.

You can launch this window manager, like others, using the `startx` command if you include the following in your home directory's `.xinitrc` file:

```
mlvwm
```

When your X session starts, you'll see a desktop as shown in Figure 5.8.

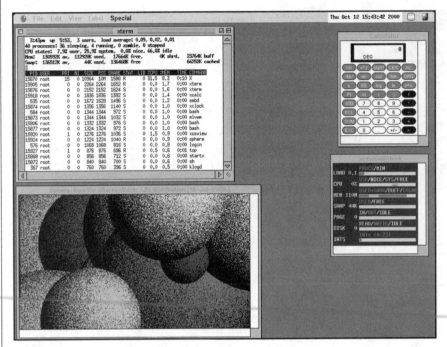

Figure 5.8 *The* `mlvwm` *window manager mimics a now-classic computer operating system interface.*

The Window Maker Window Manager

The Window Maker window manager, like AfterStep, mimics the NeXT computer interface. Like AfterStep, Window Maker provides a wharf (also known as an *application dock*), extensive desktop menus, and virtual desktops (or *workspaces*).

Window Maker provides virtual desktops that you can access by clicking on the pager in the upper-left corner of the display. The window manager features a configurable application dock and provides icon handling on the desktop. Another feature is the ability to "pin" menus to the desktop display, making the task of choosing new clients to run a bit easier.

Systemwide configuration files are located under the /usr/X11R6/share/wmakerconf directory. User defaults are stored under the GNUstep/Defaults directory in a user's home directory. Window Maker also supports different styles and themes.

You can launch this window manager, like others, using the startx command if you include the following in your home directory's .xinitrc file:

```
Wmaker
```

When your X session starts, you'll see the Window Maker desktop, which should look similar to Figure 5.9.

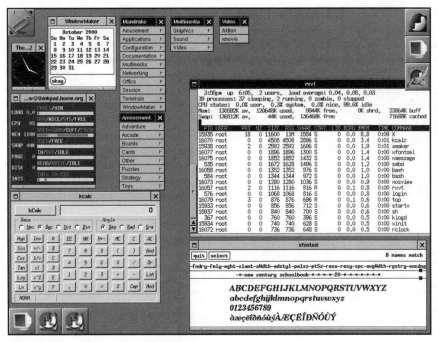

Figure 5.9 *The Window Maker window manager, like Afterstep, aims to provide a NeXTSTEP-like graphical interface for the X desktop.*

The IceWM Window Manager

The IceWM window manager, according to its developers, was "coded from scratch in C++ for performance and size." Like other window managers, IceWM provides window management, decorations, virtual desktops, and themes. IceWM comes with a graphical configuration tool (as shown in Figure 5.10) that you can use to customize the look of the taskbar, fonts, and windows, the size of elements, the theme, and the desktop background's image or color.

You can access virtual desktops by clicking on the desktop's taskbar. A familiar Start menu provides client launching.

Systemwide configuration files and themes are located under the `/usr/X11R6/lib/X11/icewm` directory. User defaults are stored under the `.icewm` subdirectory (in a file named preferences) in a user's home directory.

You can launch the IceWM window manager using the `startx` command if you include the following in your home directory's `.xinitrc` file:

```
icewm
```

When your X session starts, you'll see the desktop as shown in Figure 5.10.

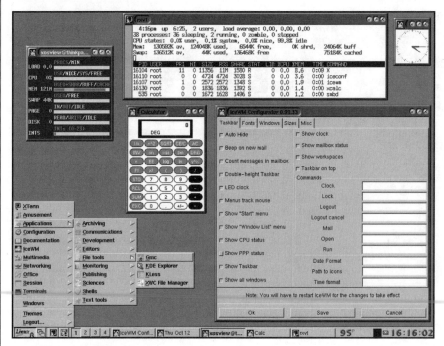

Figure 5.10 *The IceWM window manager, according to its developers, was built for speed and ease of use, and offers no-nonsense features.*

The Sawfish Window Manager

The Sawfish window manager is one of the newest window managers developed for compatibility with the GNOME software libraries. Previously named Sawmill, its name was changed to avoid a trademark dispute. Unlike other window managers, the `sawfish` client uses a scripting language for configuration and features. Although most popularly used with GNOME, `sawfish` functions quite well as a standalone manager, and provides window management, decorations, virtual desktops, and themes.

Themes, systemwide configuration settings, and internationalization files are usually stored under the `/usr/share/sawfish` directory, with user defaults stored in the `.sawfish` subdirectory in the user's home directory. Hand-coded customization may also be saved in a file named `.sawfishrc` in the home directory.

This window manager, like Enlightenment and some others, also provides a way to save a session *state*—that is, to perform *session management*. This means that the window manager will remember open clients, window positions, and settings, and restore them for the next X session.

To invoke the Sawfish window manager using the `startx` command, include the following in your home directory's `.xinitrc` file:

```
sawfish
```

When your X session starts, you'll see the desktop as shown in Figure 5.11.

Note that this window manager also comes with a user-interface configuration tool. To launch this tool, you can click the middle mouse button to select the Customize menu, or from the command line of an X terminal window type the `sawfish-ui` command as follows:

```
# sawfish-ui &
```

After you press Enter, you'll see the configuration tool as shown in Figure 5.11.

The wm2 Window Manager

The `wm2` window manager, by Chris Cannam, wins the award for being one of the smallest window managers for X. The greatest feature of this window manager (and a slightly more capable sibling known as `wmx`) is its lack of features! This means that `wm2` provides only a minimal handle for dragging and resizing windows, but no code is included to support icons, minimizing, maximizing, or virtual desktops. A single-item root menu, accessed by left-clicking, brings up an `xterm` terminal window.

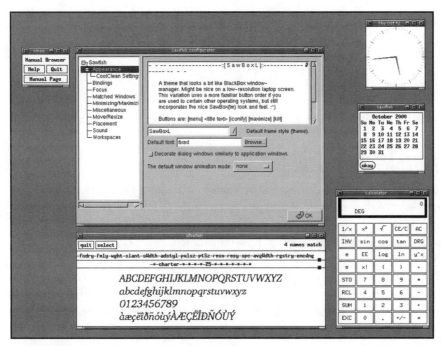

Figure 5.11 *The Sawfish window manager is GNOME-compliant, and also features session management and a graphical configuration tool.*

This window manager is less than 32KB in compressed source form, and is built from nine source files of C++ code. The resulting binary is less than 120,000 bytes! This means that wm2 can be an excellent choice for X users with computers that have low-capacity hard drives or less than optimal memory for X. For a few more features, such as virtual desktops (or "Channels," to use the author's terminology), minimizing, and more extensive menus, use the wmx window manager.

The wm2 window manager features no configuration file. All configuration is done in the file Config.h when building the binary. The steps to build and install wm2 are quite easy. After downloading the file (as root), decompress the file by entering the following command:

```
# tar xvzf wm2-4.tar.gz
```

Next, navigate to the resulting directory and edit (if required) the file named Config.h:

```
# cd wm2-4
```

```
# pico -w Config.h
```

Save any changes, then build wm2 and copy it to your system's /usr/X11R6/bin directory:

```
# make
```

```
# cp wm2 /usr/X11R6/bin
```

To launch this window manager using the startx command, include the following in your home directory's .xinitrc file:

```
wm2
```

When your X session starts, you can build your wm2 desktop, as shown in Figure 5.12.

The mwm Window Manager

The mwm window manager, perhaps better known as the Motif window manager, was originally part of the commercial and proprietary OSF/Motif programming libraries (Toolkit) from The Open Group, Inc. However, starting before 1994, a group of developers began developing a Motif 1.2–compatible Open Source distribution that included programming libraries and development files. Today, the result is LessTif 0.91.8. This distribution is compatible with Motif 1.2, and will soon be compatible with Motif 2.0. You can download, build, and install the LessTif software from various sites on the Internet, and some Linux distributions, such as Mandrake and SuSE, include LessTif, its development libraries, and associated clients (one of which is mwm).

The mwm window manager included with LessTif is a functional clone of the commercial mwm window manager, and can even use the same configuration files. You'll get a definable root menu, along with the ability to page between virtual desktops.

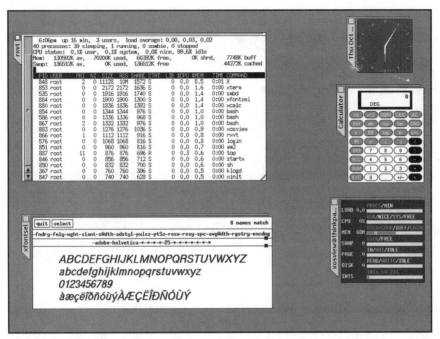

Figure 5.12 *The* wm2 *window manager is a minimalist window manager for X sessions, and can be quite useful when running X on resource-starved platforms.*

The systemwide configuration file, named `system.mwmrc`, is found under the `/usr/X11R6/lib/X11/mwm` or `/etc/X11/mwm` directories. The individual user configuration file is named `.mwmrc` and resides in a user's home directory.

When Is Free Not Free?

On May 15, 2000, The Open Group, Inc., released the source code to OSF/Motif 2.1.30 and created a pseudo–Open Source project, distributing the software under the name Open Motif. However, although the software is free for personal use when used with a free operating system, you cannot develop binary-only applications or sell applications created with the software. To do this, you must use a commercial operating system and have a license for Motif from The Open Group. Browse to **http://www.opengroup.org** for more details. Commercial distributions of Motif are available for Linux, and you can get one from Metro Link, Inc., or Xi Graphics.

How Many Window Managers?

Many other window managers are available for XFree86. Some of these include ctwm, olvwm, Blackbox, YAWM, wmG, aewm, lwm, flwm, and many others. Unless the window manager's author has made a special effort to build a version for your version of Linux and XFree86, you'll most likely need to download and build the window manager from scratch. As you can see from the wm2 example, this procedure is not always difficult. However, some window managers, especially those under rapid and active development, may require additional, cutting-edge software. This can hamper your desire to use the "latest and greatest" version of your favorite window manager. However, as you have seen so far, many other window managers are available for you to explore in your quest for the perfect X desktop.

The mwm configuration file defines the root desktop menu (accessed by right-clicking in a blank area of the desktop), along with window actions to be carried out in response to keyboard presses (known as *key bindings*) or mouse presses (known as *button bindings*).

As with other window managers, you can start an X session using mwm by editing your .xinitrc file and adding the following:

mwm

When your X session starts after you invoke the startx command, you'll see a desktop such as that shown in Figure 5.13.

An Overview of Desktop Environments

This section introduces three desktop environments for XFree86 and Linux. X desktop environments are similar to window managers (as a window manager is required to support client windows), but differ significantly in scope, size, and approach to providing a graphical interface for your X session. The environments described in this section have several traits or features in common:

- An underlying support structure consisting of one or more software libraries that provide standardized graphical interfaces for clients developed for the environment. In other words, developers creating programs for the environment can reuse a standard base of code (or, in the parlance of commercial operating systems, a base set of application programming interfaces, or *APIs*) for drawing windows, menus, buttons, scrollbars, file open and save dialog boxes, and so on.

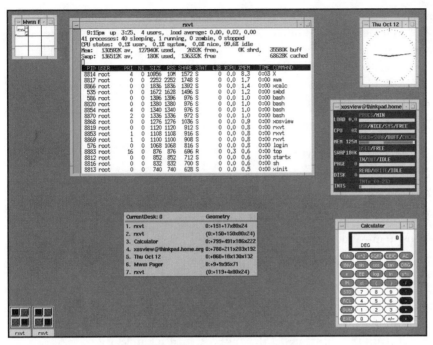

Figure 5.13 *The* mwm *window manager, part of the LessTif distribution, is an exact clone of the OSF/Motif* mwm *window manager.*

- Standardized interclient communications protocols, so that clients may more easily share data, either via drag-and-drop, object linking, or other means.

- A base set of essential clients specifically tailored to take advantage of the common code base. This means that all programs have common features, such as File, Edit, or Help menus, that all file operation dialog boxes should look and work the same, and that the same keyboard commands should control menuing. This also means that taken collectively, the entire suite of clients, along with window management, creates a singular, unique look and feel integrated into the desktop.

- The benefits of sharing a common code base and libraries, as well as features such as session management (state saving), graphical configuration tools, and, for some environments (such as KDE), transparent network access.

The Common Desktop Environment

Although many of these features have long been present for Apple Macintosh MacOS users, it was only until the introduction of the Common Desktop Environment (CDE) that UNIX and X users could enjoy a similar desktop. Based on OSF/Motif 1.2.5, CDE first became available for Linux in 1996 as a commercial add-on in a client version (see Figure 5.14) and developer's version for Red Hat, Inc.'s Red Hat Linux 4.2. Although marketed for only a relatively short time (about 18 months) and not generally considered a commercial success, CDE is still in use with commercial versions of UNIX, such as HP/UX. You can still purchase CDE for Linux from Xi Graphics, Inc., which offers the environment as a relatively inexpensive product known as DeXtop 2.1.

Some of the features of CDE include the following:

- A base set of productivity tools
- Graphical configuration
- Context-sensitivity and online help
- Data interchange, such as drag-and-drop messaging
- Consistent window and icon management
- Session management
- Graphical development tools

The original CDE client distribution for Linux required nearly 45MB disk space and included more than 60 CDE clients. The system resided under the `/usr/dt` file system tree, with the clients under the `/usr/dt/bin` subdirectory.

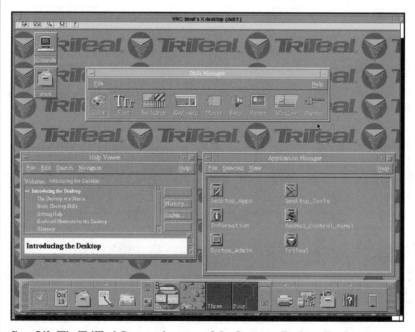

Figure 5.14 *The TriTeal Corporation port of the Common Desktop Environment (CDE) was one of the first integrated X desktops for Linux and was based on OSF/Motif 1.2.5.*

The objective of CDE was to provide a single, unifying desktop and set of APIs for developing graphical clients for the hodge-podge of commercial UNIX operating systems offered by members of the The Open Group. How well CDE has achieved this objective may be in doubt. However, although commercial developers may desire a single GUI for Linux to ensure some market success, the Linux and X user base has still not singled out a definitive GUI. The truth is that many users like the idea of having the freedom to choose a GUI, window manger, or desktop environment. The following sections discuss two of the most popular desktop environments: the K Desktop Environment (KDE) and the GNU Network Object Model Environment (GNOME).

The K Desktop Environment

In 1996, a German Linux software developer named Matthias Ettrich introduced the K Desktop Environment (KDE) for Linux and XFree86. Since then, KDE has gone through several major revisions, with vast improvements included with every release. KDE is a graphical desktop environment that runs on a variety of Linux and UNIX systems and provides all the features of a modern graphical, networking computer interface.

The suite of KDE clients grows weekly, and typical distributions include nearly 200 or more KDE applications. The current stable version of KDE is 1.1.2; the next anticipated version is 2.0, which is slated to include a full-featured office suite named KOffice, a C/C++ integrated development environment (IDE), and hundreds of clients. The current version of KDE uses a window manager named kfm, which will be replaced with a client named konqueror.

KDE is typically started from the command line or through an X11 *display manager*, or X graphical login. To start KDE from the command line using the startx command, you should insert the following into your .xinitrc file:

```
startkde
```

If you're using the current stable version of KDE (version 1.1.2), after you start your X session you should see the desktop shown in Figure 5.15.

KDE may be located under the /opt/kde directory or, if you use Mandrake or Red Hat Linux, integrated under the /usr/bin directory. Configuration files are stored in a subdirectory named .kde in a user's home directory.

One issue that potentially clouds the appeal of KDE for developers is whether or not KDE is truly free. The source code for KDE is certainly free and open; what has been in question is whether or not the Qt software libraries—which provide the base set of development functions and APIs, and which were developed by an independent company named Trolltech—are also free. According to Trolltech, the Free Edition of the Qt libraries for KDE are indeed free. However, unlike other software libraries

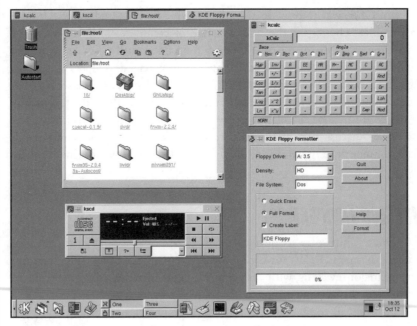

Figure 5.15 *KDE version 1.1.2 uses the* `kfm` *client for window management and provides a comprehensive desktop and suite of clients for XFree86.*

distributed under the GNU Library or Lesser GNU General Public License, commercial software developers must purchase a "Professional/Enterprise Edition" license from Trolltech before using the QT libraries.

Of course, this issue should not affect the user. KDE is an extremely friendly and usable environment that, until recently, was viewed as the "cutting edge" desktop environment for XFree86. Unless you're interested in developing and distributing proprietary programs, KDE is a viable desktop environment.

The GNU Network Object Model Environment

The GNU Network Object Model Environment (GNOME) is a project that Miguel de Icaza started in August 1997. The environment was born out of the development of software libraries created for the GNU Image Manipulation Program (GIMP) and the need for a base set of APIs to create a desktop environment that could be distributed under the GNU General Public License. This is in direct contrast to KDE, which depends on the Qt software libraries. Licensing issues have been a bone of contention between various camps of Open Source software developers in the past few years. Note, however, that other issues have also affected KDE and GNOME developers, such as the primary use of the C++ language for KDE development and the use of C for GNOME coding.

Another difference between GNOME and KDE is that GNOME consists of software libraries (such as GTK), clients that use the drawing functions provided by the libraries, and any window manager created or revised to take advantage of the GNOME libraries. Thus you can choose the type of window manager that you use with GNOME. Some of the window managers that work with GNOME include the following:

- Sawfish, available at **http://sawmill.sourceforge.net**
- Enlightenment, available at **http://enlightenment.org**
- Window Maker, available at **http://www.windowmaker.org**
- IceWM, available at **http://www.icewm.org**
- Scwm, available at **http://scwm.mit.edu**
- FVWM (version 2.3), available at **http://www.fvwm.org**

Like KDE, GNOME provides a user-friendly suite of applications with a consistent and easy-to-use desktop. Also, the GNOME developers, like the KDE developers, have been crafting an office suite of complex applications for the desktop environment. The current, stable version of GNOME is 1.2, although a newer release, 2.0, is planned for late 2000 or early 2001.

GNOME usually is installed when you install X along with Linux, and is a staple feature of nearly all Red Hat Linux–based distributions. The individual GNOME clients usually reside under the `/usr/bin` directory, whereas configuration files, libraries, and other files are stored under the `/etc/gnome` and `/usr/share/gnome` directories. Individual settings are stored in a user's home directory under a subdirectory named `.gnome`.

You can start an X session using GNOME by including the following under your `.xinitrc` file:

```
exec gnome-session
```

When X starts, you'll see a desktop similar to that shown in Figure 5.16.

Ximian GNOME

Although Red Hat, Inc., first started GNOME, and continues to support GNOME development, two of the original GNOME developers, Miguel de Icaza and Nat Friedman, created a company named Helix Code, Inc., in Cambridge, Massachusetts in mid-1999. The company's first and main product, Helix GNOME, is a polished, professional collection of GNOME clients. Another product, named Evolution, is a groupware suite with mail, calendar, addressing, and instant messaging features. In January 2001, Helix Code, Inc. changed its name to Ximian.

Ximian GNOME is unique in that it enables users to install and update the software quickly over the Internet. You can install a custom version for your Linux distribution

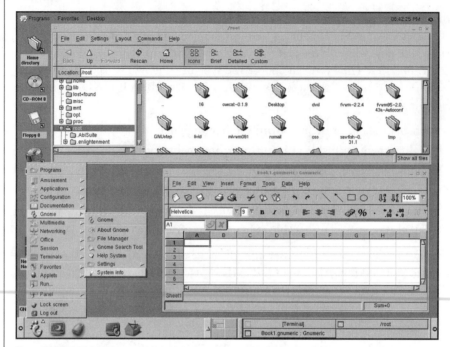

Figure 5.16 *GNOME 1.2 works with a variety of X window managers, and is a staple desktop environment for many different Linux distributions, especially Debian and Red Hat Linux.*

quickly over the Internet if you have broadband access (640Kbps download or better). You can also get the distribution on CD-ROM from Ximian.

The first step is to navigate to the Ximian Web site at **http://www.ximian.com/desktop/download.php3**, as shown in Figure 5.17.

Click the drop-down menu to select the supported Linux distribution that matches your installed distribution. The program then provides directions for you to follow as root to download the Ximian GNOME installer. For example, if you use the text-only lynx Web browser, the program might instruct you to enter the following on the command line:

```
# lynx -source http://go-gnome.com/ | sh
```

This command downloads the initial installer (currently a compressed 2.1MB file). After downloading, the installer appears as shown in Figure 5.18.

To begin the installation, click the Next button (as shown in Figure 5.18). The installer then asks you to select a package source, such as a Ximian mirror site. Click through the next several dialog boxes until the installer asks you to choose the

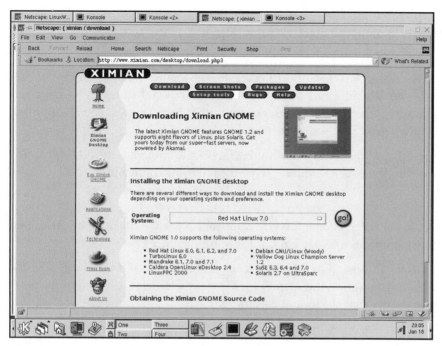

Figure 5.17 *To begin installation of Ximian's GNOME distribution over the Internet using broadband access, navigate to* ***http://www.ximian.com/desktop/download.php3***.

Figure 5.18 *The Ximian GNOME installer is used to select a download site, then to select and download the basic components of the Ximian GNOME desktop.*

software packages. Note that a full install of everything from Ximian is (currently) more than 75MB of software and 100 software packages! When finished selecting the desired components and packages, click the Next button to download the software.

A progress dialog box appears, showing the download and percentage of files retrieved. The files, in RPM format, will be retrieved and stored in your system's /tmp directory. After the download is complete, the installer uses the rpm command to install the software on your system.

After installation, you can log into Ximian GNOME through the GNOME display manager, gdm. If gdm is not running, type the following command:

gdm

After you press Enter, choose GNOME for your X session, then log in. After your session starts, you'll see the desktop, as shown in Figure 5.19.

Note that the Ximian GNOME desktop in Figure 5.19 looks much like the GNOME desktop shown in Figure 5.16. Most of the differences between the desktops lie in the updated clients and documentation.

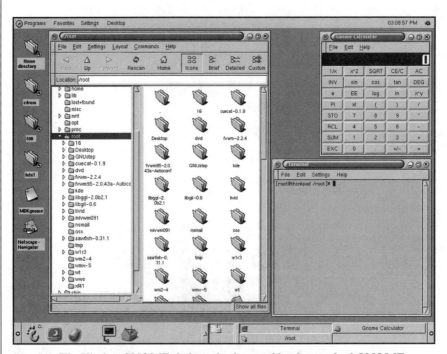

Figure 5.19 *The Ximian GNOME desktop closely resembles the standard GNOME desktop, but features updated clients and extra documentation.*

Resource Information

http://www.xfree86.org—the starting point for learning more about XFree86 and X clients included with the XFree86 distribution.

ftp://ftp.x.org—a potential source of alternative window managers for use with XFree86; the site usually provides the window managers in source code form, which you must then decompress, build from scratch, install, then configure for your system.

http://www.fvwm.org—the official home page for the fvwm window manager.

ftp://mitac11.uia.ac.be/html-test/fvwm95.html—home page of the FVWM95 window manager.

http://www.afterstep.org—home page for downloading the latest version of the AfterStep window manager (in source or binary form), and the place to browse for additional themes and icons for the desktop.

http://www.enlightenment.org—the official home page for Rasterman's E window manager.

http://e.themes.org—a linux.com Open Source site for downloading additional Enlightenment themes.

http://www2u.biglobe.ne.jp/~y-miyata/mlvwm.html—home page for the mlvwm window manager, which mimics the early Apple Macintosh desktop.

http://www.windowmaker.org—the official home page for the Window Maker window manager.

http://icewm.sourceforge.net—the IceWM window manager development page (and source to the latest versions).

http://sawmill.sourceforge.net/—home page for sawfish development.

http://www.all-day-breakfast.com/wm2

http://www.all-day-breakfast.com/wmx—the author's home pages for the wm2 and wmx minimalist window managers.

http://www.lesstif.org—home page of the Hungry Programmers, developers of the LessTif project, bringing Motif 1.2-compatible development to XFree86 and Linux.

http://www.openmotif.org—a site devoted to OpenMotif and other information.

http://www.metrolink.com/productindex.html—source for a commercial version of OSF/Motif for Linux.

http://www.suse.com—source for the SuSE Linux distribution.

http://www.xig.com/Pages/DeXtopGUI.html—information about Xi Graphics' DeXtop port of CDE for various Linux distributions.

http://www.opengroup.org—TOG's Web site, where you can learn more about Motif, CDE, and other software.

http://www.x.org—curators of X11.

http://www.kde.org—the definitive site for the latest news and KDE software.

http://www.trolltech.com/developer/faq/free.html—discussion and frequently asked questions (FAQ) from Trolltech concerning the Free Edition of the Qt software libraries.

http://www.gnome.org—the main site to begin to learn about how GNOME works and where to get GNOME software.

http://www.gnome.org/faqs/users-faq/—the GNOME FAQ, with answers to more than a dozen questions about GNOME.

http://www.ximian.com—home page for Ximian GNOME, a sophisticated port of GNOME software specifically designed for variants of the Linux operating system.

http://xwinman.org—the best place to browse and learn about X window managers and desktop environments.

PART II

Using the X Window System

Chapter 6: Starting X11

Choosing a starting method

Using a display manager

Using the startx script

Starting X remotely

his chapter provides an overview of the ways in which you can start your X session. You'll learn how to use the Linux command line to launch your system's X server, get an introduction to a number and type of X *display managers*, or X login choosers, and also learn how to use the startx command to customize your X session. You'll also learn one way to start XFree86 remotely over a network.

Understanding your options when using XFree86 is part of the X and Linux experience, and can help you get the most out of your system. Although many X users simply sit down at a terminal, log in, and go to work, creating the optimal X login, session, and desktop is critical if you want to ensure the most efficient, trouble-free system for you or for your system's users. This task, of course, usually falls on the shoulders of a system administrator in a large computing environment, but when using Linux and X on a standalone computer, you, the user, must assume some administrative tasks.

Granted, installing and configuring Linux and X become easier with each new distribution and release, but a little knowledge can go a long way toward transforming you from just another X user to a more savvy and experienced desktop technician. We hope that the information that this chapter presents will help you make more informed choices when developing personal tastes for your X environment.

Choosing a Starting Method

An X *display manager* is an X client that graphically manages who may log in to an X session, and depending on the display manager, use a specific window manager somewhere on a network. This means that you can set up your computer to offer a login to an X session running locally or on a different computer on your network (or anywhere in the world).

Several display managers (such as the xdm configuration used by a now ancient Red Hat Linux 4.2 system shown in Figure 6.1) are available for XFree86 and are usually included with most Linux distributions. The X display manager, or xdm, is an X client and part of the XFree86 distribution. KDE includes the K display manager, or kdm, and GNOME provides the gdm client.

You do not need to use a display manager to start your X session. XFree86 comes with a shell script named startx that you can use to start X. In fact, the startx command has been the staple way to start X sessions for Linux and XFree86 until very recently. Newer Linux distributions now configure X during installation, but this was not the case until recently; until now, the normal procedure was first to install Linux and X, then to configure and test X before committing the system to a graphical login.

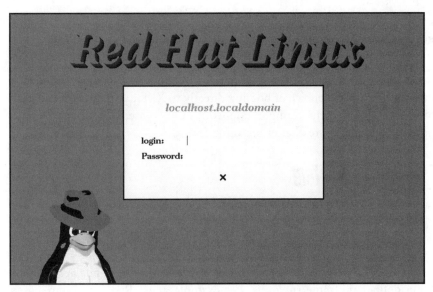

Figure 6.1 *A display manager, such as this* xdm *client for an early version of Red Hat Linux, offers a single point for logging in to Linux and starting an X session.*

The startx command (discussed in more detail later in this chapter; see the section "Using the startx Script") has several advantages over the graphical login offered by a display manager because of its flexibility and command-line options. On the other hand, a display manager can offer more security (when X is properly configured) and combine into a single step the processes of logging in to Linux and starting X. Newer display managers, such as kdm and gdm, also offer drop-down menus that enable the user to choose a window manager for the X session.

Whether or not you use a display manager can be a matter of personal preference or a need dictated by your computing environment. Certainly, one of the first choices you'll need to make when using X is whether or not to use a graphical login. In some environments, using a display manager can help offload system requirements (such as hard drive space) from the local workstation by booting to an X session using remote resources, or even simplify the task of logging in to a working X session. If you're using Linux on a network appliance, you may or may not need a display manager, depending on how the system is configured.

Using a Display Manager

This section introduces three display managers commonly used with XFree86 and Linux. The first display manager, xdm, is part of the XFree86 distribution. xdm was the first display manager available for XFree86. (The next oldest display manager was dtlogin, included with TriTeal's CDE for Red Hat Linux; although this product is no longer supported, you can still get CDE for Linux from Xi Graphics, Inc.) The other display managers discussed are KDE's kdm and GNOME's gdm.

If you successfully configure X during an initial Linux installation, many of today's distributions offer you the choice of booting directly to X. This option is adequate if you're absolutely sure that the configuration works. Otherwise, a better and perhaps safer approach is to configure X after installing Linux.

Configuring the System

Use of a display manager is generally controlled by a runlevel entry in the Linux system initialization table /etc/inittab. This text file is used by the /sbin/init command, the first command that Linux runs after booting. init is responsible for first starting processes in memory according to the *runlevel*—that is, the system state into which Linux is booting. However, you should be aware that not every Linux distribution defines the same runlevels. For example, most Red Hat Linux-based distributions define the following:

```
# Default runlevel. The runlevels used by RHS are:
# 0 - halt (Do NOT set initdefault to this)
# 1 - Single user mode
# 2 - Multiuser, without NFS (The same as 3, if you do not have networking)
# 3 - Full multiuser mode
# 4 - unused
# 5 - X11
# 6 - reboot (Do NOT set initdefault to this)
```

For Red Hat, the runlevels most commonly used after booting Linux are the following:

- 1, or *single-user* mode, used for file system repair or administrative work
- 3, for normal console-login *multiuser* mode
- 5, for multiuser mode with a graphical X login using a display manager

When you boot this system to the text-only or *console* mode, you're booting to runlevel 3. When you boot directly to a graphical login through X, you're booting to runlevel 5.

On the other hand, SuSE Linux defines these runlevels:

```
# runlevel 0 is halt
# runlevel S is single-user
# runlevel 1 is multi-user without network
```

```
# runlevel 2 is multi-user with network
# runlevel 3 is multi-user with network and xdm
# runlevel 4 is unused
# runlevel 5 is unused
# runlevel 6 is reboot
```

Note that you can boot SuSE Linux to a full (networking) multiuser, console-only mode by choosing runlevel 2, whereas by choosing runlevel 3 you boot to a graphical login using a display manager and X. Regardless of whether you are running a Red Hat or SuSE Linux-based system, you specify the default runlevel by using the initdefault setting in the /etc/inittab file. Under Red Hat Linux, booting to runlevel 5 (to use xdm) requires the following setting:

```
id:5:initdefault:
```

Under SuSE Linux, use the following initdefault setting:

```
# default runlevel
id:3:initdefault:
```

You can also switch to a specified runlevel by using the init command, followed by a runlevel number. For example, when using Red Hat Linux, to jump to a graphical login using the default display manager, use the init command followed by the appropriate runlevel, as follows:

```
# init 5
```

You can also do this directly at the LILO boot prompt by passing a kernel *argument* or boot message, entering the linux keyword and the runlevel as follows:

```
boot: linux 5
```

The default display manager is generally specified in /etc/inittab with a runlevel description. For example, an entry for a Red Hat Linux–based system to boot directly to xdm might look like the following:

```
x:5:respawn:/usr/bin/xdm -nodaemon
```

However, both SuSE and Red Hat Linux use more complicated means to determine the default boot manager. Under SuSE Linux, system initialization scripts (which are actually shell scripts) contain the logic to determine the default boot manager:

```
13:3:wait:/sbin/init.d/rc 3
```

Under Red Hat Linux–based systems, a shell script named prefdm, found under the /etc/X11 directory, is run to determine the display manager used:

```
x:5:respawn:/etc/X11/prefdm -nodaemon
```

The script contains logic that chooses the display manager, based on the contents of the file named `desktop` under the `/etc/sysconfig` directory:

```
...
# Run preferred X display manager
preferred=
if [ -f /etc/sysconfig/desktop ]; then
        if grep -q GNOME /etc/sysconfig/desktop 2>/dev/null; then
                preferred=gdm
        elif grep -q KDE /etc/sysconfig/desktop 2> /dev/null; then
                preferred=kdm
        elif grep -q AnotherLevel /etc/sysconfig/desktop 2> /dev/null; then
                preferred=xdm
        fi
fi
...
```

The preceding excerpt is just a portion of the `prefdm` shell script used by Mandrake Linux 7.0. However, as you can see, the desktop file is parsed for the keywords GNOME, KDE, and AnotherLevel to determine the display manager. You don't have to use this approach; instead, you can define your own runlevel entry to determine the display manager. However, if you choose to define your own entry, then depending on your system, other configuration scripts or clients may or may not work properly. The best approach is to understand the runlevel configuration system used by your distribution.

Using and Configuring xdm

The `xdm` client is controlled by a series of files under the `/etc/X11/xdm` directory. These files, listed in Table 6.1, determine the X server to use, access permissions, the hosts that you may log on to or from, the default appearance of the chooser dialog box, and security settings for failsafe or terminal usage. Some Linux distributions also use third-party commands, such as the `xbanner` client, to spiff up the initial display (which can be handy for customizing `xdm` logins in an academic or corporate environment).

You'll also find a subdirectory named `authdir` under the `/etc/X11/xdm` directory. This directory might also contain another directory named `authfiles`, which contains authentication files used for security to enable the X session; also note that on some systems, the directory may be a link to the `/var/lib/xdm` directory.

If you have properly installed and configured X, but generally use a text-only display, you can start the `xdm` client (as root) from the command line using its `-nodaemon` option as follows:

```
# xdm -nodaemon
```

Table 6.1 xdm Configuration Files

Filename	Description
GiveConsole	A permission-control script for a user failsafe terminal
TakeConsole	Console permission control script for root
Xaccess	A script that controls remote access
Xresources	A script that controls the appearance of the xdm screen
Xservers	A script that designates the local X server to use
Xsession	A shell script that sets up an X session and determines the window manager to use
Xsetup_0	A shell script to launch clients in the xdm display
xdm-config	Overall resource listing for xdm

After you press Enter, the screen clears and you see a login screen, as shown in Figure 6.2.

To log in, type your username and password. After you press Enter, you enter an X session using the default window manager. You can choose this window manager by using the window manager designated in the .xinitrc file in the user's home directory.

login:

Password:

Figure 6.2 *The* xdm *display manager, included with XFree86, offers a one-step login to Linux and X.*

Alternatively, if appropriate entries exist in the Xresources and Xsession files, you can press an appropriate Ctrl+F*n* key combination at the login screen. However, more commonly with today's Linux distributions, *session-management* clients specific to your Linux distribution are used to determine the default window manager.

For example, Red Hat Linux uses the switchdesk client (shown in Figure 6.3), which enables the user to choose a default client. You can launch this client from the command line of an X11 terminal by entering the following command:

```
# switchdesk &
```

After you press Enter, the client gives you a choice of window managers for your X sessions.

The switchdesk client uses configuration files found under the /usr/share/apps/ switchdesk directory. On the other hand, Mandrake Linux (which is also Red Hat–based) allows you to choose a different utility named chksession. You can use this client to add or remove window manager choices for the gdm and kdm display managers. See the chksession man page for more information.

Figure 6.3 *Red Hat's* switchdesk *client is used to set the default window manager for* xdm *logins.*

Using and Configuring kdm

The kdm client is part of the KDE X desktop suite, and provides a comprehensive graphical login to Linux and X. You can specify this client in your system's /etc/inittab file or in a system-specific configuration file. The client then will be launched automatically at the start of the proper runlevel.

For example, on Red Hat Linux–based distributions, you can boot Linux directly to a kdm login by first editing the file /etc/sysconfig/desktop by inserting the following phrase:

```
DESKTOP="KDE"
```

Next, edit /etc/inittab by changing the default runlevel entry to the following:

```
id:5:initdefault:
```

Save the file and exit your editor. The next time that you start Linux, you'll see the kdm login dialog box, as shown in Figure 6.4.

The kdm dialog box provides Login and Password fields, along with a drop-down menu offering a choice of window managers for your X session, a Go! button to launch the session, a Cancel button to cancel your login, and a Shutdown button that you can use to shut down, reboot your system, or restart your X server.

To log in, type your username, then your password. Before pressing Enter or clicking the Go! button, click the drop-down menu to select a window manager to use for your session. After you log in, you can configure kdm (as root) by using the kdmconfig client. You can launch this client through the KDE desktop panel's Start menu or from the command line of an X11 terminal window, as follows:

```
# kdmconfig
```

After you press Enter, you'll see the dialog box shown in Figure 6.5.

Use the different tabs at the top of the dialog box to navigate to different configuration screens. For example, click the Background tab, then click to select a type of wallpaper as a background to the login desktop display, as shown in Figure 6.6.

You can also control user access to your system by clicking the Users tab, then selecting various users allowed to log in. You can also assign a graphic (or scanned photo) to each user, as shown in Figure 6.7.

Figure 6.4 *KDE's* kdm *display manager offers sophisticated controls for selecting users, window manager sessions, and system states.*

Figure 6.5 *KDE's* kdmconfig *client is used to configure many different aspects of the* kdm *display manager desktop.*

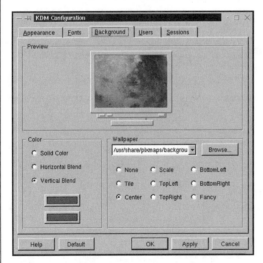

Figure 6.6 *KDE's* kdmconfig *client can set the background display of your login desktop.*

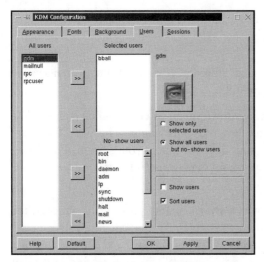

Figure 6.7 *You can also use the* kdmconfig *client to control user access and login by selectively including or excluding users.*

Using and Configuring gdm

The gdm client is part of the GNOME libraries. Like kdm, gdm provides a graphical login to Linux and X. This client, which actually launches the gdmlogin client, may be specified in your system's /etc/inittab file or in a system-specific configuration file. The client will then be launched automatically at the start of the proper runlevel for multiuser mode and X. The examples used in this section apply to Red Hat Linux.

Another way to boot Linux directly to a gdm login on Red Hat Linux–based systems is to edit /etc/inittab directly and use a gdm-specific entry for runlevel 5. Open the file, then look for the default entry, which looks like this:

```
x:5:respawn:/etc/X11/prefdm -nodaemon
```

You can then change this entry to use gdm instead by editing it as follows:

```
x:5:respawn:/usr/bin/gdm -nodaemon
```

Note that this approach also works for kdm. Of course, you can also use the traditional method by first editing the file /etc/sysconfig/desktop and inserting the following phrase:

```
DESKTOP="GNOME"
```

Next, edit /etc/inittab and change the default runlevel entry as follows:

id:**5**:initdefault:

Save the file and exit your editor. The next time that you start Linux, you'll see the gdmlogin dialog box as shown in Figure 6.8.

The gdmlogin dialog box provides a drop-down menu offering a choice of window managers for your X session, a menu to select a support language for your X session, and a System menu that you can use to shut down or reboot your system. The dialog box also provides a Login field that changes to a Password field after you enter your username.

To log in, type your username, then your password. Before pressing Enter, click the drop-down Session menu to select a window manager. After you log in, you can configure gdm (as root) by editing the file gdm.conf under the /etc/X11/gdm directory. Open this file using your favorite text editor and scroll through to find entries of interest.

The file is organized according to function, such as daemon, security, xdmcp, gui, greeter, debug, and servers. The greeter section contains settings that you can use to change the appearance of the gdmlogin dialog box. Note the following example:

```
...
Icon=/usr/share/pixmaps/gdm.xpm
LocaleFile=/etc/X11/gdm/locale.alias
Logo=/usr/share/pixmaps/gnome-logo-large.png
Quiver=0
SystemMenu=1
Welcome=Welcome to %n
...
```

Figure 6.8 *The* gdm *display manager uses GNOME's* gdmlogin *client to offer a choice of window manager sessions and system states.*

For example, in this partial output, you can see where to change the icon, logo, and welcome message of the dialog box. The available *sessions*, or window managers available through this login dialog box, are defined in the /etc/X11/gdm/Sessions directory. The default session is a symbolic link to the Default filename. You select a window manager by executing a corresponding shell script, as in the following example:

```
$ ls -l /etc/X11/gdm/Sessions
total 16
-rwxr-xr-x    1 root     root              40 Aug 13 21:51 Default
-rwxr-xr-x    1 root     root              49 Aug 13 21:51 Failsafe
-rwxr-xr-x    1 root     root              46 Aug 13 21:51 Gnome
-rwxr-xr-x    1 root     root              44 Aug 25 06:50 KDE
lrwxrwxrwx    1 root     root               7 Sep 21 05:35 default -> Default
```

The other files are short shell scripts that use the Xsession script under the /etc/X11/xdm directory to launch a particular window manager. For example, the GNOME script contains the following:

```
#!/bin/bash
exec /etc/X11/xdm/Xsession gnome
```

This script passes the variable gnome to the Xsession script. If you examine the pertinent logic in the Xsession script, you'll see the following:

```
...
# now, we see if xdm/gdm/kdm has asked for a specific environment
case $# in
1)
    case $1 in
    failsafe)
        exec xterm -geometry 80x24-0-0
        ;;
    gnome)
        exec gnome-session
        ;;
    kde|kde1)
        exec /usr/share/apps/switchdesk/Xclients.kde
        ;;
    kde2)
        exec /usr/share/apps/switchdesk/Xclients.kde2
        ;;
    anotherlevel)
         # we assume that switchdesk is installed.
        exec /usr/share/apps/switchdesk/Xclients.anotherlevel
        ;;
    esac
esac
...
```

As you can see, the script uses the information passed by gdm to launch X using a specified window manager. Other files in various directories under the /etc/X11/gdm directory are used to configure the login background and other settings, and are merely symbolic links to counterpart scripts under the /etc/X11/xdm directory.

Using the startx Script

The startx client (which is actually a shell script) is included with XFree86, and is used to initiate an X session on a local workstation. This script uses the xinit client, and can (or perhaps *should*, according to its man page) be customized for use at larger computing sites.

When you use startx to launch your X session, the client looks for a file named .xinitrc in your home directory. This file can contain a completely customized X session, replete with clients to launch and a designated window manager. You'll find a default .xinitrc file installed under the /etc/X11/xinit directory. On Red Hat Linux systems, this directory also contains a shell script named Xclients that uses logic to determine the default window manager to launch for your X session.

You can copy these files to your home directory with the names .Xclients and .xinitrc. If you plan to use startx exclusively, you should edit these files to customize your X session. A simple .xinitrc file could contain the following:

```
xsetroot -solid lightblue
rclock -fg white -bg blue -geometry 100x100-5+5 &
xcalc -geometry -155+5 &
rxvt -geometry 80x50-5+15 &
exec twm
```

These settings will launch X, change the desktop background to light blue, put a clock in the upper-right corner of your display, and place a calculator next to the clock. The settings will also place along the left side of the display an X11 terminal window that is 80 characters wide and 50 lines long. Finally, the settings specify that the twm window manager will be used for your X session.

After saving the file, you then use the startx command to launch the X server and your session, as follows:

```
# startx
```

After you press Enter, you'll see your desktop, as shown in Figure 6.9.

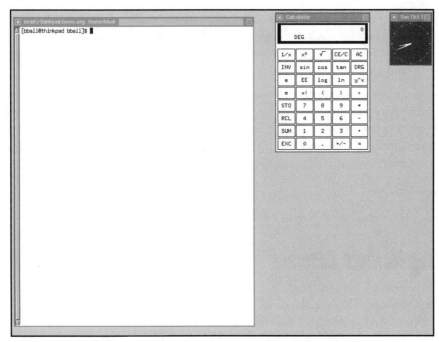

Figure 6.9 *You can use the* `startx` *client, along with your .xinitrc file, to craft custom X desktops for work.*

Passing Arguments and Options

The `startx` command can also launch X using different color depths. As long as you have configured X to support different color depths on your system, you can use the `-depth` option to specify a variety of color depths for your X sessions.

> The color depth settings are contained in your system's `XF86Config` file, usually found under the `/etc/X11` directory. See Chapter 3, "Configuring XFree86," for details on setting up XFree86.

To start an X11 session using millions of colors, use the `startx` command, along with the `-depth` option and a number representing the number of color bit planes, as follows:

```
# startx — -depth 24
```

After you press Enter, X will start, and the XFree86 server will determine whether your system can support the requested color depth and resolutions defined for your system. Typical values used for different color depths are 8, 15, and 16.

Another option commonly used is to start an X session using a different number of dots-per-inch (dpi) resolution. This can be helpful to provide better-looking fonts and help displays with large resolutions (such as 1,600×1,200), or perhaps to work around font support problems for X clients used during your X sessions. The default setting is to support 75-dpi fonts. But you can bump this up to 100 dpi by using the `startx` command and its `-dpi` setting, followed by 100, as follows:

```
# startx — -dpi 100
```

After you press Enter, your session will be at 100=dpi resolution.

Starting Multiple Sessions

If you have enough system memory, you can use the `startx` command to launch multiple X sessions. This can be useful to test new window managers or run X sessions at different color depths. Thanks to support under Linux and XFree86 for *virtual consoles*, or console displays accessible through the keyboard, you can quickly and easily jump back and forth between sessions.

You first need to boot Linux to a non-X multiuser mode, such as runlevel 3 for Red Hat or Mandrake Linux. After you log in, you can start your first X session by using the `startx` command, a *display number*, which specifies an X server instance in this example, and a number representing a virtual console. Many Linux distributions use console 7 for X; if this is the case for your distribution, you can start your X session as follows:

```
# startx — :0 vt7
```

After you press Enter, X starts. To start another X11 session, press Ctrl+Alt+F2. You'll find yourself at a text-only login prompt. Log in, and again use `startx` to start another X11 session, as follows:

```
# startx — :1 vt8
```

You'll end up in another X11 session running a different instance of your X server (`:1`) and at a different virtual console (`vt8`). You can verify this by using `grep` to print the output of the `ps` command to show the `startx` and X server processes, as follows:

```
$ ps aux | fgrep X
bball   1130  0.0  0.7  2000   952 tty1   S   21:22   0:00 sh /usr/X11R6/bin
root    1136  0.3  6.0 16972  7744 ?      S   21:22   0:00 /etc/X11/X :0 vt7
bball   1173  0.0  0.7  2000   952 tty3   S   21:22   0:00 sh /usr/X11R6/bin
root    1179  0.4  6.0 16972  7756 ?      S   21:22   0:01 /etc/X11/X :1 vt8
```

To go to the other X session, press Ctrl+Alt+F7, and press Ctrl+Alt+F8 to return. From your current session, you can go to another text-only console by pressing Ctrl+Alt+F3. To go back to either X session, press Alt+F7 or Alt+F8.

In general, the `startx` client provides an easy way to pass command-line arguments to the X server `XFree86`. To get a better idea of the number of available arguments, see the `XFree86` man page.

Starting X Remotely

Many Linux and XFree86 users are quite satisfied to install Linux and run X as a standalone system. However, X supports networking graphics, and was originally designed to work well on networks with 10,000 or more workstations. This means that you can combine the power of Linux and X and adapt XFree86 to provide services well beyond the capabilities of a single workstation.

One of the greatest features of Linux is that it works well on legacy computer hardware. While commercial software users are crying in their beer as their recently purchased hardware is quickly outdated by bloated products from the software monopoly, Linux users happily scour corporate dump sites for ancient 486 and Pentium computers, reaping bargains at a fraction of the hardware's original cost. Even better, the legacy hardware performs quite well, even using X!

For a modest investment, Linux users can assemble relatively inexpensive local networks, with critical expenditures focused on one or two higher-powered servers. By configuring XFree86, it is possible to sit down at a recycled workstation and log in to and run X from the high-powered server. This section explains how to do so.

Install and configure XFree86 to work properly on each remote workstation. For example, on a workstation named `stinky`, edit the file `Xaccess` under the `/etc/X11/xdm` directory. Look for the following section of code:

```
...
#
# The nicest way to run the chooser is to just ask it to broadcast
# requests to the network - that way new hosts show up automatically.
# Sometimes, however, the chooser can't figure out how to broadcast,
# so this may not work in all environments.
#

*                   CHOOSER BROADCAST        #any indirect host can get a chooser

#
# If you'd prefer to configure the set of hosts each terminal sees,
```

```
# then just uncomment these lines (and comment the CHOOSER line above)
# and edit the %hostlist line as appropriate
#


#%hostlist      host-a host-b


#*             CHOOSER %hostlist      #
```

This section of the file provides several ways for X to broadcast the availability of X hosts for terminal logins. Edit this section to comment out the CHOOSER BROADCAST line (using a pound sign), uncomment the hostlist line, and uncomment the CHOOSER line. Then insert the name or names of your servers, such as wonderdog and supercat (replacing the host-a and host-b entries):

```
...
#
# The nicest way to run the chooser is to just ask it to broadcast
# requests to the network - that way new hosts show up automatically.
# Sometimes, however, the chooser can't figure out how to broadcast,
# so this may not work in all environments.
#


#*             CHOOSER BROADCAST        #any indirect host can get a chooser


#
# If you'd prefer to configure the set of hosts each terminal sees,
# then just uncomment these lines (and comment the CHOOSER line above)
# and edit the %hostlist line as appropriate
#

%hostlist      wonderdog supercat


*              CHOOSER %hostlist      #
```

Save the file and exit. Repeat this process for every workstation on your network. On your servers, wonderdog and supercat, check the Xaccess file to ensure that the following line is uncommented (that is, make sure that the line does not begin with a pound sign):

```
*                              #any host can get a login window
```

Then, start the xdm client on each server:

```
# xdm
```

Ensure that all your users have accounts on your servers. Users on your network can now sit down at a workstation, then log on to either server by using the Xwrapper command with the XFree86 server's -broadcast option like this:

```
# Xwrapper -broadcast
```

The Xwrapper command (part of the XFree86 distribution) allows nonroot users to directly launch the X server. Using this example command line, an xdm login appears from the server wonderdog, as it is the first server listed in the workstation's Xaccess file. If wonderdog is offline, the xdm login for supercat appears. To log on to a specific server, workstation users should use the Xwrapper command and the XFree86 server's -query option, followed by a server's name, as follows:

```
# Xwrapper -query supercat
```

After pressing Enter, the xdm login screen appears for supercat, even though wonderdog is online and listed first. Note that your network's users don't have to have an account on the workstation!

One approach for providing X sessions for your users is to set up each workstation on your network with a minimal Linux and XFree86 installation with only a single root account, and perhaps an open work account used to provide the xdm login screen.

For example, as root, create a user named xlogin with a password on each workstation. Next, edit the /etc/passwd file and look for the following line:

```
xlogin:x:501:501::/home/xlogin:/bin/bash
```

Replace /bin/bash in the password entry (which designates the login shell for the user) with the pathname to a special shell script, such as remotex:

```
xlogin:x:501:501::/home/xlogin:/usr/local/bin/remotex
```

Save the passwd file. Next, create the remotex shell script:

```
/usr/X11R6/bin/Xwrapper -broadcast
```

Save the script under the /usr/local/bin directory, then use the chmod command to make the script executable:

```
# chmod +x /usr/local/bin/remotex
```

Don't forget to use the passwd command to assign a password for the new xlogin user! Then, when any user on your network sits down at any workstation, the user can boot Linux and log in with the xlogin username and password. After entering the password and pressing Enter, the xdm login screen for the first available server appears. This provides an additional level of security by requiring users to know how to log in to a workstation and then use a personal username and password before running X on a server.

This example approach also provides for simplified system maintenance; your system administrator can simply clone a single hard drive for use on all workstations on your network (if the workstation hardware is compatible, the system has been properly configured for security, and so on).

This example approach is not the only way to use XFree86 remotely. There are other means to providing remote X access. See Chapter 9, "Using X11 on a Network," for more detailed information about X and network activity.

Resource Information

http://www.xfree86.org—the starting point for learning more about XFree86 and X clients included with the XFree86 distribution.

http://chaos.fullerton.edu/XBanner/—Amit Margalit's home page for XBanner, a utility client used to decorate xdm login screens.

http://linux.about.com/compute/linux/library/weekly/aa11098a.htm—an About.com article regarding xdm and Linux.

http://www.linuxgazette.com/issue34/tag/xdm.html—a *Linux Gazette* article on using xdm for remote logins.

http://www.mozilla.org/unix/dpi.html—description of resolution problems for the Mozilla browser.

http://vip.hpnc.com/~cbbrowne/xwindows.html—Chris Browne's X Web site, with views and overviews of X technology.

http://www.linux.org.tw/CLDP/HOWTO/mini/FDU.html—one source for the XFree86 Font Deuglification mini-HOWTO; describes how to use better-looking fonts with XFree86.

This chapter introduces some of the basics when first using XFree86. You'll learn about logging in, using an X11 *terminal*, or shell window, configuring various terminal clients, launching X clients, and using various graphic software tools to manage processes during your X session. Finally, you'll learn how to stop or log out of your X session.

Starting an X Session

As you learned in previous chapters, there are a number of ways to start an X session. Once X is properly configured for your system, you can use the startx command, log in locally through an X display manager, or query for specific hosts on your network to log in to.

Fortunately, to keep things simple, X does not require a separate username or password in order for you to initiate an X session. But you are required to have a valid account on the local or remote computer. If you manage one or more workstations, you should also know that it's not a good idea to log in as the root operator and use Linux or X directly. As root, you are the *superuser*, and can do anything to the system, including wreaking havoc through inadvertent file deletion by entering a command such as the following:

```
# rm -fr /
```

This command line instructs Linux not only to destroy the root filesystem, but also any other mounted filesystem—such as a mounted Windows, DOS, or Network File System (NFS) filesystem—under the root directory. If you need to use root access to edit system configuration files, a much safer approach is to limit root activity to a specific task. For example, you can become root by using the su command as follows:

```
$ su
Password:
#
```

But a much better way to use su is to specify the task:

```
$ su -c "pico -w /etc/X11/XF86Config"
Password:
```

After you press Enter, you can then edit the file (in this example, the command specifies the pico editor with line-wrapping disabled). When you exit the editor, you return to normal user status. Using su at least provides a small precaution, because you'll need to examine the task, press Enter, enter a password, and then press Enter again to launch the task.

Obviously, if you use startx to launch a local X session, you have already logged in. But if you log in to Linux and X using xdm, you may be able to use various editing keys when entering your username and password. These keys are listed in Table 7.1.

Table 7.1 xdm Login Editing Keys

Key	Description
Ctrl+a	Jump to the beginning of the entry
Ctrl+b	Move back one character (nondestructive)
Ctrl+d	Delete the next character
Ctrl+e	Jump to the end of the entry
Ctrl+f	Move forward one character
Ctrl+h	Move back one character, erasing that character
Ctrl+k	Delete to the end of the entry
Ctrl+r	Restart the login
Ctrl+x	Delete the entire entry
Ctrl+u	Delete the entire entry

Note that most but not all the keystrokes listed in Table 7.1 correspond to keystrokes used with the bash shell command line and the emacs editor. You can also use the left and right cursor keys when editing your entries. If you type an incorrect username or password and press Enter, the display manager should respond with an error and replace the entry cursor on the login: prompt for you.

Using X11 Terminal Clients

This section introduces terminal clients for X. Just as you have a vast choice of window managers to use for your X sessions, you will also find a number of different X terminal clients included with your Linux distribution, especially if you install KDE and GNOME. Your choice of a favorite terminal might be driven by practicality, a need for features, or simply personal preference. Some terminal clients have special features that require certain software support libraries, whereas other clients may be used as standalone terminals or with any window manager.

Exploring Terminal Features

Nearly all X terminal clients support display features similar to common hardware-based terminals. Note that there is a difference between an X terminal client and a hardware terminal. In the past, when UNIX was a character-based system and X was yet to be developed, users logged in to UNIX over serial lines using a variety of display devices with attached keyboards or character-based terminals. These terminals had different hardware features, worked at different speeds, and in many cases, responded to entirely dissimilar software commands.

To get an idea of the vast number of different terminals (many if not most of which now line landfills across the world), take a look at your system's terminal capabilities database, /etc/termcap. This file, consisting of nearly 15,000 lines of terminal definition and configuration values, is one indication of the complexity of supporting character-based terminals under UNIX and, of course, now Linux. Note that you cannot use X with a character-based terminal—the point is that this limitation has been inherited by Linux. When working at the console or using a console-based text editor in an X11 terminal window, programmers need to adhere to a standard set of software codes that will make the cursor *addressable*. Specifically, programmers need to be able to place the cursor anywhere in a display that traditionally (but not always) is 80 characters wide by 24 or 25 lines.

Although Digital Equipment Corporation's VT52 terminal of 1974 was one of the first with an addressable display, the standard for cursor addressing grew out of DEC's VT100 hardware, which featured a screen, keyboard, and serial input line. The software codes used to control the display evolved into today's VT100 emulators. Other standard sets of cursor control still in use include VT102, VT220, VT320, and so on.

The Linux console emulates the DEC VT220 terminal, but adds color support. You'll find terminal information files regarding various X terminal clients under the /usr/share/terminfo directory. These files are compiled parts of a database of terminals used by today's Linux screen–oriented programs. Read the terminfo man page for information regarding the database, and the term man page for information regarding the format of the compiled database entry for each terminal. The ncurses software library and functions are used to handle cursors in Linux programs.

Choosing a Terminal Client

Fortunately, choosing which X terminal client to use today is a lot easier than it was to choose which hardware terminal to use 20 years ago. Features that are desirable today include the following:

- The ability to be reconfigured to recognize different terminal codes
- Scrolling, with a *history* feature that enables the user to view past pages

- Extensive window controls, such as the ability to minimize (iconize or dock into a taskbar), maximize, or close, and controls for resizing or dragging
- The ability to change foreground and background colors (or at least use reverse colors and handle color) easily
- The ability to use different fonts and font sizes
- The ability to mimic one or more terminal standards, or perhaps use different keys
- The ability to use images in the background or perhaps support transparency

Some X terminal clients have all these features, including some not listed, such as the ability to remember sessions and settings, use images for window decoration backgrounds, use minimal memory, or launch actions with user-defined hot keys. Nearly all X terminal clients obey a similar subset of command-line options (which you'll learn about in Chapter 8, "Using X11 Clients").

Table 7.2 lists several X terminal clients included with most Linux distributions.

Table 7.2 X Terminal Clients

Name	Description
aterm	AfterStep X VT102 terminal emulator
Eterm	Enlightened terminal emulator for X
gnome-terminal	GNOME X terminal emulator
konsole	KDE terminal emulator
kterm	Multilingual terminal emulator
kvt	KDE terminal emulator (deprecated; use konsole or another client)
rxvt	An X terminal emulator
xiterm	An X international terminal
xterm	The X terminal emulator

Configuring a Terminal Client

How you configure your terminal depends, in most cases, on the features supported by the client. Terminal clients supported by KDE and GNOME, for example, generally provide menus and dialog boxes that list options that you can use to change the appearance or capabilities of a client. However, other terminal clients require that you enter command-line options to take advantage of different features.

For example, you can launch KDE's `konsole` client from KDE's desktop panel or the command line of another terminal client (even if you're not using KDE) as follows:

```
# konsole &
```

After you press Enter, the terminal appears, as shown in Figure 7.1.

Note that Figure 7.1 shows the KDE `konsole` client running under the FVWM window manager, yet still features a menu bar. This menu bar provides a way for you to start another terminal window or select various options for the terminal, such as whether or not to display a menu, what type of font to use, and what the size of the terminal window (measured in characters and lines) should be.

On the other hand, the `xterm` client, included with XFree86, provides few hints about how you should graphically configure the terminal. You need to read its man page or other documentation in order to learn that you can change its fonts and size

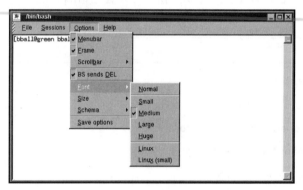

Figure 7.1 *The* konsole *client is a terminal emulator with menuing options included with KDE.*

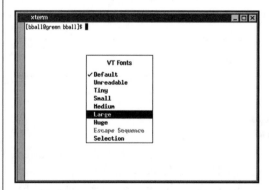

Figure 7.2 *The* xterm *client, part of the XFree86 distribution, features pop-up configuration menus.*

on the fly by pressing Ctrl+right-click. For example, you can launch the terminal with the following command:

```
# xterm &
```

The terminal appears on your desktop. Press Ctrl+right-click and you'll see a pop-up font menu, as shown in Figure 7.2.

Scroll through the list of fonts and select a different size; the terminal window then changes accordingly. Other terminal clients, such as rxvt (and nearly all X clients), can also accept command-line options to change font size, type, and other characteristics—or even launch programs. For example, to start the rxvt terminal and run the top command in the terminal with white letters on a blue background, specify the -fg (foreground), -bg (background), and -e (execute) options as follows:

```
# rxvt -fg white -bg blue -e top &
```

After you press Enter, you'll see the rxvt window as shown in Figure 7.3 (press **q** to exit the top command and quit the terminal).

Additionally, nearly every X11 client can take advantage of special configuration files, known as *resource files*, containing text strings, or *resource settings*. (Although this chapter introduces the concept of resource settings, Chapter 8, "Using X11 Clients," discusses the topic in greater detail.)

Resource settings may be stored in a number of places in your filesystem. One common directory used by many X clients is the /usr/X11R6/lib/X11/app-defaults directory. Other resource settings may be stored under the /usr/share/apps/kdisplay/app-defaults file (these settings help provide hints for client displays when using KDE).

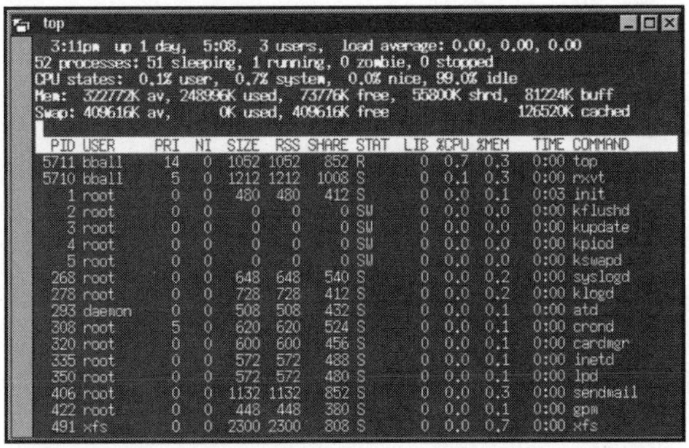

Figure 7.3 *The* rxvt *client also obeys command-line options to customize the display for use.*

Resource settings are sets of text strings that define display or other characteristics for an X client. If you look at the defaults for X clients, you'll see the following files:

Beforelight	NetHack.ad	XGammon	XPat	Xfd
Bitmap	Netscape	XGetfile	XPlaycd	Xfm
Bitmap-color	Viewres	XISDNLoad	XPlaymidi	Xgc
Chooser	X3270	XLoad	XRn	Xloadimage
Clock-color	XBanner	XLock	XScreenSaver	Xmag
Editres	XCalc	XLogo	XSm	Xman
Editres-color	XCalc-color	XLogo-color	XSysinfo	Xmessage
Fig	XClipboard	XMailbox	XSysinfo-color	Xmh
Fig-color	XClock	XMascot	XTerm	Xvidtune
Freeciv	XConsole	XMdb	XTerm-color	
GV	XDaliClock	XMixer	Xditview	
GXditview	XDbx	XOsview	Xditview-chrtr	
KTerm	XFontSel	XPaint	Xedit	

If you examine the settings for the xterm client, you'll see (in part) the following:

```
...
*fontMenu.Label:                VT Fonts
*fontMenu*fontdefault*Label:    Default
*fontMenu*font1*Label:          Unreadable
*VT100*font1:                   nil2
*IconFont:                      nil2
*fontMenu*font2*Label:          Tiny
*VT100*font2:                   5x7
*fontMenu*font3*Label:          Small
*VT100*font3:                    6x10
*fontMenu*font4*Label:          Medium
*VT100*font4:                   7x13
*fontMenu*font5*Label:          Large
*VT100*font5:                   9x15
*fontMenu*font6*Label:          Huge
*VT100*font6:                   10x20
*fontMenu*fontescape*Label:     Escape Sequence
*fontMenu*fontsel*Label:        Selection
```

This part of xterm's resource file defines systemwide defaults for xterm's font menu (as shown in Figure 7.2). As you can see, each resource setting takes the following form:

```
widget*resource: value
```

In the `XTerm` file, this form translates to the following:

```
*fontMenu*font5*Label:   Large
```

This means that the menu entry for `xterm`'s font menu uses the text string "Large" for the `font5` menu item. You can also define specific client resources in a file named `.Xdefaults` or `.Xresources` in your home directory. In this instance, you would use a resource string setting such as the following:

```
client*resource: value
```

For example, to turn off the use of color by `xterm`, use an entry such as the following:

```
xterm*VT100*colormode: off
```

Finally, you can also specify resource settings on the command line. For example, to turn off the use of color by the `xterm` client, enter the `-xrm` or X resource option followed by the name of the resource and its setting, as follows:

```
# xterm -xrm '*VT100*colorMode: off' &
```

Not all X terminal clients behave this way. For example, you can build the `rxvt` terminal emulator with or without resource setting support. Additional special X client command-line options, known as XToolkit options, are covered in greater detail in Chapter 8, "Using X11 Clients."

Exploring Special Terminal Features

X and (more specifically) X terminal clients support text copy-and-paste operations between clients. Using your pointer, click to activate a terminal window. To copy a single word, double-click the selected word, then move your pointer to another window and press the middle mouse button (that is, click mouse button 2, or simultaneously click the left and right mouse buttons if you use a two-button mouse and have enabled three-button mouse emulation). To copy a line of text, triple-click the desired line, then again click the middle mouse button to paste the text.

To copy a selection of text, known as a *region*, left-click and hold down the mouse button, then drag up or down to highlight a region of text. Again, move your pointer to a desired window and click the middle mouse button. Note that although pasting text by using the middle mouse button works with X terminal clients, you should use Ctrl+v to paste text into other clients, such as StarOffice. Not all X clients respond to copy-and-paste operations, or respond to them in the same way.

XFree86 also comes with at least two clients that you can use to copy and paste text: `xclipboard` and `xcutsel`. These clients perform the same operation, but you can also use `xclipboard` to save copied text to a file.

Starting X11 Clients

When you run a terminal client, you use a Linux *shell*, or interactive command line. Using the shell, you can launch X clients in the *background* (memory) and go right back to work. A proper X client will "detach" from your terminal window and appear in its own window as long as you use the proper shell operator, the ampersand (&), or the proper background operator on the command line, as follows:

```
$ xterm &
```

When you launch an X client using the background operator, the program becomes a *background process*. Using the background operator is essential under X11, as you can repeatedly launch clients from a single terminal window.

Another way to launch multiple clients is through your home directory's .xinitrc file. This file, as you've learned, can contain directions to launch clients and a specific window manager for your X session if you launch X from the console. You can also craft your own shell scripts to launch multiple clients with a single command, as follows:

```
#!/bin/bash
xterm &
xcalc &
netscape &
```

Save the file with a name such as myx, then use the chmod command and its +x option to make the file executable:

```
$ chmod +x myx
```

You can then launch several clients at once with the following command:

```
$ ./myx
```

Note that you don't have to use a background operator because all the clients that you launch will launch into the background. After you press Enter, your shell prompt returns.

Stopping X Clients

Each background process (such as an X server) is assigned a unique process number, or *process ID*. Various programs display the IDs of some or all processes, whereas others may be used to control processes. Unless you are the superuser root, you will be able to control only the processes that you own. One simple way to view process IDs is to use the ps (process status) command, along with fgrep search command. For example, use the ps command along with its -e command line option (to display all processes), then pipe the output through the `fgrep` command to search for certain processes, as follows:

```
$ ps -e | fgrep kvt
  6068 tty1      00:00:14 kvt
  9646 tty1      00:00:00 kvt
```

In this example, the search was for any running instances of KDE's kvt terminal. As you can see, there are two terminals. When you view the kvt windows on the KDE desktop, one terminal is labeled "Terminal <2>." That terminal has been assigned a process ID of 9646 in this example, as it was started after the previous terminal, which has a smaller process ID. Although you can use your desktop pointer to click the terminal's close box, if you know the process ID, you can destroy the window by using the `kill` command from the command line of another terminal, as follows:

```
$ kill 9646
```

After you press Enter, the terminal disappears. If you used that terminal to launch other clients, they too will exit, because they are inherited processes. This behavior is why an application dock, desktop panel, or root display menu can be handy to launch independent processes during your X session.

Keep in mind that even though a client may be minimized, iconized, or docked, that client is still using system memory. On a workstation with little memory (such as 32MB), a local X session can quickly exhaust the system's resources by running too many processes. It is much better to stop unneeded clients and keep as much memory free as possible for system performance.

You can also use the `killall` command, included with many Linux distributions, to kill a process by name. Using the previous example, you would kill all the instances of the kvt client as follows:

```
$ killall kvt
```

After you press Enter, the terminals' windows disappear. If you use `killall`'s `-i` (interactive) option you can selectively kill clients.

Using Process Management Clients

The previous examples of process management used simple shell command-line utilities. However, many different and capable clients are available for XFree86 that offer more sophisticated views of memory and processes. This section highlights just a few of the more recent and popular clients included with your Linux distribution.

One of the most venerable legacy clients for monitoring the demands of your system's memory and keeping track of your system's CPU usage is the `xload` client. This client displays a graph of the activity of your computer, or the *load average*. The load average graph compiles the number of tasks run over a certain period of time. xload measures CPU usage as the average amount of time that the CPU was not idle. Other X clients, such as xosview, also display these and other system statistics, such as hard drive activity and swap space usage. Both clients are shown in Figure 7.4.

KDE and GNOME offer more sophisticated utilities that combine graphing with actual process listings. If you run these utilities with root permission, you can control and monitor any process on your system. For example, to launch the KDE process visualization client, kpm, enter the client name on the command line of a terminal window using the su command to grant root permission:

```
$ su -c kpm
Password:
```

Suppose that you see an error message like the following after pressing Enter:

```
Password:
Xlib: connection to ":0.0" refused by server
Xlib: Client is not authorized to connect to Server
kpm: cannot connect to X server :0.0
```

You can temporarily grant permission and rescind permission for the task time of the client by entering a command like the following:

```
$ xhost +localhost ; su -c kpm ; xhost -localhost
```

When the client starts, you'll see a display similar to that shown in Figure 7.5.

Note that kpm combines the output of the ps command with the graphics features of the xosview and xload clients. You can control a specific process by first clicking it in the window, then selecting an item from the Process or Signal menus. A similar

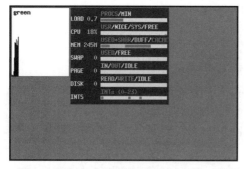

Figure 7.4 *The* xload *and* xosview *clients offer system monitoring for your X session.*

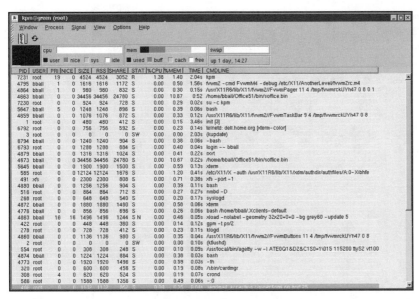

Figure 7.5 *The* kpm *client can selectively list and control processes on your system and also provides convenient graphic monitoring tools.*

client but one with more advanced memory graphing features is included with the GNOME distribution. You'll find the initial display of the gtop client to be somewhat familiar to the output of the top command (shown in Figure 7.3).

As with kpm, you can launch the gtop client from the command line of a terminal window or select the client from the GNOME desktop panel's menu. When you launch, gtop, the initial display looks like that shown in Figure 7.6.

Unlike kpm, the gtop client cannot be used to control specific processes. Note that gtop, like nearly all GNOME clients, features a menu bar and a toolbar with buttons; however, gtop's interface also includes three tabs. The default tab shows all processes. The far-right tab, Filesystems (free), shows the amount of available hard drive space on all mounted filesystems. If you click the center tab, Memory Usage (resident), you'll see a display similar to that shown in Figure 7.7.

The graphic shows the top 15 processes in terms of memory usage, along with the client requiring the most memory, and related processes. This format can help you monitor the relative memory requirements for various clients used on your system.

Stopping an X11 Session

This section introduces the techniques for properly logging out of an X session. There are brute-force methods that you can use when things go awry, and more

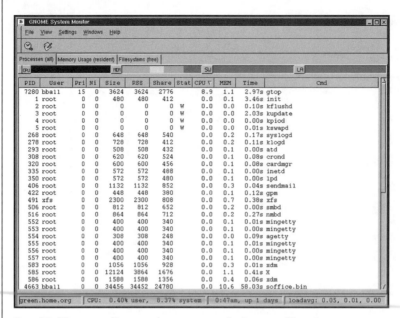

Figure 7.6 *The* gtop *client monitors processes during your X session.*

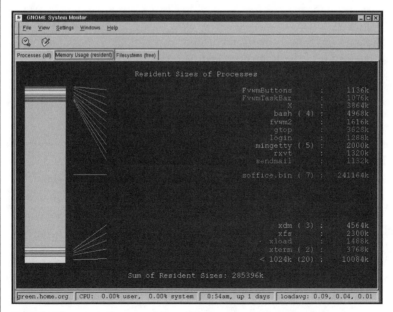

Figure 7.7 *The* gtop *client provides sophisticated graphing of processes in your system's memory.*

standard ways to exit your session and return either to the Linux console or an xdm login screen.

Logging Out

Most window managers offer a mechanism for logging out of an X session gracefully. You'll find a Log Out menu item on KDE's desktop panel and the GNOME panel. Other window managers, such as Motif, twm, and FVWM, offer Log Out menu items from root display menus.

Logging out of your X session gracefully is the best way to end your X session. You can run the chance of corrupting your filesystem if you exit Linux or X11 by turning off your computer, and you can lose session management or other settings that you configured during your X session.

Using the Keyboard

XFree86 offers some basic keyboard controls that you can use either to exit an X session to the Linux console or to kill the current X server. The Linux kernel included with most distributions offers six virtual consoles. As you learned in Chapter 6, "Starting X11," you can jump to a text-only console by pressing Ctrl+Alt+F*n*, where *n* is a virtual console from 1 through 6. For example, to return to the third virtual console, you would press Ctrl+Alt+F3. Usually you then return to the X session by pressing Alt+F7.

One of the options that you can include in your system's XF86Config ServerFlags section controls the ability to kill the current X server session by pressing Ctrl+Alt+Backspace. The section appears as follows:

```
Section "ServerFlags"

    # Uncomment this to disable the <Crtl><Alt><BS> server abort sequence
    # This allows clients to receive this key event.
    #DontZap


EndSection
```

Although the logic may seem backward, if you enable this feature, you won't be able to use this method to kill the X session. However, if you're still determined to kill the session, you can still do so even with this feature enabled. Simply use the su command, and then as root, kill the current X server by entering the kill command with the server's process ID.

Resource Information

http://www.xfree86.org—the starting point for learning more about XFree86 and X clients included with the XFree86 distribution.

http://www.rxvt.org—home page of the "ouR eXtended Virtual Terminal" client, or rxvt. You'll find an FAQ, a manual, and a source code for the current version of this fabulous client.

http://208.201.97.5/pubs/gbb/0805/pcx.htm—a (somewhat) dated overview of commercial X terminal packages for Windows.

http://www.cs.utk.edu/~shuford/terminal/dec.html—a short history of the ubiquitous Digital Equipment Corporation VT100 terminal.

http://www.geocities.com/SiliconValley/Pines/5004/linux-console.html— a thorough description of control codes recognized by the Linux console.

XF86Config man page—describes X server options to control keyboard killing of the X server.

Chapter 8: Using X11 Clients

Understanding the X Toolkit options

Using client resources

This chapter provides an introduction to using X11 clients, X command-line options (known as *X Toolkit* options), and X resources, which were introduced in Chapter 7. Building on information that you've learned so far, the chapter aims to help you build expertise when using X clients from the command line.

Understanding the options that you can use during your X sessions can help you build better, more efficient desktops with properly configured application windows. Some of the issues discussed in this chapter are critical, especially if your system has limited real estate (for example, if your system's resolution is less than 1,024×768), and can help you overcome obstacles with client placement and organization on the root display.

XFree86 and the X protocol provide the user with a great deal of flexibility and control, and you'll benefit from greater knowledge of this flexibility.

Understanding the X Toolkit Options

One of the benefits of using X is standardization. One of the downsides of using X is nonstandardization. How can this be true? Although X provides the basic underlying protocol and drawing routines for creating interactive clients and a robust graphical networking system, there are few standards (if any) regarding how clients should provide menus or other window decorations. But one standard shared is by nearly all X clients using functions outlined in the Xt (X Toolkit) library: the availability of standard options that can be used to control the initial size and placement of windows, font usage, color, and, as shown in the last chapter, resource settings.

These options are available through resource files or the command line. This section demonstrates how to use common X Toolkit command-line options.

Using the Command Line

The Linux command line, known as the shell, offers quite a bit of power to the user. When you use the shell with special commands known as *filter* programs, you can use the output of one command to feed the input of another command, and thereby build complex commands from a single command line. For example, to search and then mail a list of matching files with a single command line, you can combine the output of the find command with the mail command as follows:

```
# find ./ -name '*.msg' | mail -s "Message List" willie@tux.org
```

Although a few X clients (such as xmessage) can work as software filters, most simply obey built-in command-line options and are meant to run as a background process with a window display on the desktop. Launching most clients is as simple as tacking on the shell's background operator, &, and pressing Enter, as follows:

```
# xterm &
```

This command launches the xterm client in a new window and frees up the command line (if launched from another terminal client). Most X clients that have been built using the Xt libraries use a "standard" set of command-line options (and corresponding resources) known as *X Toolkit options*. The most commonly used options are listed in Table 8.1.

Table 8.1 Common X Toolkit Options

Command-line Option	Description
+rv	Do not use reverse video
-background *color*	Use a specified *color* for background drawing
-bd *color*	Use a specified *color* for the window border
-bg *color*	Use a specified *color* for background drawing
-bordercolor *color*	Use a specified *color* for the window border
-borderwidth *n*	Set the window border width to *n* pixels
-bw *n*	Set the window border width to *n* pixels
-display *display*	Use a specific *display* (or remote host)
-fg *color*	Use the specified *color* for foreground drawing
-fn *font*	Use a specified *font* for text drawing
-font *font*	Use a specified *font* for text drawing
-foreground *color*	Use a specified *color* for foreground drawing
-geometry *spec*	Specify the width, height, and location of the client
-iconic	Start the client in a minimized state
-name *name*	Load the client resources to be found under *name*
-reverse	Use reverse video if possible
-rv	Use reverse video if possible
-title *str*	Set the window title to *str*
-xrm *resourcestr*	Set and use the designated *resourcestr*

Note that some X clients may not honor these options, nor use the same resources. You can usually get a list of a client's options by using the -h, -help, or --help command-line options. For example, to see a list of the rxvt's options, use -h:

```
$ rxvt -h
```

```
Usage v2.6.1 : (XPM,utmp,menubar,graphics,XGetDefaults)
rxvt [-help]
 [-display string] [-tn string] [-geometry geometry] [-C] [-iconic] [-/+rv]
 [-/+ls] [-/+sb] [-/+sr] [-/+st] [-/+si] [-/+sk] [-/+ip] [-/+ut] [-/+vb]
 [-bg color] [-fg color] [-pixmap file[;geom]] [-fb fontname] [-fn fontname]
 [-name string] [-title string] [-n string] [-cr color] [-pr color]
 [-bd color] [-sl number] [-mod modifier] [-e command arg ...]
```

Some clients, such as xterm, have an astounding number of command-line options (68!). For example, to display an xterm window with a blue cursor, yellow highlighting, a red pointer, a scrollbar on the right, PeachPuff as the background color, magenta as the foreground color, a 9×15-pixel font, and the title "Every day is a holiday, and holidays are for every day," use a command such as the following:

```
$ xterm -cr blue -hc yellow -ms red -rightbar -bg PeachPuff \
-fg magenta -font 9x15 \
-title "Every day is a holiday, and holidays are for every day."
```

After you press Enter, you'll see a terminal window such as that shown in Figure 8.1.

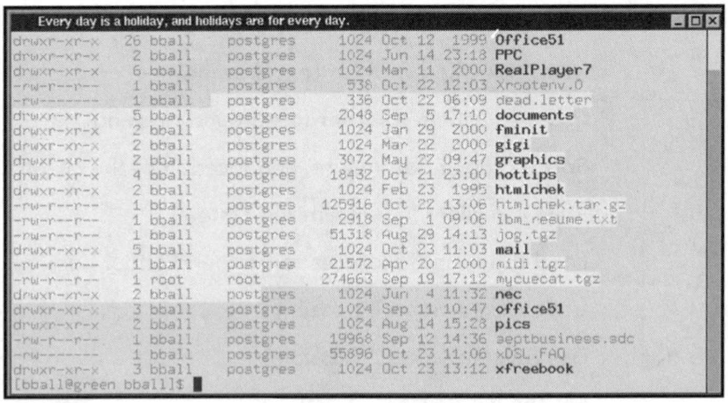

Figure 8.1 *The xterm client features many different command-line options, including several common X Toolkit options.*

---

xterm Exception!

Be careful when using geometry settings to start an `xterm` client—the values do not correspond to pixels. When you use geometry settings with `xterm`, the width and height settings designate the number of characters and lines of the new terminal window.

X Toolkit geometry settings can be especially useful to build working desktops and to place windows in exact positions on the display. As a system administrator, you can help new users learn X by crafting default desktops with helpful tools on the screen, using client listings with geometry settings in default `.xinitrc` files. Geometry settings take the following form:

```
-geometry WidthxHeight+/-Xoffset+/-Yoffset
```

Although the syntax may look complicated, it is quite easy to use geometry settings. In fact, a few "tricks of the trade" are documented in the X man page regarding the use of X and Y offsets. For example, you can use the `-geometry` option to create and place an `xclock` window that is 100 pixels wide and 80 pixel high with a negative X offset and a positive Y offset, as follows:

```
# xclock -geometry 100x80-0+0 &
```

After you press Enter, the clock will appear in the upper-right corner of your display. This means that you can use the following offsets to control corner displays of clients:

Offset	Position
+0+0	Upper-left corner
-0-0	Lower-right corner
-0+0	Upper-right corner
+0-0	Lower-left corner

Another interesting use of geometry settings is to place clients offscreen in a virtual desktop. If you know your desktop size in pixels and the geometry of your virtual desktops (such as 2×2, 3×2, and so on), you can then use geometry settings to position client windows on other desktops relative to desktop one, the starting desktop. For example, if your display is $1,024 \times 768$ and you use a 2×2 virtual desktop, start the `xclock` client with the following geometry setting:

```
$ xclock -geometry 80x80+1025+0
```

After you press Enter, the new `xclock` will appear in the upper-left corner of the virtual desktop adjacent to the first desktop. Unfortunately, this approach will not work with every window manager. However, KDE, GNOME, and other window managers have a feature that you can use to make a client appear in the same position in every desktop. For example, in the KDE desktop, if you start a console, then click in the upper-left corner of the client window, you'll see the drop-down menu shown in Figure 8.2.

Note that aside from the usual maximize, iconify, resize, and close settings, you can also choose the Sticky menu item, which places the same client in each virtual desktop, or the To Desktop menu item, which allows you to send the client to the chosen desktop. This feature can help you quickly build a fully populated session, perhaps with each desktop devoted to a special purpose (such as mail, graphics, word processing, and so on).

Whereas some older window managers depend on your home directory's `.xinitrc` file to provide guidance on which clients and where they should be positioned initially, newer window managers will remember your settings using session management features.

Using Client Resources

As you learned in Chapter 7, "First Steps with X11," X clients built using the Xt or X Toolkit library can also use resource files and resource settings as default guides to a number of characteristics. You can apply these settings on a systemwide basis in client-specific files under the `/usr/X11R6/lib/X11/app-defaults` directory,

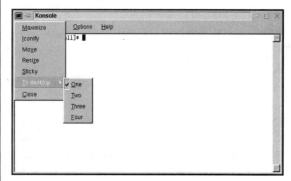

Figure 8.2 *The KDE window manager offers a "sticky" option and desktop navigation for its clients.*

included in a file named .Xdefaults in your home directory, or specify the settings on the command line using the -xrm X Toolkit option. Some window managers may use other locations, such as KDE's /usr/share/apps/kdisplay/app-defaults file.

The values of the default locations of client resources may be the same throughout the system or different for each user. The definition of in-memory variables, or *environment variables*, may also determine these values. The environment variables include the following:

- XUSERFILESEARCHPATH. This variable defines the location of resource settings (usually, and more efficiently, in your home directory in a subdirectory named app-defaults).

- XAPPLRESDIR. A holdover from earlier versions of X, this client resource pathname variable is still supported for compatibility.

- XFILESEARCHPATH. This variable can define multiple locations of app-defaults directories on your system.

- XENVIRONMENT. This variable can define the name of a resource file; if the variable is undefined, X looks in your home directory for a file named .Xdefaults-*hostname*, where *hostname* is the hostname of your system (and usually defined by the shell environment variable HOSTNAME).

As you also learned, X11 client resource settings take the following form:

```
*widget*resource: value
```

The widget portion designates a client-specific feature, such as a menu or internal value used to use a setting or toggle a feature. Xt library clients are crafted around a widget *tree*, or hierarchy of resources. The resources for a client use the widget name, and the resource portion of the setting may be one or more widgets that respond to the value portion of the setting.

Resource strings in your home directory's .Xdefaults file may look like this:

```
client*resource: value
```

The client portion is usually the name of the X client (or the name specified by using the -name X Toolkit option). Again, the resource and value portions are used to effect a setting on a particular client resource (such as a scrollbar). You can change these settings to suit your system or personal preferences.

You usually can read a comprehensive list of a client's resources by looking at the client's corresponding file in the app-defaults directory. Another place to check is the client's man page. You can also use the appres X client to list resources for a specific client. For example, to view the resources of the xmag client (which magnifies a portion of your display), use the appres client as follows:

```
$ appres Xmag
*pane2*orientation:      horizontal
*pane2*showGrip:         False
*Scale.baseTranslations: #augment  <EnterWindow>: set-colors()\n\
                                    <LeaveWindow>: unset-colors()\n\
                                    <Btn1Down>:popup-pixel()\n\
                                    Button1<Enter>:popup-pixel()\n\
                                    <Btn1Motion>:update-pixel()\n\
                                    <Btn1Up>:popdown-pixel()\n\
                                    <Leave>:popdown-pixel()\n\
                                    <Key>n:new()\n\
                                    <Key>q:close()\n\
                                    Ctrl<Key>c:close()\n\
                                    <Key>space:replace()
*pixLabel.Translations:  <Enter>:popdown-pixel()
*helpLabel.font:         8x13bold
*helpLabel.label:        xmag
*close.accelerators:     #augment    <Key>q:set()notify()unset()\n\
                         Ctrl<Key>c:set()notify()unset()
*VT100.Translations:     #override <Key>BackSpace: string(0x7F)\n\
<Key>Delete: string("\033[3~")\n\
<Key>Home: string("\033[1~")\n\
<Key>End: string("\033[4~")
*replace.accelerators:   #augment   <Key>space:set()notify()unset()\n\
                                    <Btn2Up>:set()notify()unset()\n\
                                    <Btn3Up>:set()notify()unset()
*scrollKey:       True
*visualBell:      true
*allowShellResize:       on
*Font:   fixed
*scrollTtyOutput:        False
```

In this example, you can see the current defaults for the xmag client, and a list of recognized settings, such as default fonts, keyboard controls, and button presses.

Using the editres Client

Yet another way to view (and change) client resources is to use the editres client, which can graphically display a client's widget tree and list resources. For example, start a client, such as xclock, then start the editres client; your desktop should then look like that shown in Figure 8.3.

Next, click the Commands menu and select the Get Tree menu item. Your pointer will turn into a cross-hair, and a message will instruct you to "Click the mouse pointer on any toolkit client." This means that you should left-click the xclock window. The editres window then shows the widget tree for the xclock client, as shown in Figure 8.4.

Note that xclock consists of three widgets: xclock, and two child widgets, shellext and clock. According to xclock's man page, the clock widget understands most of the client's core resource names. To view the clock widget's resources, first select the clock widgets in the tree by left-clicking them. Next, use the Command menu to select the Show Resource Box menu item. A new window, as shown in Figure 8.5, appears with a listing of resources recognized by the clock widget.

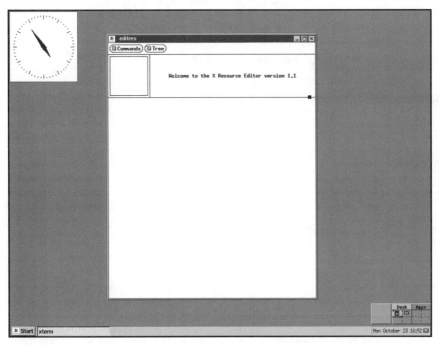

Figure 8.3 *The* editres *client is an X resource editor.*

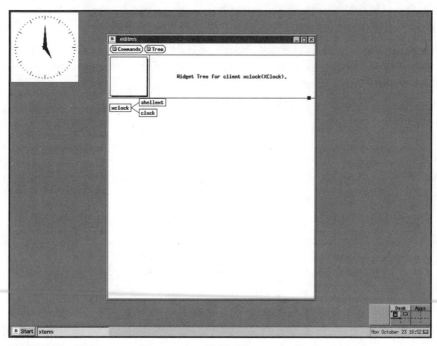

Figure 8.4 *Use the* editres *client to view X Toolkit–aware client widget trees.*

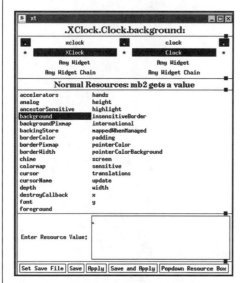

Figure 8.5 *The* editres *client displays the resources of a selected client widget, and may be used to change settings while the client runs.*

The editres resource box displays the resources of the selected widget. Click to select the widget names, then click to select a resource that you would like to edit, such as the background, and type a new value in the Enter Resource Value text field. When finished, click the Apply button to view your changes.

The new settings are created on the fly, and may be saved to a file. First, click the Set Save File button and enter a filename, such as xclock.rsrc. Change a setting, then click the Save and Apply button; the new resource setting is then appended to your new xclock.rsrc file.

You can repeat this step as often as you wish until you achieve the desired effect, as shown in Figure 8.6.

Following changes to the hands, foreground, background, and update resources, the xclock client now uses a red background with yellow hands, including a second hand to update the time each second. The corresponding resource settings, saved in the xclock.rsrc file, are the following:

.XClock.Clock.hands: yellow

.XClock.Clock.background: red

.XClock.Clock.foreground: yellow

.XClock.Clock.highlight: yellow

.XClock.Clock.update: 1

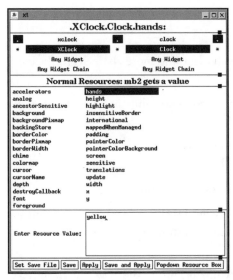

Figure 8.6 *After you make changes using the* editres *client, the* xclock *client displays a red background, with a yellow foreground and hands, and is updated once each second.*

The X Resource Database

You can also set systemwide resources on a per-server basis by using the `xrdb` client. This client is usually run from the Xsession script (found under the `/etc/X11/xdm` directory) and may be used to read in resource information from a variety of sources. On a Mandrake Linux system, two sources are a file named `.Xresources` under the `/usr/X11R6/lib/X11/xinit` directory or your home directory's `.Xresources` file. Under Red Hat Linux, two sources are `/etc/X11/Xresources` or your home directory's `.Xresources` file.

You can then copy, paste, and save these settings in your `.Xdefaults` file. Subsequently, each time that you launch `xclock`, it uses the new resources.

You'll have to decide whether it is easier to use the `editres` client, to use preference menus in newer X clients for KDE and GNOME, or to edit resource-setting text files. On the one hand, placing resource settings outside of a client can reduce the client size. On the other hand, providing comprehensive graphical interfaces for preference settings can be overwhelming and lead to "code bloat," especially if a client is used for a single purpose.

Resource Information

http://www.xfree86.org—the starting point for learning more about XFree86 and X clients included with the XFree86 distribution.

xterm man page—descriptions of the nearly 70 command-line options of this X terminal client.

X man page—descriptions of the X Toolkit options, with details on how to use geometry settings and X environment variables.

editres man page—directions for using this resource editor.

http://www-sop.inria.fr/koala/jml/xres/xres.html#HDR3—Jean-Michel Leon's Web page, featuring an abstract titled "End-user Customization of Xt Applications."

ftp://ftp.crl.research.digital.com/pub/X11/contrib/faqs/—the FTP site to retrieve FAQs about X, Motif, and the latest version of X11R6.

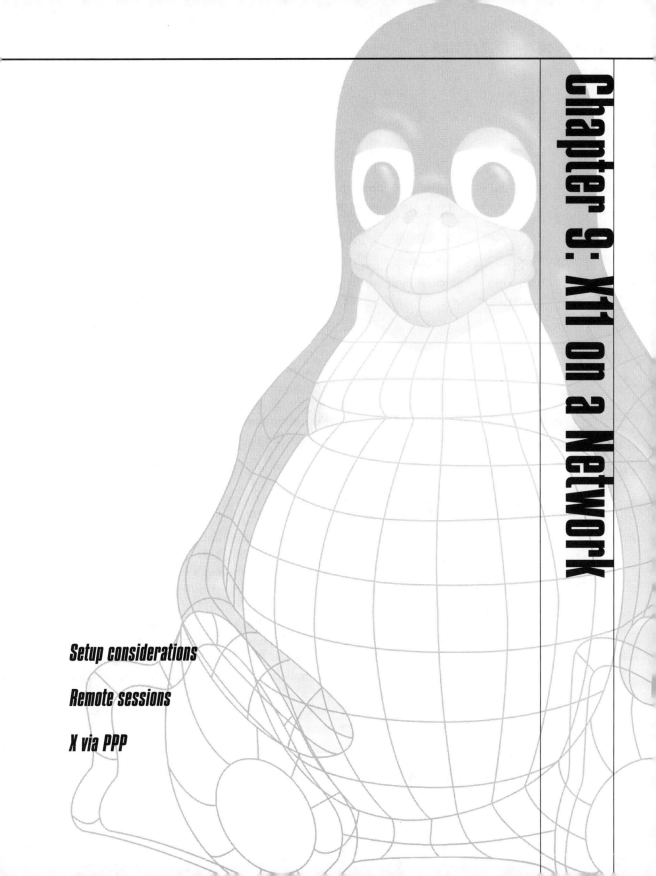

Chapter 9: X11 on a Network

Setup considerations

Remote sessions

X via PPP

This chapter provides information on how to use X on a network, and builds on topics previously introduced regarding how to start X, launch clients, and use terminal clients. You'll see how to use X to build a powerful but flexible graphical network using simple techniques and a minimum of rote skills. This chapter will cover some initial considerations in setting up a network, then provide the details on how to perform remote logins and launch clients, even over a dial-up PPP connection.

Even though XFree86 performs admirably on a standalone workstation and provides a superior graphical interface for Linux users, the real power of X quickly becomes apparent when used with other workstations or servers. X has a long history of network reliability, and was designed from scratch with networking in mind. As you learned in Chapter 6, "Starting X11," low-end Linux workstations, along with the right displays, can be part of a cost-effective but efficient LAN. This chapter builds on the concept of using XFree86 in a network environment. You'll learn the basic concepts of using X on a network, configure remote logins, and see how to launch clients locally from a remote station or remotely from a local workstation. This chapter will also cover some basic security issues that you should be aware of, with potential solutions and troubleshooting suggestions hopefully providing answers to common problems.

Setup Considerations

When you are setting up XFree86 to work on a network, the same basic considerations that go into planning an efficient network for other operating systems can apply. These considerations include an outline and thorough review of the purpose, requirements, cost limits, user needs, security, and support issues facing the network. One of your least worries is about using Linux and XFree86, as both distributions are flexible enough to conform to many different situations, from a wide area network (WAN) to a local area network (LAN), a company intranet, or even embedded device development. Other factors in favor of Linux and XFree86 as a cost-effective solution include the fact that both distributions are royalty and license free, work on nearly any hardware platform, and come with source code. Linux and X are a bargain, considering that the cost of using commercial operating systems with server features is nearly $1,000 for only five users.

Overview of Clients and Servers

The networking aspect of X is based on a client/server model, with the X server handling nearly every aspect of client display, such as drawing, providing fonts, transmitting pointer and keyboard events, and so on. The X server handles these tasks, so that only the graphics hardware hosting the server is of any importance to the underlying code. This abstraction, in response to client requests, allows the server to create desktops and displays on remote hardware successfully without having to know about the particulars of the remote hardware, and increases the portability of the server code.

The basic components of the X client and server model include the X display server, which reacts to requests (or commands) sent by X clients (applications). These requests are in the form of X protocol requests, and the clients may be running locally or from a remote computer. This model can be confusing initially, but once you understand the basic concepts, you'll soon see that you can configure X flexibly to fit a variety of network models.

Aspects of the X model parallel file and disk server networks. Although you can use X in this way (using X terminals focused on a central server), you can also use X in a way that models a distributed network. Again, you can launch X clients locally or remotely on any workstation running an X server, as long as proper permissions exist. By transmitting and receiving graphics drawing requests and keyboard and mouse input events, the X display server allows local client launch and display, remote client launch and display, and local display of remote client launches. This means that you can run and display remote X clients locally on an Intel-based PC, even if the remote computer is an Apple Macintosh running XFree86 (or the reverse—and run Intel-based X clients, such as Sun's StarOffice suite, to display on your Macintosh).

Linux, with its vast support of networking protocols and filesystems, is a perfect complement to the capabilities of XFree86. By using a combination of each system's features, you can quickly craft creative solutions to provide pinpoint computing solutions suitable for a wide array of computational needs and budgets.

For example, in a text-based environment without the benefits of using X, Linux supports the ability to log in and work on remote workstations or servers (through the `telnet` or `ssh` utilities). Linux also supports the mounting of remote filesystems locally, even in a heterogeneous system (using the Network File System, or NFS, NetaTalk, and Samba). When you factor in a networking graphical system such as X, which supports display and use of clients locally or from a remote computer, you'll quickly realize the benefits of using Linux and X.

Considerations

Every network design involves planning considerations of needs, requirements, availability, flexibility, use, access, security, and costs. A variety of yardsticks are used, such as total cost of ownership, cost per seat, and even performance benchmarks. Obviously, the target is to get the most computational "bang for the buck," but other factors can be important, such as future upgrade, maintenance, or administration costs.

Some factors in favor of X include its independence of operating systems. There are X servers and clients (or close variants) for almost every hardware platform available, even Personal Digital Assistants (PDAs)! In the recent past, dedicated X terminals— or hardware with adequate display, input, and performance to support a minimal X server—were part of the formula in X network design. X terminals generally lacked traditional hard drive, RAM, and other storage space, and therefore cost less than workstations that could also function in a server capacity. Today, these terminals are being resurrected as *network appliances,* and again can be part of the equation in efficient network design.

Obviously, no one would seriously consider building an X network consisting of PDAs, but hardware costing the same or less can today be purchased and put to work as X terminals. When companies face *horizontal scaling* (adding more workstations to the network), expenses can mount quickly. Obviously, the capabilities of the hardware on the network will vary, and depend on the functions or processing needs of parts of the network (in other words, the design and shipping departments will have different workstations).

However you design your network, you'll find XFree86 a solution that provides benefits of flexible user interaction, graphics output, transparent networking, hardware interoperability, and room to grow.

Remote Sessions

There are a number of ways to conduct an X session on a network. For example, you can log in to Linux on your workstation, start X, then launch clients that display locally. Another way is to use an X display manager to log in to a remote computer and run a remote X session on your local display. And yet another way is to launch a local X session, use the `telnet` command to log in to the remote computer, launch clients from the remote server, then have them display locally.

A properly defined $DISPLAY environment variable is crucial when using X. A display name is assigned to every X server on your network, and usually consists of the hostname, a display number, and a screen number. Knowing the display is necessary if you want to launch remote clients for local use or launch a client for use on a remote display.

For example, when you log in to Linux and launch X on the workstation named `stinky`, the $DISPLAY environment variable for your session will look like this:

```
stinky:0.0
```

The variable could also look like this:

```
:0.0
```

You can quickly determine your $DISPLAY variable by piping the output of the shell's env command through fgrep like this:

```
$ env | fgrep DISPLAY
DISPLAY=dell.home.org:0.0
```

This example (after using telnet to access a remote host) shows the hostname, display, and screen number, and refers to your workstation, not the display of the remote host. Another way to see your shell's $DISPLAY variable quickly is to use the echo command (or your shell's built-in echo command), as follows:

```
$ echo $DISPLAY
dell:0.0
```

And yet another way is to use the xdpyinfo client as follows:

```
$ xdpyinfo | fgrep display
name of display:    dell.home.org:0.0
```

If more than one X session is running locally on a server, you may see something like the following:

```
name of display:    :1.0
```

In this example, the user is logged in and using a second X session (display) on the workstation.

Remote Client Execution

There are also a number of ways to launch clients on an X network. For example, if you log in to Linux and start an X session locally, you can display a local client on a remote display by using the -display X Toolkit option along with the remote computer's display name. If you're sitting at a workstation named greenie, you can launch the xcalc client and display it on the remote X display on stinky like this:

```
$ xcalc -display stinky:0.0 &
```

However, if you do not have access or permission to run clients on the remote computer, you will see something like this:

```
Xlib: connection to "stinky:0.0" refused by server
Xlib: Client is not authorized to connect to Server
Error: Can't open display: stinky:0.0
```

The xhost command is used to control server access under X. Use this client to add or remove hostnames or usernames to or from a server's connection list. In the previous example, you would use xhost on the remote computer stinky as follows:

```
$ xhost + greenie
greenie being added to access control list
```

After you press Enter, the user on greenie could then execute the xcalc client, and xcalc would appear on stinky's display. However, after using the xcalc client, you should then remove greenie's access, as follows:

```
$ xhost - greenie
greenie being removed from access control list
```

A more common approach, especially on small networks, is first to grant access to a more powerful workstation or server, then log in using a telnet session, as follows:

```
[bball@thinkpad bball]$ xhost + dell
dell being added to access control list
[bball@thinkpad bball]$ telnet dell
Trying 192.168.2.35...
Connected to dell.home.org.
Escape character is '^]'.
Welcome to SuSE Linux 7.0 (i386) - Kernel 2.2.16 (3).

dell login: bball
Password:
Last login: Mon Oct 30 16:14:09 from green.home.org
Have a lot of fun...
bball@dell:~ > env | fgrep DISPLAY
DISPLAY=thinkpad.home.org:0.0
bball@dell:~ > office52/soffice &
```

> You can also log in remotely for access to launch X clients by using xterm's -e command-line option along with the telnet command, as follows:
>
> ```
> xterm -e telnet remotehostname
> ```

In this example, display access to the local X server is granted to the workstation named dell. Next, the telnet command is used to open a session to dell. As you can see, after the user logs in to dell, the $DISPLAY environment variable is still for the local workstation (named `thinkpad`, in this example). Finally, the StarOffice suite is launched on the `dell` workstation, and will be displayed on `thinkpad`. Note that it was unnecessary to use the `-display` option (although you could choose to use the option). After the session has ended, you should again use the `xhost` command to remove display access.

Displaying remote clients on a user's screen in a network environment can also take some thought. For example, if a user logs in to X via `xdm` into a remote server (using `X -broadcast` or `X -query` *hostname*), that user can display an X client remotely by specifying the hostname of the user's workstation, not the remote computer. For example, if a user on `stinky` logs in to X via `xdm` and runs a session on `greenie`, a user on `thinkpad`, given proper access, would display the `xcalc` client using the following command:

```
$ xcalc -display thinkpad:0.0 &
```

In this example, `thinkpad` displays the `xcalc` client, even though the user is logged in to `greenie`.

In some instances, you may have to set your `$DISPLAY` variable manually, especially if you use the `rlogin` or `rsh` command to log in to a remote box. You can do this easily from the command line by using the shell's variable definition assignment. After logging in remotely, if you use the `bash` shell, use the `bash export` command followed by the definition, like this:

```
$ export DISPLAY=myhostname:0.0
```

After you press Enter, your workstation will display locally any X clients launched on the remote computer (again, you may first have to grant access using `xhost`).

X via PPP

Another method of allowing remote access is to use low-bandwidth X with the `lbx-proxy` client. This method is generally used to provide remote X sessions via modem dial-in, and allows X to work via Serial Line Internet Protocol (SLIP), compressed header SLIP, or more commonly, Point-to-Point Protocol (PPP).

One method of easily establishing X sessions via dial-up and getting a bit better performance is to use the `dxpc` client (which acts as a client or server, depending on command-line options). This software, originally by Zachary Vonler and now maintained by Brian Pane, works by caching X Protocol messages in order to provide compressed X requests over slower transmission lines. This provides remarkable performance and greatly speeds up the display of clients, even when using slow serial lines.

First, you'll need to download and install the dxpc software package. This software, available through **http://www.vigor.nu/dxpc/**, is packaged as source code in a 123K compressed tarball. To build and install the software, use the tar, cd, configure, and make commands (as root) like this:

```
# tar xvzf dxpc*gz
# cd dxpc*
# ./configure ; make install
```

Next, you'll need to set up PPP service on the intended server, named stinky for this example. You can quickly perform this setup (as root) by creating a user account named ppp. Next, in the user's /etc/passwd entry, replace the shell entry with the pathname to a shell script (named doppp in this example):

```
ppp:x:502:502::/home/ppp:/usr/local/bin/doppp
```

Don't forget to assign a password for the new PPP user by using the passwd command. Next, create the shell script with the following command:

```
exec /usr/sbin/pppd -detach
```

Save the file and use the chmod command to make it executable. Your system's /etc/inittab file should already be set up to accept dial-ins via modem. The following entry, which uses the agetty command, allows dial-ins at 38400 on /dev/ttyS2:

```
3:2345:respawn:/usr/local/bin/agetty -w -I 'ATE0Q1&D2&C1S0=1\015' \
115200 ttyS2 vt100
```

Next, to assign a static IP address for the dial-in user, create a file named options.ttyS2 in the /etc/ppp directory with the following command:

```
192.168.2.37:192.168.2.41
```

In this example, the remote caller will be assigned the IP 192.168.2.41, whereas the IP of the server host (stinky) is 192.168.2.37. Finally, create your /etc/ppp/options file with the following commands:

```
asyncmap 0
netmask 255.255.255.0
proxyarp
lock
crtscts
modem
```

Save the file. At this point, you can dial from a remote computer, named greenie in this example, into your server. To do so, enter the username and password, then establish a PPP connection with the assigned IP address.

Now dial in to the server named `stinky` and establish a connection. On the remote computer (`greenie`), open two X terminal windows. On one, use the `telnet` command to get on the server and ensure that the `$DISPLAY` variable is set to the `$DISPLAY` of the remote computer, as follows:

```
[stinky]$ export DISPLAY=greenie:0.0
```

Next, run the dxpc program in this window as a client:

```
[stinky]$ dxpc -f -s1
dxpc proxy running in CLIENT mode
```

The dxpc command will show a status report (in client mode on the remote server). The extra options cause the process to fork and enable compression reports to stdout. Next, reset the `DISPLAY` variable as follows:

```
 [stinky]$ export DISPLAY=unix:8
```

The `unix:8` display used by the dxpc command (when the computer is running as a server), provides an address used to display clients – the dxpc command is "mimicking" an X server, and uses the `unix:8` display. Now, on the terminal window of the remote computer (`greenie`), use the dxpc command in server mode, specifying the remote computer as follows:

```
[greenie]$ dxpc -f stinky -s1
dxpc proxy running in SERVER mode
```

After you press Enter, the dxpc command will run as a server and intercept requests from remote clients, then display them locally. You can now launch clients from the server's terminal window (`stinky`'s in this example) and they will run over your serial PPP connection. Versions of dxpc are available for a number of computer platforms and operating systems, including Solaris, Windows, HP/UX, and Digital Unix. You can use this software to easily set up a telecommuting connection, and with faster serial lines, even run graphical clients remotely with acceptable performance. Browse to **http://www.vigor.nu/dxpc/** for more information.

Virtual Networks

Another solution, using X-based server software, is Xvnc, a collection of server and client software for a number of different computer platforms. This software is from AT&T Labs Research in central Cambridge, England, and works on Intel-based PCs running Windows or Linux, Solaris (SPARC), Macintosh (68K and PPC), DEC Alpha, Windows CE, or any Java-enabled display. This software is becoming a standard addition to a number of Linux distributions because it is free, comes with source code, and is easy to use and set up. Xvnc allows you to sit at your Linux workstation and display the desktop of another computer running a totally different operating system. You can also, for example, sit down at a Macintosh computer, and display a Linux X session in a floating window. After downloading and installing the software from the Xvnc home page (see "Resource Information" at the end of this chapter), you can start it as a server on a desired platform (that may or may not being running XFree86).

For example, start the Xvnc server on a remote computer running Linux on your LAN like this:

```
[green]$ vncserver -geometry 800x600


New 'X' desktop is green:1


Starting applications specified in /home/bball/.vnc/xstartup
Log file is /home/bball/.vnc/green:1.log
```

As you can see, you can use geometry settings to determine the initial desktop size. The Xvnc server starts, and the "virtual" session is assigned a display number. A file named xstartup under the .vnc directory of the remote computer determines the virtual X session, and will automatically be created when you first use Xvnc. This file may look like this:

```
#!/bin/sh
xrdb $HOME/.Xresources
xsetroot -solid grey
xterm -geometry 80x24+10+10 -ls -title "$VNCDESKTOP Desktop" &
twm &
```

The startup script shown here will first read in any session preferences from your .Xresources file, then set the root display color, start the xterm client, and then launch the twm window manager. To view this remote session, enter the vncviewer command along the name of the remote display, like this from a different computer on your LAN:

```
$ vncviewer green:1
```

```
VNC server supports protocol version 3.3 (viewer 3.3)
Password:
VNC authentication succeeded

...
```

After you press Enter, the program asks you to enter a password (assigned after you run the `vncserver` client for the first time on the remote machine). A window then appears, as shown in Figure 9.1.

The remote session appears in a window the size of the remote session's desktop (800×600 in this example). This software makes it extremely easy to run remote sessions of computers on a single display, even on widely disparate platforms such as Windows, as shown in Figure 9.2.

Security Issues

Although security perhaps is not a problem on a small network, you should always consider security when running remote clients, especially when using the keyboard. For the best security, you should always launch your X terminal locally, then use `tel-net` to access the remote machine. Even better, you can also first set `xterm` to use a secure keyboard during your session.

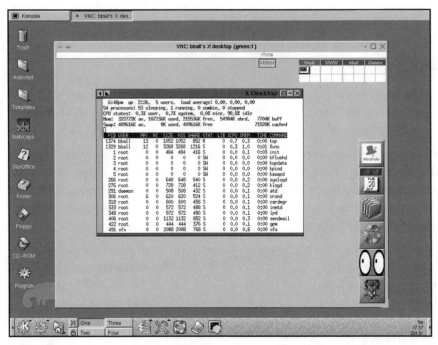

Figure 9.1 *The* `vncviewer` *client and the* `Xvnc` *server software allow you to run virtual networks and remote computers across networks and platform systems.*

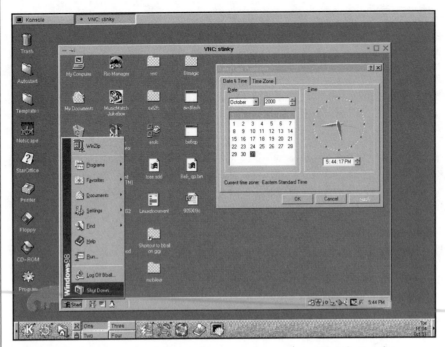

Figure 9.2 *The* Xvnc *server and client software works even on outdated operating systems such as Windows.*

Start the client during your local X session as follows:

```
$ xterm &
```

Next, move your mouse button to a blank area of the terminal window, then hold down the Ctrl key and left-click the mouse button. A pop-up menu appears, from which you should select the Secure Keyboard option, as shown in Figure 9.3.

The xterm window uses reverse background and foreground colors while in secure keyboard mode. This mode forces all keyboard input to the xterm window for the duration of the mode, so if you launch another client or Netscape, you will not be able to enter input into other windows or text fields. Turn off the secure keyboard mode by iconifying the window or using the pop-up menu.

If you want to allow external access to your network's internal X servers, consider setting up an X firewall proxy using the xfwp client. You'll also need to run an X proxy manager, but once in place, the addresses of your LAN's X servers will be protected, and only authorized clients will be allowed to connect. The xfwp client is generally used on a firewall computer, but you may have to do some additional configuration with your existing firewall software to allow access to your LAN's X servers.

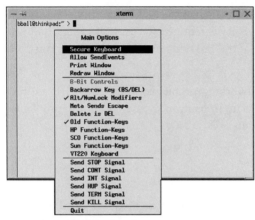

Figure 9.3 *The* xterm *client features a Secure Keyboard option for increased security.*

Some general pointers on security include the following:

- Check your xhost settings and always reset them.
- Regularly upgrade your software to include bug and security fixes; periodically check the home pages for your distribution, and check the XFree86 security pages for updates.
- Limit physical access to your network, protect passwords, and ensure that passwords are changed regularly.
- Protect open ends of your network using firewalls, and disable unneeded services (usually listed in inetd.conf or /etc/xinetd).
- Limit shell accounts or dial-in access; unless remote administration is really needed, consider alternatives that allow limited access.
- Edit your /etc/hosts.deny and /etc/hosts.allow files. Fortunately, all Linux distributions use TCP wrappers, but you should edit these files nevertheless.
- Regularly check system logs.

Troubleshooting

Most problems with remote execution of clients under X involve the incorrect use of $DISPLAY variables, the -display option (specifying an incorrect hostname, display, or screen number), and permissions involving the xhost command.

Problems can arise from mistyped passwords, incorrect `.xinitrc` or `.xsession` files, or corrupt filesystems (a home directory is required for using X locally, and you must have a user account in order to use the `telnet` command to gain access to a remote computer).

Another problem can arise through networking problems, routing, and IP address assignment. In general, if your network is up to par, you shouldn't run into problems. XFree86 is a robust and stable distribution of X.

Resource Information

http://webopedia.internet.com/TERM/c/client_server_architecture.html—a traditional definition of the client/server architecture, applied to networking; note that although you can use this type of networking with X, the definition doesn't apply to X's service model.

http://www.esri.com/library/userconf/proc95/to100/p067.html—a description of client/server networking, incorporating X terminals.

http://www.thinknic.com—the New Internet Computer, a $199 Linux terminal that comes with Ethernet, sound, CD-ROM, a keyboard, and a mouse; add a monitor, and you have an X terminal!

http://www.abs.net/~lloyd/csfaq.txt—the Client/Server FAQ (this site is no longer actively maintained).

http://www.xfree86.org/security/—home page for security issues, vulnerabilities in distributions, and fixes for XFree86.

http://www.motifzone.com/tmd/articles/webenx/webenx.html—an article on how to set up Web-enabled remote X client execution.

http://www.landfield.com/faqs/x-faq/part1/section-14.html—an article describing LBX, or low-bandwidth X.

http://www.vigor.nu/dxpc/—home page for the `dxpc` client, used with Linux and XFree86 to set up X sessions via a PPP connection.

http://www.uk.research.att.com/vnc/xvnc.html—home page of the X-based virtual network computer server; from this site, you can download documentation, source, and precompiled binaries for your system.

http://www.xmission.com/~howardm/Xwoes.html—an outline of common problems with XFree86 and Linux.

Chapter 10: XFree86 X11 Clients

This chapter introduces a number of XFree86 clients included with the latest XFree86 distribution. Several of these clients have been covered elsewhere in this book; this chapter will mention those clients, but also provide an overview of some commonly used applications.

XFree86 comes with more than 100 different clients that you can use to configure, manage, and run X. Table 10.1 lists the clients included with XFree86 4.0.1, specifies the client's file size, and briefly describes each command. You can use this table as a quick reference, or to decide whether you really need to install the client on your system. Thus the table can help system managers trim the contents of the /usr/X11R6/bin directory on those systems with limited resources.

Exploring Base Clients

This section presents a table listing XFree86 4.0.1's clients. The chapter then proceeds to describe briefly some of the more interesting or useful clients that you'll likely use during your X sessions. Note that not all the clients listed in Table 10.1 provide a graphical interface.

Table 10.1 Base X Clients

Client	Size (Bytes)	Description
appres	14,994	Lists X application resource database
atobm	16,366	Converts from ASCII to bitmap
bdftopcf	35,014	Converts a font from .bdf to .pcf format
beforelight	23,327	Provides a screensaver for X
bitmap	86,655	Launches a simple bitmap editor
bmtoa	14,959	Converts from bitmap to ASCII
cxpm	27,891	Checks the X pixmap file format
dga	29,622	Tests clients for X11's Direct Graphics Access extension
editres	59,375	Edits a client's resource settings
fsinfo	39,737	Provides a font server information client
fslsfonts	45,910	Lists fonts from an X font server
fstobdf	45,420	Creates a .bdf font from a font server
iceauth	31,590	Provides an ICE file editor and display client

Table 10.1 Base X Clients *(continued)*

Client	Size (Bytes)	Description
ico	52,704	Demonstrates animation
imake	29,037	Creates makefiles
lbxproxy	332,203	Provides a low-bandwidth X proxy utility
listres	17,073	Launches a widget resource listing client
lndir	16,190	Creates a directory of symbolic links
makedepend	32,555	Creates makefile dependencies
makeg	419	Creates an executable file with debugging information
makepsres	36,858	Creates a PostScript font resource database
makestrs	21,494	Builds string table source files, with headers in C
mergelib	2,295	Provides a shell script to merge software libraries
mkcfm	135,501	Displays font metrics summaries
mkdirhier	1,019	Creates directory hierarchy
mkfontdir	40,073	Builds an index of X fonts in a directory
mkhtmlindex	1,229	Creates index files of HTML man pages
oclock	25,159	Provides a clock client
proxymngr	34,115	Launches an X proxy manager
pswrap	86,162	Generates a PostScript-to-C procedure
resize	18,740	Generates a shell command to reset xterm
revpath	12,035	Generates a reverse path
rman	108,104	Converts man pages to HTML
rstart	1,863	Launches a remote X client
rstartd	1,455	Launches a remote start helper client
sessreg	16,517	Authorizes system users to start an X server
setxkbmap	95,136	Provides a map keyboard using a specified layout
showfont	45,138	Displays fonts known to the X server
showrgb	13,582	Displays an RGB color database
smproxy	26,526	Enables nonsession X clients to launch
startx	1,626	Starts an X session
SuperProbe	100,540	Probes the system's graphics hardware
sxpm	24,032	Displays and converts an X pixmap
twm	156,440	Launches the Tab window manager
viewres	28,107	Displays widget classes of the Athena Widget set
x11perf	110,099	Launches an X session performance monitor client

Table 10.1 Base X Clients (continued)

Client	Size (Bytes)	Description
x11perfcomp	2,643	Merges x11perf output into a table format
xauth	42,160	Edits and displays X authority information
xbiff	22,602	Launches an e-mail notification client
xcalc	35,258	Provides a calculator client
xclipboard	23,256	Launches an X copy-and-paste utility
xclock	25,705	Provides a clock client
xcmsdb	33,837	Launches a Device Color Characterization utility
xconsole	23,408	Provides a console message monitor
xcutsel	17,853	Launches an X copy-and-paste client
xditview	74,026	Displays ditroff files
xdm	1,162,78	Launches an X display manager
xdpyinfo	55,372	Displays information about the X session and server
xedit	94,188	Launches a simple text editor for X
xev	25,802	Displays the X keyboard and mouse events
xeyes	23,868	Provides a follow-the-pointer client
xf86cfg	290,021	Launches a graphical XF86Config editor
xf86config	59,651	Provides a console-mode XF86Config editor
xfd	24,277	Displays the specified font's characters
xfindproxy	19,704	Discovers and displays proxy services
xfontsel	39,278	Launches an X font display client
XFree86	1,686,751	Provides the new, modular X server
xfs	103,420	Launches the X font server
xfwp	40,379	Provides an X firewall proxy
xgamma	27,317	Monitors the gamma correction client
xgc	69,271	Demonstrates X graphics and widgets
xhost	18,469	Manages server display access control
xieperf	259,959	Tests and demonstrates the XIE protocol
xinit	20,750	Launches the client used to initialize and start the X server
xkbbell	17,772	Provides a keyboard bell control client
xkbcomp	263,997	Creates a keyboard description for xmodmap
xkbevd	91,064	Launches the keyboard event daemon
xkbprint	161,956	Prints a keyboard description
xkbvleds	26,808	Displays keyboard LEDs

Table 10.1 Base X Clients (continued)

Client	Size (Bytes)	Description
xkbwatch	23,540	Displays codes returned by a specific key press
xkill	18,583	Kills the X client (command-line or pointer)
xload	20,322	Shows the system load average
xlogo	18,770	Displays the X logo
xlsatoms	15,329	Lists X server internal atoms
xlsclients	16,291	Lists the running X clients
xlsfonts	27,247	Lists fonts known to the X server
xmag	41,739	Magnifies portions of the desktop
xman	60,420	Displays the man pages
Xmark	27,499	Summarizes statistics from x11perf output
xmessage	23,735	Displays a designated message
xmkmf	1,007	Creates a makefile from an imake file
xmodmap	35,131	Changes pointer and keyboard characteristics
Xnest	982,501	Launches a nested X server
xon	2,195	Launches an X client on a remote computer
xprop	36,040	Displays window and font properties from the X server
Xprt	2,520,562	Launches the X print server
xrdb	30,308	Provides an X resource database client
xrefresh	16,825	Refreshes the root display
xset	40,505	Sets various modes for X
xsetmode	14,246	Sets a mode for the pointing device
xsetpointer	14,415	Changes the X pointer
xsetroot	21,076	Sets X root window characteristics
xsm	86,577	Launches the X session manager
xstdcmap	18,518	Defines colormaps
xterm	229,227	Launches the X terminal client
Xvfb	4,034,759	Invokes the Vesa framebuffer server
xvidtune	45,309	Fine-tunes the video settings
xwd	32,203	Captures an X window
xwininfo	33,868	Displays window information
xwud	29,302	Displays X window dumps

Unlike most XFree86 clients, a number of the clients in Table 10.1 do not have a corresponding man page. This is because the clients, such as the xkb series, are part of X.org's (the steward consortium for X) series of unsupported clients, testing applications, or utilities. However, don't let the lack of a man page deter you from experimenting!

Setting Preferences with the xset Client

The xset client is used to display and set preferences for local or remote X sessions. This client controls many different aspects of your session, including the following:

- **Terminal bell**—xset can turn this feature on or off, and can set the volume, pitch, and duration of your system beep.
- **Keyclicks**—The client can control the volume of your system's keyclick sound, or turn the keyclick on or off; xset can also control your keyboard's autorepeat feature or rate.
- **Display Power Management Signaling (DPMS)**—xset can control the Energy Star features of your monitor (if the monitor supports these features).
- **Screensaving**—The client enables you to turn your session's screensaving features on or off; if you activate the features, and the client also enables you to set an interval before activation.
- **Fonts**—The client can add or remove a font to or from your X session.
- **LEDs**—You can use xset to control your keyboard's Light Emitting Diodes.
- **Pointer**—You can set your pointer's acceleration and threshold (the distance traveled relative to movement) values.

Use xset's q option to display your current settings, as follows:

```
# xset q
Keyboard Control:
    auto repeat:  on     key click percent:  0    LED mask:  00000000
    auto repeat delay:  500     repeat rate:  5
    auto repeating keys:   00ffffffdffffbbf
                           fa9ffffffffdffdff
                           7f00000000000000
                           0000000000000000
    bell percent:  75    bell pitch:  800    bell duration:  100
Pointer Control:
```

```
   acceleration:  2/1     threshold:  4
Screen Saver:
   prefer blanking:  yes      allow exposures:  yes
   timeout:  0     cycle:  600
Colors:
   default colormap:  0x21     BlackPixel:  0     WhitePixel:  65535
Font Path:
   unix/:-1
Bug Mode: compatibility mode is disabled
DPMS (Energy Star):
   Standby: 1200     Suspend: 1800     Off: 2400
   DPMS is Disabled
Font cache:
   Server does not have the Font-Cache Extension
```

After you press Enter, you'll see default values for a number of settings. Use the s and on options as follows to turn on screensaving:

```
# xset s on
```

Next, select an interval, in seconds, before screensaving is activated, like this:

```
# xset s 60
```

To use graphics and a background (instead of a blank screen) for screensaving, use the noblank option like this:

```
# xset s noblank
```

After the specified interval (60 seconds in this example), the screen clears and you'll see the display shown in Figure 10.1.

To turn off screensaving, use the s and off options as follows:

```
# xset s off
```

You can also use this client to control features of remote displays, but be mindful when using the -display option. If you log in to X on a remote server through xdm, the display is not local. For example, if you start an X session from a workstation named tinky, but log in to a remote computer named froggy, your xset commands will apply to froggy and won't be active for your display on tinky unless you use the -display option like this:

```
# xset -display tinky:0.0 m "default"
```

Figure 10.1 *X features built-in screensaving facilities that you can control by using the* xset *client.*

Screensaving Necessary?

Modern color monitors with energy saving features and active-matrix liquid crystal displays (LCDs) for laptops are immune to static displays of information that 10 years ago would have been cause for concern. Monitor "burn-in" hasn't been an issue to worry about for a number of years, but screensavers live on as an art form. Probably better termed as "eye candy," screensavers are really no longer needed, but you'll find a healthy selection of more than a hundred included with every Linux distribution. Unless you need to use a screensaver with password protection, it's always a good idea to turn off electrical devices if you're not using them (to save energy). Whether or not you use a screensaver is a personal, but not necessary, choice.

Capturing and Displaying Screens

The xwd and xwud clients are used to capture and display the local or remote contents of a window or entire display. To capture the contents of a window, use the xwd command on the command line of a terminal window, along with its -out option and a filename, like this:

```
# xwd -out mygraphic.xwd
```

After you press Enter, your pointer will turn into a cross-hair. Move your pointer to a window to capture, then press the left mouse button. Your graphic (in X Window bitmap format) will be saved in the current directory. You can capture the entire display (without using your pointer) by using the -root option, like this:

```
# xwd -root -out mygraphic.xwd
```

You can also capture the contents of a display on a remote computer by using X Toolkit -display option and the name of a remote display, like this:

```
# xwd -root -display stinky.home.org:0.0 -out stinkygraphic.xwd
```

This example assumes that you have access to the remote computer's display (granted by using the xhost command on the remote computer, as you learned in Chapter 9, "Using X11 on a Network"). To display your graphic, you can use the xwud client, which will "undump" your capture and display it in a window. Like xwd, the xwud client also features X Toolkit options; in this case, you can use xwud to display the graphic in a scaled window. Use the -scale option, along with a -geometry setting, to display the captured window at 320×200 pixels, like this:

```
# xwud -scale -geometry 320x200 -in mygraphic.xwd
```

The -in option allows you to specify a filename on the command line. If you do not use any command-line options, you could also just display the graphic, by using the standard input redirection operator, <, like this:

```
# xwud <mygraphic.xwd
```

Linux distributions typically include hundreds of graphics utilities for X, including one of the best graphics manipulation clients, the GIMP. See Chapter 12, "X11 Multimedia Clients," for more information about graphics and XFree86.

NOTE

Setting the Display Background

The KDE and GNOME desktop environments have distribution-specific tools that you can use to set the background, or root display. When you use a simpler window manager or run a less complex X session, use the xsetroot command to change the color of the root display or to place an image in the root display. This client works from the command line of an X terminal window, and you can use xsetroot, like many X clients, for effect on a local or remote display.

For example, to set the background of your root display to light blue, use the xsetroot command and its -solid option as follows:

```
# xsetroot -solid lightblue
```

After you press Enter, the background will become light blue. The color name derives from the X RGB database, and should be listed in the file rbg.txt under the /usr/X11R6/lib/X11 directory. You can also specify a patterned background by using the -bitmap option followed by the pathname to an X bitmap file, as follows:

```
# xsetroot -bitmap /usr/X11R6/include/X11/bitmaps/escherknot
```

After you press Enter, your display will look like that shown in Figure 10.2.

Figure 10.2 *The* xsetroot *client can change the background color of your root display or place a bitmap in the background.*

The `xsetroot` command is only one of many different clients you can use to display images in your root window. Read the `man` pages for the `xv`, `xli`, `xpmroot`, `xscreensaver`, `bseroot`, and `display` clients. You can use these clients to display nearly any type of graphic image, including animations, in your desktop.

Receiving Mail Notification

You can use the `xbiff` client to notify you when electronic mail arrives in your inbox (most likely the file with your username under the `/var/spool/mail` directory). This client, a latter-day counterpart of the console-mode `biff` command, is typically launched automatically when an X session starts, and is positioned in an out-of-the-way corner of the desktop. `xbiff` can use most X Toolkit options, but it also recognizes several other helpful options, such as the following:

- `-file` *path*, where *path* is the complete pathname to the user's mailbox file
- `-update` *n*, where *n* is how often (in seconds) to check for new mail
- `-volume` *%*, where *%* is a loudness level between 0–100 for the notification bell

For example, you can run `xbiff` like this:

```
# xbiff -update 15 -volume 100 -geometry 100x100 -fg white -bg blue &
```

After you press Enter, a 100×100-pixel mailbox with a blue background will appear in the upper-left corner of your display, as shown in Figure 10.3.

When you receive mail, you'll hear a loud beep, the mailbox handle (flag) will pop up, and the image will be reversed, as shown in Figure 10.4.

Figure 10.3 *The* `xbiff` *client monitors your system's mailbox.*

Figure 10.4 *"You've got mail!" the* `xbiff` *way!*

Displaying Eyes and the Logo

Two fun clients, xeyes and xlogo, are also included in the XFree86 distribution. These clients really don't do much, but can be fun to watch or to use to dress up a plain desktop. The xeyes client features a pair of graphic eyes that follow your pointer. The xlogo client simply displays a floating window with the X.org logo. Both clients obey a subset of the X Toolkit options.

You can start both clients like this:

```
# xeyes -fg red -center yellow  & ; xlogo -fg black -bg lightgreen &
```

After you press Enter, you'll see a pair of floating eyes and the X logo, as shown in Figure 10.5.

Displaying the Time

You'll find two clock clients included with XFree86: xclock, which displays the time in analog (clockface) or digital format; and oclock, which displays a round clock face. These clocks may be started by entries in your .xinitrc file or from the command line of an X terminal. They obey a subset of the X Toolkit options.

The xclock client has a number of interesting options, such as the ability to use different clock faces and to offer a chime (beep) once on the half-hour and twice on the hour. You can also enable a seconds hand on the xclock client by using the -update option with a value of 1 (in seconds). For example, you can use the following command lines to see the difference between oclock and xclock's digital and analog modes:

```
# oclock -fg yellow -bg red -bd blue &
# xclock -geometry 100x100+125+10 -update 1 -fg yellow -bg red &
# xclock -geometry +235+10 -d -fg green -bg black &
```

After all three clients are launched, you'll see them in the upper-left corner of your display, as shown in Figure 10.6

Figure 10.5 *The* xeyes *and* xlogo *clients can dress up your desktop.*

Figure 10.6 *You can use the* oclock *and* xclock *clients to display the time as colorful analog clocks; the* xclock *client also features a digital mode.*

Clocking Out the Time

Many different clock clients are available for XFree86 and Linux. You'll find clocks of every imaginable type. Some of the most popular include the `rclock` client (which features a timer, alarms, and an appointment reminder), `xdaliclock` (with melting clock faces), and `asclock` (the After-Step clock that can be docked into your desktop panel).

Linux uses two types of time: the hardware time, set inside your computer; and the system time, set by Linux upon startup. Use the `date` command to set the Linux system date and time manually. Use the `hwclock` (as root) to set either your computer's internal (hardware) clock, the system time from the hardware clock, or the hardware clock from the system time. You can also use the `rdate` command to retrieve the correct time from an Internet time server, as in the following example:

```
rdate -s time.nist.gov
```

This example works well if you're at a workstation in a fixed location. However, if you're a laptop user on the road, ensure you start with accurate time, and then change your system's timezone settings during your travels. See the man page for the `tzselect` command, or if you're a Red Hat or Mandrake Linux user, use the `timeconfig` command.

The `-fg` and `-bg` options are used to set the foreground and background colors. You can use the geometry settings for the two `xclock` modes to place the clocks next to the `oclock` client (on the far left in Figure 10.6). The last command line's `-d` option forces `xclock`'s digital mode. Note that you can also use geometry settings to resize the clocks.

Magnifying a Portion of the Display

Use the `xmag` client to magnify (and copy) a portion of your desktop. Start the client from the command line of an X terminal window as follows:

```
# xmag
```

After you press Enter, your pointer will turn into a 90-degree *L* shape. Next, left-click on the upper-left area of the desktop that you would like to magnify. The `xmag` client then displays the area in a floating window, as shown in Figure 10.7. You can then paste this graphic into a compatible X graphics application (such as `xpaint`).

Figure 10.7 *You can use the* xmag *client to capture and magnify a portion of your desktop display.*

Resource Information

ftp://ftp.x.org/pub/unsupported/test/Xkb/programs/README—a note regarding the xkb-series of clients. Note that these clients do not have man pages.

http://www.gw.total-web.net/~dperr/dpms.htm—technical specifications for Display Power Management Signaling.

http://www.epa.gov/energystar/—home page for the U.S. Environmental Protection Agency's Energy Star program, with links to products, manufacturers, and retailers, and an FAQ concerning the Energy Star program.

http://www.ee.surrey.ac.uk/Personal/L.Wood/screensavers/—a Web page with links to numerous screensaver pages, including those for X.

A Quarter Century of UNIX, Salus, Peter H., Addison-Wesley Publishing Company, 1994, pp. 169–170—the true story of John Foderero's biff command and Biff the dog, who unfortunately died in 1993 at the age of 15.

http://www.broadwayinfo.com/bwdemo.htm—live demonstrations of various X clients, including xeyes. To view the demonstrations, you need a Netscape remote X application plug-in named libxrx.so.6.3-linux2, found at ftp://ftp.x.org/pub/R6.4/plug-ins/.

http://www.crathva.fsnet.co.uk/penguineyes.html—home page to download the penguineyes X client for Linux, GNOME, and XFree86.

http://www.geocities.com/SiliconValley/Lakes/3767/xlogo-index.html—home page for the Xlogo project (not to be confused with the xlogo client; XLogo is the use of Logo turtle graphics with the XML markup language).

http://tycho.usno.navy.mil/what.html—the current U.S. Naval Observatory time, with links to animated clocks.

Chapter 11: Popular X11 Clients

- Commercial application suites

- Free application suites

- Productivity clients

This chapter introduces some commercial office suites and free software productivity tools that are popular among Linux and XFree86 users. You'll see how some of the packages are installed, learn about the installation and use requirements, see how to set up backup preferences, and get solutions to some common problems that arise when setting up or using the programs.

One of the biggest arguments against using Linux in recent years—spouted by early Linux foes, industry nay-sayers, and the so-called professional but biased PC media still in the grip of the software monopoly—was that there was a lack of solid, capable, and "professional" software suites available for Linux. (These same pundits have now moved onto other excuses, such as scalability, accountability, and total cost of ownership, or whatever fear, uncertainty, and doubt [FUD] tactics are currently being espoused by the software monopoly.)

The fact is that great software has been available for Linux and XFree86 almost since the first releases and distributions. In this chapter, you'll learn about Applixware, a legacy office suite that has recently been substantially improved. You'll also learn about the very latest office suite from Corel, WordPerfect Office 2000 Deluxe for Linux.

Palm PDA users will also find out how to use a graphical X client to back up or install software on their PDAs. And you'll get an overview of some of the more popular free productivity software packages included with nearly every Linux distribution for XFree86.

Linux and XFree86 users enjoy a special relationship with their operating system, and as you'll soon see, they can find "professional-quality" software that exceeds other commercial operating system software in ease of installation, configuration, stability, and features.

Commercial Application Suites

Although the majority of Linux users quite happily continue to use free software instead of commercial applications, a number of commercial applications appeal to a segment of the Linux market. In particular, those sites that need or require service and support for daily operations may want to consider using commercial software.

An office suite is generally a collection of individual software packages with common functions, interdependence, and a code- and data-sharing base. Most office suites combine a word processor, spreadsheet, image or presentation editor, and perhaps a database manager. Modern office suites add additional functions, such as electronic mail handling and perhaps a development package. A code- and data-sharing base enables you to create documents that contain common data. For example, a word processing document might include numbers from a spreadsheet or a graphic from an image editor. Also, each suite element can benefit a common module, such as a spelling checker.

Some suites may also offer productivity applications such a personal information manager (PIM). Some PIM modules include an address book, To-Do or contact list manager, scheduling and appointments manager, and project management functions.

Applixware Office for Linux

First offered for Linux in conjunction with Red Hat Linux 4.2 in 1997, the Applixware Office suite can create and read documents across a dozen different operating systems. To use Applixware on an Intel-based PC running Linux, you need XFree86, at least 32MB RAM, a Pentium-class 166MHz CPU, and 133MB, 236MB, or 500MB hard drive storage.

Applixware Office for Linux, now marketed by VistaSource, Inc., combines a number of different software tools in an integrated environment for developing numerous types of documents, databases, and clients. The following are the basic elements:

- **Data**—a database client for accessing database information. The client uses a spreadsheet interface to interface with the free Postgresql and MySQL systems, along with the commercial ADABAS database (and others).

- **Directory Displayer**—an explorer-type dialog used for file navigation and launching.

- **Graphics**—a graphics client that you can use with 32 different graphics formats. This client is also part of the Presents presentation module.

- **HTML Author**—a Webcentric incarnation of the Applixware Words word processing client, used to create, edit, and publish Web pages.

- **Macro editor**—a suite-wide macro editor that you can use to create repeatable shortcuts of common actions.

- **Mail**—an electronic mail manager that is MIME-compliant and that can also serve as a Post Office Protocol 3 (POP3) gateway.

- **Presents**—a presentation manager that you can use to create, import, or export a variety of presentation document formats. This application features transition effects, templates, and drawing and graphics tools.

- **SHELF/Builder**—an object-oriented client builder used to create standalone applications that work on a variety of computer platforms.

- **Spreadsheets**—a modern 3D spreadsheet that can create, import, and export more than a dozen spreadsheet document formats. The application features embeddable "live" links that can be updated in real time, along with a sophisticated graphing package.
- **Words**—a word processor that you can also use to create HTML Web pages. The application features include "live" links and the import and export of nearly two-dozen document formats.

The Applixware Office suite features extensive context-sensitive, built-in help, along with tutorial modes and online reference books.

Installing Applixware

Insert and mount your Applixware CD-ROM. Then (as root) start the installation using the setup shell script as follows:

```
# ./setup
```

After you press Enter, the installation begins. Earlier versions of Applixware used a text-only interface, but if you have the proper GNOME libraries installed, you'll see a graphical install, as shown in Figure 11.1.

Figure 11.1 *The Applixware install features a graphical interface.*

Use the drop-down menus and dialog buttons to install the suite. By default, the software is installed under the `/opt/applix` directory (although you can change this path). The process can take nearly 10 minutes, depending on your computer.

After installation, you can start Applixware by using the pathname to the `applix` executable, as follows:

```
# applix
```

After you press Enter, you'll see the initial splash screen, as shown in Figure 11.2, along with a floating toolbar window that you can use to launch any of the suite's components.

> If you install Applixware while using KDE (except when using KDE under Corel's Linux distribution), restart the desktop's panel after installation. You'll then find an Applixware menu under the panel's Applications menu item.

NOTE

Use the tutorials or demonstration modules to learn how to use Applixware. Like other X clients, Applixware also obeys a number of command-line options, such as `-display`, used in conjunction with a remote hostname and display number to launch the suite remotely or on a remote computer. If you don't want to use the floating Applixware toolbar, you can launch a single suite component, such as Spreadsheets, from the command line like this:

```
# applix -ss
```

After you press Enter, the Spreadsheets client appears. Table 11.1 lists other command-line options.

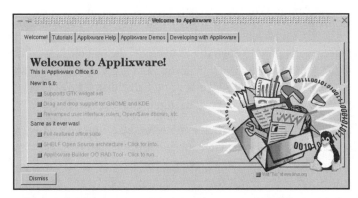

Figure 11.2 *The Applixware suite features a tutorial mode for beginners.*

Table 11.1 Applixware Command-Line Launching Options

Command-Line Option	Action
-db	Launches the Applixware Data client
document.ext	Launches Applixware by opening *document* according to its extension (such as .aw for Words, .as for Spreadsheets, .ag for Graphics, .ap for Presents, or .ppt for PowerPoint)
-gr	Launches Applix Graphics
-help	Launches Applix help
-mail	Begins composing e-mail
-me	Starts the Applix macro editor
-presents	Launches Applix Presents
-ss	Launches Applix Spreadsheets
-wp	Launches Applix Words

Setting Preferences

Unless you're employed in a unique business setting or graphics shop, chances are pretty good that the one component of any office suite you'll use will be the word processor. Nearly every user spends a large percentage of time editing text, Web pages, or source code. If you work with documents very often, you'll want to ensure that the system creates backup documents, so knowing how to set this preference is important.

To set backup preferences for word processing, click the Applix Words icon on the floating toolbar to launch the Applix Words word processor, then click the Applixware menu item in the Applix Words menu bar. You'll see a drop-down menu, as shown in Figure 11.3.

Select the Words Preferences menu item to open the Preferences dialog box. Note that this menu, which is available whenever you run any of the suite's modules, also allows you to launch another component. When the Words Preferences dialog box appears, as shown in Figure 11.4, you'll see a variety of options and preference settings.

Click the Create Backup Copy radio button, then enter a time, in minutes, between backups. The application then will save backup documents at the set interval. You can specify a value of zero (0) to turn off this feature, even if you have selected the Create Backup Copy option. Unfortunately, this feature does not apply to any currently open document. Ideally, you should set this preference before beginning a word processing session.

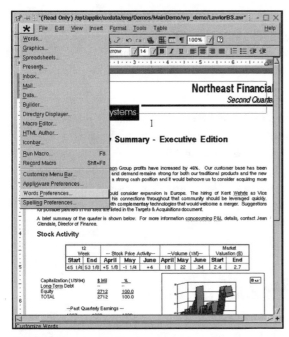

Figure 11.3 *Use the Applixware menu in any component to launch other suite components or to set preferences.*

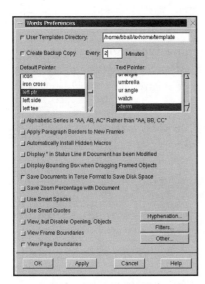

Figure 11.4 *Use the Words Preferences dialog box to set preferences, such as backups, used during word processing sessions.*

Backup files are, by default, saved in a directory named axhome/backup in your home directory. However, you can change the location of your backup files by changing the auto-save directory specified in the Applixware Preferences' Directories dialog box, which, as with Words Preferences, you can access through the Applixware menu.

Browse to **http://shelf.sourceforge.net/projects/** to see a list of projects being built and supported by Applixware's internal command language, ELF. The ELF language has a syntax similar to extended Beginners All-purpose Basic Instruction Code (BASIC). VistaSource, Inc., is creating and supporting a number of Open Source projects using this language. This means that you can use the language to create separate clients or add functions to Applixware under XFree86.

Corel's WordPerfect Office 2000 for Linux

Corel, Inc., has had a rocky road with lots of financial ups and downs, but continues to support Linux and XFree86 with some major products. Starting in December 1998 with the release of a free version of WordPerfect 8 for Linux (see the section "Corel's WordPerfect 8 for Linux" later in this chapter), Corel promised to bring its office suite and related products to the Linux market. In the summer of 2000, Corel released WordPerfect Office 2000 (along with its premier graphics program, Corel-DRAW) for the Linux community.

Part of the incentive and aid for the port came from the Open Source community's Wine project. Wine, which aims to provide clone software libraries comparable to those used in the commercial Windows operating system, attempts to enable users to run programs written for Windows under XFree86 and Linux (along with FreeBSD and Solaris). In 1998, Corel adopted the project, which so far has had great success in allowing Linux and XFree86 users to run hundreds of Windows programs without problems.

As a result, Corel contributed code back to the Wine project, and at the same time used parts of Wine to port WordPerfect Office 2000 and its graphics application. Corel's actions provide one of the biggest examples of collaboration between the Open Source developer community and a corporate enterprise.

The office suite consists of five base applications:

- **WordPerfect 9**—an updated version of WordPerfect with graphics and charting features, along with Internet publishing and HTML editing.
- **Quattro Pro 9**—a spreadsheet client with all the features of modern 3D spreadsheets, including Internet publishing and HTML editing.

- **Corel Presentations 9**—a presentation editor that incorporates a drawing editor and graphics-editing module.
- **Paradox 9**—a relational database manager client that, like other sophisticated database environments, allows creation of customized database programs.
- **CorelCENTRAL**—a PIM supporting scheduling, reminders, and contacts; other features include support for launching browsers on internal URLs.

Like Applixware, Corel's office suite is also tied together with an internal macro language (named PerfectScript) that can communicate across the suite's clients. The suite also includes a CD-ROM with 1,000 fonts, 12,000 clipart images, and 200 photos for use in documents.

Installing WordPerfect Office 2000

Corel's WordPerfect Office 2000 for Linux is primarily contained on two installation CD-ROMs, although four CD-ROMs are included in the package. (The CD-ROMs include a copy of Corel's Linux distribution and a limited version of Loki's Railroad Tycoon, and more.) The suite is aimed at Linux systems using a 2.2-series Linux kernel and X. The minimal system requirements, according to Corel, are a 200MHz CPU and 64MB RAM. However, these suggested requirements specify an unrealistic minimum; you can achieve better performance with a faster CPU and twice as much memory. (Applixware, on the other hand, is quite fast even on lower-end Pentium CPUs and 32MB XFree86 Linux systems.) You'll also need more than 400MB hard drive space for a full installation, not counting fonts, clipart, or photo images.

Start the installation (as root) by inserting and mounting CD-ROM Disk 1. Next, use the setup command on the CD-ROM as follows:

```
# ./setup
```

After you press Enter, you'll see a splash screen as shown in Figure 11.5.

Trouble Installing?

The Corel WordPerfect Office 2000 for Linux package is quite particular about the type of software library support installed, and requires a minimum of the glibc 2.0 software libraries. Out of the box, this office suite will not install on some Linux distributions, such as SuSE Linux 7.0, even though the distributions were introduced after the office suite came on the market. Browse to **http://linux.corel.com** for updates or bug fixes for this office suite.

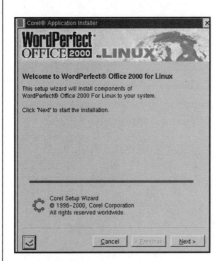

Figure 11.5 *Corel's office suite for Linux features a graphical installation.*

Click the Next button to continue the installation. You can choose a minimal or full installation of the suite's components. Unlike Applixware, Corel has chosen the installation directory (/usr/lib/corel) for you, so you cannot specify a different installation directory. Installation can take up to 10 or more minutes, depending on your setup and computer system.

After installation, if you use KDE and Corel Linux for your XFree86 sessions, you'll find a WordPerfect Office 2000 menu available under the desktop panel's Applications menu, as shown in Figure 11.6.

Trouble Launching Corel's Office 2000?

Despite the ease of installation, the Corel office suite will refuse to launch on a number of Linux distributions, such as Red Hat Linux, unless you prepare your system by performing a complex series of software package installations in a specific order using the rpm command. Probably the best advice is to install Corel's version of Linux first, then install and use WordPerfect Office 2000. This sequence will avoid many problems with missing software libraries, software configuration errors, and other impediments to using WordPerfect Office 2000.

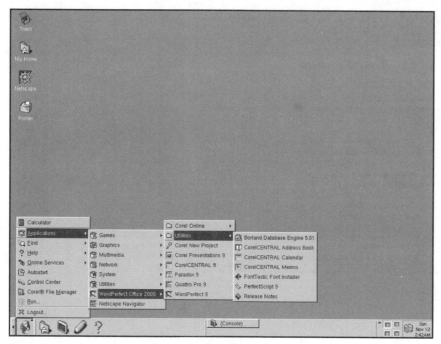

Figure 11.6 *You can easily launch a word processing session after installing WordPerfect Office 2000 for Linux.*

Click the Applications menu, then select WordPerfect Office 2000, then WordPerfect 9 to launch WordPerfect 9 from the desktop's panel. Expect to wait up to 60 seconds, even on a 300MHz system with 128MB RAM, before the application launches and appears, as shown in Figure 11.7. The reason for this delay is that a considerable number of software libraries and a substantial amount of support code from Corel's version of Wine must be loaded into memory.

WordPerfect 9, along with other Office 2000 components, can be launched from the command line of an X11 terminal window like this:

```
# wordperfect
```

Table 11.2 lists this and other command lines for launching elements of Core's office suite.

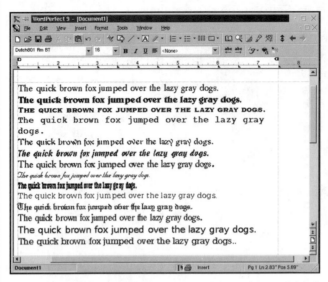

Figure 11.7 *Corel's WordPerfect 9 is the word processing module of WordPerfect Office 2000 for Linux.*

Table 11.2 WordPerfect Office 2000 for Linux

Command	Description
ccaddressbook	Launches an address book client
cccalendar	Launches a planner/calendar client
cccardfile	Launches a minidatabase client
ccmemos	Launches an appointments/reminders memo client
ccrepair	Launches a database repair client
paradox	Launches the Paradox 9 database client
perfectexpert	Launches the Office 2000 template manager
perfectscript	Launches the PerfectScript macro editor client
presentations	Launches the Corel Presentations 9 client
prplayer	Launches the Presentations document player
quattropro	Launches the Quattro Pro 9 spreadsheet client
wordperfect	Launches the WordPerfect 9 word processor

Setting Preferences

Each client provides preferences settings that enable you to configure how the suite will work for you. Fortunately, because of the clients' design consistency, you can find these settings as a Settings menu item under each client's Tools menu. For example, to set backup creation and its timed interval for WordPerfect 9, first launch the client, then click the Settings menu item under WordPerfect 9's Tools menu. You'll see a Settings dialog box, as shown in Figure 11.8.

Click the Files icon on the dialog box shown in Figure 11.8, and you'll see the Files Settings dialog box, as shown in Figure 11.9. You can use this dialog box to enable or disable various file settings, such as the default name and pathnames for documents, templates, and other elements associated with WordPerfect 9 documents.

By default, the suite saves backup documents in the .wpo2000/Backup directory in your home directory. You can change the location of the backups and then save your changes using the Files Settings dialog box. You can also change the time interval between saves and specify whether to save the original or changed document.

Figure 11.8 *Use preference settings to change default behavior of each WordPerfect Office 2000 client.*

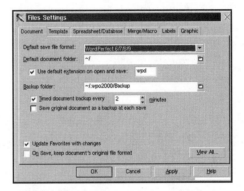

Figure 11.9 *Use the Backup Folder field and Timed Document check box to enable autosaving of backup documents when you work with WordPerfect 9.*

Having Trouble with Fonts?

If you find that fonts are unavailable when you use WordPerfect Office 2000 for Linux, make sure that Corel's office suite is able to access the proprietary font server, fonttastic. This font server by Bitstream, Inc., replaces or augments the XFree86 FontPath, and is a daemon like the xfs font server. To add the fonttastic fonts to your X session's FontPath settings, use the xset command and its +fp command-line option like this:

```
xset +fp tcp/localhost:7102/all
```

Free Application Suites

This section introduces a number of free software office suites, word processors, text editors, and various productivity applications that you'll find available for Linux and XFree86. Just because these applications are free does not mean that the software is of lower quality than many commercial software products. In many cases, these clients are even better, more stable, and much more popular because they have withstood the ravages of hard use and the scrutiny of their source code by hundreds of thousands of advanced users and programmers around the world.

StarOffice

StarOffice, at one time a proprietary commercial office suite, was acquired in 1999 by Sun Microsystems, Inc., which then released the multiplatform suite free for Linux, Solaris, Windows NT, and Windows 95. In October 2000, Sun then released the source code to StarOffice under the GNU General Public License and Sun Industry Standard Source License. These bold maneuvers by Sun have resulted in StarOffice becoming one of the most popular applications for Linux, and a viable, economical alternative to expensive commercial office suite software for other operating systems.

The StarOffice suite consists of a word processor, spreadsheet, organizer, graphics editor, presentation manager, and database manager wrapped together in an integrated desktop that can function as a window or complete desktop during your X session. This office suite's main desktop window can also function as a Web browser. The following are the main components of StarOffice:

- **Words**—a word processor that can import and export 16 different document formats; the application also includes extensive support for HTML document editing, revision marking, spell-checking, a thesaurus, and automatic correction.
- **Spreadsheets**—a modern spreadsheet with numerous graphing facilities that can generate data and graphics for embedding in other StarOffice documents.
- **Presentations or StarImpress**—a presentation creation and display client with integrated drawing and image editing tools.
- **StarDraw**—a drawing and image editing client used to generate or modify artwork for use in StarOffice documents.
- **Mail**—an electronic mail manager.

New improvements added to recent versions of StarOffice are the ADABAS database manager, expanded Java language support, and better documentation of StarOffice's internal language, StarBASIC. Expect additional features as the Open Source version of StarOffice matures.

Installing StarOffice

StarOffice is included as a standard feature with many Linux distributions. If you did not get a copy with your distribution, you can download a binary install version from Sun at **http://www.sun.com/staroffice**. The download for version 5.2 requires as little as 95MB for the main installation file.

To begin the installation, log in as root, then run the file named `so-5_2-ga-bin-linux-en.bin`, as follows:

```
# ./so-5_2-ga-bin-linux-en.bin
```

If you have an older version of Linux or an incompatible set of software libraries, you can also download version 5.1a, which consists of a 70MB tape archive file. You can then extract the file like this:

```
# tar xf so51a_lnx_01.tar
```

After decompression, you can then start the installation (of either version) by using the included `setup` command (as root) like this:

```
# ./setup /net
```

In this example, the `/net` command-line option allows the root operator to install a system-wide StarOffice configuration in which individual users can then perform minimal installs (otherwise, the command will install the entire 150MB StarOffice system in each user's home directory).

After you press Enter, you'll see a splash screen, as shown in Figure 11.10.

Click the Next button to continue the installation, then select an installation directory for the main StarOffice components, such as `/opt/Office51`. After installation, individual (nonroot) users can then run the `setup` or `soffice` command to configure StarOffice in the local home directory, like this:

```
# /opt/Office51/bin/setup
```

After you press Enter, you'll again see a splash screen. Click the Next button to navigate through the installation until the program asks you to select the type of installation, as shown in Figure 11.11.

Click the Standard Workstation Installation, then click the Next button to continue the install. The install program will create in your home directory a subdirectory named `Office51` (or `Office52`, depending on the version that you are installing).

> If you use KDE, you will find a StarOffice menu item on the desktop panel's menu after a StarOffice install.

NOTE

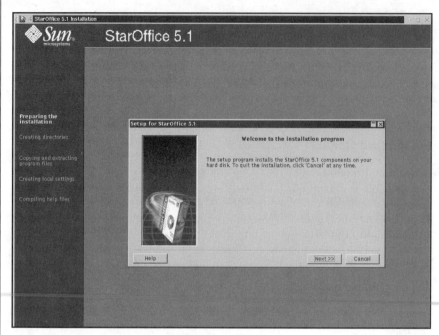

Figure 11.10 *StarOffice for Linux features a graphical install and is available for older or newer Linux distributions.*

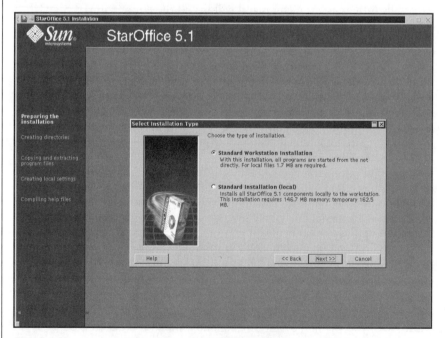

Figure 11.11 *You can install StarOffice as a 1.7MB workstation configuration (assuming that a system-wide install has already taken place), or you can install the entire suite in a user's home directory.*

You can then start StarOffice by using the `soffice` command like this:

```
# ./Office51/bin/soffice &
```

Or, if you've installed StarOffice version 5.2, use the following command:

```
# ./Office52/soffice &
```

After you press Enter, you'll see the StarOffice start screen (as shown in Figure 11.12), through which you can set initial Internet settings and view tips on usage.

If you use the Internet during your X sessions, you can integrate various StarOffice functions (such as Web browsing, downloading, and electronic mail) into your system. If you do not use the Internet, click the Don't Use the Internet button. You can always change your settings later.

Setting Backup Preferences

Universal preferences for nearly any StarOffice suite component are available through the Options menu item of the StarOffice desktop's Tools menu. Click the Tools menu, then click Options to view the Options dialog box, as shown in Figure 11.13.

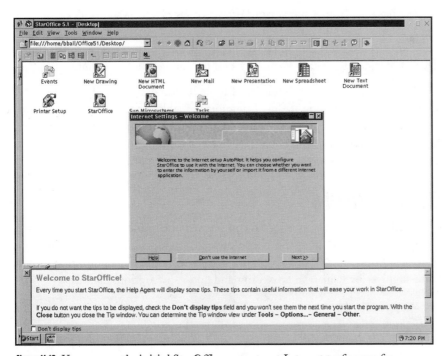

Figure 11.12 *You can use the initial StarOffice screen to set Internet preferences for workstations in a networked environment.*

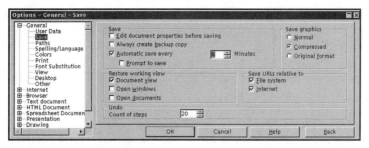

Figure 11.13 *You can use the StarOffice Options dialog box to set backup preferences easily.*

To create backup documents, click the Always Create Backup Copy check box. You can specify the interval (in minutes) that StarOffice automatically saves documents, and you can have StarOffice prompt you to save the document. You can also use the Options dialog box to change settings for the Internet, browsing, word processing (such as display characteristics), HTML editing, spreadsheets, presentations, and graphics.

Corel's WordPerfect 8 for Linux

WordPerfect has long been a staple word processor for UNIX systems. A Linux version was developed several years ago, and has been available as a commercial product for a number of years. However, in December 1998, Corel, Inc., which had acquired WordPerfect, decided to release WordPerfect 8 for Linux as a free client.

WordPerfect 8 for Linux is nearly identical to its brethren available for commercial operating systems and its now-defunct commercial sibling for Linux. (Corel once offered a low-cost commercial version, but that version is no longer on the market.) This free word processor is an excellent choice for performing word processing functions under Linux and XFree86, especially on older Linux systems.

Installing WordPerfect 8

The WordPerfect 8 download is a 38MB compressed binary file consisting of a number of tape archives that must be decompressed after download. Download the archive, named GUILG00.GZ, and save it in a directory. You can then decompress and extract the archives by using the tar command and its xf options, as follows:

```
# tar xv GUI*
```

You can then verify the contents with the ls command as follows:

```
$ ls
```

GUILG00.GZ	b_ins00	b_req01	g_req01	g_us00
Readme	b_ins01	b_us00	g_req02	g_us01
Runme	b_req00	g_req00	g_req03	

To begin installation, log in as root, then use the `./Runme` script as follows:

```
# ./Runme
```

After you press Enter, the installation script begins. If your system supports a graphical install, you'll see a dialog box that will take you through the install process. If your system does not support a graphical install, the program will ask you questions using a text-based screen, as shown in Figure 11.14.

If your system supports a graphical installation, you'll see an initial splash screen as shown in Figure 11.15.

The install asks you to accept licensing terms, then enables you to designate an installation directory (most users choose to use /opt/wp8) and a type of installation. A full install requires about 70MB of hard drive space.

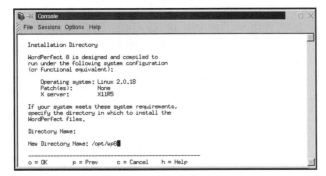

Figure 11.14 *The free WordPerfect 8 for Linux install screen may be graphical or text-based, depending on your system.*

Having Trouble Installing WordPerfect?

If you find that the WordPerfect installer fails, make sure that your Linux system has libc5-compatibility libraries installed. WordPerfect depends on older software libraries that are sometimes not installed by some of today's Linux distributions.

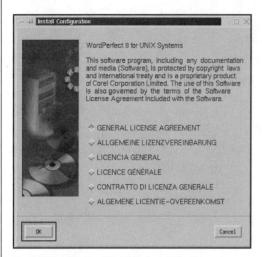

Figure 11.15 *The free WordPerfect 8 for Linux graphical install offers a much easier way to install WordPerfect 8 for Linux.*

Continue through the installation, and install any desired printer drivers. You can install all printer drivers at this time without a penalty in hard drive storage, although many Linux systems require only a single printer driver named Passthrough Post-Script. After completing your installation choices, the install progresses quite rapidly, and compiles in less than a minute or two, depending on your system. Following completion of the install, you can then start your copy of WordPerfect like this:

```
# /opt/wp8/wpbin/xwp &
```

After you press Enter, you'll see the main WordPerfect window, as shown in Figure 11.16.

The screen asks you to enter a license key to enable unlimited usage of WordPerfect for your system. You can get this free key by browsing to **http://venus.corel.com/ nasapps/wp8linuxreg/register.html**. The application asks you to enter some information and then displays a license key right away.

Setting Up for Printing

To enable printing on your Linux system, launch WordPerfect, then select the Print menu item from the File menu. You'll see a Print dialog box as shown in Figure 11.17.

Click the Select button at the top of the dialog box. You'll then see a Select Printer dialog box. Click its Printer Create/Edit button, then click the Add button in the Printer Create/Edit dialog box. Select the Passthru PostScript printer driver in the Add Printer Drive, then click OK until you return to the Printer/Create dialog

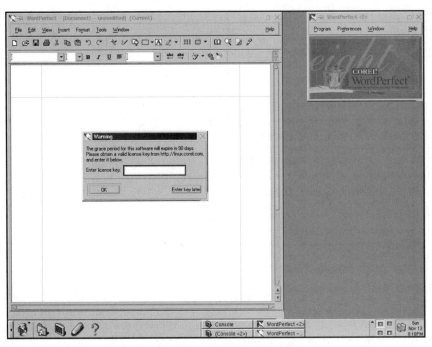

Figure 11.16 *You can obtain a free license key from Corel, Inc., for your copy of WordPerfect 8 for Linux.*

Figure 11.17 *Set up printing under WordPerfect 8 for Linux by using the Print dialog box.*

box. You'll then see the Passthru PostScript driver with a destination of None. Click the Setup button, then click the Destination button and select your system's default printer. The Select Printer dialog box then appears as shown in Figure 11.18, showing the Passthru PostScript driver selected for your printer.

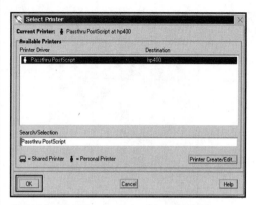

Figure 11.18 *WordPerfect 8 for Linux prints to a designated printer using a specific printer driver.*

Next, click the OK button again, and you'll be at your original Print dialog box, but now with a designated printer and printer driver selected.

Productivity Clients

This section introduces a number of productivity clients for XFree86. GNOME and KDE include some of these clients, whereas others are among the vast collection of X11 clients that you can use with XFree86.

KDE Clients

The K Desktop Environment includes numerous clients that you can use as productivity applications. These clients usually have a single purpose and range in capability from very simple to extremely complex (although you'll find most of them fairly easy to use).

Table 11.3 lists some common KDE productivity clients.

GNOME Clients

The GNOME desktop for Linux also includes many different productivity clients, and more than 80 different clients are available through the GNOME home page (see "Resource Information" at the end of this chapter). Table 11.4 lists some popular clients that you may find on your system if you use GNOME.

Table 11.3 KDE Productivity Clients

Name	Description
kab	KDE address book client
karm	Time-tracking client
kcalc	Calculator client
kcminfo	System information client
kedit	Simple KDE editor
kfinger	GUI client for finger
kfsstatus	System filesystem graphing client
kless	GUI text file browser
klipper	KDE clipboard client
kmag	KDE display magnification
knetload	GUI network load monitor
knotes	Simple note client
korganizer	Complex planner and calendar client
krecord	Voice recording client
kruiser	Filesystem explorer
ktail	Graphical tail client
kteatime	Reminder client
ktelnet	Graphical telnet client
ktop	Graphical system monitor
kvoice	KDE voice-answering interface to mgetty
kweather	KDE weather-recording client
kworldwatch	KDE Mercator sunclock
kwrite	Simple KDE text editor
vigmeup	Alarm clock with .mp3 player and snooze button

Palm PDA Clients

There are a number of Linux programs and clients that you can use with the Palm PDA. Because of Palm Computing's good hardware design, open relationship with developers, availability of documentation, source code, and operating system programming interfaces, the Palm PDA has become a major success in the hand-held computing market, much to the detriment and chagrin of the software industry monopoly.

Table 11.4 GNOME Productivity Clients

Name	Description
gbonds	Treasury bond calculator
gdiskfree	GUI filesystem monitor
gedit	Capable GNOME text editor with many plug-ins
gless	GNOME text file browser
gmc	GNOME file manager and desktop
gnofin	Simple checkbook client
gnomba	GNOME Samba client
gnome-edit	Link to the GNU emacs editor
gnome-cal	GNOME calculator client
gnome-card	Address book client
gnome-pim	GNOME calendar and address clients
gnotepad	Simple notepad client
gnumeric	Complex and capable spreadsheet client
gtimetracker	Time-tracking client
gxedit	Graphical text editor

Because of the open support, Linux developers have crafted numerous tools for working with the Palm PDA under Linux. One of the most popular tools, the pilot-link suite of programs, forms the basis for many graphical clients for XFree86, the Palm, and Linux.

The pilot-xfer Client

The commands for Kenneth Albanowski's pilot-link suite are text-based, and meant to be used from the command line in conjunction with a Palm PDA attached to your computer's serial or USB port. This section covers the pilot-xfer program, part of the pilot-link suite. Table 11.5 lists pilot-xfer and the other commands included with the suite.

The most capable client, and probably the one that most Linux users will use with the Palm PDA, is pilot-xfer. For example, to back up your PDA quickly, you can log in as root, then create an environment variable named PILOT_RATE, like this (if you're using the bash shell):

```
# export PILOT_RATE=57600
```

Table 11.5 pilot-link Palm Productivity Programs

Name	Description
addresses	Creates a text file of PDA's addresses
install-datebook	Uploads datebook data to PDA
install-memo	Uploads memos to PDA
install-todos	Uploads To-Do lists to PDA
install-user	Changes PDA's user settings
memos	Downloads memos to a UNIX mailbox
pilot-addresses	Uploads and downloads PDA addresses
pilot-clip	Uploads and downloads the PDA clipboard
pilot-mail	Sends and retrieves mail to and from PDA
pilot-schlep	Installs a PDA client
pilot-undelete	Converts PDA records settings
pilot-xfer	Provides comprehensive PDA installation and backup
read-expenses	Retrieves a PDA expense database
read-ical	Retrieves and converts the PDA datebook and To-Do lists
read-todos	Retrieves the To-Do database and converts it to text
reminders	Retrieves the PDA datebook to the database file

Next, attach your Palm in its cradle to your computer's serial port, then use the pilot-xfer command, along with the designated serial port device, the -b or backup option, and the name of directory to hold the backup, as follows:

```
# pilot-xfer /dev/ttyS0 -b piii
```

In this example, after you press Enter and then press your Palm's HotSync button, the program will retrieve the contents of your PDA and save the files in the directory named piii.

You can also use a USB serial adapter to back up your PDA if your computer does not have a serial port. In this case, ensure that USB services are enabled, then use the insmod command to load the Linux usb-serial module as follows:

```
# insmod usb-serial
```

Next, use the output of the dmesg command to check for a recognized serial device, or specify the first device (generally /dev/usb/ttyUSB0), as follows:

```
# pilot-xfer /dev/ttyUSB0 -b piii
```

The kpilot Client

One of the most popular graphical clients for interaction with the Palm PDA is Dan Pilone's kpilot client, usually included with KDE and many Linux distributions. You can launch this client from the command line of an X terminal window, as follows:

```
# kpilot&
```

After you press Enter, you'll see the main kpilot window, as shown in Figure 11.19. kpilot can be used to synchronize data between your Linux system and a Palm-OS PDA, and will automatically start communicating with your PDA when you press your PDA's software or hardware synchronize button.

To begin using kpilot, first select the File menu, then click Settings. The KPilot Options dialog box appears, as shown in Figure 11.20.

Use this dialog box to select the correct serial port (perhaps a symbolic link named /dev/pilot that points to the correct port, such as /dev/ttyS0). Next, click the drop-down Speed menu, then select a speed for transferring files. Most computers will easily support the value 57600, but you can try the faster 115200 if you like. If you click the Start KPilot at Hot-Sync option, kpilot will automatically launch if its kpilotDaemon is active (you can start the daemon manually from the command line) and you press the Palm PDA cradle's HotSync button. When finished, click the OK button.

To begin, insert your Palm in its cradle and connect the cradle to your computer. You can then start kpilot, click the Backup menu item from its File menu, then press your Palm cradle's HotSync button to back up your PDA.

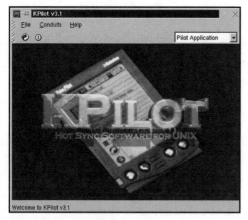

Figure 11.19 *The* kpilot *client is a HotSync software application for the Palm PDA, X, and various UNIX systems, including Linux.*

Figure 11.20 *To set up* kpilot, *first select the correct device and baud rate for your computer's serial port.*

X11 Clients

There are numerous X11 productivity clients. Some of these programs are legacy applications developed over the years on various UNIX systems, which have then been ported to XFree86 and Linux. One client that you're sure to find with your Linux distribution is Sanjay Ghemawat's `ical`, a visual calendar and planning client that you can also use to print one-, two-, six-, nine-, or twelve-day calendars or monthly calendars.

Start `ical` from the command line of your terminal window like this:

```
# ical &
```

After you press Enter, you'll see `ical`'s main window, which defaults to an appointment view of the current day, as shown in Figure 11.21.

This client has a number of command-line options that you can use to import, print, or display your calendar. `ical` also obeys a subset of X Toolkit options, so you can specify foreground and background colors. Another feature is the ability to set appointments (also known as notices), repeating items, and alarms. To use the alarms feature, you'll need to run `ical` either all the time on your system or every time that you log in for an X session.

Other productivity clients for XFree86 include `plan` (which calculates loan amortization), `grok` (which creates databases), and `plan` (which offers calendar and appointment functions). You're sure to find many more productivity clients with a little searching on the Internet.

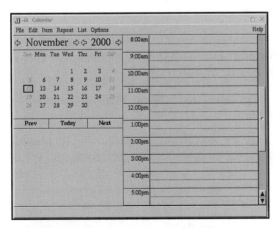

Figure 11.21 *The* `ical` *client is a popular X11 productivity application.*

Resource Information

http://koffice.kde.org/—home page for the KOffice office suite for KDE.

http://members.iinet.net.au/~cam/faq.html—Cameron Newham's Applixware FAQ (which is outdated).

http://www.vistasource.com/products/axware/—home page for the Applixware Office Suite for Linux.

https://sourceforge.net/project/showfiles.php?group_id=3854—a page listing add-ons, extras, and macros for Applixware for Linux, including a calculator, a falling blocks game, a solitaire card game, and macro editors.

http://linux.corel.com/—the home page for Corel Linux products, such as WordPerfect Office 2000 and CorelDRAW Graphics Suite.

http://linux.corel.com/products/wp8/download.htm—the Web site from which you can get a free version of WordPerfect 8 for Linux.

http://www.winehq.com—the Wine development headquarters, and the site from which to download the latest set of Windows emulation libraries.

http://opensource.corel.com/—the home page of the Corel, Inc., Open Source project pages, where you can get source code for Corel's Linux distribution and its version of the Wine libraries.

http://www.sun.com/staroffice—the starting point for downloading binary versions of StarOffice for Linux.

http://www.staroffice.org—the starting point for downloading source code versions of StarOffice for Linux.

http://www.kde.org—a comprehensive site about KDE with links to many different KDE clients for Linux.

http://mobilix.org/pda_linux_palm.html—a site with links to all types of Linux applications for the Palm PDA, including IrDA utilities.

http://www.icsi.berkeley.edu/~minenko/PalmVNC/—the home page for the Palm VNC client, which allows you to use the Palm PDA as an X11 network terminal.

http://www.gnome.org—the home page for the GNOME project, with links to many additional clients for your GNOME system.

Chapter 12: X11 Multimedia Clients

Graphics clients

Audio clients

Video and animation clients

This chapter introduces a number of multimedia clients that you can use with XFree86 and Linux. These clients cover a wide range of applications, including graphics, audio, video, and animation. You'll learn about some of the premier applications that you can use as an artist or to boost creativity when building various multimedia products using Linux and XFree86.

Many of the clients, like games, will tax your system's resources. In many but not all cases, you should have a properly configured sound system. Your X11 sessions should provide a resolution of at least 1,024×768 and thousands of colors. Although this may be a problem for legacy hardware, most modern-day Intel-based PCs can boast this capability. Laptop users with recent models will also benefit, as higher resolution seems to be a stock feature, with 800×600 displays relegated to only the lowest-end models.

Graphics Clients

Graphics clients play an important part when you are using XFree86 and Linux. The clients described in this section offer expanded or added graphics capability to your system. Graphics are used throughout the X desktop to build icons, background pixmaps, and root displays. Graphics may also play an important role when creating technical documents, drawings, brochures, and even faxes.

Using the GIMP

The GIMP is the premier graphics creation and editing client for Linux and XFree86. This application and its custom software toolkit spawned a new generation of graphics clients and other applications by providing a base set of routines eventually incorporated into and expanded by the GNOME project. As an Open Source project, the GIMP is distributed free, with source code, which has helped increase its popularity and improve its finesse, as developers contribute improvements and features. It is one of the lightning rods of success that many advocates of Open Source point to when talking about the viability of the Open Source model of building projects.

Nearly every Linux distribution includes the GIMP. As an interactive image editor for XFree86 and Linux, the GIMP is without peer. In fact, many of its features, such as scripting and advanced filters, rival that of commercial alternatives on other computer platforms and operating systems.

The GIMP may be installed on your system in several locations. Although the main client binary will be found under the `/usr/bin` directory, support files, libraries, and various filters will be found under the `/usr/share/gimp` and `/usr/lib/gimp` directories. The GIMP user manual may be installed under the `/usr/doc/gimp` or `/usr/share/doc/gimp` directories. You'll need at least 25MB to install version 1.0. The current version is 1.1.30, although new releases are made regularly. According to GIMP developers, major improvements are slated for version 2.0 of this client.

You can launch the GIMP via your favorite desktop panel or through the command line, as follows:

```
# gimp &
```

> The GIMP also features a number of command-line options. You can get a list by using its -h or -help options. The GIMP seems to support only one X Toolkit option: -display, followed by a remote hostname and display number.

If you're running the GIMP for the first time, when you press Enter after the pre-ceding command, you'll see the user installation dialog box shown in Figure 12.1.

Figure 12.1 *The GIMP requires a quick installation when you run it for the first time.*

Click the Continue button to start the install. You'll then see a dialog box that provides a list of contents intended for your personal GIMP directory, which, if you're using version 1.1, will be named `.gimp-1.1` in your home directory. Click the Continue button to create the directory and install the five files and 15 directories. The install program again asks you to confirm the install, so click the Continue button. The program then asks you, as shown in Figure 12.2, whether you'd like to specify the file cache size and a swap file location.

When finished, click the Continue button to accept the settings. The install program then asks for your monitor resolution. You can set the resolution of your images from the currently running X session or specify a different number of pixels per inch (ppi). You should enter a number that matches your display so that you can view images properly in a correct size. Click the Continue button when finished. You'll then see a short splash dialog box, and the GIMP will start as shown in Figure 12.3.

Each time that you start the GIMP, you'll see a tip of the day (unless you disable this feature by deselecting the Show Tip check box the next time that the GIMP starts). The main GIMP window is a floating dialog box of drawing tools with a File, Xtns, and Help menu. You can use the File menu to begin your editing session by opening an existing image file or creating a new image file from scratch.

Table 12.1 lists the types of graphics files that you can import or export when you use the GIMP.

After creating or opening an image, right-click on the image window to access the GIMP's menus as shown in Figure 12.4.

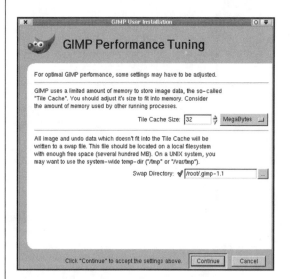

Figure 12.2 *The GIMP can use large amounts of file cache and a swap file located elsewhere on your filesystem.*

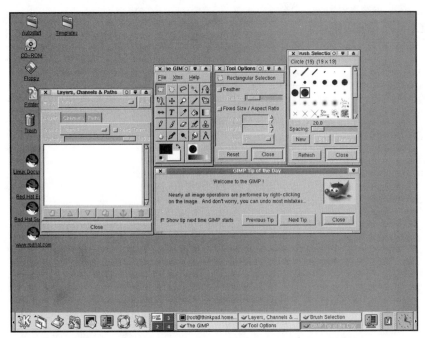

Figure 12.3 *The GIMP offers a tip of the day, and opens with a floating menu, toolbar, and several open utility windows.*

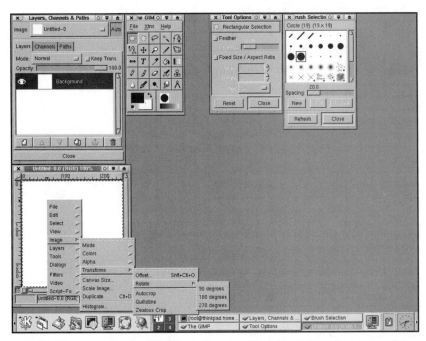

Figure 12.4 *You can access the GIMP's main menus by right-clicking the image-editing window.*

Table 12.1 GIMP Image Formats

Type	Description
BMP	Windows and OS/2 bitmap graphic
bzip2	Block-sorted compressed image
CEL	Lumina CEL file (read-only)
Fax G3	G3 fax format graphic
FITS	Flexible Image Transport System
FLI	Autodesk Animator file (read-only)
GBR	GIMP brush file
GIcon	Glowicon icon format (read-only)
GIF	Graphics interchange format (read-only)
gzip	Compressed GNU file
HRZ	Slow scan TV file
jpeg	Joint Photographics Experts Group (JPEG) graphic
PAT	PaintShop Pro pattern file
PCX	PCX graphic
PIX	Alias image file
PNG	Portable network graphic
PNM	Portable anymap graphic
PostScript	PostScript document/graphic
PSD	Adobe PhotoShop bitmap
PSP	PaintShop Pro image file
SGI	Silicon Graphics image
SUNRAS	Sun rasterfile
TGA	Truevision Targa File
Tiff	Tagged Image File Format graphic
URL	Web address
WMF	Windows metafile graphic
XBM	X bitmap graphic (read-only)
XCF	GIMP image format
xjt	Layered jpeg graphics format
Xpm	X pixmap graphic
XWD	X window dump

Using Scanners

Scanners are useful devices that can copy and import images and documents. Although scanners initially were an expensive hardware add-on for any computer system, prices have dropped and even the cheapest models currently on the market now have features that rival or exceed those of the most expensive models of only a few years ago. Scanners come in all different shapes and sizes, and can use a variety of input/output (I/O) ports on your system. This includes the serial and parallel port, Small Computer System Interface (SCSI) PC ports, Personal Computer Memory Card Interface Adapter (PCMCIA) slots, and today, the more common Universal Serial Bus (USB) port.

Before contemplating a purchase of a scanner for Linux, first check for the availability of a driver or user-space application that can enable your scanner to be recognized and used under Linux. Although some scanners require a specific set of loaded kernel modules, you can use other scanners from a command-line program. Depending on the type of scanner and supporting software, you may not need to use X or have a running X session in order to perform a scan. However, it is much more convenient to use a graphical interface when scanning, as most supporting applications provide convenient preview, cropping, contrast, brightness, and color controls. One of the most popular software support programs for using scanners is the Scanner Access Now Easy (SANE) package.

SANE

SANE is a scanner support package split into two components: a *back-end* (or low-level driver), and a *front-end* (or graphical interface) to the driver and scanner hardware. The back-end support comes in the form of background drivers, whereas the front-end may be one or more supporting command-line, X, or network clients, such as the following:

- xsane, which can function as a GIMP plug-in
- xscanimage, which can function as a GIMP plug-in
- scanimage, a command-line version of xscanimage
- xcam, a GUI for cameras
- saned, a network daemon to support scanning over a network

For example, the xscanimage client, which may be used as a standalone program or as a plug-in with the GIMP, provides a number of controls and settings, depending on the supported driver. Settings for xscanimage are stored in several resource files found under the subdirectory `xscanimage` inside the directory `.sane` in your home directory. The resource files include the following:

- `xscanimage.rc`, which sets user preferences
- *`devicename`*`.rc`, a resource file with the name that consists the scanner's driver, such as `as6edriver.rc`; this file generally contains the last or current settings for the driver
- *`preview-devicename`*`.ppm`, a saved preview from a previous preview acquisition

You can start this client from the command line as follows:

```
# xscanimage &
```

After you press Enter, insert a photo into your scanner, click the Preview Window button, then click the Acquire Preview button as shown in Figure 12.5.

You can then use the various controls to set the type of scan, resolution, brightness, and contrast. Other drivers (the one shown in Figure 12.5 is for an Artec AS6E) may provide fewer or more controls.

Optical Character Recognition

Free optical character recognition (OCR) packages are still in their infancy for Linux, but at least one package stands out from the crowd and appears to provide results that are as good as those of the early commercial OCR packages. Joerg Schulenburg's GNU OCR/JOCR package, which is distributed under the GNU GPL, can be used

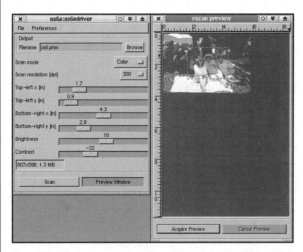

Figure 12.5 *The* `xscanimage` *client displays a floating dialog box of controls, along with an image preview window.*

to generate OCR scanned sheets of text quickly. This software builds quickly and easily from source under current Linux distributions, and has a graphical front-end built using GNOME.

To use GOCR, download the GOCR package, decompress the software, navigate to the directory, then configure, build, and install the package as follows:

```
# ./configure ; make ; make install
```

After a minute or so, you can then use the gocr command from the command line to perform OCR. First, scan a sheet of text in line-art (black-and-white) mode at 300dpi (dots per inch). Next, save the file as a .pbm, .pnm, .jpg, .tiff, .gif, or .bmp graphic. You can then perform OCR by using the gocr command as follows:

```
# gocr -v 1 page1.pnm >page1.txt 2>>ocr.log
```

The -v option denotes a level of information to be saved in the OCR log file. You can also use the gtk-ocr client during an X session to perform OCR for scanned pages. Start the client from the command line of an X terminal as follows:

```
# gtk-ocr &
```

After you press Enter, you can click the Setting button to enter defaults for the client. When you want to perform OCR, first click the Add button, then add files to the list of files (most likely a series of pages) to convert. To begin OCR, click the Convert button (as shown in Figure 12.6).

If you click the View button, the ImageMagick display client launches to display your scanned text. You can use this as a "preflight check" before performing OCR to see whether the page was scanned cleanly and straight. For example, suppose that the original text (from a printout of a text file included with gocr's source code) was as follows:

```
Note: this info is related to example files, used to test gOCR. As of this
writing, these files are not available to non-developers. So, if you aren't
a developer, forget about this file.

...
```

Figure 12.6 *The* gtk-ocr *client is a front-end to the* gocr *command.*

The resulting OCR text is as follows:

```
Mote. this info is related to example files, used to test gOCR. As of this
writing, these files are not available to non-aevelopers. So, if yau aren 't
a aeveloper, forget about this file.

...
```

The results are fairly consistent and show that OCR under Linux is feasible. Keep in mind that each scanned page (letter size at 300dpi) requires nearly 8MB hard drive space. The gocr client is quite memory-intensive, and requires nearly three times the size of your scanned image in order to work. OCR of a full page of text was accomplished in 1 minute and 11 seconds on a 500MHz Pentium computer with 128MB RAM.

Siemens PocketReader

An alternative to performing OCR in software is to use a hardware decoder. One such device, the Siemens PocketReader, is a small, hand-held reader pen that the user swipes over text line by line to perform OCR. The device then saves the resulting data inside the reader's 40,000-character memory.

A small X client, pocketreader, is provided for Linux and allows you to download the contents of the OCR pen. You must first build and install the client (which requires the GNOME GTK+ libraries). Next, start the client from the command line as follows:

```
# pocketreader &
```

After you press Enter, use the client's POCKETREADER menu (as shown in Figure 12.7) to configure the software to use the correct serial port (such as /dev/ttyS0) and speed (38,400 baud).

After you have configured the software, scan some text with the pen, then connect the included serial cable to your computer. Next press Ctrl+R or select the Read Text menu item from the client's POCKETREADER menu. The text then appears in the client's window, as shown in Figure 12.8.

Using the same printed text as in the example for gocr, the scanned result (of an untrained hand) is as follows:

```
IOte: this into is related to exalnpLe files used to test qOCR.
As of this vriting , these files are n lot available to non-developers .
So, if you arenft a developer , forget about this file.
```

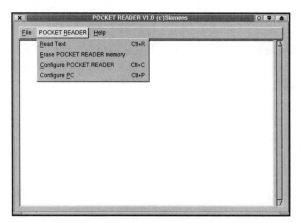

Figure 12.7 *To transfer text from the OCR pen, you must first configure the software for your computer's serial port.*

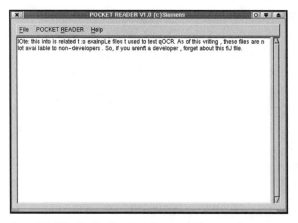

Figure 12.8 *The PocketReader client quickly transfers scanned text from the pen via your computer's serial port.*

Using Digital Cameras

Just as with scanners, the ever-increasing popularity of digital cameras in the market-place has spurred greater support for these devices under Linux and X11. This section describes one of most popular digital camera support clients for X: the GNOME-enabled gPhoto, which supports more than 100 different types of cameras.

Using gPhoto

Until this year, gPhoto was not a staple addition to most Linux distributions. However, with digital cameras becoming commonplace, many Linux distributions now include this capable software package. gPhoto, which uses the GTK+ libraries, provides a healthy selection of photo-handling utilities in addition to being a transport agent for digital images.

Start gPhoto from the command line of terminal window as follows:

```
# gphoto&
```

After you press Enter, click the Configure menu, then select the Select Port/Camera Model menu item. You'll the see the dialog box shown in Figure 12.9.

Select the proper serial port, then click the Camera Model drop-down menu, and scroll through the list of cameras to select your particular model. Click the Save button when finished.

Next, to save time before a long download, you can use gPhoto to download *thumbnails*, or a reduced-view index of the contents of your digital camera. Click the Camera menu, select Download Index, then click the Thumbnails menu item. You can also press Ctrl+i or use a toolbar button to download the thumbnails. gPhoto then downloads miniature pictures of the images in your camera and displays them in the main window, as shown in Figure 12.10.

When you decide what pictures to download, click to select them, then again use the Camera menu to download the pictures as shown in Figure 12.11. Note that you can also use one of the toolbar buttons to download the selected photos.

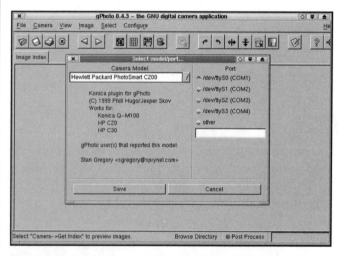

Figure 12.9 *When you first use gPhoto, use its configuration dialog box to select the proper camera and transfer port.*

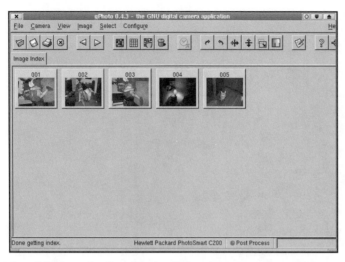

Figure 12.10 *Downloading thumbnails is a great way to save time when deciding what pictures to download from your digital camera.*

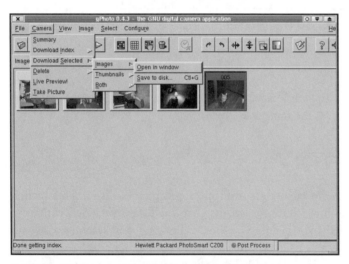

Figure 12.11 *Click to select thumbnails, then use the Camera menu to download the selected pictures.*

After the picture or pictures download, they are displayed in tabbed windows in gPhoto's main window, as shown in Figure 12.12. The toolbar buttons provide rudimentary but important editing options, such as rotation, flipping, scaling, brightness, color, and contrast controls.

Figure 12.12 *gPhoto can make the task of quickly editing digital images easy.*

After you are satisfied with your image, you can then save the images using gPhoto's File menu. The client saves the images in .jpg format.

Audio Clients

Literally hundreds of audio clients are available for Linux and X11. This section introduces some of the more common clients that you'll find included with your Linux distribution. To use these clients, you should configure your system to use your computer's sound hardware. This hardware can include a microphone, lines in, audio out, CD audio, and so on. If you need help configuring your sound system to work with Linux, read the Sound-HOWTO, Sound-Playing-HOWTO, or sound documentation included with the Linux kernel. You can also turn to alternative free sound systems for Linux, such as the ALSA project, or use the commercial sound drivers from 4-Front Technologies.

Audio Mixer Clients

After configuring your sound, you should be able to adjust the volume, balance, and other features using a variety of graphical clients. This section covers some common audio mixers that you'll find included with your Linux distribution.

One of older audio mixers for X and Linux is Olav Woelfelschneider's xmixer client, shown in Figure 12.13. This client has basic controls that you can use to handle sound for your microphone, speakers, headphones, CD audio, and synthesizer.

You can adjust the controls by clicking on the left, right, or both sliders and dragging up or down. Click the Exit button to quit this client. If you use KDE, you'll find Christian Esken's kmix audio mixer client included with your system. This client, shown in Figure 12.14, features a sliding balance control.

If you click on the light buttons by each audio feature—such as volume, speaker, or microphone—you can toggle the feature on or off (toggling the feature off actually mutes the line). You can also use kmix to save your audio preferences for use the next time that you start KDE or use sound. If you use GNOME, you'll also find the gmix client available for your desktop. This client, shown in Figure 12.15, features rudimentary controls, but offers mute buttons and works with the GNOME esd sound daemon.

Figure 12.13 *The* xmixer *client allows you to control your computer's sound system during your X session.*

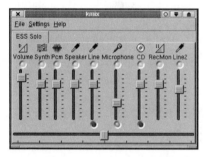

Figure 12.14 *The* kmix *client features button controls and a sliding balance control.*

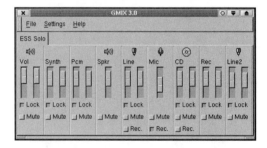

Figure 12.15 *The* gmix *client for GNOME also features button controls for muting and locking sound levels.*

Sound Players

There are many different types of sound players for Linux, but few for X11, unless you count some of the more esoteric sound editors such as the snd client. Most sound players for Linux are command-line utilities, and the most common is the sox command with its symbolic link, the play command. This command is typically used to play a .wav file, as in the following example:

```
# play /usr/share/sndconfig/test.wav
```

Audio CD Players

Some of the most popular sound clients for X are audio CD players. There are number of players, but the newer ones have some interesting features.

xplaycd

Again, one of the oldest graphical audio CD players for Linux is Olav Woelfelschneider's xplaycd client. This client, shown in Figure 12.16, provides the basic audio CD controls, but also includes a remarkable feature: You can drag and drop the track number buttons to reorder the audio track play.

kscd

If you're a KDE fan and have access to the Internet, you can use the kscd client not only to play audio CDs, but also to retrieve automatically the CD title, track, author, and track titles. This network-aware client, shown in Figure 12.17, features button controls and a number of configuration dialog boxes that you can use to change the number of Internet music databases searched or the appearance of the client's window (such as the background or foreground colors).

You can use this client to build gradually a local database of all your audio CDs or even to contribute information about an obscure CD to the Internet databases.

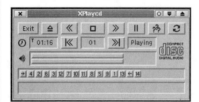

Figure 12.16 *The* xplaycd *client is an early version of a graphical audio CD player for X and Linux.*

Figure 12.17 *The* kscd *client not only plays CDs, but also searches the Internet for track and title information about your CD.*

.mp3 Players

The latest rage in audio music seems to be the .mp3 audio format. All the machinations of the music industry aside, this audio format has become the *de facto* standard for compressed digital-quality audio files. You'll find a number of .mp3 or MPEG audio players available for Linux and X. The command-line version for non-X users is the mpg123 command, which you can use to play one or more audio files as follows:

```
# mpg123 *.mp3
```

After you press Enter, the player loads the first of any found files and starts playing them through your computer's sound system. The premier graphical audio player for X is the xmms client. This client, shown in Figure 12.18, features a graphic equalizer, a playlist editor, and the ability to use different audio and visual plug-ins.

Another great feature of this client is that you can minimize it to occupy very little space on your screen without losing any of the client's controls. This feature alone endears this client to Linux and X laptop users. However, if you enable the equalizer and visual plug-ins, as shown in Figure 12.19, this player can take up a lot of your display.

Figure 12.18 *The* xmms *.mp3 player client for X has many different features, including a graphic equalizer.*

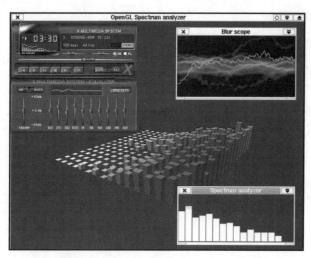

Figure 12.19 *The* xmms *client also has visualization plug-ins for viewing your music graphically.*

.mp3 Rippers

One of the nice features about using .mp3 audio is that you can fit nearly 10 audio CDs of music on a single CD-R. This also means you can carry around 20 or 30 CDs of music and use only a few gigabytes of hard drive space on your laptop. You can also preserve your entire audio collection in digital format on a small server on your LAN.

There are a number of front-end clients that you can use to automate the process of converting audio CDs into .mp3 format. If you use KDE, you'll definitely want to use Adrian Schroeter's krabber client. You can start this client from the command line of an X11 terminal window as follows:

```
# krabber &
```

After you press Enter, krabber looks for the cdparanoia, cdrecord, sox, and mpg123 commands, as well as various .mp3 encoders such as lame. The main interface looks like that shown in Figure 12.20.

This client features a number of options, including sound filters, the ability to set CPU priority (to devote more or less CPU usage to the encoding task), and the ability to set the quality of the digital conversion. Better quality means larger encoded files. Songs played with average sound quality typically take up to 1MB of hard drive storage per minute.

All you have to do is click the buttons labeled 1–4 in sequence. Clicking the first button enables you to choose the audio tracks of any inserted audio CD. Like the kscd client, krabber will query remote Internet music databases and automatically name

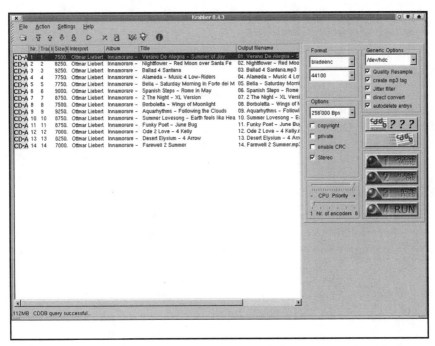

Figure 12.20 *The* krabber *client is a graphical front-end that automates the task of converting audio CDs into .mp3 files.*

and label your tracks if the client finds the CD. Clicking button 2 enables you to choose the directory in which to save your audio database. Then click button 3 to name your tracks. When you are finished, click button 4 to start reading the audio files from CD and encoding them in .mp3 format. You'll see a progress indicator, as shown in Figure 12.21.

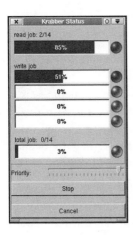

Figure 12.21 *The* krabber *client also presents a progress indicator during the process of ripping and encoding your audio files.*

Video and Animation Clients

Video and animation playback, first ushered into the personal computer realm only a few years ago, is now almost a necessity for online viewing, especially now that personal computers feature more RAM and hard drive storage. With the advent of the next phase of the communications revolution and the introduction of universal broadband access for most Internet users, the capability to watch video and animation locally or over the Internet is finally being realized.

Animation Clients

One animation and video clip playback client is Mark Podlipec's xanim player. This client is a staple addition to many Linux distributions, and can play back more than a dozen different animation and video clips formats, including QuickTime and .avi clips.

You can start this client from the command line, specifying the command along with the name of the video clip, like this:

```
# xanim *.avi
```

After you press Enter, the xanim client plays the animation (and sound), as shown in Figure 12.22.

Figure 12.22 *The* xanim *client can play a variety of video and animation clips.*

Video Clients

A variety of video clients are available for Linux. These programs are sometimes used with a video device driver and kernel modules to provide service for all users or implemented as *user-space* applications (as owned processes by users) running in system memory. Using video hardware with Linux depends on the availability of such software, so you should always check the status of support for such hardware before contemplating its purchase.

However, watching video requires another type of client for X11. Often included with Linux distributions is Real's RealPlayer, which you can use as a standalone program to listen to music or watch streaming audio files. Most often, however, Netscape's Navigator launches RealPlayer while the user is Web browsing, to aid the user in viewing video or listening to audio. For example, if you have broadband access, you can use RealPlayer to watch movies over the Internet, as shown in Figure 12.23.

Other devices, such as Web cams, can be used with Linux and X11 with few problems. Generally, these device offer a less-expensive video solution that usually provides minimal video resolutions of 640×400 pixels or less. Newer models can use a USB port, whereas older models may hook into the parallel port to transmit data.

At least one computer manufacturer, Sony, has incorporated a digital camera into its line of computers. The Sony Picturebook includes a swivel-mounted color camera that you can use to take single snapshots or digital movies. In particular, the Sony C1XS, a diminutive laptop with a 1,024×480 display but sporting up to 128MB RAM and a 12GB hard drive, is well supported under Linux. Its built-in digital camera can take 640×480 .jpeg snapshots (as shown in Figure 12.24) or record digital movies in .avi format. The Picturebook's camera is supported by Andrew Tridgell's capture client, which displays a "live-motion" screen while waiting for a press of the Picturebook's camera exposure button. To initialize the client, enter the following:

```
# capture -s
```

Figure 12.23 *The RealPlayer client plays streaming audio or video during your X sessions.*

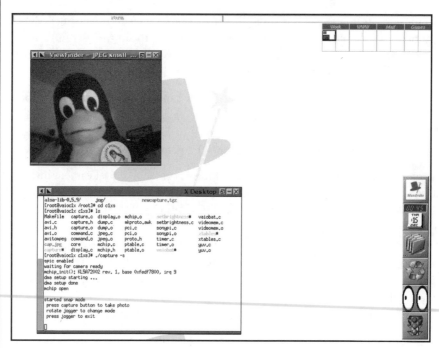

Figure 12.24 *The* capture *client for select Sony Picturebooks can also be used to display images over a network, as well as to capture .jpeg snapshots or .avi movies.*

After you press Enter, you'll see an initial small video window, as shown in Figure 12.24.

Additional video devices and software for Linux enable you to perform digital editing of movies or view cable TV through your computer's video card adapter.

DVD Players

At the time of this writing, the only way to play DVD movies legally using Linux is to use enabling drivers and DVD hardware cards from manufacturers such as Creative or Matrox. Although you can quite easily patch the current Linux kernel to read the DVD filesystem, then use software to watch DVD movies, a paranoid movie industry has seen fit to try to prosecute anyone (even a 16-year-old boy) caught distributing software to decode DVD movies. Although several companies touted announcements in early 2000 for bringing out DVD playing software for Linux, those products have yet to come to market.

The good news is that there are projects aimed at developing Open Source DVD players for Linux and XFree86. If you'd like to learn how to play DVDs under Linux right away, read the OMS-HOWTO. The Open Media System (OMS) DVD

Player for Linux from the LiViD (Linux Video and DVD) project shows great promise, and with the introduction of the 2.4 series of the Linux kernel it is no longer necessary to patch the kernel to support the DVD filesystem.

Resource Information

http://www.gimp.org—home page of the GIMP, and the location for downloading the latest version.

http://www.ibiblio.org/pub/Linux/apps/graphics/capture/—FTP site for all sorts of scanning software "front-ends."

http://users.yoobay.at/preader/_pr_e.htm—support page for the Siemens Pocketreader hand-held OCR scanner.

http://www.buzzard.org.uk/jonathan/scanners.html—parallel-port scanners supported under Linux and XFree86.

http://www.buzzard.org.uk/jonathan/scanners-usb.html—USB scanners supported under Linux and XFree86.

http://www.cica.indiana.edu/graphics/image.formats.html—the Center for Innovative Computer Applications provides a comprehensive list of graphics formats.

http://www.mostang.com/sane/—the SANE home page, the starting point for checking on support for your scanner under Linux.

http://www.vividata.com/pricelist.html—a price list for commercial OCR packages for Linux.

http://www.math.nwu.edu/~mlerma/locr/—home page for the Linux OCR (LOCR) project, an alternative OCR project for Linux.

http://altmark.nat.uni-magdeburg.de/~jschulen/ocr/—home page for the GOCR project.

http://www.gphoto.org/—home page for the gPhoto project, with support for more than 100 different digital cameras. Chances are good that if you own a digital camera, Linux supports it.

http://www.linuxvideo.org/docs/Linux-DVD-HOWTO/en/html/Linux-DVD-HOWTO-en.html

http://www.linuxvideo.org/docs/OMS-HOWTO/Linux-DVD-HOWTO-en.html—a site that provides directions for setting up your Linux system to play DVDs.

http://www.stellarsphere.com/tidbits/articles/vol1_imgformats/imgformats.html#bas1—an online tutorial about popular Web graphics formats.

http://www.alsa-project.org—home page of the Advanced Linux Sound Architecture sound drivers.

http://www.opensound.com—home page of the commercial Open Sound System sound drivers from 4-Front Technologies.

http://www.axis.com/products/cam_2120/index.htm—home page for the AXIS 2120 Linux-enabled network Web camera.

http://www.linuxvideo.org/docs/OMS-HOWTO/—download site for the OMS HOWTO.

Chapter 13: Popular X11 Games

Free X11 games

Commercial X11 games for Linux

This chapter introduces a number of popular free and commercial games for Linux and XFree86. Until recently, most of the amusement and past-time clients (games) for X resided in the realm of legacy clients that were ported over time to work with Linux. However, as Linux and XFree86 have increased in popularity over the last two years, commercial game producers have seen a new, expanded marketplace for selling games for Linux.

Now more than a dozen commercial games are available for Linux, thanks to the programming efforts of at least one company, Loki Entertainment, Inc. Table 13.1 lists some of the most popular games.

Commercial games for XFree86 are, of course, the equivalent to counterparts for other commercial operating systems. However, some of these games require special graphics hardware and software libraries to support 3D rendering and feasible game play. Fortunately, you can download nearly all-commercial games as demos, so you can try the game before purchasing it. This idea has merit, as it can save you time, effort, and money. Commercial games are covered in the section "Commercial X11 Games for Linux," later in this chapter.

The good news is that you'll find many other games available for X that do not require a major reinvestment of graphics hardware, video memory, or additional download and installation of special software libraries. Nearly every Linux distribution includes a variety of games for X, and many have become classic additions to the /usr/X11R6/bin directory tree.

This chapter covers nearly 30 great games, both arcade and strategy, that will work on nearly every computer system. Keep in mind that an 800×600 display with 256 colors is generally required. Realistically, most games function best when played on a 1,024×768 desktop with thousands of colors.

Free X11 Games

This section introduces several free strategy and arcade games for X, along with miscellaneous fun clients that you can use on your system. The strategy games cover the more traditional board games, although some strategy games also involve graphics, sound, and music. The arcade games include some traditional ones, as well as a few with unique twists.

Table 13.1 Commercial Games from Loki for Linux

Name	Description
Civilization: Call to Power	Strategy
Descent3	Arcade
Eric's Ultimate Solitaire	Strategy card game
Heavy Gear II	Real-time strategy arcade
Heretic II	Arcade first-person shooter
Heroes of Might and Magic III	Real-time strategy
Kohan: Immortal Sovereigns	Real-time strategy
MindRover	Arcade
Myth II: Soulblighter	Real-time strategy
Quake III: Arena	Arcade first-person shooter
Railroad Tycoon II	Strategy
Sid Meier's Alpha Centauri	Strategy
Simcity 3000 Unlimited	Strategy
Soldier of Fortune	Arcade first-person shooter
Unreal Tournament	Arcade

Strategy Games

Strategy games usually involve some sort of logic and thinking. Traditional strategy games are board games, and quite a few of these clients are available for X. Some have been around for quite some time, whereas others are new to the scene. You'll also find a good selection of card solitaire and mah-jongg solitaire clients for X, with some included as part of the KDE or GNOME desktop environments.

Board Games

Board games for X are usually modeled after their real-world counterparts, and games such as chess and backgammon have been around for computers since the first interactive teletypes. Many of these games feature computer-versus-human play, along with strong internal intelligence through the use of quite robust algorithms. You can expect a good challenge. When you add X for graphics support, you also find a colorful display and intuitive use of your pointer for piece movement.

Playing Chess with xboard

The xboard client is a graphical interface to the GNU chess program. This client provides a colorful board in a variety of sizes and also obeys a subset of X Toolkit options for window placement. Start this game from the command line of a terminal window as follows:

```
# xboard &
```

After you press Enter, you'll see a window, as shown in Figure 13.1.

This client offers play against the computer or play against another human; also, you can set up a game between two computers. You can also use this client to play chess over a network or by electronic mail. X users with a display smaller than 1,024×768 should use xboard's -size option as follows:

```
# xboard -size small
```

Playing Chess with GLChess

The glchess client plays chess in 3D within a floating window on your screen. Start the client from the command line as follows:

```
# glchess &
```

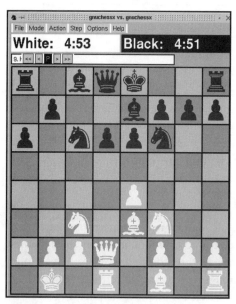

Figure 13.1 *The* xboard *client is a graphical front-end for the GNU chess program.*

The game displays a chessboard in a floating window, as shown in Figure 13.2. After you launch the client, press the 2, 3, or 4 keys to change the board's highlighting. You can also rotate the x, y, and z axes of the board by using the cursor keys. To begin play, click to select a piece, then click a valid destination square on the board.

Playing Backgammon with xgammon

Lambert Klasen and Detlef Steuer's xgammon client is a fun-filled and accurate rendition of classic backgammon. This game, like xboard, also features computer-against-computer play. You can launch xgammon from the command line as follows:

```
# xgammon &
```

After you press Enter, you'll see two windows, as shown in Figure 13.3.

This client has more than 20 different command-line options, and like most well-behaved X clients, xgammon obeys resource settings.

Solitaire Card Games

Card games have always been popular, and especially so with computer users. The energy used playing solitaire on desktops across the world for so many hours could probably run a small nation-state. If you're a solitaire card game fan, you won't be disappointed when you look at what's available for X. This section features several clients that are sure to keep your interest for hours on end.

Figure 13.2 *The* glchess *client plays chess on a 3D chessboard.*

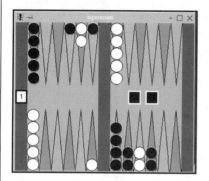 

Figure 13.3 *The* xgammon *client plays a good game of backgammon.*

Solitaire with xpat

Heiko Eissfeldt and Michael Bischoff's xpat2 solitaire game features more than just one version of solitaire. You'll find Spider, Gypsy, Klondike, Seahaven Towers, Free Cell, Idiot's Delight, Monte Carlo, Midnight Oil, Calculation, Canfield, Fantasy, a modified Canfield, Royal Cotillion, and Baker's Dozen.

Start the client from the command line as follows:

```
# xpat2 &
```

After you press Enter, you'll see a window as shown in Figure 13.4.

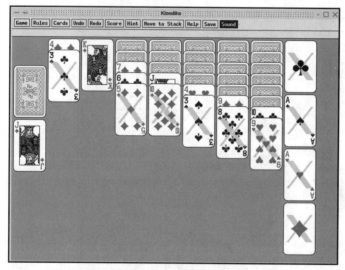

Figure 13.4 *The* xpat2 *client features 13 different card solitaire games.*

Select a game by using the Rules menu. The client automatically places the cards for you, so you don't have to drag cards between piles. While this may not be as flexible as other solitaire games, it does speed up play.

Solitaire with kpat

The kpat client, by Paul Olav Tvetei, is included with KDE and is another combination solitaire game for X. You'll need to have KDE and its support libraries installed in order to play kpat. This game features nine different card games. Although you normally launch a KDE client from the desktop's panel menu, you can launch this game from the command line as follows:

```
# kpat &
```

After you press Enter, you'll see the window shown in Figure 13.5.

To select a game, choose New Game from the Game menu. You can drag and release cards during game play.

Solitaire Games

There are many other types of solitaire games besides card games. Although some fall into the category of board games, others (such as ksame, discussed later in this section) could not be played without the help of graphics animation and X. Some solitaire games can be played quickly, in less than a minute, whereas others may require nearly an hour.

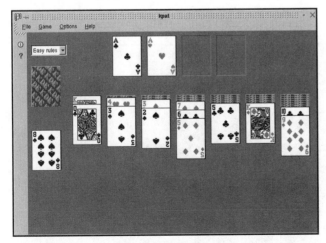

Figure 13.5 *The* kpat *client plays nine different solitaire games and is part of the KDE games suite.*

Play Mah-Jonng with xmahjongg

Jeff S. Young's xmahjongg game was first developed more than 10 years ago for X11R3, yet remains just as playable today. The object of xmahjongg, as with nearly all other Mah-Jongg computer games, is to remove as many tiles as possible from the board by first clicking a tile, then clicking a matching tile. The game ends when no more matching tiles are available.

> Computer Mah-Jongg games are not the same as the real game of Mah-Jongg (which can be traced back to the late 1800s in China). Rules are extensive, four players are usually required, and setup of the initial board is quite different. Browse to **http://www.mahjongg.com** to learn more about this game.

This client features a large, colorful display, allows you to build your own games, and requires a display of at least 1,024×768. A nice feature of this client is that it does not require 256 colors, and may be played on a 4 bit planes per pixel or 16-color display.

Start this client from the command line of a terminal window as follows:

```
# xmahjongg &
```

After you press Enter, you'll see the window shown in Figure 13.6.

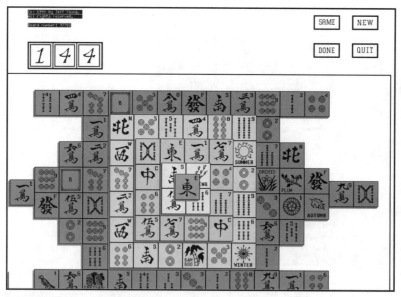

Figure 13.6 *The* xmahjongg *client has survived through three revisions of the X Window system, largely due to its good game play and portability.*

Play Mah-Jongg with kmahjongg

KDE's kmahjongg client features a beautiful tile set and built-in help. You can play this game on a display of at least 800×600, which makes this client a good choice for smaller notebook displays.

Start kmahjongg from the command line of a terminal window as follows:

```
# kmahjongg &
```

After you press Enter, you'll see the window shown in Figure 13.7.

This game also has a "cheat" mode in which any matching tiles blink when you click on a tile.

Games Modeled After SameGame

KDE's ksame client plays a game of matching balls, popularized by an Apple Macintosh game named *SameGame* (and probably ported to many different computer platforms). Click on adjacent, matching balls to make them disappear; the game's object is to remove as many as possible from the playing field.

Start ksame from the command line of a terminal window as follows:

```
# ksame &
```

After you press Enter, you'll see the window shown in Figure 13.8.

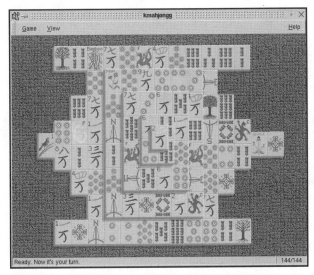

Figure 13.7 *The* kmajongg *client features built-in help, beautiful tiles, and options for changing the background.*

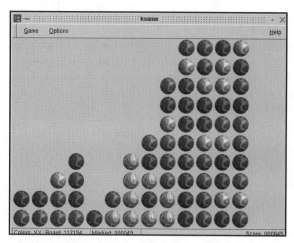

Figure 13.8 *The KDE* ksame *game plays the same game as SameGame.*

If you're a fan of GNOME, you can play the same game as ksame by using the same-gnome client. Start same-gnome from the command line of a terminal window as follows:

```
# same-gnome &
```

After you press Enter, you'll see the game window shown in Figure 13.9.

Note that both ksame and same-gnome allow you to use different themes and ball colors between plays.

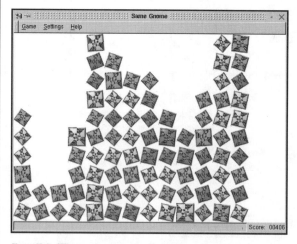

Figure 13.9 *The* same-gnome *client plays the same game as SameGame and* ksame, *but with a twist!*

Puzzles

A computer puzzle can be confounding, astounding, and even a game! One fun client for X that offers a puzzle on each playing level is xsok, included with many Linux distributions. This game, based on a game called Sokoban (from Japan), involves using the cursor keys to move a little man through a maze (represented by a warehouse). The object is to have the man push the jewels (boxes) through the maze to correct destinations.

Start xsok from the command line of a terminal window as follows:

```
# xsok &
```

After you press Enter, you'll see the window shown in Figure 13.10.

You'll find variations of this game for GNOME (gsokoban) and KDE (ksokoban).

Other Puzzling Clients for X11

Many different puzzle clients are available for XFree86. Some clients are based on the sliding tiles games of 15 (arranging 15 tiles in sequential order on a 16-tile field), whereas others, such as xjig, can be used to create onscreen jigsaw puzzles out of .gif images. The xpuzzles client provides a complete set of geometric puzzles.

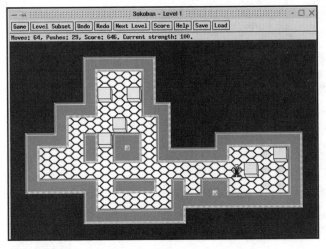

Figure 13.10 *The* xsok *client for X11 appears simple, but grows increasingly frustrating and challenging.*

Strategy Simulation with LinCity

Although not in the board, solitaire, or puzzle category, other games for X11, such as simulations, can require thinking and strategy. One of the most popular free software simulation games is *LinCity* by I. J. Peters. This client comes in two versions: one for the console, and the other for X. The console version is named `lincity`, and you can start it, like `xlincity`, from the command line. To run the X version, open a terminal window and launch the `xlincity` client as follows:

```
# xlincity &
```

After you press Enter, you'll see an initial splash window; press the spacebar to begin. If you choose to load a default scenario, you may see the display shown in Figure 13.11.

`xlincity` features built-in help to aid in game play. You can also choose different simulation speeds, build your own simulations from scratch, and save simulations in progress.

Arcade Games

Arcade games have been popular ever since the first commercial pong games were introduced to the public in the 1970s. Even though today's commercial arcade games are much more than simple paddle-driven court games and more like military flight and combat simulators, simple arcade games for X continue to be popular and hold attention. This section includes a small selection of some of the more popular games.

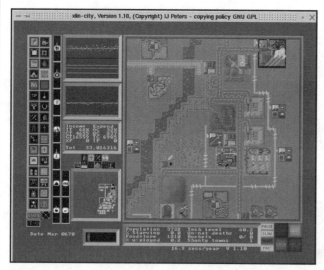

Figure 13.11 *The* `xlincity` *simulation game offers a number of complex controls that you can use to build simulations that will run for days.*

> ## *Wherefore Is DOOM?*
>
> *DOOM*, the first-person shooter game by iD Software that has spawned a foul legion and host of bloody arcade games for PCs, is available in source code form from **http://sourceforge.net/project/showfiles.php?group_id =3586**. You'll also need a DOOM WAD (data) file and a music server (available in source from the sourceforge site). Building and installing the shareware version of *DOOM*, named `lxdoom`, takes about three minutes on a 500MHz Pentium computer, and game play works quite well, even at large resolutions, such as 1,024×768. Although there is no commercial version of *DOOM* for Linux, iD Software still retains the copyright, and you must still use commercial *DOOM* WAD files for full play.

Unlike board games, most arcade games will use your system's sound card. You'll need to have a properly configured sound card for your system in order to take full advantage of these clients. Do you have to use sound? Of course not! Many of the clients covered here provide sound control, either through the command line or via a graphical interface.

Action Arcade with abuse

For its arcade action with a unique interface and playing field, abuse has acquired a legion of fans, especially Linux X game players. This game, from the company Crack dot Com, is now distributed in source code form. You can find a copy at Jonathan Clark's Web site, **http://jonathanclark.com/crack.com/abuse/downloads.php3**. The abuse client runs in a small 320×200 window, but features 3D animation and sound effects.

Start abuse from the command line of a terminal window as follows:

```
# abuse &
```

After you press Enter, you'll see the window shown in Figure 13.12.

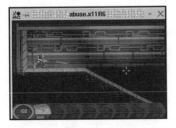

Figure 13.12 *The game* abuse *features different levels, controls, weapons, and monsters in a quest through an underground maze.*

The game is played with the cursor keys and mouse buttons, along with a number of other controls.

Maelstrom from the Mac

Maelstrom, by Andrew Welch, is a shareware arcade game originally developed for the Apple Macintosh. What is interesting about this game—besides its excellent animation, fast play, and great sounds—is that the original interface is relatively unchanged from the Macintosh version.

Start *Maelstrom* from the command line of a terminal window as follows:

```
# Maelstrom &
```

After you press Enter, you'll see an initial splash window. Press the spacebar, and you'll see a window of controls that allow you to change keyboard settings, high scores, and the volume. When ready, press the *P* key, and the game begins, as shown in Figure 13.13.

This game is somewhat like the old classic *Asteroids* arcade game, but it is more like 3D *Asteroids* on steroids! You use various keys to maneuver, thrust, and fire at oncoming asteroids. As with the classic *Asteroids*, playing this game for any length of time requires dexterity and good aim.

Classic Arcade with xgalaga

A whole generation of arcade game players grew up flinging weeks' worth of allowances and spending money into game machines. You can relive some classic

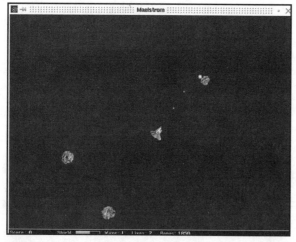

Figure 13.13 *Life in space doesn't last too long when asteroids are around and you're playing Maelstrom during your X session!*

arcade action when you play `xgalaga` on your desktop. This game, like the original *Galaga* (or *Galaxian*), features hordes and phalanxes of enemy ships streaming down the screen while you try to dodge and take out as many enemies as you can.

Start `xgalaga` from the command line of a terminal window as follows:

```
# xgalaga &
```

After you press Enter, you'll see an initial window; press any key to begin the play, as shown in Figure 13.14.

Retro-arcade with xinvaders

One of the games that started it all was *Space Invaders*. One of the first invader clones of the commercial arcade version appeared as C source code for the CP/M console. Then, as personal computers gained the ability to use color and graphics, innumerable clone games appeared on the scene. The `xinvaders` client by Jonny Goldman closely mimics the feel and play of the original arcade game.

Start `xinvaders` from the command line of a terminal window as follows:

```
# xinvaders &
```

After you press Enter, you'll see an initial window; press the Play button to begin, as shown in Figure 13.15.

Press the z key or spacebar to fire, and use the left- and right-mouse buttons to move your spaceship from left to right.

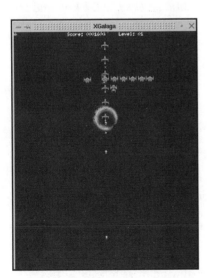

Figure 13.14 *The* xgalaga *client features similar play to the successor game of Galaxian.*

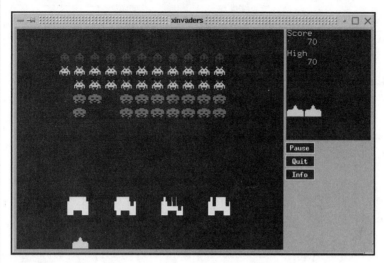

Figure 13.15 *The* xinvaders *client is a retro-classic game of intergalactic dueling.*

Falling Blocks with xtetris

The game of *Tetris* caused a sensation when it first appeared on the IBM PC in the mid-1980s after Vadim Gerasimov ported Alexey Pazhitnov's falling blocks game. Next appearing on the Apple II, the game of *Tetris* soon spawned an immense legion of users, and a long, sad 10-year story for its inventor, who received nearly nothing for his work while British, U.S., and Japanese companies reaped a fortune.

This version of the falling blocks game uses the traditional *h, l, j,* and *k* keys and the spacebar for left, right, clockwise, counterclockwise, and dropping movement of the falling piece. Start xtetris from the command line of a terminal window as follows:

```
# xtetris &
```

After you press Enter, you'll see an initial window; press the New Game button to begin, as shown in Figure 13.16.

The Classic Pac-Man

The kpacman client included with KDE closely mimics the original version of *Pac-Man*, first released in 1980 for commercial arcades. Home PC versions quickly followed, and over the last 20 years a number of additional versions have continued to be marketed. If you're a fan of "Blinky, Pinky, Inky, and Clyde," you're sure to like Joerg Thoennissen's kpacman.

Start kpacman from the command line of a terminal window as follows:

```
# kpacman &
```

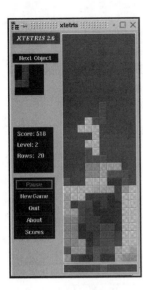

Figure 13.16 *The* xtetris *client plays a traditional game of falling blocks.*

After you press Enter, you'll see a splash screen introducing the characters. Press F2, and when the game prompts, use your cursor keys to guide your man through the maze. A demo screen is shown in Figure 13.17.

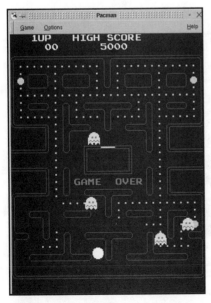

Figure 13.17 *The* kpacman *client mimics the fun and excitement of the original arcade game.*

Rocking with rocksndiamonds

If you like the classic game of *Loderunner* or *Dig-Dug*, you're sure to like a version for X with lots of variations, sounds, and musical themes. Holger Schemel's rocksndiamonds game for X offers hundreds of levels and variants of different games, including *Boulderdash*.

Start rocksndiamonds from the command line of a terminal window as follows:

```
# rocksndiamonds &
```

After you press Enter, you'll see a splash screen. You can then select a game level and type of game. The object in most versions (such as the one shown in Figure 13.18) is to collect as many points as possible, usually by finding or touching gold or jewels.

Penguins as Lemmings in pingus

A relatively new game for X, based on a commercial game named *Lemmings*, is taking the Linux game-playing community by storm. pingus, by Ingo Ruhnke, offers a chance to save hundreds of penguins by selecting the right penguin for the right job at the right time.

Start pingus from the command line of a terminal window as follows:

```
# pingus &
```

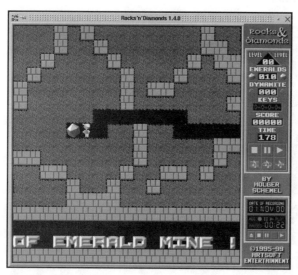

Figure 13.18 *Game play is fun and musical when playing* rocksndiamonds.

After you press Enter, you'll see a splash screen. You can then select a game level and then play, as shown in Figure 13.19.

Miscellaneous Fun Clients

If you read the documentation included with many X games, you'll find that many clients take advantage of X's networking capabilities, allowing game play via a network. This section describes several fun clients for X that don't fall into the categories of a game.

Ugh!

The xroach client displays a horde of roaches that initially scurry around the desktop, but then quickly hide under any open windows (if you close or iconify the window, you'll uncover a morass of the buggers, and they'll scurry around again). You can use this client to great effect with its -display option, so that if you have correct permission, you can send a horde to a remote display on your LAN.

Start xroach from the command line of a terminal window like this:

```
# xroach -rc brown -rgc green -squish -speed 1 &
```

After you press Enter, you'll see 10 brown roaches scurry around your screen (as shown in Figure 13.20). The -squish option allows you to click on a roach, which results in a green splatter on your desktop.

Figure 13.19 *Penguins as lemmings do your bidding when you play* pingus.

Figure 13.20 *You can play exterminator when you use the* xroach *client.*

Here Kitty, Kitty!

You can quickly and easily change your X pointer using a number of utility clients included with XFree86. But you can also have your pointer turned into a mouse and chased by a cute little cat named Oneko when you use Masayuki Koba and Tatsuya Kato's oneko client.

Start oneko from the command line of a terminal window as follows:

```
# oneko &
```

After you press Enter, you'll see a little cat as shown in Figure 13.21.

X Aquarium

If you can't have a fish tank in your computing center or your room, then the xfishtank client may be the next best thing. This client puts a designated number of animated fish and bubbles in the root display of your desktop. Start xfishtank from the command line of a terminal window as follows:

```
# xfishtank &
```

After you press Enter, you'll see a desktop as shown in Figure 13.22.

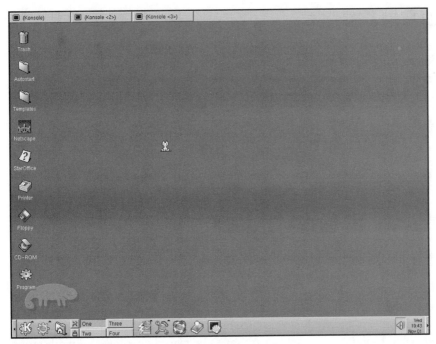

Figure 13.21 *The* oneko *client creates a cat that chases your mouse.*

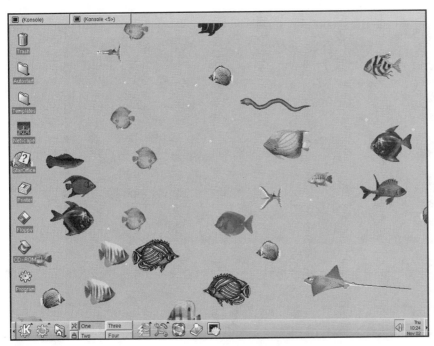

Figure 13.22 *The* xfishtank *client creates a virtual aquarium.*

Virtual Santa Claus

If you have a holiday spirit, the xsnow client can be a fun animation for your root display during the special time of the year. This client features falling snow that accumulates on icons and the bottom of your screen, then shows a special jolly someone with 12 reindeer flying across the screen.

Start xsnow from the command line of a terminal window as follows:

```
# xsnow &
```

After you press Enter, you'll see a desktop as shown in Figure 13.23.

Commercial X11 Games for Linux

Selecting commercial games for Linux and X may require some deliberation before purchase. On the one hand, these games are professional and polished, and will hold your interest for many hours of play. On the other hand, some of these games require enormous amounts of hard drive storage, require advanced and in some cases expensive video hardware, and are huge resource hogs for CPU cycles and system memory while they are running. Most are not meant to be played on a low-end workstation and, unlike Linux and XFree86, have minimum system requirements, even for Pentium-class computers.

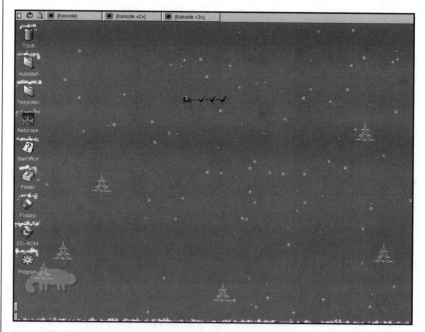

Figure 13.23 *The* xsnow *client can be fun for at least one month each year.*

Even grant that today's PCs are getting faster and more capable, and that many users now have access to broadband technologies such as DSL, some of these games are still out of play for many PCs still in use. On the other hand, if you want to play some of the hottest first-person, 3D real-time arcade or strategy games, you'll find many of those listed in Table 13.1 quite up to snuff.

This section covers a number of commercial arcade and strategy games for Linux and X. If you're interested in any of these games, try downloading a demo first. But be warned: Although most demos are in the 50–60MB download range, some, such as *SimCity 3000*, require more than 180MB just to install the compressed archive.

Strategy Games

Commercial strategy games have traditionally been board games or simulations. However, in the last few years, the difference between animated arcade games, strategy or role-playing games, and simulations has blurred. Today, a number of quite sophisticated strategy simulation games are on the market. This section covers a sampling of these new games for Linux and XFree86.

Call to Power

Civilization: Call to Power, or *CivCTP,* is a strategy civilization game in which the object is to wisely guide the growth of your civilization through thousands of years in sped-up time. This game requires more than 400MB hard drive space, and an X display of at least thousands of colors. As is true for nearly all games discussed throughout the rest of this chapter, installation is script-driven and automatic.

After installation—which can take nearly 10 minutes, depending on your CD-ROM drive's speed—you can start the game play as follows:

```
# civctp
```

After you press Enter, you'll see a splash intro movie. You can then choose the type of civilization and its initial ruler before launching into the simulation, as shown in Figure 13.24.

SimCity 3000

SimCity 3000 is an amazing city simulation and strategy game. Over the years, the popular *SimCity* series of computer games has grown in sophistication, but you have to see this product's details to fully appreciate the game. You can actually see people walking around your city when you play this game, and the level of detail is quite astonishing.

Game play is typical of other simulations as shown in Figure 13.25, which is a shot of a demo version of the game.

Figure 13.24 *CivCTP combines animation and strategy for compelling game sessions in which you guide a civilization from its early stages to maturity.*

Figure 13.25 *SimCity 3000 features extremely fine detail and realism in its city simulation.*

Heroes III

Heroes of Might and Magic is a strategy simulation on a par with *Call to Power*. *Heroes* invites you to build a powerful kingdom over which you rule. This game, like the others, features sound and animation, and requires at least thousands of colors for your X session. Game play is as shown in Figure 13.26, which is a screenshot of a demo version of the game.

Railroad Tycoon II

Railroad Tycoon II combines the strategy simulation features of other games discussed so far with simulation detail that almost rivals that of *SimCity 3000*. One interesting feature of this simulation if that as you buy and build your railroad empire, you can watch trains run across the track that you've laid and bridges that you've built.

Game play is as shown in Figure 13.27, which is a shot of a demo version of the game.

Arcade Games

Commercial arcade games for the PC are very resource-intensive, and seem to extract every resource available on your system. These games have grown ever more sophisticated, and many require the latest hardware, drivers, and software libraries in order to display ever-increasing levels of realism. Some of the games discussed in this section will work on most ordinary X displays of thousands of colors, whereas others are quite picky about video hardware. Carefully examine the system requirements before you buy.

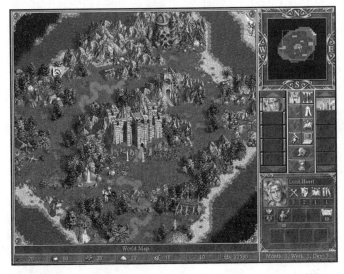

Figure 13.26 *Heroes III features sound and animation as you build a kingdom from scratch.*

Figure 13.27 *Watch your railroads run in Railroad Tycoon II's railroad empire-building strategy and simulation game.*

Quake II and Quake III Arena

Quake, iD Software's killer first-person shooter follow-up to the popular *DOOM* title, has spawned several versions, many additional software scenario add-ons, and even international network competitions. One version, *Quake II,* works well on most types of hardware. *Quake III Arena* (from Loki and iD) requires special hardware, such as a 3dfx Voodoo or Matrox G200/G400 video card and OpenGL software libraries for rendering.

Both versions require nearly 400MB of hard drive space. You can install *Quake II* using as little as 206MB. After installing the binaries and data files (under the /usr/local/games/quake2 directory), you can start the game as follows:

```
$ cd /usr/local/games/quake2
$ ./quake2
```

After you press Enter, you can start play (as shown in Figure 13.28). Press the Esc key to access Quake2's menus and option. Control is via the cursor keys, mouse buttons, and the Shift key, but you can customize all controls.

Figure 13.28 *Quake II is a further adventure into first-person shooter arcade games for Linux and X.*

Heretic II

Heretic II is a commercial version of the original *Heretic* game from iD Software. There is also an Open Source version (albeit still copyrighted by iD) in source code or binary form available at **http://heretic.linuxgames.com/homepage3.html**.

Game play is like that of most first-person shooters, as shown in Figure 13.29, which shows a demo version of the commercial *Heretic II* game.

Figure 13.29 *Heretic II features improvements over the original Heretic, but works on most X displays.*

Resource Information

http://www.lokigames.com—home page for the premier porting and programming shop of commercial games for Linux and X. You'll find links to order games online or to download demos of games that interest you.

http://www.happypenguin.org/—home page for nearly all games for Linux, including some of the best of the latest free role-playing games.

http://www.pimpernel.com/mahjongg/—a Web page where you can play an online (Java) version of mah-jongg.

http://luthien.nuclecu.unam.mx/~pancho/mahjongg/—home page for the GNOME version of mah-jongg.

http://www.mahjongg.com/history.htm—history of the game of mah-jongg.

http://www.floot.demon.co.uk/lincity.html—home page for *LinCity*, a free simulation game for X. You can find active development on new versions through ftp://ftp.eecs.umich.edu/people/gsharp/.

http://jcomm.uoregon.edu/~stevev/Linux-DOOM-FAQ.html—the Linux *DOOM* FAQ.

http://rumsey.dhs.org/xgal.html—home page for the xgalaga game.

http://harkavyr.home.mindspring.com/galaga/galagainfo.htm—the *Galaga* Worship Page, full of history and other lore accumulated by one aficionado. (Note that *Galaga* is a trademark of Namco, Ltd.)

http://www.atarihq.com/tsr/special/tetrishist.html—the history of Alexey Pazhitnov's *Tetris*.

http://www.classicgaming.com—links to interesting histories of classic arcade games.

http://www.linuxquake.com—home page for all you need to know about *Quake* and *Linux*.

http://heretic.linuxgames.com/np/heretic2.shtml—links to versions of *Heretic*, including one for the *Samsung Yopi*.

PART III

Managing the X Window System

Chapter 14: Configuring X11 Input

A USB primer

Keyboard issues

Pointer issues

This chapter introduces software tools and methods that you can use to control, configure, or manage X input. You'll learn about a number of clients used to create, modify, or manage the keyboard and mouse. You'll also learn about issues regarding various new devices supported under Linux and XFree86. Understanding how to install and configure a new pointing device or keyboard for XFree86 can help you overcome obstacles that you face in creating an efficient desktop system for yourself or, if you're a system administrator, other users on your network.

Some of the clients discussed in this chapter are included with XFree86, whereas others may be downloaded from the Internet. Although some issues of pointer support are XFree86 problems, others, such as installing a Universal Serial Bus (USB) mouse, are not. Supporting new devices can require that you work with the Linux kernel. You may have to learn a little about Linux kernel modules and configuration, but you'll find all the information that you need in this chapter.

Linux and XFree86 support a great wealth of input devices. These devices include keyboards, pointing devices as such mice, infrared remote control, touch screens, and voice control via a microphone. This chapter does not cover all these devices, but you can check various Web sites for more information.

Versions of XFree86 prior to 4.0 provided support for a number of graphic input devices, such as tablets and touchscreens. These versions supported joystick input, for example, with a drop-in driver. The "Module" section of the `XF86Config` file specified these supporting drivers , and the "Xinput" section of `XF86Config` required a corresponding entry. Newer versions of XFree86, such as 4.0.1, now include at least five loadable input modules (found under the `/usr/X11R6/lib/X11/modules/input` directory), which are documented in short man pages included with the XFree86 distribution. Currently, Dynapro, MicroTouch, and Wacom drivers are included, along with a mouse, and a *void*, or null-input device (which is used to run X without a pointer or keyboard). To configure the devices that these drivers support, you need to make appropriate entries in your `XF86Config` file's "InputDevice" section.

> Commercial versions of X from companies such as Metro-Link, Inc., provide additional drivers for other input devices, such the Magellan Space Mouse or Labtec SpaceOrb.

Many new devices appearing for the PC market are USB input devices such as keyboards and mice. The next section explains how to incorporate support for this device on a properly configured Linux system so that you can use the USB device during your X sessions.

A USB Primer

Support for USB devices will become a reality with the release of the Linux 2.4 series of kernels. At the time of this writing, the Linux community was poised to receive the new kernel after a long and much anticipated wait during the year 2000. The current stable kernel at the time of this writing is 2.2.18, but many Linux users still use earlier 2.2-series kernels (and 2.0.38 and 1.2.13 kernels).

Because of the popularity of USB, support for these devices was *backported*, or inserted in Linux kernels, starting with 2.2.15. You can now use many USB devices with 2.2.15, 2.2.16, 2.2.17, and 2.2.18. All that is required is the application of a single *patch* file such as `usb-2.4.0-test2-pre2-for-2.2.16-v3.diff.gz`, and a quick recompile of your kernel (see the "Resource Information" section at the end of this chapter). The good news is that most Linux distributions, such as Mandrake 7.2, SuSE 7.1, and Red Hat 7.0, have included USB support in the distributed kernel.

Linux now supports nearly 60 USB input devices such as joysticks, keyboards, and mice. Table 14.1 lists the supported devices.

Table 14.1 Linux Supported USB Devices

Name	Description	Manufacturer
104	Keyboard	Belkin
3-button USB	Mouse	Belkin
3D USB	Mouse	Agiler
9000U Multimedia	Keyboard	BTC
ACK-298	Keyboard	SOLID YEAR
ACK-595U	Keyboard	Solidtek
Ami Mouse USB	Mouse	Trust
Cobra USB Gamepad	Joypad	Creative
Cordless wheel mouse	Mouse	Logitech, Inc.
Cue:CAT USB	Barcode reader	Digital Convergence
F-16 Combat Stick	Joystick	CH Products
FlightSim Yoke LE	Aircraft-style joystick	CH Products
Gamepad Pro USB, Model #4211	Joystick	Gravis
Graphire USB	Graphics tablet (pen and wheel mouse)	Wacom
iMac	Mouse	Apple
KU-8933	Keyboard	Chicony
LYNX 96 USB	Mouse	Micro Innovations

Table 14.1 Linux Supported USB Devices *(continued)*

Name	Description	Manufacturer
M-BA47	Wheel mouse	Logitech, Inc.
M-BB48	Wheel mouse	Logitech, Inc.
M-BD58	Optical wheel mouse	Logitech, Inc.
M-UB48	Wheel mouse	Logitech, Inc.
Model 3B USB	Mouse	Kye/Genius
Mouse	Mouse	Macally
Mouse-in-a-Box Optical Pro	Mouse	Kensington
MY3000 USB 4A CYA	Keyboard	Cherry
Orbit USB/PS2	Trackball	Kensington
PCG-UMS1	Mouse	Sony
Pro Pedals USB Rudder Pedals	Joystick add-on	CH Products
RM-203u (USB-Nest)	USB-to-joystick port	Rockfire
scroll mouse	Mouse	Agiler
T-BB12	Trackball	Logitech, Inc.
T-RA18	Cordless trackball	Logitech, Inc.
Type-6 USB	Keyboard	Sun Microsystems
USB Apple mouse	Mouse	Mitsumi
w/PS/2 mouse port	Keyboard	Keysonic
WingMan Extreme Digital 3D	Joystick	Logitech, Inc.
WingMan Gamepad	Joypad	Logitech, Inc.
WingMan Gaming	Mouse	Logitech, Inc.

Many additional USB pointing devices may be supported by the time you read this book. Check **http://www.linux-usb.org** for details, descriptions and drivers for newly supported devices.

Usually you configure a mouse by using a graphical administration tool included with your Linux distribution, such as the `mouseconfig` command included with Red Hat or Mandrake, or the `yast` command included with SuSE Linux. Newer distributions from Mandrake and Red Hat (version 7.0 and higher) provide for USB mouse configuration via a graphical tool. You can also configure your system manually by loading the correct kernel modules using the `insmod` command.

Directions for configuring a USB mouse for your system will be found in the file named `input.txt` under the `/usr/src/linux/Documentation/usb` directory. One quick way to add support involves loading a proper set of kernel modules (as root) from the Linux input drivers. If your system has USB support, you'll find the modules under the `/lib/modules/2.2.XX/usb` directory, where *xx* is the version of your Linux kernel.

You can check the version by using the `uname` command with its `-r` (revision) command-line option, as follows:

```
# uname -r
2.2.16
```

In this example, the modules will be found under the `/lib/modules/2.2.16/usb` directory. Next, attach your USB mouse, then load the following modules:

```
# insmod input
Using /lib/modules/2.2.16/usb/input.o
# insmod mousedev
Using /lib/modules/2.2.16/usb/mousedev.o
# insmod usbcore
Using /lib/modules/2.2.16/usb/usbcore.o
# insmod usb-uhci
Using /lib/modules/2.2.16/usb/usb-uhci.o
# insmod hid
Using /lib/modules/2.2.16/usb/hid.o
```

This example uses the `usb-uhci` kernel module, which matches the type of USB controller. If you receive an error message, try using the `usb-ohci` kernel module instead to match your computer's hardware. You can then verify the actions of loading the modules by examining your Linux kernel messages using the `dmesg` command:

```
# dmesg
...
usb.c: registered new driver usbdevfs
usb.c: registered new driver hub
usb-uhci.c: $Revision: 1.232 $ time 20:14:50 Aug  2 2000
usb-uhci.c: High bandwidth mode enabled
usb-uhci.c: Intel USB controller: setting latency timer to 0
usb-uhci.c: USB UHCI at I/O 0x1060, IRQ 11
usb-uhci.c: Detected 2 ports
usb.c: new USB bus registered, assigned bus number 1
usb.c: USB new device connect, assigned device number 1
hub.c: USB hub found
hub.c: 2 ports detected
```

```
usb.c: USB new device connect, assigned device number 2
usb.c: This device is not recognized by any installed USB driver.
usb.c: registered new driver hid
mouse0: PS/2 mouse device for input0
input0: USB HID v1.00 Mouse [ USB Mouse STD.  ] on usb1:2.0
...
```

In this example, a generic USB mouse has been detected and mapped to correspond to a PS/2 mouse. If your system's device directory, or /dev, is set up correctly, a subdirectory named input will be under /dev, and you'll find the corresponding mouse device:

```
crw-r--r--   1 root     root      13,  63 Jul 29 07:48 mice
```

You can then use the mouse under the Linux console by first stopping the gpm mouse driver, then restarting it with the following command:

```
# gpm -t ps2 -m /dev/input/mice
```

After you press Enter, you can use your USB mouse at the Linux text console. If you load the module keybdev.o right after the mousedev.o module, your USB keyboard should start working right away. Another way to verify that the modules have loaded is to use the lsmod command, as follows:

```
# /sbin/lsmod
Module              Size   Used by
hid                 11516  0  (unused)
usb-uhci            21604  0  (unused)
usbcore             42760  0  [hid usb-uhci]
mousedev            3724   0  (unused)
input               2908   0  [hid mousedev]
```

Manually loading kernel modules is one way to add USB support. You'll find that newer Linux distributions from vendors such as Red Hat, Mandrake, or SuSE include USB startup scripts under the /etc/rc.d or /etc/rc.d/init.d directory. When in doubt, follow your distribution's documentation and use any graphical administration tools (such as mouseconfig or yast) to add USB support. Note that you'll still need to edit your XF86Config files for now, as many of these tools do not yet automatically update the X configuration file!

Pre-4.0 XFree86 Setup

To use your USB mouse under pre-4.0 versions of XFree86, edit your system's XF86Config file and modify the "Pointer" section. For example, if you have generally used a two-button PS/2 mouse, this section will look like the following:

```
# ********************************************************************
# Pointer section
# ********************************************************************


Section "Pointer"
    Protocol      "PS/2"
    Device        "/dev/psaux"
# Emulate3Buttons is an option for 2-button Microsoft mice
# Emulate3Timeout is the timeout in milliseconds (default is 50ms)
    Emulate3Buttons
    Emulate3Timeout    50
EndSection
```

To add your USB mouse, edit this section to look like the following:

```
# ********************************************************************
# Pointer section
# ********************************************************************


Section "Pointer"
    Protocol      "ImPS/2"
    Device        "/dev/input/mice"
# Emulate3Buttons is an option for 2-button Microsoft mice
# Emulate3Timeout is the timeout in milliseconds (default is 50ms)
    Emulate3Buttons
    Emulate3Timeout    50
EndSection
```

If you're running an X session, log out and restart X. You'll now be able to use your USB mouse.

XFree86 4.0.1 Setup

If you're using the new version of XFree86, you'll again need to edit your XF86Config file. Note that XFree86 supports any number of pointing devices, using the "InputDevice" section to define keyboard, mouse, and other pointing devices. To use your USB mouse, first locate the original mouse "InputDevice" section, which may look like the following:

```
Section "InputDevice"
    Driver        "mouse"
    Identifier    "Mouse[1]"
```

```
    Option          "Device"            "/dev/pointer0"
    Option          "Protocol"          "ps/2"
    Option          "Emulate3Buttons"
EndSection
```

Edit this definition to use your USB mouse instead:

```
Section "InputDevice"
    Driver          "mouse"
    Identifier      "Mouse[1]"
    Option          "Device"            "/dev/input/mice"
    Option          "Protocol"          "ImPS/2"
    Option          "Emulate3Buttons"
EndSection
```

Save your changes, then restart your X session. You'll now be able to use your USB mouse. However, you can also set up your XF86Config file and be able to use more than one pointer at a time. Using the previous example, create a second "InputDevice" section for your USB mouse, and use an identifier such as the following:

```
    Identifier      "Mouse[2]"
```

You'll end up with two "InputDevice" sections that look like the following:

```
Section "InputDevice"
    Driver          "mouse"
    Identifier      "Mouse[1]"
    Option          "Device"            "/dev/pointer0"
    Option          "Protocol"          "ps/2"
    Option          "Emulate3Buttons"
EndSection


Section "InputDevice"
    Driver          "mouse"
    Identifier      "Mouse[2]"
    Option          "Device"            "/dev/input/mice"
    Option          "Protocol"          "ImPS/2"
    Option          "Emulate3Buttons"
EndSection
```

Next, locate the "ServerLayout" section, which should look like this:

```
Section "ServerLayout"
    Identifier      "Layout[all]"
    InputDevice     "Keyboard[0]"       "CoreKeyboard"
```

```
    InputDevice    "Mouse[1]"         "CorePointer"
    Screen         "Screen[0]"
EndSection
```

Add your USB mouse identifier (`Mouse[2]`) to this section like this:

```
Section "ServerLayout"
    Identifier     "Layout[all]"
    InputDevice    "Keyboard[0]"      "CoreKeyboard"
    InputDevice    "Mouse[1]"         "CorePointer"
    InputDevice    "Mouse[2]"         "SendCoreEvents"
    Screen         "Screen[0]"
EndSection
```

Save your file, then restart XFree86. You can now use both pointing devices.

But what if you want to choose which pointer to use when you first start XFree86? That's easy! First, edit your new "ServerLayout" section and *comment out* each mouse's InputDevice entry—that is, insert a pound sign (#) at the beginning of each mouse's InputDevice entry—like this:

```
#   InputDevice    "Mouse[1]"         "CorePointer"
#   InputDevice    "Mouse[2]"         "SendCoreEvents"
```

If you use the `startx` command to begin your X sessions, specify the desired pointer, such as the new USB mouse, by using its name along with the XFree86 server's `-pointer` option, as follows:

```
# startx -- -pointer "Mouse[2]"
```

When X starts, your PS/2 mouse won't work, but your USB mouse will.

Another useful option to add to your `XF86Config` file allows you to start an X session even if the mouse isn't working. Use the `AllowMouseOpenFail` option in a separate "ServerFlags" entry, as follows:

```
Section "ServerFlags"
    Option         "AllowMouseOpenFail"
EndSection
```

Note that this entry will only work if your "ServerLayout" section has a valid "Core-Pointer" entry. In other words, if you try to start an X session without any defined "CorePointer" entries, X will fail to start. If you have a defined "CorePointer" entry and the mouse is not attached or available, the `AllowMouseOpenFail` option will work and allow X to start.

You can use the technique of multiple input device definitions to make additional devices, even keyboards, available during your X sessions. The XFree86 server also recognizes a -keyboard command-line option, and you can define additional keyboards as "CoreKeyboard" input devices. The next section expands on the use of keyboards for XFree86.

Keyboard Issues

Keyboards are an important part of your X session. Using the right keyboard of the right size and at the right height for typing can help reduce the risk of Carpal Tunnel Syndrome. This is a serious condition, usually brought on by severe repetitive stress injury that can eventually become disabling. Affected areas include the back, neck, shoulders, arms, hands, and, more commonly, the wrists and forearms. Symptoms include pain, stiffness, coldness, tenderness, swelling, and numbness.

Some general tips, compiled from various computer manufacturers that want to combat problems and help ensure comfort, include the following:

- Adjust your body position.
- Distribute your weight evenly.
- Keep your elbow height near your keyboard.
- Keep your head vertical and comfortable.
- Keep your keyboard in front of you.
- Keep your thighs level.
- Keep your wrists straight when typing.
- Let go of your mouse when you're not using it.
- Move around occasionally.
- Relax your fingers and thumbs when you type.
- Rest your feet on the floor.
- Support your lower back.
- Take short breaks.
- Type softly.
- Use arm supports if available.
- Vary your posture.
- When typing, use your arm instead of reaching with fingers.

Other factors included the comfort and placement of frequently used keys, the availability of various characters, and the readability of the keyboard during the work session. Fortunately, using Linux and X, you can completely redefine your keyboard and remap keys to accommodate a wide variety of styles and needs. It is up to you, however, to equip your workspace with ergonomics in mind and to make your sessions as comfortable as possible.

Remapping Keys

You can remap the keys on your keyboard using the `xmodmap` client. This client was designed to change the keymap table, which interprets X keyboard events and returns keyboard symbols. This means that you can use this client to swap keys quickly around your keyboard, or even design entirely new keyboards using the command line.

For example, one common gripe among experienced computer users is the loss and replacement of the Ctrl key where the Caps Lock key is now located on QWERTY U.S. keyboards. Many favorite applications, such as editors for Linux, can still use the now legendary *cursor diamond* for cursor movement:

```
    e
asdf
    x
```

Early display terminals usually provided a small Ctrl key, accessed by the left hand's pinky finger. While the user pressed the Ctrl key, the rest of the user's left hand was free to navigate in the direction indicated by the cursor diamond. For example, you could press Ctrl+s to move one character left, Ctrl+a to move one word left, Ctrl+d to move one character right, Ctrl+f to move one word right, Ctrl+e to move up one line, and Ctrl+X to move down one line.

Unfortunately, on most modern U.S. keyboards, the left Ctrl key is placed below the left Shift key. You can quickly remedy this by placing the following key definitions into a file named `.Xmodmap` in your home directory:

```
remove Lock = Caps_Lock
remove Control = Control_L
keycode 0x42 = Caps_Lock
keycode 0x25 = Control_L
add Lock =  Control_L
add Control = Caps_Lock
```

Save the file, which uses the value of the Ctrl and Caps Lock keys in hexadecimal, and then use the `xmodmap` file to read in your definitions to swap the keys for your X session:

```
# xmodmap .Xmodmap
```

Note that your `.Xmodmap` file is generally read in before you start an X session. You could also identify the `Caps_Lock` and `Control_L` keys as follows:

```
remove Lock = Caps_Lock
remove Control = Control_L
```

```
keysym Control_L = Caps_Lock
keysym Caps_Lock = Control_L
add Lock = Caps_Lock
add Control = Control_L
```

Note that in this example, the names of the keys are used instead of numeric keyboard values. One way to verify key definitions and values is to use the xev client, or X event client. Start xev from the command line of a terminal window as follows:

```
# xev
```

After you press Enter, another window will appear, as shown in Figure 14.1.

To find the value for your keyboard's Ctrl key, press the key; then depress the key to release events printed in your original terminal window. As you can see in the strings of output text in the xev window, the values returned by the Ctrl and Caps Lock keys are 66 and 37 decimal, which translate to 0x42 and 0x25 in hexadecimal. Note that xev also reports on pointer movement and mouse button events.

Programming Help

One quick way to translate numbers from one base system to another is to use a programmer's calculator. Although the venerable xcalc client does not offer this feature, the kcalc client included with KDE can translate four different base values. Simply select the input number's base (either decimal, hexadecimal, octal, or binary), enter the number, then click a different base. Note that binary translations work only up to 32,767 decimal.

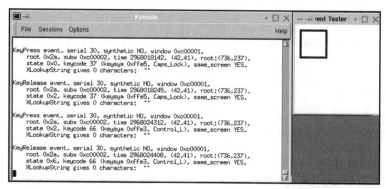

Figure 14.1 *The* xev *client displays mouse, window, and keyboard events.*

Setting Keyboards

Another way to view the values of your keyboard's keys is to use the `xkeycaps` client (not part of the standard XFree86 4.0.1 distribution), which can graphically display nearly 200 different keyboards. You can see a list of the keyboards by using xkey-cap's `-help` option as follows:

```
# xkeycaps -help
   Amiga          - Amiga Non-A1000 (German)
   Mac            - Apple Extended II (MacX; US)
   MkLinux-de     - Apple Extended II (MkLinux; German)
   MacADB         - Apple Standard ADB (NetBSD; US)
   TT             - Atari TT (US)
   Presario       - Compaq Presario 1655 (XInside; US)
...
   TEK401US       - Tektronix Tek-LK401 (US)
   TEK401SF       - Tektronix Tek-LK401 (Swedish TTY)
   TEK401SFDP     - Tektronix Tek-LK401 (Swedish DP)
   TEKsun4        - Tektronix Tek-Sun Type4 (US)
   TEKXN11        - Tektronix XN11 Terminal (Swedish/Finnish)
   TM4000M        - Texas Instruments TravelMate 4000M (US)
   Explorer       - Texas Instruments Explorer (US)
   Tecra          - Toshiba Tecra 500CDT (US)
```

Note that the preceding listing does not show all the command's output. To use xkeycaps, start the client from the command line. After you press Enter, you'll see two windows as shown in Figure 14.2.

If you do not specify a known keyboard type by using xkeycap's `-kbd` option, you can use the smaller, initial window to select a keyboard close to the one that you're using. Scroll through the list, then select your keyboard and click the OK button. The keyboard window will change to reflect the keyboard that you selected, as shown in Figure 14.3.

The type of keyboard that you use for your X sessions should be set in your `XF86Config` file:

```
Section "InputDevice"
   Driver        "Keyboard"
   Identifier    "Keyboard[0]"
   Option        "Protocol"       "Standard"
   Option        "XkbLayout"      "us"
   Option        "XkbModel"       "pc101"
   Option        "XkbRules"       "xfree86"
EndSection
```

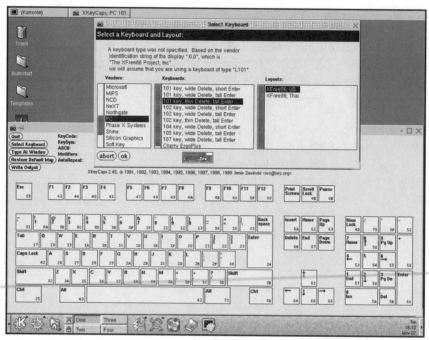

Figure 14.2 *You can use the* xkeycaps *client to display and edit your X11 keyboard.*

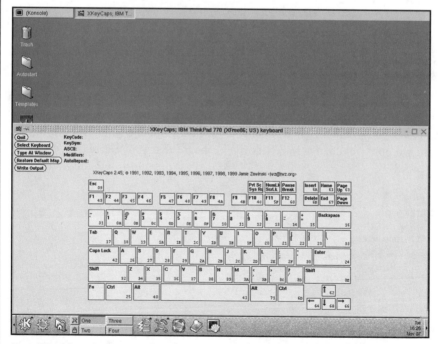

Figure 14.3 *After selecting your keyboard, you can edit or change keys, then save your changes.*

The keyboard rules for this example definition correspond to a set of keyboards defined in the file named `xfree86` under the `/usr/X11R6/lib/X11/xkb/keymap` directory, and the codes are defined in a file named `xfree86` under the `/usr/X11R6/lib/X11/xkb/keycodes` directory. You can use the new selected `xkeycaps` keyboard to match a newly installed keyboard and even remap your entire keyboard. However, this client is best used to make convenient changes to an existing, matching keyboard.

In this example, the selected keyboard is for an IBM ThinkPad laptop. Note that the default key values are shown in hexadecimal. If you right-click on a key, you can exchange that key for another, duplicate it, disable the key, restore its default value, or edit its value. You can then make the key print or return a special character, send a special event to a window manager, or even simulate a type of pointer movement or mouse button event. When finished, click the OK button, then click the Write Output button. You can save the entire keyboard values or just the changed values for the keys that you modified.

The changes will be saved in your home directory in a file named `.xmodmap-`*hostname*, where *hostname* is the name of your system. You can then try the changes using the `xmodmap` command; if you like them, put the changes into your `.xmodmap` file.

Finally, yet another way to view your keyboard and its values is to use the `xkbprint` client. This command generates a printable image of your system's keyboard that you can display using one or more X11 graphics clients. For example, use the `xkbprint` client, along with its `-color` and `-o` command-line options, like this:

```
# xkbprint -color -o mykeyboard.ps :0.0
```

After you press Enter, a PostScript document with the name `mykeyboard.ps` will be saved in the current directory. You can then use the `gv` client to display the keyboard as follows:

```
# gv mykeyboard.ps
```

After you press Enter, you'll see a graphic such as that shown in Figure 14.4.

Pointer Issues

The typical pointing device for X is a three-button mouse. In this configuration, the mouse buttons are labeled (with typical right-handed bigotry) left, middle, and right, or 1, 2, and 3. The right button, or mouse button 3, usually is used to bring up a menu of information about an object, or to display information about an item. You'll notice this behavior if you right-click on an icon or a blank area of the root display.

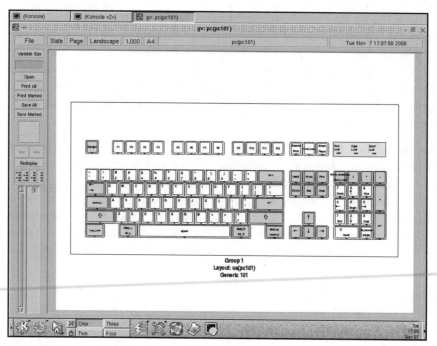

Figure 14.4 *You can use the* xkbprint *client to display a graphic of the currently defined keyboard for your X session.*

The left button, or mouse button 1, is used to select an object, designate an insertion point, display a menu, launch an executable (with a double-click), or drag for multiple selection. You can demonstrate these general actions by clicking in a terminal window and dragging with the left mouse button held down, clicking on a scrollbar and dragging, double-clicking an executable file or icon when using a window manager that supports launching, or clicking in the blank area of the root display.

Finally, the middle mouse button, or mouse button 2, is used to paste copied information, such as text, from one client to another, or to bring up a window menu in the root display. You can see pasting by first highlighting text in one terminal window, then clicking the middle mouse button in another X terminal window.

Some left-handed users will benefit by remapping the mouse buttons, using the xmodmap client to reverse their action. For example, use xmodmap and its -e and pointer options as follows:

```
# xmodmap -e "pointer = 3 2 1"
```

After you press Enter, the buttons will be reversed.

Making Your Keys Easily Accessible

If you don't have a mouse attached to your computer, but you do have a keyboard with a keypad, you can still move your cursor around the screen. The XFree86 server has built-in mouse support that you can enable from the keyboard. To activate this feature, press Ctrl+NumLock. You can then use the keypad on your keyboard to move your cursor, as outlined in Table 14.2.

Table 14.2 XFree86 Keypad Mouse and Pointer Movement

Keypad Key	Action
1	Pointer southwest
2	Pointer south
3	Pointer southeast
4	Pointer west
5	Left- click
6	Pointer east
7	Pointer northwest
8	Pointer north
9	Pointer northeast
.	Release click and hold
0	Click and hold
/	Set 5 to the left mouse button
-	Set 5 to the right mouse button
•	Set 5 to the middle mouse button
Ins	Accelerate pointer

Laptop users will have to hold and depress the special function key, generally used to enable the keypad built into the laptop's keyboard (look to see whether you have a keypad painted along the bottom edges of your *7, 8, 9, 0, u, i, o, p, j, k, l, ;, m, <, >,* and *?* keys).

Yet another way to use the keyboard instead of a mouse is to define keyboard keys to pointer movement in your window manager's resource file. For example, if you use fvwm2 window manager, define the Alt+Ctrl+ (left, right, up or down) cursor keystroke to move your pointer 1/100th across the screen. Edit the file named .fvwm2rc in your home directory and insert the following:

```
# move 1/100th across desktop with Atl+Ctrl+Cursor
Key Left        A       CM       CursorMove -1 +0
Key Right       A       CM       CursorMove +1 +0
Key Up          A       CM       CursorMove +0 -1
Key Down        A       CM       CursorMove +0 +1
```

Save the file, then start your window manager session. If you then press and hold down the Alt+Ctrl keys plus a cursor key, you will move the pointer access the screen. Other window managers support this feature, too.

Changing Pointers

As you probably realize by now, X uses a fairly concise set of pointers. But this doesn't mean you can't change your pointer. You can view a number of available cursors for your pointer by using the xfd client and its -fn option, as follows:

```
# xfd -fn cursor
```

After you press Enter, you'll see the window shown in Figure 14.5.

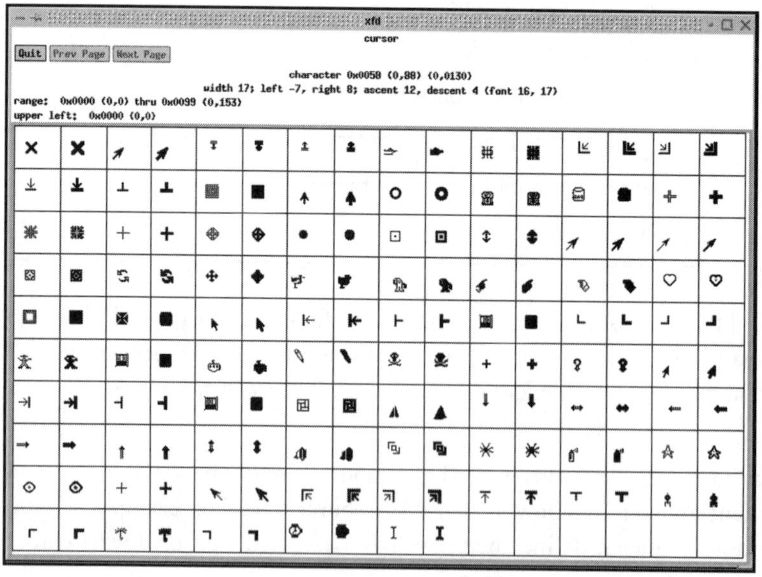

Figure 14.5 *The xfd X client displays the available characters in a designated X font.*

The xfd client displays all the characters available in a specified font. X pointer cursors also have designated names, and are defined in the file cursorfont.h, found under the /usr/X11R6/include/X11 directory if you have installed support for X development on your system. This file lists a name for each character in the font. Use the character's name and the xsetroot client with its -cursor_name option to change your pointer, like this:

```
# xsetroot -cursor_name pirate
```

After you press Enter, your pointer will become a skull and crossbones. For a lighter touch, try the following command:

```
# xsetroot -cursor_name gumby
```

To reset your cursor, use this command:

```
# xsetroot -cursor_name X_cursor
```

Setting Pointers

You can use the xset command to control the speed and threshold setting of your pointer. Simply use the m option and a single integer (to control acceleration) or a set of integers (to control acceleration and threshold) with the command, as follows:

```
# xset m "1 6"
```

After you press Enter, your pointer will move only a short distance relative to movements of your pointer device. On the other hand, you could use the following command:

```
# xset m "30 10"
```

After you press Enter, your pointer will rapidly jump from one end of the screen to another. To reset your pointer value, use the default option as follows:

```
# xset m "default"
```

You can put these xset settings into your system's .xinitrc or .Xdefaults file to customize your X session.

You'll also find a number of clients included with GNOME and KDE that you can use to configure your keyboard and mouse. These clients provide a graphical interface to device administration, and represent a movement away from command-line utilities toward a point-and-click administration of the X desktop. Chapter 16, "Window Manager Configuration," discusses these GUI software tools in greater detail.

NOTE

Resource Information

http://www.xfree86.org/4.0.1/mouse.html—configuration of pointer devices supported under XFree86 4.0.1.

http://www.the-labs.com/HomeAppliance/input.html—links to various input hardware and software driver support pages.

http://atrey.karlin.mff.cuni.cz/~vojtech/input/—home page to the Linux Input Drivers, one of the first places to go if you're looking for support for nearly 200 input devices.

http://www.suse.cz/development/usb-backport/—SuSE's home page for the Linux USB drivers backport.

http://www.linux-usb.org—home page of the Linux USB project.

http://www.suse.cz/development/linux-usb/—a mirror of the home page of the Linux USB project.

http://www.qbik.ch/usb/devices/—a site that keeps tracks of the USB devices that are working with Linux.

http://www.ctsplace.com/—a Web site dedicated to information about Carpal Tunnel Syndrome and computer keyboards, with links to additional information, wrist exercises, an FAQ, and other resources.

Chapter 15: Configuring the X11 Display

Handling resolutions

Managing fonts

Enabling screensaving and enhancing security

Using multihead displays

In this chapter, you proceed with configuring and managing your X system. You'll learn about managing various aspects of your system, such as the display, keyboard, fonts, virtual desktops, and access. You'll also learn about configuring multihead X displays using some of the new features of the XFree86 distribution.

For several reasons, it is important to know how to manage your X display. First, you'll be able to track down and fix any problems quickly, and quickly determine whether a difficulty requires a hardware or software fix. Next, you'll be able to configure more efficient systems, and squeeze the best performance out of your system or systems.

You will put these skills to good use when administering your own system or an entire LAN.

Handling Resolutions

As you've already learned, you can never have too much screen real estate when using X. If you are fortunate enough to have a graphics system capable of resolutions of $1,600 \times 1,200$ at 24-bit-plane color depth or millions of colors, you won't experience the problems of trying to run an X client that needs $1,024 \times 768$ on an 800×600 display.

Although Linux and XFree86 are portable enough to squeeze onto many embedded systems, some of which have displays of 160×160, for all practical purposes displays of at least $1,024 \times 768$ are preferable and the most usable. If your system does not support this resolution, chances are good that you are using a specialized display, perhaps on a notebook such as the Sony Picturebook (which sports $1,024 \times 480$ resolution), legacy computer equipment with a less-capable graphics card and monitor combination, or an embedded device.

You can do a few things in software, however, to overcome display obstacles posed by limited hardware. This section introduces some solutions that you can attempt when using `XFree86` and some window managers.

Using Keyboard Controls

On systems that support X at multiple resolutions, you can define multiple modes in your `XF86Config`'s "Screen" section. For example, a large monitor and graphics card with lots of memory may have a "Modes" line such as the following:

```
...
    Subsection "Display"
```

```
        Depth        16
        Modes        "1600x1200" "1024x480" "800x600" "640x480"
    EndSubsection
```

. . .

In this example, you have a choice of resolutions to use for your X session. You can toggle through these resolutions using your keyboard's keypad if your XF86Config's "ServerFlags" section has disabled the DontZoom feature as follows:

. . .

```
#    DontZoom
```

. . .

You can toggle resolutions on the fly by pressing Ctrl+Alt+[+]/– (that is, the keypad's plus or minus keys). Laptop users usually need to press and hold a special Fn key while performing this toggle to enable the embedded keypad set in the laptop's keyboard. The resolutions will be used in the order in which they appear on the "Modes" line. Most users place the highest resolution first, even though most configuration utilities generate the "Modes" line from lowest to highest resolution by default.

For systems with limited resolution, one possible solution involves the use of a panning virtual desktop, a feature sometimes provided by the window manager used for your X session. Some virtual desktops allow clients to span the current desktop while also allowing transparent borders that move. This capability enables you to *pan*, or shift a window through the desktops using either your pointing device or designated keystroke combinations.

For example, the fvwm2 window manager features settings for control language keywords, such as Scroll, in its resource file, which is either .fvwm2rc in your home directory or system.fvwm2rc under the /etc/X11/fvwm2rc directory:

```
# Let's bind some keys to pan the desktop around
Key Left      A      C      Scroll -100  0
Key Right     A      C      Scroll +100  +0
Key Up        A      C      Scroll +0    -100
Key Down      A      C      Scroll +0    +100
Key Left      A      M      Scroll -10   +0
Key Right     A      M      Scroll +10   +0
Key Up        A      M      Scroll +0    -10
Key Down      A      M      Scroll +0    +10
```

These settings enable the user to press Shift+Ctrl+ a cursor key (left, right, up or down) to move the pointer, and Alt+Shift+ a cursor key to pan the desktop.

Editing XF86Config

Another solution involves modifying the resolution settings in your system's XF86Config file. XFree86 provides special keywords that you can use in the file to specify a larger display than your system's hardware can ordinarily allow. These displays are known as a *virtual* resolutions. The Xfree86 server handles the panning or shifting of the display automatically, regardless of the window manager used for your X session.

Configuring Virtual Resolution Settings

If you examine your current XF86Config file, you may or may not see any virtual resolution settings. The file most likely will provide these settings when you are using X at less than optimal resolutions. The amount of video memory installed on your system can also determine whether the file displays the settings. For example, if your system sports 2MB of video RAM, and an optimal (that is, hardware-limited) display resolution of 1,024×768, you may not be able to use a virtual desktop larger than the optimal resolution. On the other hand, you most certainly will be able to use a virtual screen during X sessions at a resolution of 800×600, because the system will not need to use extra video RAM. The color depth of your X session will also have bearing, as extra video memory is required as more bit-planes are used.

Virtual resolutions are entered in the "Display" subsection of your XF86Config's "Screen" section, and two keywords are particularly pertinent to the settings. The first is the Virtual keyword, followed two integers: a value of X for horizontal pixel width, and a value of Y for vertical pixel height. These entries specify the virtual resolution, with one caveat: X must be a multiple of either 8 or 16 for color, and a multiple of 32 for the monochrome X server. The second keyword that you can use is ViewPort. Like Virtual, the ViewPort setting also requires trailing X and Y entries, but in many cases, these entries are set to zero (0). This is because the ViewPort setting tells the X server where to place the initial upper-left corner of the display.

Therefore, a system with the capability to display X at 1,024×768 at thousands of colors, but only 800×600 at millions of colors, will limit the size of the virtual display. In the following example, not all Virtual settings will be available at higher resolutions, especially at greater color depths. This example can be a good place to start, but you will have to experiment with your system to determine the limits of resolution and virtual settings:

```
Section "Screen"

                ...

    Subsection "Display"
        Depth       8
        Modes       "1024x768"   "800x600"   "640x480"
```

```
                    Virtual      1600 1200
    EndSubsection
    Subsection "Display"
        Depth       16
        Modes       "1024x480"   "800x600" "640x480"
                    Virtual      1280 960
    EndSubsection
    Subsection "Display"
        Depth       24
        Modes       "800x600"    "640x480"
                    Virtual      800 600
    EndSubsection
EndSection
```

After experimentation in using different color depths and resolutions, this section could look like:

```
Section "Screen"

                    . . .

    Subsection "Display"
        Depth       8
        Modes       "1024x768"   "800x600" "640x480"
                    ViewPort     0 0
                    Virtual      1280 960
    EndSubsection
    Subsection "Display"
        Depth       16
        Modes       "800x600"    "640x480"
                    ViewPort     0 768
                    Virtual      1024 768
    EndSubsection
    Subsection "Display"
        Depth       24
        Modes       "640x480"
                    Virtual      800 640
    EndSubsection
EndSection
```

In this example, an X session started with 256 colors would have a 1024×768 screen starting at the upper-left corner of a 1280×960 display. If the session is started with thousands of colors (a color depth of 16), the 800×600 display will be started at the lower-left corner of a 1024×768 display. When millions of colors are requested, the 640×480 display will be centered in an 800×640 virtual window.

Managing Fonts

Font use under X11R6 can seem mysterious and difficult to set up and administer, but the fact is that fonts are quite easily managed using X11, on a workstation or even across a network. XFree86 has built-in facilities and comes with a number of clients that you can use to manage fonts on your system. You'll find plenty of documentation and guidance on using fonts included with your system.

Using the xfs Font Server

The `xfs` font server is a critical element in managing fonts when using X in a networked environment. Using `xfs`, you can offload font storage to faster computers on your LAN or to computers with more storage. The server also responds dynamically to requests to add or remove fonts from a particular X session.

You do not have to use `xfs` for your X session, particularly on a standalone workstation. If you do not, a correct FontPath entry in your system `XF86Config`'s "Files" section is essential. For example, on a standalone workstation with adequate storage and resources, you can dispense with the font server and simply tell the X server where to find the system fonts, like this:

```
...
Section "Files"
     RgbPath     "/usr/X11R6/lib/X11/rgb"
     FontPath    "/usr/X11R6/lib/X11/fonts/misc/"
     FontPath    "/usr/X11R6/lib/X11/fonts/75dpi/:unscaled"
     FontPath    "/usr/X11R6/lib/X11/fonts/100dpi/:unscaled"
     FontPath    "/usr/X11R6/lib/X11/fonts/URW/"
     FontPath    "/usr/X11R6/lib/X11/fonts/Type1/"
     FontPath    "/usr/X11R6/lib/X11/fonts/Speedo/"
     FontPath    "/usr/X11R6/lib/X11/fonts/75dpi/"
     FontPath    "/usr/X11R6/lib/X11/fonts/100dpi/"
EndSection
...
```

Note that the preceding listing does not show all the output of the `XF86Config` file. The "Files" section, which also tells the server the location of the 8-bit-plane color database, can contain detailed listings and pathnames of the locations of different fonts.

Note that you can also use NFS- or Samba-mounted filesystems to store your X fonts; they do not have to reside on the local filesystem, although most Linux users choose to install thousands of fonts locally so that they can access the fonts quickly. However, if you're going to resort to networked storage for providing fonts, a better approach is to use xfs font server.

You'll find a number of X font utilities included with Linux and XFree86, such as the following:

- afm2tfm, which converts a font-metrics file to a TeX font metrics file
- bdftopcf, which converts a binary format font to .pcf format
- chkfontpath, a FontPath utility for the xfs font server
- getafm, which creates a font-metrics file from a PostScript font
- fsinfo, which displays font server information
- fslsfonts, which displays fonts known by the xfs font server
- fstobdf, which converts an xfs server font into a .bdf font file
- ftinfo, which displays information about a TrueType font
- mkfontdir, which creates an index of a font directory
- showfont, which prints specified font data
- xfd, which displays a font's characters
- xfontsel, which displays available X fonts and enables you to select one
- xlsfonts, which displays your system's installed and recognized X11 fonts

Installing Fonts

Fonts are usually installed under the /usr/X11R6/lib/X11/fonts directory in a subdirectory associated with the type of font. For example, you'll now find a Type1 font directory included with newer XFree86 distributions such as 4.0.1:

```
$ ls /usr/X11R6/lib/X11/fonts
100dpi/    PEX/      Type1/      mdk/     mozilla-fonts/
75dpi/     Speedo/   drakfont/   misc/    pcf_drakfont/
```

Each directory will contain one or more additional files, such as fonts.dir, an index of the directory's fonts, and fonts.alias, an index of short names of fonts. Outside of this index of shortened names, font names can be as long as the following example:

```
-adobe-courier-bold-r-normal--25-180-100-100-m-150-iso8859-2
```

XFree86 can use a variety of fonts during your X sessions. Fonts are distributed in binary, ASCII, outline, and portable formats. You'll find the more common ASCII or ISO8859-1 Latin 1 character set used during most sessions, but also European language fonts, Asian language fonts, and Unicode fonts. These additional fonts were developed to support the world's languages and to provide for characters with accents or characters in graphic form. Thus Xfree86's fonts can support languages, such as Japanese or Korean, that require thousands of characters.

The most critical FontPath entry in your XF86Config file is for the fonts contained in the misc directory. If the X server is unable to find this directory, launching your X session will fail and the server will abort.

Changing Font Use with xset

Use the xset client to add or remove fonts during your X session. You can use this client to alter the xfs font server's font path on the fly, by using the client's +fp command-line option as follows:

```
# xset +fp /usr/local/share/fonts/misc
```

After you press Enter, fonts under the specified directory will become available for your X session, and will be added to the beginning of your FontPath. You can also specify remote displays by using the -display option like this:

```
# xset -display dell:0.0 +fp /usr/X11R6/lib/X11/fonts/mdk
```

This command enables your local X session to use the fonts from the mdk directory on the remote host named dell.

Using TrueType Fonts

A great feature of the new XFree86 4.0.1 distribution is built-in support for True-Type fonts. If you use a previous or 3.3-X-series of XFree86, you'll need to resort to using a specialized font server, such as xfstt.

One quick and easy way to add fonts to your system, especially if you use a dual-boot system, is to copy the Type1 or TrueType fonts included with the Windows operating system installed on your system. If you copy these fonts into an X11R6 font directory, you can use them during your X sessions (you may as well get some use out of what is otherwise worthless software, right?).

Although you can use any directory, the best approach is to create a directory (perhaps named winfonts) under the /usr/X11R6/lib/X11/fonts directory to hold the fonts. Next, copy all .ttf files from your Windows partition into the new directory. You can quickly locate these fonts if you have the partition mounted, by using the find command as follows:

```
# find /mnt/dos -name *.ttf -print | less
```

After you press Enter, you may find the fonts under the /mnt/dos/windows/fonts directory. Press the **q** key to quit the less browser, then copy the files like this:

```
# cp /mnt/dos/windows/fonts/*.ttf /usr/X11R6/lib/X11/fonts/winfonts
```

After the copying is done, use the ttmkfdir and mkfontdir commands to make the requisite fonts.scale and fonts.dir files in the new fonts directory, as follows:

```
# cd /usr/X11R6/lib/X11/fonts/winfonts
# ttmkfdir -o fonts.scale
# mkfontdir
```

To use these new fonts during your X session, you can either add the new directory to your XF86Config's FontPath section or, if you use the xfs font server, add the new directory to the xfs configuration file, found under /etc/X11/fs:

```
...
# where to look for fonts
#
catalogue = /usr/X11R6/lib/X11/fonts/misc:unscaled,
4        /usr/X11R6/lib/X11/fonts/75dpi:unscaled,
         /usr/X11R6/lib/X11/fonts/misc,
         /usr/X11R6/lib/X11/fonts/Type1,
         /usr/X11R6/lib/X11/fonts/Speedo,
         /usr/X11R6/lib/X11/fonts/75dpi,
         /usr/share/fonts/default/Type1,
         /usr/X11R6/lib/X11/fonts/winfonts
...
```

Finally, restart xfs (if you're using a Red Hat–based system), as follows:

```
# /etc/rc.d/init.d/xfs restart
```

You'll now be able to use the new fonts!

Enabling Screensaving and Enhancing Security

Just because Linux and XFree86 are Open Source doesn't mean that you'll always want anyone to be able to see what you're doing during your X sessions. Using a screensaver is one way to secure your system, and to make your X sessions and workstation secure from prying eyes during and even after a workday.

Security is an issue that is facing more and more computer users every day. Your personal information is coming under closer scrutiny every day; from surreptitious

Dealing with Privacy and Unwanted Mail

Intrusions on your privacy today also include getting unwanted Internet email from nuisances such as electronic mail spammers; these foul miscreants and scofflaws deserve far more than just the castigation and scorn of today's online society. Their offal litters the hard drives of millions of computer users, and their unwanted intrusion, even if inadvertently invited, can be more than just a nuisance. If you live in a state that provides remedies against unwanted electronic mail, pursue your rights! Some states, such as California, Virginia, and Washington, allow for a fine of up to $500 per instance for unwanted electronic mail. Some ISPs, such as FlashNet, issue a fine of $1 per sent email and a $1,000 cleanup fee. Even if your suit in small claims court is against an out-of-state party, you should then forward claims and complaints to the pertinent state's attorney general for prosecution.

The best approach is first to get a good education on the types of violations that can incur penalties in your state. If your state does not have laws with penalties regarding unwanted electronic mail, contact your local elected representative and demand action. You don't have to live with spam. For those spam emails arriving from overseas, you should carefully examine the electronic email headers to find out where the mail entered your system, then sent a complaint to your ISP. If your ISP is unresponsive, you can also send your complaint to the Mail Abuse Prevention System LLC, which maintains the Realtime Black Hole (RBL). ISPs that find themselves on the RBL will quickly realize the importance of not functioning as a gateway for spammers.

commercial software that uploads the contents of your hard drive over the Internet, to greedy corporate data mining of your consumer habits, this information begs for protection.

Using xset

The xset client is a versatile program that you can use to set many different user preferences during your X sessions. You can also use the client to control screensaving. To turn on screensaving, first use the xset command, along with its s option, followed by the number of seconds before screensaving is to start, like this:

```
# xset s 60
```

Next, to enable screensaving, use a pertinent keyword, such as on, as follows:

```
# xset s on
```

To turn off screensaving, use the `off` keyword, as follows:

```
# xset s off
```

Blanking the screen is one way to provide privacy of the display when a workstation is not in use, but it doesn't provide any measure of security. Other clients, discussed in the next few sections, provide a bit more security.

Using xlock

The `xlock` client, part of the XFree86 contributed software, can be used to provide password protection for an idle X session. This client has an extensive list of command-line options, and features many different screensaving effects. To see a sample of the effects right away without password protection, use its `-nolock` and `-mode` options as follows:

```
# xlock -nolock -mode random
```

To "lock" your display right away, simply use `xlock` without its `-nolock` option, as follows:

```
# xlock
```

After you press Enter, the display will turn blank and screensaving will start. To return to your session, click a mouse button or press a keyboard key. The program then prompts you to type your password and press Enter before you can return. To see a list of `xlock`'s options, read its man page, or use its `-help` command-line option as follows:

```
# xlock -help
```

Using xscreensaver

The `xscreensaver` client features a client/server model in which it is a daemon component and resides in memory as a process. The `xscreensaver-command` client is then used to control screensaving. Start the process by invoking `xscreensaver` as follows:

```
# xscreensaver &
```

After you press Enter, you can control screensaving with the `xscreensaver-command` client and its command-line options. For example, to start screensaving, use the client like this:

```
# xscreensaver-command -activate
```

To see the current settings, use the `-prefs` option as follows:

```
# xscreensaver-command -prefs
```

After you press Enter, you'll be able to enter settings in a graphical dialog box and selectively choose password requirements. This client features many different settings, such as password-entry timeouts, fading, and nearly 100 different screensaving effects. You can use many of the effects in the root display, or background of your desktop, providing animated X sessions.

For the best security, always use passwords for screensaving and never leave workstation passwords in your work area. Also, make sure to take advantage of your computer's BIOS password facilities. If your equipment is stolen, the thieves may never be able to change your system settings. Laptop users can benefit from this approach, as laptops also offer BIOS password protection from suspend, sleep, and hibernation modes.

Using Multihead Displays

One of the new features of the XFree86 4.X series of X distributions is the support of Xinerama, the use of multihead displays, similar to a feature supported by the Apple Macintosh for nearly 15 years. To take advantage of this feature, you must use the new XFree86 4.0.1 server and have one or more compatible graphics cards installed on your system.

XFree86 offers several types of support for use of multiple monitors. First, having multiple instances of the X server, such as running multiple X sessions, can support the use of one or more monitor resolutions and color depths. Second, you can have one or more monitors display simultaneous desktops during a single X session. Finally, a single instance of the X server can be used as a session that takes advantage of Xinerama, which allows windows to span physical borders (that is, the monitors' borders).

The current limitation is that you cannot associate different color depths with each display when using a single instance of the X server with the desktop as a contiguous display. One possible solution may be to run multiple instances of the X server using different color depths (provided you have adequate memory). Clients then may be started remotely between displays, and the user can activate displays through the use of keyboard commands, such as Ctrl+Alt+Fn (that is, a specified function key).

Choosing a Video Card

Any supported video card should enable you to use Xinerama, but peculiarities of your system's motherboard could cause big problems. You'll need to decide if you want to use two peripheral component interconnect (PCI) video adapters, a single multihead video card, or one accelerated graphics port (AGP) video card and one PCI video adapter. Although an AGP adapter is not necessarily faster than a PCI video card, your choice may be determined by whether your motherboard has a limited number of PCI slots. Also, if your video subsystem is integral to your computer's motherboard, check whether the subsystem is automatically disabled when another video card is detected.

Some of the better cards include those from Matrox, which have built-in dual- or quad-head support. This support will save you from having to buy an additional card, and is the perfect solution for a dedicated system that requires a single graphics card. The Matrox G400 multihead card (an AGP card) is used in the examples described in the following sections.

Compliant Clients and Window Managers

Currently, the window managers that best support multihead displays are Enlightenment, sawfish, and perhaps Window Maker. There are problems, at the time of this writing, even with the latest version of KDE 2.0 (such as dialog boxes spanning displays when they open), and even with this desktop environment you must use an alternative window manager instead of kfm.

Configuring XF8Config

You'll need to create several specialized sections in your XF86Config file to craft support for multiple monitors. Support for multiple devices, monitors, screens, and layouts is built into XFree86 4.0.1. Your first task is to create unique entries for each monitor, video device, and screen.

For example, if your system will use two monitors—with one a 15-inch liquid crystal display (LCD) and the other a 17-inch multisync display—create a "Monitor" section for each, and provide a unique identifier like this:

```
Section "Monitor"
    Identifier   "NECXV17"
    HorizSync    31-65
    VertRefresh  55-100
EndSection


Section "Monitor"
    Identifier   "LCD"
    HorizSync    31-65
    VertRefresh  56-75
EndSection
```

In this example, the X session will use an NEC XV17 labeled "NECXV17" and a Samsung LCD monitor labeled "LCD." If you plan to use two video cards, you'll need to determine the BusIDs reported by your cards. To find out the BusID for your video cards, you can use the X server with its -scanpci command-line option, as follows:

```
# XFree86 -scanpci

...

Probing for PCI devices (Bus:Device:Function)

...

(1:0:0) Matrox unknown card (0x2179) using a Matrox MGA G400 AGP

...
```

This example shows the results (1:0:0) on a desktop PC, using a Matrox G400 dual-head AGP video card. Note that the G400 card does not report two PCI BusID numbers, even though two video adapters are built into the card. If you have two cards installed, the X server should report two unique BusIDs.

You should next define your graphics devices. Again, include a unique identifier for each device, in a "Device" section like the following:

```
Section "Device"
     Identifier     "G4001"
     Driver         "mga"
     Option         "DigitalScreen" "yes"
     BusID          "PCI:1:0:0"
     Screen         0
     VideoRam       32768
EndSection


Section "Device"
     Identifier     "G4002"
     Driver         "mga"
     BusID          "PCI:1:0:0"
     Screen         1
     VideoRam       32768
EndSection
```

In this example, note that each device is assigned a unique identifier. The Driver field specifies the XFree86 driver mga_drv.o, so that is the driver that will be loaded from the /usr/X11R6/lib/modules/drivers directory when X starts. The DigitalScreen option is required for this driver if the display is an LCD panel (in this case, the "yes" setting indicates that the LCD will be used for a particular card). Next, note that each Device definition is assigned a screen number, starting with 0 for the first screen.

Now that you have defined your monitors and video devices, you'll need to create a separate "Screen" section for each, using the screen number, device identifier, and monitor identifier, like this:

```
Section "Screen"
     Identifier        "Screen 0"
     Device            "G4001"
     Monitor           "LCD"
     DefaultDepth      16


     Subsection "Display"
         Depth          16
         Modes          "1024x768"  "1280x1024"
         Virtual        1024         768
     #   ViewPort       0            0
     EndSubsection
EndSection


Section "Screen"
     Identifier        "Screen 1"
     Device            "G4002"
     Monitor           "NECXV17"
     DefaultDepth      16


     Subsection "Display"
         Depth          16
         Modes          "1024x768"  "1280x1024"
         Virtual        1024         768
     #   ViewPort       0            0
     EndSubsection
EndSection
```

Each "Screen" section uses your previous definitions and also includes a "Display" subsection with color depth and resolution settings. To avoid any problems, this example uses identical settings that work on each monitor. As you can see, the "Screen" section determines the assignment of a card to a display as well as the display's characteristics.

When you decide how to arrange your monitors, you'll need to create or edit one or more ServerLayout sections. Each section will use at least two screen numbers, along with a screen ID and position information or a placement keyword to specify which display to place where in relation to the main display. The ServerLayout section uses information derived from at least two "Screen" sections.

For example, to define a layout named "Dual-head" using the monitors side by side with the LCD on the left, create a ServerLayout section like this:

```
Section "ServerLayout"
    Identifier  "Dual-head"

    Screen  "Screen 0" LeftOf "Screen 1"
    Screen  "Screen 1"

    InputDevice "Mouse1" "CorePointer"
    InputDevice "Keyboard1" "CoreKeyboard"
EndSection
```

This layout creates a contiguous display in which you can drag windows or active clients across a virtual border between the monitors. After editing your XF86Config, start your X session using the startx command. You'll also need to use the +xinerama command-line option as follows to enable your layout:

```
# startx -- +xinerama
```

Your XF86Config file can also have multiple ServerLayout sections. For example, if you simply want a simultaneous display instead of a contiguous display between monitors, use a layout like the following:

```
Section "ServerLayout"
    Identifier  "Simultaneous"

    Screen  "Screen 0"
    Screen  "Screen 1"

    InputDevice "Mouse1" "CorePointer"
    InputDevice "Keyboard1" "CoreKeyboard"
EndSection
```

In this example, both monitors will display the same X session at the same time. You can choose which layout to use by using the X server's -layout command-line option, along with the layout's name, as in either of the following two examples:

```
# startx -- +xinerama -layout Dual-head
# startx -- +xinerama -layout Simultaneous
```

If you have defined multiple layouts, but don't choose one on the command line, X will use the first defined layout.

Resource Information

http://www.xfree86.org—home page for XFree86, and the place to start if you want to learn more about font handling and security using XFree86.

http://mail-abuse.org/—Home page for the Realtime Blackhole list, *the* place to go for information about dealing with spammers and unresponsive ISPs that allow spam email through their servers.

http://dlis.gseis.ucla.edu/people/pagre/spam.html—an early article on dealing with spammers.

http://www.mcnichol.com/spam.htm—Washington state's antispam laws explained.

http://www.math.utah.edu/~beebe/fonts/X-Window-System-fonts.html—a thorough discussion of fonts and X11.

http://www.linuxdoc.org/HOWTO/mini/FDU/index.html—Doug Holland's guide to better use of X fonts.

http://www.xfree86.org/4.0/RELNOTES2.html—release notes regarding Xinerama use, with cautions regarding color depth across displays.

http://www.xfree86.org/4.0.1/RELNOTES.html—release notes for XFree86 4.0.1 and Xinerama use.

http://www.linuxdoc.org/HOWTO/Xinerama-HOWTO.html—Dennis Baker's how-to on using two or more displays to take advantage of XFree86 4.0.1's Xinerama extensions.

http://www.kde.org/documentation/faq/index.html—KDE 2.0 FAQ at the KDE home page.

http://www6.tomshardware.com/graphic/98q3/980702/—Tom Pabst's hardware page, with information regarding the difference between AGP and PCI video adapters.

http://www.matrox.com/mga/support/drivers/latest/home.cfm—home page for the latest XFree86 drivers for various Matrox graphics cards.

Chapter 16: Window Manager Configuration

his chapter introduces configuration of various popular window managers for XFree86. You'll find an amazing variety of window managers for Linux and X, and choosing a favorite can be difficult. You'll also learn about some of the unique features of each window manager and how you can configure each to work the way you want.

One of the best reasons to use Linux and XFree86 is to be able to choose an alternative window manager for use during an X session. Choosing which window manager to use from the hundred or so available for X can be a challenge, but as you gain experience, your personal tastes and needs will dictate your favorite environment. A number of the window managers discussed in this chapter support different *themes*, or desktop schemes, in which various sets of window controls, colors, and decorations are available, with each set radically or subtly different.

Although some window managers may be a challenge to configure, nearly all respond to changes in configuration text files stored on your system. In most cases, if a graphical configuration tool is offered to change the theme or configuration of a window manager, you should probably use the supplied tool.

Remember that although a window manager is nothing more than an X11 client, using XFree86 without a window manager isn't much fun. This chapter covers some of the more popular window managers for XFree86:

- AfterStep, which features a *wharf*, or docking station for icons and windows
- fvwm, which features basic window management, including virtual desktops
- fvwm2, an improved version of fvwm
- GNOME-aware window managers, which include Enlightenment and sawfish, two of most popular window managers used with GNOME
- KDE, one of the newer desktop environments for XFree86, includes a suite of hundreds of clients
- mlvwm, a window manager that mimics the classic MacOS desktop
- mwm, which is the original Motif and LessTif clone window manager with virtual desktops and a configurable desktop menu
- twm, which is included with XFree86 and provides minimal window management
- Window Maker, the GNU X11 window manager with improved features from AfterStep
- wm2, a window manager with a limited set of features

You'll probably find a number of these window managers available on your Linux distribution's CD-ROMs (especially if you use SuSE Linux). KDE and GNOME are the most popular desktop environments for most Linux users. You'll also see how easy it is to build and install some window managers from scratch.

> You'll find many additional window managers for Linux and XFree86 at **http://www.plig.org/~xwinman/**.

Configuring the twm Window Manager

The twm, or Tab window manager, is installed by default under the /usr/X11R6/bin directory, and is included with every XFree86 distribution. Originally developed by Tom LaStrange, twm offers only the most basic features for supporting window management, such as a root menu, basic window controls, and the use of icons.

You can find the twm window manager's system-wide configuration file, system.twmrc, under the /etc/X11/twm directory, although older versions of XFree86 or other Linux distributions may locate this file under the /usr/X11R6/lib/X11/twm directory. (New distributions use symbolic links that point to /etc/X11/twm.) Users can customize the system-wide file by copying it with the name .twmrc into the home directory.

Some Linux distributions allow you to specify a desired window manager on the startx command line as follows:

```
# startx twm
```

However, most Linux users who use the startx command will enter the following lines into the .xinitrc file in their home directory:

```
exec xterm &
exec twm
```

This example launches the xterm client and then the twm window manager. After you start your X session, you can access twm's root menu by left-clicking in a blank area of the desktop. This menu is defined in your copy of .twmrc in your home directory. You can use favorite text editor, such as pico, to edit this file, as follows:

```
# pico -w .twmrc
```

This command line disables line-wrapping with pico's -w command-line option. When you examine the file, you'll find twm's root menu defined in the defops section:

```
menu "defops"
{
"Twm"             f.title
"Iconify"         f.iconify
"Resize"          f.resize
"Move"            f.move
"Raise"           f.raise
"Lower"           f.lower
""                f.nop
"Focus"           f.focus
"Unfocus"         f.unfocus
"Show Iconmgr"    f.showiconmgr
"Hide Iconmgr"    f.hideiconmgr
""                f.nop
"Kill"            f.destroy
"Delete"          f.delete
""                f.nop
"Restart"         f.restart
"Exit"            f.quit
}
```

In some older distributions of XFree86 and Linux, the default configuration does not include a menu item to launch a terminal window. This means that unless you first launch a terminal window and then start twm, you have no way to access a terminal window. Fortunately, newer Linux and XFree86 distributions (such as Mandrake) now include a menu item for at least launching the xterm client. To insert a menu item for xterm or another terminal client, add a definition such as the following:

```
"Launch xterm client"  f.exec  "exec xterm &"
```

Save the file, then restart X. The next time that you use twm, you'll be able to launch a terminal window easily.

Configuring the fvwm2 Window Manager

The original fvwm window manager, a descendant of twm, was created by Robert Nation and is usually found with other X clients under the /usr/X11R6/bin directory. This window manager has now been superseded by a newer version named fvwm2, but with the name fvwm. Both versions support virtual desktops, offer win-

Confused After Building from Source?

New Linux and XFree86 users can become confused when switching between Linux distributions; likewise, users who are accustomed to using a particular Linux distribution can become disoriented when building software from scratch. This is because not every Linux distribution places configuration files under the same paths or includes the same versions of window managers. If you build fvwm from scratch using default settings and source code from its home page (see "Resource Information" at the end of this chapter), you'll find fvwm installed under the /usr/local/bin directory with the name fvwm2. However, fvwm's system-wide configuration file will not be installed during the build. (You'll need to copy the file manually from the source's fvwm-2.2.4/extras/FvwmScript/Scripts/ directory into a new fvwm directory under /etc/X11, then edit the file for your system.) The new version may also be three times the size of the installed version from your commercial distribution. Keep in mind that building and installing a window manager from scratch can often involve additional configuration tasks not required when using the same window manager installed from a commercial Linux distribution.

dow controls, and provide support for loadable modules that can add additional window management features. The system-wide older fvwm configuration file is named system.fvwmrc, and is usually located under the /etc/X11/fvwm directory. Like twm, this file may be copied as .fvwmrc and saved your home directory for per-user customization. The newer fvwm2 window manager's system-wide configuration file is named system.fvwm2rc, and is found under the /etc/X11/fvwm2 directory. It too may be copied as .fvwm2rc and saved in your home directory.

As an example resource file change, you can customize the number of virtual desktops available for your X sessions when using fvwm2 by editing the desktop section, which may look like this:

```
DeskTopSize 2x2
```

This section defines the default number of virtual desktops, which appear in the desktop's pager window, and which you can access by left-clicking on the appropriate square in the pager's window. To add 12 more desktops, change the entry as follows:

```
DeskTopSize 4x4
```

When you restart fvwm2, you'll see a small grid of 16 desktops in the pager.

Configuring the fvwm95 Window Manager

The fvwm95 window manager, by Robert Nation, is based on fvwm2 and adds improvements such as a hierarchical start menu and a taskbar. As with the earlier versions, you can build custom menus and change effects by editing a configuration file.

If you build and install fvwm95 from source, the majority of this window manager's support files will be located under the /usr/local/lib/X11 directory. To build and install fvwm95, download and decompress the source, navigate into the source directory, then use the package's configure script and the make command like this:

```
# tar xvzf fvwm95-2.0.43a-Autoconf.tgz
# cd fvwm95*
# ./configure ; make install
```

The system-wide configuration file, system.fvwm95rc, will be found under the /usr/local/lib/X11/fvwm95 directory. Again, as with twm and fvwm2, copy the system.fvwm95rc file as .fvwm95rc and save it in your home directory to make your customizations. The configuration file consists of sections for fonts, windows, modes, menus, startup, and mouse and keyboard bindings.

For example, one mode customization issue regarding pointer movement and window placement is that of *focus,* or when or how a window should be made active. You can select from one of the following operating modes:

```
Style "*" ClickToFocus
#Style "*" MouseFocus
#Style "*" SloppyFocus
```

This example, taken from the default system.fvwm95rc file, does not make a window active until the user clicks the window or its contents. If you prefer that a window becomes active when the pointer merely hovers over a part of the window and then becomes inactive when the pointer does not hover over any portion of the window, *uncomment* the MouseFocus line—that is, remove the pound sign (#) in front of the line—and place a pound sign in front of the ClickToFocus line. If you use the SloppyFocus setting, a window will become active after the pointer passes over the window, but will stay active even after the pointer is no longer hovering over a part of the window.

Another mode to enable in conjunction with focus is whether or not to have a window that is made active will be placed over any other windows. To do this, you'll also need to uncomment the following section:

```
#+ "I"  Module FvwmAuto 500
```

In this example, if you click on a window's title bar, it will automatically be placed on top of any other overlapping windows.

Configuring the K Desktop Environment

Version 1.0 of the K Desktop Environment (KDE) for Linux and X was released in July 1998. Since then, KDE has become one of the most popular desktop environments and suite of X clients for XFree86 and Linux. KDE and its host of accompanying programs provide many features not supported by legacy window managers. Some of these features include session management, Network Transparent Access (NTA) (which allows the user to drag and drop files via remote file lists), mounting of filesystems with a mouse click, graphical control of window hints, sounds for system events, *sticky buttons* (which place an instance of a single client on each virtual desktop), and a pop-up command-line interface (CLI). This section introduces configuration tips for managing logins, managing the desktop's panel, and graphically configuring KDE using the KDE Control Center.

Using kdm

As you already know, to configure the X display manager (xdm) for use, you edit the system's /etc/inittab file, or initialization table. The entry in inittab that boots Linux to a multi-user X session might look like this:

```
id:5:initdefault:
```

However, other Linux distributions, such as SuSE, may use a different run-level, such as the following:

```
id:3:initdefault:
```

Note that in this example, SuSE Linux uses run-level 3 for a multi-user X session. The other required entry in your inittab file specifies a display manager for the run-level and manages logins. A corresponding run-level entry (such as for Red Hat Linux) will look like this:

```
x:5:respawn:/usr/bin/X11/xdm -nodaemon
```

KDE in Transition

At the time of this writing, KDE 2.0 had just been released. A long-awaited sequel to the previous 1.1.2 stable version, KDE 2.0 introduces new software libraries, many updated clients, a new window manager, and a fledgling office suite. For all discussions regarding KDE, this book refers to KDE 2.0 even though many readers may still be using the older version.

To use KDE's display manager instead of xdm, change the entry and specify the correct path to the kdm client, as follows:

```
x:5:respawn:/usr/bin/kdm -nodaemon
```

When you restart Linux, the kdm client will then manage logins to your X sessions. If you'd like to try kdm before committing your system to a particular run-level, you can also (as root) use kdm from the text-only console as follows:

```
# kdm -nodaemon
```

After you press Enter, the screen will clear and you'll see a kdm login window. You can manage kdm via the KDE Control Center (see the following section, "Using the kcontrol Client").

NOTE

Make sure that you have correctly configured XFree86 to work with your system before you edit your system's initialization table. If you find that your system, upon rebooting, alternately flashes a blank screen and tries to run X, there's a problem. If this happens, press Ctrl+Alt+Del to reboot your system, then enter the kernel argument **linux single** at the LILO boot: prompt to reboot Linux into single-user mode. You can then undo any changes made to your inittab file or fix the problem (which could range from a bad XF86Config file to an incorrect entry in your .xinitrc file).

Using the kcontrol Client

The KDE Control Center, named kcontrol, is a graphical utility used to control many different aspects of a KDE session. Table 16.1 lists the controls that this client provides.

Click the application starter button on your panel, then click the Control Center menu item. The client will appear as shown in Figure 16.1.

For example, to change settings for kdm's login display, users, and sessions, click the System list item in the kcontrol window. Next, click the Login Manager in the drop-down list. Note that you must be running as root in order to change any of these settings. The Login Manager dialog box appears as shown in Figure 16.2.

You can change the greeting text, show a custom logo, display the time, and alter language and country settings for the display. To change fonts, the background, or user access, or to add or remove X session types from the kdm login screen, click on the appropriate tab in the dialog box.

Table 16.1 KDE kcontrol Functions

Module	Controls
File Browsing	File associations; file management, behavior, and appearance; trashcan behavior
Help	Search engine control and pathnames; language settings
Information	System hardware, filesystem, network, sound, and X server status
Look & Feel	Colors, fonts, icons, keys, panel, screensaver, taskbar, themes, window behavior, desktop background, borders, and virtual desktops
Network	Talk and Windows shares configuration
Peripherals	Keyboard and mouse settings
Personalization	Accessibility, country and language, cryptographic, email, keyboard layout, and password controls
Power Control	Display Power Management System (DPMS) control
Sound	Midi, mixer, system bell, and system and event sound controls
System	Date, time, and kdm login display and management controls
Web Browsing	Controls for konqueror file manager and Web browsers, such as Netscape; display of bookmarks

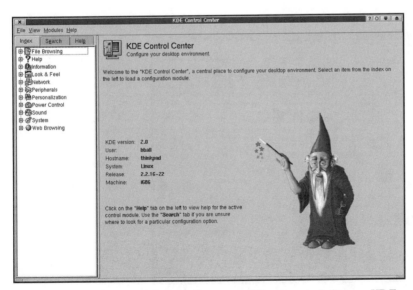

Figure 16.1 *The KDE Control Center offers many different controls for your KDE logins and sessions.*

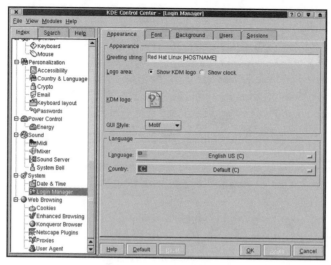

Figure 16.2 *The Login Manager is used to change the appearance, permissions, and actions provided by* kdm.

Changing Color Schemes

Click the Look & Feel item, then click the Colors list item to alter the color scheme used for your KDE session's windows. A dialog box, as shown in Figure 16.3, appears.

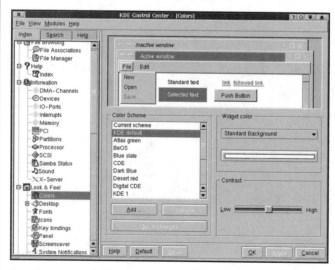

Figure 16.3 *Change color schemes used by all windows during your KDE sessions by using* kcontrol's *Colors dialog box.*

Scroll through the list of schemes, then click the Apply button. Another unique feature is the ability to change the contrast of the colors by using the slider control.

Changing KDE Themes

Although changing color schemes can make your KDE sessions look radically different, a new feature introduced with KDE 2.0 is advanced *theme management,* or the ability to change nearly every aspect of all windows, dialog boxes, and controls used during your KDE session. Again click the Look & Feel item, then click the Themes list item, then click the Style list item to select a new KDE theme, as shown in Figure 16.4.

Scroll through the list of themes, then click the Apply button to use your new settings.

Changing the Desktop Wallpaper

KDE 2.0 comes with more than two dozen different .jpg files you can use as wallpaper for the background of your desktop. You can also use nearly any .jpg file for this task. To do so, click the Look & Feel item, then click the Desktop list item. Scroll through kcontrol's Desktop items, then click Background. You'll then see the dialog box shown in Figure 16.5.

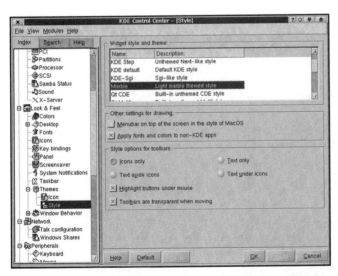

Figure 16.4 *Select a new KDE theme for your KDE sessions by using* kcontrol's *Style dialog box.*

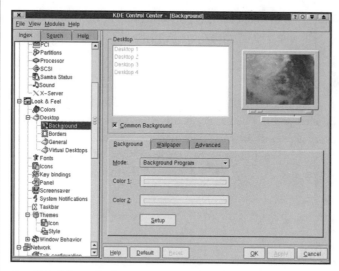

Figure 16.5 *Select a background program or a wallpaper to use in the root display during your KDE sessions.*

Click the Background tab in the dialog box, then click the Mode drop-down menu list and select Background Program. Next, click the Setup button, then click to select a client to run in the root display, as shown in Figure 16.6.

When finished, click the OK button, then click the Apply button. You'll then see the program running in the root display, as shown in Figure 16.7.

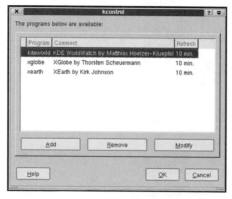

Figure 16.6 *Select a client to run in the background using KDE 2.0's Background Program feature in the* kcontrol *window.*

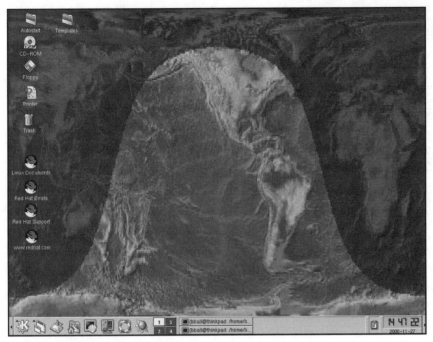

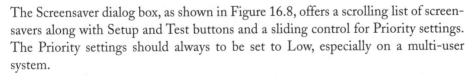

Figure 16.7 *KDE 2.0 supports running selected clients (such as* kworldwatch *shown here) in the root display of your desktop during your KDE sessions.*

Configuring Screensaving

KDE 2.0 comes with 27 different screensavers that you can set up and test using the Screensaver list item from kcontrol's Look & Feel function.

> You don't always have to launch kcontrol to configure or activate settings for your KDE sessions. You can also select the panel's Preferences menu item followed by an appropriate menu item to change various settings.

The Screensaver dialog box, as shown in Figure 16.8, offers a scrolling list of screensavers along with Setup and Test buttons and a sliding control for Priority settings. The Priority settings should always to be set to Low, especially on a multi-user system.

If you click the Require Password check box, KDE will require you to enter your password before returning from a screensaving session. Unfortunately for fans of the earlier version of KDE, it is no longer possible to set up special active "hot corners" of the display to turn on screensaving immediately.

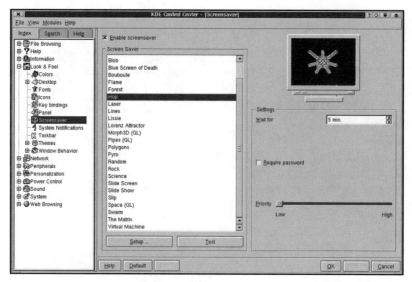

Figure 16.8 *The Screensaver dialog box also offers password control for KDE session screensaving.*

Using KDE System Sounds

Although changing your KDE windows or background or using a different theme can provide visual stimulation, you can also use a specific sound for specific KDE or AOL Instant Messenger events during your X sessions. KDE 2.0 recognizes 38 separate system notifications and window events to which you can assign a sound. Table 16.2 shows a list of these events, such as opening or closing windows, along with integral AOL Instant Messenger chat events.

Table 16.2 KDE and AOL IM System Sound Events

System	Events
System Notification	No match found; more than one match found; cannot open the file; serious program error and exit; log out; start up; program error; miscellaneous; desktop has changed
Window Event	Another is active; close; restored; deleted; virtual desktop selected; iconified; maximized; done moving; new window; done resizing; begin resizing; shade up; made sticky; dialog box deleted, new dialog box
AOL Event	Buddy list member offline; buddy list member online; message arrival; message sent; now offline; now online; warning

To assign sounds, first ensure that you have properly configured Linux to work with your computer's sound card. Next, click the Look & Feel list item, then click the System Notifications list item. You'll see a dialog box, as shown in Figure 16.9, that you can use to assign a sound to a system event.

You can also have KDE notify you visually by displaying a message box, sending a message to the standard output, or creating a log entry in a specified file, which can be handy to track users.

Configuring the Keyboard and Mouse

Even though you can use the xset and xmodmap clients to control your pointer and keyboard for your X sessions, KDE includes graphic keyboard, mouse, and pointer controls. For example, to change the order of your mouse buttons, the behavior of mouse clicks, and even the shape and size of your pointer, click the Mouse list item under the Peripherals drop-down list menu. You'll see the Mouse dialog box shown in Figure 16.10.

To change how fast or slow your mouse moves across the screen, click the Advanced tab. You can then set threshold and acceleration values similar to those settings offered by the xset command.

When finished, click the Apply button. Note that if you change the cursor size, you'll need to restart your KDE 2.0 session.

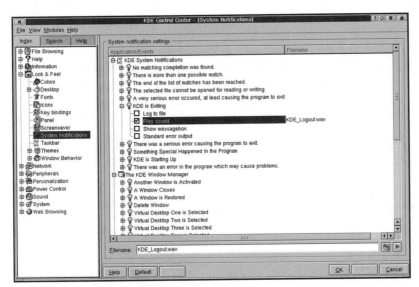

Figure 16.9 *Assign sounds to a system notification or window event using System Notifications.*

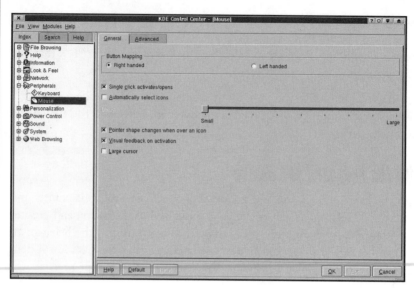

Figure 16.10 *The General tab of the Mouse dialog box offers changes to button mapping and pointer size.*

Just Mousing Around!

You can specify other mouse actions by using the Mouse Behavior dialog box. To access this dialog box, click the Window Behavior menu item under Look & Feel list item. You use this dialog box to determine window behavior according to the type of mouse click. Other settings dependent on your pointer include active or inactive desktop borders. By changing the defaults in the Borders dialog box (which you can access by clicking Look & Feel, then Desktop, then finally Borders), you can set KDE to allow you to navigate to different virtual desktops by moving your mouse to the current desktop border. You can also set up KDE so that you can navigate through the desktops by pressing Ctrl+Tab.

Configuring the Panel

The typical KDE panel provides an application starter menu, client icons, session control buttons (such as buttons to lock the screen or log out), virtual desktop buttons, and other program icons and information, such as the clock and calendar at the far right. To configure the desktop panel, click the application starter button, then select the Panel menu, then Configure, then the Settings menu item.

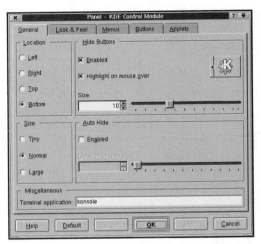

Figure 16.11 *The KPanel Control Module dialog box is used to configure panel settings for your KDE session.*

The KDE Control Module dialog box will appear as shown in Figure 16.11. From this dialog box, you can configure different settings, including the following:

- *Location* enables you to set the location of the panel on the display, the panel's size, and the panel's behavior.
- *Look & Feel* allows you to add animation effects and use themes in the background of the panel.
- *Menus* enables you to configure the number of menu entries to display, as well as the behavior of the application starter menu.
- *Buttons* allows you to specify the behavior and display of panel buttons.
- *Applets* enables you to configure which applets, or embedded clients, are used in the panel.

When you are finished configuring your settings, click Apply, then click the OK button.

You can manually configure the panel by right-clicking an icon, then selecting Remove, Move, or Properties from a small pop-up menu. The Move item allows you to drag the icon across the panel and release it in a different place. Clicking Remove deletes the icon. By clicking the Properties item, you can change the name, permissions, action, icon image, and pop-up name for the icon.

Editing the Panel Menu

Use the Menu Editor item from the Configure submenu of the panel's Panel menu to change the desktop's application starter menus. The KDE Menu Editor dialog box

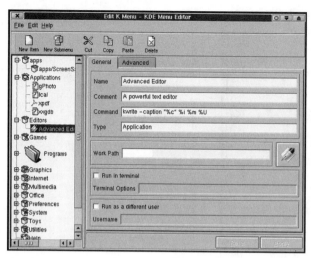

Figure 16.12 *The Menu Editor dialog box enables you to add or remove menu items from the panel's menus.*

then appears as shown in Figure 16.12. You can then use the different fields to edit an existing menu or create a new menu for your KDE session.

You can also add applications to the panel by selecting the Add menu item from the Panel menu's Application submenu.

Configuring the GNOME-aware Window Managers

GNOME (GNU Network Object Model Environment) is a programming project derived from earlier work and development of the GTK++ libraries used to create the GNU Image Manipulation Program, or the GIMP. GNOME programmers distribute their work under the GNU GPL, which allows anyone to share source code or build programs. Unlike using Qt software libraries for KDE, which still requires licensing if you want to build binary-only software, using GNOME projects is royalty- and license-free.

GNOME is a set of software libraries and a suite of clients that use the software libraries. These libraries provide sophisticated windowing, event, and drawing capabilities in a unique X session. One of the reasons that GNOME is unique is that it provides a framework that enables any GNOME-aware window manager to support features such as a desktop panel, session-management, drag-and-drop, animation, and a consistent client interface during the X session.

Configuring GNOME

Configuring GNOME while running a GNOME session is actually the act of configuring the window manager used to support the session. You select many of the configuration options, including the choice of the window manager to use with GNOME, through the GNOME Control Center, as shown in Figure 16.13.

For example, after launching the Control Center via the panel's Start menu, click the Desktop item, then click the Window Manager list item. You'll see a list of recognized, GNOME-aware window managers listed in the dialog box. Using this dialog box, you can alternatively try or reset your choice of window manager on the fly.

Other configuration options offered by the Control Center include document handling, sound, external filesystems, session startup, and user interface elements, such as windows, buttons, and dialog boxes. Many of these settings are also available via the panel's Start menu, as shown in Figure 16.14.

Like KDE, GNOME offers settings to handle the background, screensaving, keyboard, mouse, and virtual desktops. And like KDE's panel, the GNOME panel may be customized with additional applets, new application buttons, and different orientations, such as along the left, right, or top of the display.

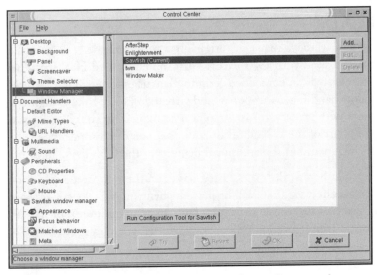

Figure 16.13 *The GNOME Control Center is used to configure nearly every aspect of your system and X session, including your choice of window manager.*

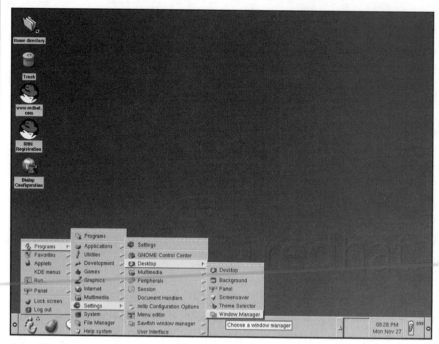

Figure 16.14 *You can also use your GNOME desktop panel instead of the GNOME Control Center to configure your X session.*

Configuring sawfish

John Harper's `sawfish` window manager, originally named `sawmill`, is now the default window manager used with GNOME as distributed by Red Hat, Inc. This window manager uses Lisp as an embedded scripting language for enabling features such as menus, window handling, focus policy, and virtual desktops. Like Enlightenment, `sawfish` comes with an easy-to-use graphical configuration tool. You'll most likely use `sawfish` as part of the GNOME desktop, but you can also use this window manager on its own, without the additional benefits of the GNOME libraries.

You can customize a number of files when using `sawfish`. In your home directory, you can create a `.sawfishrc` file that will be parsed when you start your X session. Many users will probably want to use `sawfish`'s built-in configuration root menus, or launch the companion configuration utility, `sawfish-ui`, as follows:

```
# sawfish-ui &
```

If you run `sawfish` by itself, you'll see the window shown in Figure 16.15 after you press Enter.

You can select different themes by clicking the Appearance item, then the drop-down menu in the editor's dialog box. Using the `sawfish-ui` client, you can change

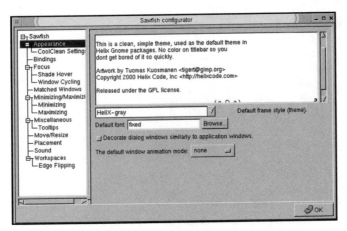

Figure 16.15 *The* `sawfish` *window manager's* `sawfish-ui` *configuration utility provides a graphic configuration tool for your X* `sawfish` *sessions.*

nearly any aspect of your X session when `sawfish` is used as the window manager. The client automatically saves any changes in a file named `custom` under your home directory's `.sawfish` subdirectory.

Configuring Enlightenment

One of the earliest window managers to support GNOME was Enlightenment, also known as E. Developed by Carsten Haitzler and Geoff Harrison, this accelerated window manager may be used with or without GNOME. Theme support was an early feature of Enlightenment. At one time, Enlightenment was destined to be the premier window manager for use with GNOME, but the client has since evolved to include many of its own desktop environment features.

Enlightenment stores most of its information on a per-user basis in a subdirectory named `.enlightenment` in your home directory. Under this subdirectory, you'll find backgrounds, icons, and themes directories, although the four default Enlightenment themes and other information are stored under your system's `/usr/share/enlightenment` directory.

Configuring Enlightenment is quite easy, as this window manager has an accompanying graphical configuration tool named `e-conf`. You can launch this tool from the GNOME window manager dialog box in the GNOME Control Center, or from the command line of an X11 terminal window, as follows:

```
# e-conf &
```

After you press Enter, you'll see Enlightenment's Configuration Editor window as shown in Figure 16.16.

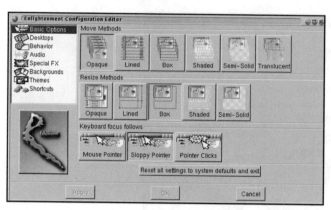

Figure 16.16 *Use Enlightenment's* e-conf *Configuration Editor to configure different aspects of the client's behavior and appearance.*

You can use the Configuration Editor to edit basic options, desktops, behavior, sound, animation, backgrounds, themes and keyboard shortcuts. For example, you can change the pointer focus with a few mouse clicks or install a new theme using the theme dialog box. Click Apply to see the effect after each change, then click the OK button to exit the editor.

You can also change many of Enlightenment's behaviors by right-clicking in a blank area of the root display. A Settings menu, as shown in Figure 16.17, then appears.

This menu is even more comprehensive than the Configuration Editor, and even includes settings for compatibility with KDE.

Figure 16.17 *Access Enlightenment's Settings menu by right-clicking a blank area of the desktop.*

Configuring the AfterStep Window Manager

Many Linux distributions include AfterStep as a legacy window manager. At one time, AfterStep had eclipsed older window managers in features, but it now seems somewhat dated compared to KDE 2.0, GNOME, and Enlightenment. Originally fashioned after the Bowman window manager (itself a modification of fvwm), After-Step was modified and improved to include many of the features of the NeXTSTEP graphical interface. AfterStep provides a *wharf* for docking client icons, as well as other expected niceties, such as a desktop menu, virtual desktops, window animation, and, in the latest version, themes and GNOME compatibility. This window manager—like fvwm, fvwm95, and others—builds from source and installs quite quickly and easily on today's PCs running Linux and XFree86. To install AfterStep, enter the following commands:

```
# tar xvzf AfterStep*gz
# cd AfterStep*
# ./configure ; make install
```

After building and installing AfterStep from scratch, you'll find its system-wide configuration files under the /usr/local/share/afterstep directory. You can then use the startx command to launch AfterStep for your X session if you enter the following line in your .xinitrc file:

```
exec afterstep
```

When you first start AfterStep, it creates a GNUStep subdirectory in your home directory. This subdirectory can contain customizations, although you can control nearly all of AfterStep features through its root menu, as shown in Figure 16.18.

Figure 16.18 *Use AfterStep's root menu by clicking in a blank area of the desktop, then selecting the Desktop menu.*

Configuring the Window Maker Window Manager

Window Maker, originally by Alfredo Kojima, is an improved version of the After-Step window manager. In its latest version, Window Maker now provides for graphical configuration, an application and workspace dock, theme support, keyboard support, virtual desktops, window and menu animation, and internationalization support for different national languages.

The actual filename of this window manager is wmaker, and in some Linux distributions its system-wide configuration files are located under the `/usr/X11R6/share/WindowMaker` directory. If you want to build and install this window manager from scratch, you'll need to download the following files:

- `libPropList-0.10.1.tar.gz`, a special software library that provides data structures and lookups
- `WindowMaker-0.62.1.tar.gz`, the source to Window Maker
- `WindowMaker-extra-0.1.tar.gz`, which provides themes, icons, and other utilities

Building and installing Window Maker is quite simple. You simply enter the following commands:

```
# tar xvzf libProp*gz ; cd libPro* ; ./configure ; make install
# tar xvzf Windo*62*gz ; cd Window* ; ./configure ; make install
# tar xvzf Win*extra*gz ; cd *extra* ; ./configure ; make install
```

After building and installing Window Maker, you then need to run the `wmaker.inst` command as follows:

```
# wmaker.inst
```

The `GNUstep` subdirectory in your home directory will be created to hold your personal settings, whereas the `/usr/local/share/WindowMaker` directory contains backgrounds, icons, graphics files, style and theme subdirectories, along with configuration and startup scripts. You can then start up `wmaker` from your `.xinitrc` file as follows:

```
exec wmaker
```

In past versions, you had to edit the file `WMRootMenu` in the `GNUstep/Defaults` subdirectory in your home directory. However, using Window Maker's root menu, as shown in Figure 16.19, you can change the appearance of your desktop to a specific background, style, or theme. You can then save the custom appearance as your own theme.

Configuring the mwm Window Manager

The Motif window manager, known as mwm, has traditionally been a part of the Motif software development library distribution from the Open Group. Motif, until

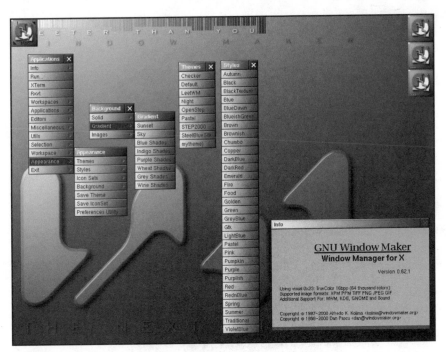

Figure 16.19 *Use Window Maker's root menu to create and then save your own custom themes for your X sessions.*

recently, was a commercial product and distributed under license. Early Linux and XFree86 adopters had to pay for a Motif distribution for Linux until the advent of the LessTif X11 Toolkit libraries, a clone of Motif available without royalties or licensing fees.

With the release of mwm, you no longer have to pay to get the LessTif mwm window manager, a functional equivalent of the legacy Motif mwm. Thanks to the efforts by the Hungry Programmers starting in 1995, Linux users can now enjoy the benefits of a highly compatible Motif 1.2 clone.

Although derived from fvwm, the LessTif mwm uses the original window manager's syntax in its resource file. As with other legacy window managers, this window manager's system-wide configuration file, system.mwmrc, is located in a directory with the window manager's name (mwm) under the /usr/X11R6/lib/X11 directory, and you can copy the file with the name .mwmrc into your home directory.

For example, you can add the xcalc client to the root menu by editing your copy of .mwmrc. Look for a menu section, which should look like the following example:

```
Menu DefaultRootMenu
{
        "Root Menu"                    f.title
```

```
"New Window"              f.exec "xterm -e /bin/bash &"
"Shuffle Up"             f.circle_up
"Shuffle Down"           f.circle_down
"Refresh"                f.refresh
"Pack Icons"             f.pack_icons
"Toggle Behavior..."     f.set_behavior
 no-label                f.separator
"Restart..."             f.restart
"Restart fvwm"           f.restart "fvwm"
"Quit..."                f.quit_mwm
}
```

As you can see in this example, the only default client available is xterm. You can add xcalc by inserting a menu definition directly after the "New Window" entry. The definition should look like the following example:

```
"Calculator"             f.exec "/usr/X11R6/bin/xcalc &"
```

Make your changes, save the file, then start your X session. You'll see the new menu, as shown in Figure 16.20.

You can build LessTif's mwm window manager using the source included with Less-Tif, although many Linux distributions, such as SuSE Linux, include a binary version of the LessTif distribution. You can use mwm for your X session by including the window manager in your .xinitrc file.

After you start your session, you can access the root menu by right-clicking in a blank area of the desktop. You can also edit mwm's app-defaults file, named Mwm, under the /usr/X11R6/lib/app-defaults directory.

See Chapter 20, "Using LessTif and Open Motif," for more information about programming with the Motif and LessTif software libraries.

Root Menu
New Window
Calculator
Shuffle Up
Shuffle Down
Refresh
Pack Icons
Toggle Behavior...
Restart...
Restart fvwm
Quit...

Figure 16.20 *Edit your* .mwmrc *root menu definition to add additional clients for your* mwm *X sessions.*

Configuring the mlvwm Window Manager

Takashi Hasegawa's `mlvwm` window manager uses a simple Apple Macintosh desktop theme that includes drop-down menus from a bar across the top of the display. This window manager features virtual desktops and a simplified "Balloon Help," (or pop-up help messages).

The program builds easily from source code. Simply enter the following commands:

```
# xmkmf
# make install
```

After building the program, copy the file `Mlvwmrc` from the `sample_rc` directory to a file named `.mlvwmrc` in your home directory. This file contains pathnames and entries in `mlvwm`'s client menu, which you can access by clicking the upper-left corner of the display, just as you would when using the Macintosh operating system. To use this window manager, add `mlvwm` to your `.xinitrc` file as follows:

```
Mlvwm
```

After you start your session, you should see a window similar to that shown in Figure 16.21.

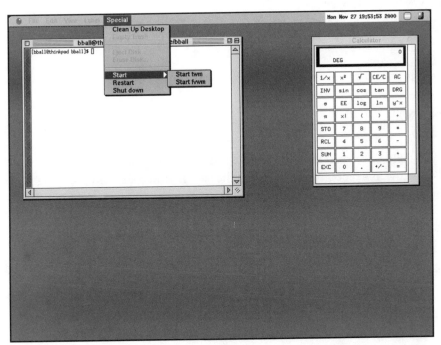

Figure 16.21 *Edit* `mlvwm`'s `.mlvwmrc` *file to build your root menu definitions when using mlvwm for your X sessions.*

Configuring the wm2 Window Manager

Chris Cannam's wm2 window manager wins the prize as the smallest window manager discussed in this book. The source code distribution consists of 32KB of compressed files, and when built, the source code results in a binary on most systems of less than 200,000 characters. This window manager's best feature is its lack of features; wm2 doesn't even provide any icons, virtual desktops, root menu, or configuration file.

The only way that you can configure the wm2 window manager is by editing a source code file named Config.h:

```
...

#define CONFIG_NEW_WINDOW_COMMAND "xterm"

...

***PD: End code
```

You can set colors by editing another portion of the file:

```
***PD: Begin code

...

#define CONFIG_TAB_FOREGROUND      "black"
#define CONFIG_TAB_BACKGROUND      "gray80"
#define CONFIG_FRAME_BACKGROUND    "gray95"
#define CONFIG_BUTTON_BACKGROUND   "gray95"
#define CONFIG_BORDERS             "black"


#define CONFIG_MENU_FOREGROUND     "black"
#define CONFIG_MENU_BACKGROUND     "gray80"
#define CONFIG_MENU_BORDERS        "black"

...
```

After you build wm2, insert wm2 into your .xinitrc file in your home directory. You can also use the xsetroot command to set the background color before starting your X session, as follows:

```
xsetroot -solid lightblue
wm2
```

Resource Information

http://www.fvwm.org—home page for the fvwm window manager.

ftp://mitac11.uia.ac.be/html-test/fvwm95.html—home page for the fvwm95 window manager.

http://www.kde.org—the home page and starting place to learn more about the K Desktop Environment. You can also download beta or newer (but perhaps unstable) versions of KDE from this site.

http://www.enlightenment.org—home page for Enlightenment.

http://www.gnome.org—home page for the GNOME project, and a great place to learn more about how to use GNOME and where to download additional GNOME-aware clients for X and Linux.

http://www.afterstep.org—home page for the AfterStep window manager.

http://www.windowmaker.org—home page for the latest version of Window Maker.

http://www.lesstif.org—home page for LessTif, a project by the Hungry Programmers, and a clone version of OSF/Motif. LessTif includes development libraries and a window manager named mwm.

http://www.plig.org/~xwinman/—the best place to cruise for related links to many different window managers.

http://www.sawfish.org—a site dedicated to distributing the latest releases of sawfish and themes.

http://sawmill.sourceforge.net/—home page for the sawfish window manager.

http://www2u.biglobe.ne.jp/~y-miyata/mlvwm.html—home page for mlvwm, a Macintosh-like window manager.

http://www.all-day-breakfast.com/wm2/—home page for wm2, a stripped-down window manager with minimal features.

PART IV

X11 Programming

Chapter 17: Building X11

Installing XFree86 development components

Building from source

This chapter covers building and installing XFree86 from source. You'll learn how to download, decompress, and build the XFree86 4.0.1 distribution from scratch. Although few if any Linux and XFree86 users perform these tasks, doing them can be informative and an integral part of the process of learning technical details about XFree86. The tasks are also necessary if a required patch or fix appears for the current distribution and you need to build a revised driver or server in order to use X11 on your new hardware.

This chapter explains how to download the essential files and components of XFree86 source distribution, and covers the essential elements required before you can build XFree86. Coverage is limited to XFree86 4.0.1, which was released July 3, 2000, and which presents a radically new architecture to support X with Linux.

According to the XFree86 Project, Inc., the organization's current work is focused on providing updates and fixes to the older 3.3.6 series and adding new features to the 4.0-series server. The next release of XFree86, according to **http://www .xfree86.org/releaseplans.html**, is to have version 4.0.2 "...available sometime in late 2000." The current version at the time of this writing is 4.0.1, and it is this new architecture that merits coverage instead of the older, multiserver distributions.

Installing XFree86 Development Components

To build XFree86, you should have a working Linux development system installed on your computer. Ideally, you should use the same versions of software and libraries that the XFree86 Project, Inc., uses to build its distribution. However, in general, you will run into fewer problems if you use a current GNU gcc compiler, along with a set of current #include files and software libraries.

You'll have even fewer problems if you're merely installing a patch and rebuilding the current XFree86 distribution. In other words, try to match the development tools with the version of XFree86 currently in use. Although you can try, it may not be possible to use an older Linux distribution, such as Red Hat 5.2, to host and build XFree86 version 4.0.1.

Although XFree86's documentation does not include specific references to recommended versions of development tools, it does refer to versions of free software development tools that should not be used. Although The Open Group touts X11R6.4, the base and source for XFree86 4.0.1, as "... the easiest release to build yet," the release has some pitfalls:

- *Applying patches.* If you need to customize a particular driver, apply the patch as directed. You'll need the `patch` command and possibly the `diff` command. There will usually be some additional patches that you'll want to apply before the build.

- *Configuration.* You'll need to configure the source for use with Linux. The configuration files include various *flags* (settings) that you need to specify before starting the build.

- *Compiling.* According to The Open Group, you cannot use the GNU `gcc` compiler version 2.5, 25.1, or 2.5.2 to build the software. In addition, some versions of Red Hat Linux include a development version of the `gcc` compiler that may or may not build portable binaries, even with compatible software libraries. You should probably use the latest stable version if possible. The compiler used to test the build for this chapter was `gcc` version 2.95.2, used under Mandrake Linux running Linux kernel 2.2.14-15mdk (Mandrake 7.0).

- *Other caveats.* You may have problems linking old libraries if your Linux distribution has a broken runtime loader. The GNU `make` command is not compatible; the XFree86 source includes a `make` command that will be built and used. According to The Open Group, the GNU `as` assembler and `ld` linker are not supported or will not work for rebuilding X (although the build and resulting binaries worked fine on the test system for this chapter). New library names will be used by the rebuilt server and X clients, even if you build a version commensurate with the installed version; the recommended approach, according to The Open Group, is to install the new libraries by symbolically linking the old library to the new one.

Downloading Source Archives

You can obtain the source code for XFree86 in a variety of ways. One of the easiest is to download the files via FTP from **ftp://ftp.xfree86.org/pub/XFree86/4.0.1/source**. You'll find the following files:

- `FILES`—a list of all files in each archive
- `SUMS.md5`—checksums of the files to ensure validity
- `SUMS.md5sum`—checksums of the archives to ensure validity
- `X401src-1.tgz`—source to the XFree86 server, clients, documentation, libraries, and contributed clients
- `X401src-2.tgz`—XFree86 fonts and font utilities
- `X401src-3.tgz`—XFree86 hardcopy documentation
- `doctools-1.2.tgz`—documentation creation tools

The XFree86 4.0.1 source distribution includes more than 11,000 files. You'll need at least 53MB to store just the compressed archives and files. When decompressed, the source code requires more than 227MB of hard drive space. According to the XFree86 folks, you can get by with using only the first archive (X401src-1.tgz) if you already have X11 fonts installed on your system. The documentation tools package is used to format the XFree86 documentation (which includes the man pages).

Another way to get the very latest work in progress (instead of a point release, such as 4.0.1) is to use XFree86's Concurrent Version System (CVS). Although having the latest release can be important, especially if you're aware of a new feature or driver release that will enable you to overcome a plaguing problem with your graphics system and X, it is not always advisable to use or build XFree86 from the CVS repository. The distribution, unless labeled as "stable," will be a work in progress, and may have some nasty bugs.

To download a current snapshot directly from the XFree86 developer's working directories, use the cvs command first to log in to the remote XFree86 CVS directory:

```
$ cvs -d :pserver:anoncvs@anoncvs.xfree86.org:/cvs login
(Logging in to anoncvs@anoncvs.xfree86.org)
CVS password:
```

The program prompts you for the password (which is *anoncvs*). Next, use the cvs checkout command to retrieve the source tree of XFree86 using the xc module:

```
$ cvs -d :pserver:anoncvs@anoncvs.xfree86.org:/cvs checkout xc
cvs server: Updating xc
U xc/INSTALL.PS
U xc/INSTALL.TXT
U xc/Imakefile
U xc/LABEL
U xc/Makefile
U xc/RELNOTES.PS
...
```

As you can see, the files will start downloading. If you just want the contributed files, use the contrib module. Other modules include test, docutils, and utils. Note that retrieving the entire source tree can take quite some time, especially if you're not using a broadband service. If you don't want to use CVS or FTP, you can also download the source code, in compressed form, via HTTP and a Web browser, such as lynx or Netscape. To download this source, browse to the following site:
http://www.doc.cs.univ-paris8.fr/mirroirs/XFree86/

or

http://ftp-stud.fht-esslingen.de/pub/Mirrors/ftp.xfree86.org/.

Examining Essential Files

To build a new version of XFree86, you must have a Linux development system installed on your computer. Although having a previous version of XFree86, or at least a previous version of the X11 development files, installed on your system will help, you won't be able to do anything without a proper C compiler, linker, loader, and associated support files installed.

After decompressing the source to XFree86, you'll find every file under a new xc directory. At the base of this directory are several essential files:

- INSTALL.PS—a PostScript version of INSTALL.TXT
- INSTALL.TXT—Kaleb Keithley's "Building and Installing X11R6.4," a must-read before attempting to build XFree86
- Imakefile—the overall Imakefile for building XFree86
- LABEL—copyright information and names
- RELNOTES.PS—PostScript version of RELNOTES.TXT
- RELNOTES.TXT—release notes concerning XFree86
- bug-report—a template for reporting bugs or other problems
- registry—documentation describing internal symbols that XFree86 uses to identify such things as organizations, key symbols, protocol names, vendors, extensions, host families, property names and types, and fonts

The base source is installed in the following subdirectories under the xc directory:

- config—a directory of configuration files used during the build to determine specific host platform features or hardware
- doc—documentation files, distributed in a compressed PostScript format or in a markup language format
- exports—header (#include) files, along with X11 bitmap and pixmap graphics and the X11 software libraries
- extras—additional font and graphics library support, such as FreeType, TrueType, Mesa rendering, and the Xpm libraries
- fonts—XFree86's font distribution
- include—#include files
- lib—source to the X11 software libraries
- nls—additional fonts
- programs—source to the X server and the suite of XFree86 clients
- util—various software utilities, such as compress and patch

Building from Source

The most important of the base documents are the build and install directions in the file INSTALL.TXT. This file, from The Open Group, provides an overview of the build and install process of X11R6.4 for a variety of computer platforms. You should definitely read the entire document before you begin the process, in order to get a better idea of proper procedures and potential problems.

However, don't be put off or intimidated. If you're worried about your current XFree86 installation, rename or move the /usr/X11R6 directory tree before installing your new version of X. Next, read the "Easy Build" portion of the document. You'll see that it contains the following simple steps and directions for building X:

1. Edit xc/config/cf/site.def.

2. To this file, add the following:

   ```
   #define LinuxDistribution XXXXXX
   ```

   where *xxxxx* may be one of the following:

   LinuxUnknown

   LinuxSuSE

   LinuxCaldera

   LinuxCraftworks

   LinuxDebian

   LinuxInfoMagic

   LinuxKheops

   LinuxPro

   LinuxRedHat

   LinuxSlackware

   LinuxTurbo

   LinuxWare

   LinuxYggdrasil

   However, you can skip this step if you use a SuSE, Red Hat, or Debian distribution, as those distributions determine this value automatically.

3. Change to the xc directory and enter the following:

   ```
   # make World >& world.log
   ```

4. To install the new distribution, enter the following:

   ```
   # make install >& install.log
   ```

5. To create and install the XFree86 and X11 man pages, enter the following:

   ```
   # make install.man >& man.log
   ```

6. Keep your fingers crossed. If a problems occurs and the build fails, you'll need to peruse the rest of the installation directions for details and carefully examine the build, install, or man logs.

The directions contain some guidance on building under different Linux distributions, and specify some possible settings that can help you avoid any problems. When the build starts, you can use the less pager to read any initial information, as follows:

```
# less world.log
...
Building on Linux 2.2.14-15mdk i686 [ELF] (2.2.14).


Linux Distribution: RedHat
libc version: 6.1.2
binutils version: 2.9
...
```

In this example, the install program has recognized the distribution as Red Hat (actually Mandrake Linux). You can watch the progress of the build by using the tail command with its -f command-line option, as follows:

```
# tail -f world.log
```

Depending on your computer system's CPU, available memory, and hard drive speed, the complete build can take nearly one hour. For example, a sample build on a 500MHz Pentium II, 128MB system required 54 minutes. Of course, if you have a low-end quad-CPU Alpha system, which can perform a Linux kernel recompile in 90 seconds (as opposed to four minutes for the Pentium), the build time will be considerably shorter.

Examining the X11 Source

The new architecture of XFree86 4.0 and higher provides a great deal of convenience, especially in those instances where you need to add support for a graphics chipset family. In the past, with the pre-4.0 XFree86 distribution, this task required patching and rebuilding an entire server binary. Today, however, you need only make changes to a driver, which enables manufacturers and XFree86 developers to add support for new hardware quickly.

For example, Jay Beal, a Sony C1VN Picturebook user whose laptop uses Transmeta's Crusoe CPU, needed to add the following patch (by Gene Ragan and "Marc at XFree86") to his system's ati_drv.o driver. With the patch added, this driver (for the ATI graphics chipset) can enable the laptop's 1,024×480 display.

```
--- xc/programs/Xserver/hw/xfree86/drivers/ati/atipreinit.c.ORIG Wed Nov 23 \
02:05:30 2000
+++ xc/programs/Xserver/hw/xfree86/drivers/ati/atipreinit.c Wed Nov 23 \
02:06:25 2000
@@ -981,7 +981,7 @@
                 * Compensate for BIOS absence.  Note that the reference
                 * frequency has already been set by option processing.
                 */
-               if ((pATI->DAC & 0x0FU) == ATI_DAC_INTERNAL)
+        if ((pATI->DAC & 0x0FU) == ATI_DAC_INTERNAL || (!xf86NameCmp(pGDev-
>clockchip, \ "Internal")))
                    pATI->ProgrammableClock = ATI_CLOCK_INTERNAL;
                else switch (pATI->DAC)
                {
```

In this example, the change of a single line in a driver makes the difference between a working XFree86 display and disappointment. As you can see from the patch source, source code to drivers is located under the `xc/programs/Xserver/hw/xfree86/drivers` directory. Table 17.1 lists the driver's directory's contents (omitting the requisite Imakefile and Makefile used during the build).

Note that not all of the drivers in the directory will be compiled and installed, such as the drivers for Sun Microsystems' hardware. Other drivers, such as glide.o, and v4l drv.o, are extension drivers to enable additional features on video cards. You should also note that at this point, not all legacy hardware support in XFree86 3.3.6 is present in the new driver set. This means that you may have to resort to using an older version of XFree86 for a while, or wait until drivers for the next XFree86 4.0 architecture are developed.

If you discover problems with a particular driver, take the time to check the latest source tree from the XFree86 Project, Inc. You may find that a newer version of the driver has been developed. Another place to check is the Web site of your graphics card manufacturer. Many enlightened manufacturers, such as Matrox, now provide support for Linux in the form of newer drivers in binary or source form, and donate any improvements to the next release version of XFree86.

Table 17.1 XFree86 Server's drivers Directory

Directory	Contents
apm/	Driver for the Alliance Promotion chipset
ati/	Driver for the ATI graphics chipset
chips/	Chips & Technologies video driver
cirrus/	Cirrus Logic chipset driver
cyrix/	Cyrix chipset video driver
fbdev/	Framebuffer device driver
glide/	Driver for Glide-enabled video (3Dfx Voodoo, etc.)
glint/	3DLabs and TI GLINT/Permedia driver
i740/	Intel video driver
i810/	Intel video driver
imstt/	Twin Turbo 128 driver
mga/	Matrox video driver
neomagic/	NeoMagic video chipset driver
nv/	NVIDIA (RIVA 128, TNT, TNT2, etc.) driver
r128/	ATI Rage 128 driver
rendition/	Rendition/Micron (framebuffer, accelerated) driver
s3virge/	S3 Virge video driver
sis/	Driver for the SiS graphics chipset
sunbw2/	Sun black-and-white video driver (not for Intel-based XFree86)
suncg14/	Sun CG14 video driver (not for Intel-based XFree86)
suncg3/	Sun CG3 video driver (not for Intel-based XFree86)
suncg6/	Sun CG6 video driver (not for Intel-based XFree86)
sunffb/	Sun Creator, Creator 3D, and Elite 3D video driver (not for Intel-based XFree86)
sunleo/	Sun Leo video driver (not for Intel-based XFree86)
suntcx/	Sun TCX video driver (not for Intel-based XFree86)
tdfx/	3Dfx video driver
tga/	Targa Graphics Adapter video driver
trident/	Trident Microsystems video driver
tseng/	Tseng Labs chipset driver
v4l/	Video 4 Linux driver
vga/	Generic VGA video driver

Testing Clients

After you build XFree86, but before you install the new version on your system, you can quickly test a few clients on your existing system by extending your system's software library path to include any required new software libraries. For example, if you navigate to the xc/programs/xclock directory, you can then use the ldd command to show any shared library dependencies of the new xclock client, as follows:

```
$ ldd xclock
        libXaw.so.7 => not found
        libXmu.so.6 => /usr/X11R6/lib/libXmu.so.6 (0x4001c000)
        libXt.so.6 => /usr/X11R6/lib/libXt.so.6 (0x4002f000)
        libSM.so.6 => /usr/X11R6/lib/libSM.so.6 (0x40081000)
        libICE.so.6 => /usr/X11R6/lib/libICE.so.6 (0x4008c000)
        libXpm.so.4 => /usr/X11R6/lib/libXpm.so.4 (0x400a4000)
        libXext.so.6 => /usr/X11R6/lib/libXext.so.6 (0x400b4000)
        libX11.so.6 => /usr/X11R6/lib/libX11.so.6 (0x400c1000)
        libc.so.6 => /lib/libc.so.6 (0x40173000)
        /lib/ld-linux.so.2 => /lib/ld-linux.so.2 (0x40000000)
```

After you press Enter, you'll see a list of libraries that the client requires. As you can see, the command did not find a new library named libXaw.so.7. You can then add the new library, found under the xc/lib/Xaw directory, as follows:

```
$ export LD_LIBRARY_PATH=/d3/x11r6xfree86/xc/lib/Xaw
```

In this example, the source and build directories reside on /d3/x11r6xfree86 in the xc directory. However, you may need to add an additional new library to this path if a new function is missing in the older libraries. For example, when you try to run the new xclock, you may see the following output:

```
$ ./xclock
./xclock: error in loading shared libraries: \
/d3/x11r6xfree86/xc/lib/Xaw/libXaw.so.7: undefined symbol: \
XmuCvtGravityToString
```

Here you can see that even though the ldd command deemed the older Xmu library sufficient, the newer library may include a new function. You can then simply add the path, again using the LD_LIBRARY_PATH environment variable:

```
$ export LD_LIBRARY_PATH=/d3/x11r6xfree86/xc/lib/Xaw: \
/d3/x11r6xfree86/xc/lib/Xmu
```

After you press Enter, you can then run the xclock client:

```
# ./xclock
```

Do You Need Help or Want to Help?

The XFree86 Project has nine different mailing lists that you can use to ask questions, receive news, or offer advice and suggestions to other users. Browse to **http://www.xfree86.org/mailman/listinfo** and take a look at a list that interests you. Many new users will want to subscribe to the `Newbie` mailing list. For general discussions about X, subscribe to the `Xpert` list. All you have to do is click on a link to the desired list, then enter your email address and a password.

This approach also works for the newly built `bitmap`, `ico`, `oclock`, `xmag`, `xbiff`, `xcalc`, `xeyes`, `xfontsel`, `xload`, `xlogo`, `xman`, `xmessage`, `xterm`, and `xwininfo` clients. Note that modifying `LD_LIBRARY_PATH` will not be necessary if you install the new server, libraries and clients.

Resource Information

http://www.xfree86.org—the starting point for learning more about XFree86.

ftp://ftp.xfree.org—the main download site for retrieving the latest binary or source distribution of XFree86.

http://www.xfree86.org/cvs/—directions for using XFree86's public CVS access system to download the latest source code for XFree86.

http://www.bastille-linux.org/jay/vaio.html—Jay Beal's Sony C1VN page (linked from the Linux Laptop pages).

http://www.cs.utexas.edu/users/kharker/linux-laptop/—the Linux Laptop pages, with links to hundreds of Web sites with solutions for getting Linux and XFree86 to work on laptops.

http://www.matrox.com/mga/support/drivers/latest/home.cfm—site of the enlightened Matrox Graphics company, with links to the latest XFree86 drivers for Linux for the Matrox product line—a model site by a model company!

comp.os.linux.x—the Usenet newsgroup with many answers regarding building, installing, configuring, managing, and using XFree86.

Chapter 18: Basic X11 Programming

Installing Xfree86 development support

Using essential programming tools

Using make, imake, and xmkmf

Creating, building, and installing a simple client

This chapter introduces the concepts, software tools, and resources such as software libraries that you'll need to begin developing simple clients for the X Window system. You'll get an overview of X programming, discover several essential utilities, learn how to use some programming tools, and then see how to build a simple X11 client.

Programming for X11 requires a basic understanding of the available resources, such as function calls provided by various software toolkits included with XFree86. One of the benefits of programming for X is *portability,* or the ability of your code to build and compile under a variety of other computer platforms, regardless of operating system or hardware. As long as the other computer supports X11 and your code is hardware-independent, your program should survive and successfully build on other machines with few, if any, changes.

Installing XFree86 Development Support

If you have installed XFree86, but want to develop programs for X using Linux, you'll need to make sure that you have also installed a working C (and possibly C++) development system. This means that you may need to install the Linux kernel `#include` files, the `gcc` compiler, and associated development software libraries and documentation. You'll also need the GNU Development Tools, such as the `as` assembler, the `ld` linker, and others. Fortunately, most Linux distributions make installing development support fairly easy using some form of package manager such as Red Hat's `rpm` command, SuSE's `yast` (which is `rpm`-based), or Debian's `app-get` system. However, you can also install the tools from compressed tarballs, such as .tgz files, using the `tar` command.

If you use an `rpm`-based Linux distribution, you can check whether the XFree86 development files are installed by using the `rpm` command's `-q` query option and the `fgrep` command as follows:

```
$ rpm -qa | fgrep XFree86-dev
XFree86-devel-4.0.1-1
```

In this example, following a query to the `rpm` database for all installed packages, an `fgrep` search of the `rpm` command output shows that the XFree86 4.0.1 development package is installed. You can then see a list of the files included in the development package by again using the `rpm` command and its query option, but this time with a list option, as follows:

```
$ rpm -ql XFree86-devel-4.0.1-1 | less
```

When you pipe the output through the `less` paging command, you can peruse the list of files. You'll see that the contents of the XFree86 development files are installed under the following directories:

- `/usr/X11R6/bin`—nine different binary software tools.
- `/usr/X11R6/include/X11`—X11 #include files, containing definitions and declarations of default values and functions.
- `/usr/X11R6/include/X11/bitmaps`—nearly 100 bitmaps that may be used when programming (note that these files are not required or exclusive).
- `/usr/X11R6/include/X11/extensions`—#include files containing defaults and definitions for extended functions.
- `/usr/X11R6/include/X11/fonts`—#include files containing information for font programming.
- `/usr/X11R6/lib/X11/config`—files containing *rulesets* (default definitions used by the local operating system and other operating systems). You use these files when building configuration files and Makefiles, which are used to build local X11 clients. The ruleset information is used by the `xmkmf` and `make` commands during the build process.
- `/usr/X11R6/lib`—X software libraries containing functions used by X clients. This directory holds several libraries, such as the basic Xlib, Xt Intrinsics, X Toolkit, and Athena Xaw libraries. In XFree86 version 4.0 and higher, you'll also find the Xpm (X pixmap) libraries in this directory.
- `/usr/X11R6/man/man3`—man pages describing X11 functions.

Installing the XFree86 development package requires an additional 9MB of hard drive space. The normal Linux development tools can require up to 20MB or more hard drive space, depending on the type of tools and libraries that you install.

Using Essential Programming Tools

Designing and writing code to create an X11 client can be very different than designing and writing code for a Linux command or a command designed to run from and use the command line. Many Linux commands derive from legacy UNIX counterparts, and follow a different design and use philosophy than a graphical X client. An example of such a command is one that is used as a *filter* program. Such a command is designed to receive input from another program, modify the input, and then pass the input along with modified data as output using the standard output, redirected standard output, or yet another pipe.

The following is an example of the command-line philosophy using filters and pipes:

```
# find /usr/share/doc -name *.txt -print | xargs cat | tr ' ' '\n' \
| sort | uniq | egrep -av [*[:digit:]] | egrep -av [*[:punct:]] \
| egrep -av [*[:space:]] | egrep -av [*[:cntrl:]] >mydict
```

In this example, the find, xargs, tr, sort, uniq, and egrep commands are used to build quickly a dictionary (albeit not spell-checked) named mydict using words found in all text files under the /usr/share/doc directory. You can then add the egrep command to the beginning of the mydict file like this:

```
#!/bin/sh
/bin/egrep -i $1 <<zzzz
```

Add the string zzzz to the end of the file, then use the chmod command with its +x option to make the entire file executable. You can then use the entire dictionary as a command that searches the dictionary itself. For example, to look up all words containing *expen,* use the following command:

```
# ./mydict expen
expendable
expense
expensive
inexpensive
```

In direct contrast to those UNIX and Linux commands that do something right away, such as print or display information or manipulate input data and output a result, nearly all X clients are *event-driven,* and spend most of the time waiting for a mouse click or button press. One example of an event-driven program for UNIX and Linux is a text-based editor. If you're familiar with programming for the Apple Macintosh and MacOS, you know that the standard operating system includes no command line for launching applications (although you can launch clients via scripts or other mechanisms), but that most MacOS applications are event driven.

The main() function in a simple Linux command in C is designed to handle command-line options and then do something:

```
main(int argc, char ** argv) {
    /* handle command-line options */
            ...
                printf("Hello, world.\n");
                exit(0);

}
```

On the other hand, the `main()` function in a simple X client in C is designed to handle command-line options and then wait to do something:

```
XtAppContext          client_context;

...

main(int argc, char ** argv) {
                /* handle X Toolkit command-line options */

                ...

                /* set up the client */

                ...

                XtAppMainLoop(client_context);
                exit(0);

}
```

In this example, the simple X client defines an identifier or context, then, in `main()`, handles command-line options, sets up the dialog box, window, or other widget, and then waits for input or an event in `XtAppMainLoop()`, a standard function included in the X11 Xt libraries. The event loop is important, as it demonstrates one method of waiting for and acting on particular events experienced by your client's widgets; you can then add functions to respond to the events, such as a button press.

You can launch X clients from the command line or through another program. X clients can also obey command-line options, known as X Toolkit options, as you discovered in Chapter 8, "Using X11 Clients." You can make the task of creating these clients a lot easier by using the programming tools discussed in the next section.

Using make, imake, and xmkmf

XFree86 includes two essential utilities that you can use to keep your work organized and make the task of programming and testing your X client a lot easier. One reason that you should turn to these clients is that the job of programming under Linux, such as creating an X client, can involve a repetitive cycle of editing, running, and testing until you are satisfied with the graphic interface and program performance. Often you will need to break up a project into multiple parts or write lengthy command lines for a rebuild.

Using `imake` and `xmkmf`, along with the `make` command (see the section "Using the make Command" next), makes the task of building and rebuilding projects easier. They give you an automatic way of tying different files in a project together, checking dependencies, and rebuilding only those files that have changed in a project. Thus these utilities can save the programmer an enormous amount of time and effort. As if this weren't enough, these software tools go even beyond basic programming support, and may also be used to test, install, uninstall, and even archive entire sets of documents or programming projects.

Using the make Command

The make command included with most Linux distributions is GNU make, and was developed by Richard Stallman and Roland McGrath. The make command has long been the standard programming assist tool, even in the face of newer software tools such as autoconf (see the section "The autoconf Command"). The make command generates new commands using directions or *rules* contained in a default file named Makefile; however, you can actually use any filename if you run make with its -f option, followed by the name of the file containing the outline of file dependencies.

This section describes a short Makefile. The structure of a basic Makefile is fairly simple, but you can quickly and easily add different elements to add to its usefulness. For example, to build a small project with a single file using gcc and the basic X11 libraries, you can enter the following:

```
CC = gcc
INSTALL = /usr/local/bin
INCLUDES = -I/usr/X11R6/include
LIBS = -L/usr/X11R6/lib -lX11 -lXaw -lXt -lXext
OBJS = main.o
myclient : ${OBJS}
        ${CC} -o myclient ${OBJS} ${INCLUDES} ${LIBS}
test :
                ./myclient
install :
        install -g root -o root myclient ${INSTALL}
clean :
        rm -fr *.o myclient
archive :
        tar cvzf ../myclient.tgz .
```

The first five lines of this example define the compiler (gcc), the directory under which the client will be installed (/usr/local/bin), the libraries required to support the client (named myclient), and the name of the object files required for linking (main.o). Following those definitions are five lines describing the commands to be created and used to build, test, install, clean up, and archive the project. Note that you must enter a Tab character at the beginning of each command-line definition.

You can type and save the listing in a file named Makefile, which is intended to reside in the same directory as the source. To build the project, use the make command as follows:

```
$ make
gcc    -c main.c -o main.o
```

```
gcc -o myclient main.o -I/usr/X11R6/include -L/usr/X11R6/lib -lX11 -lXaw -lXt -
lXext
```

After you press Enter, the make command generates the proper command line. Note that you can also enter the following command:

```
$ make myclient
gcc     -c main.c -o main.o
gcc -o myclient main.o -I/usr/X11R6/include -L/usr/X11R6/lib -lX11 -lXaw -lXt -
lXext
```

If you edit and make any changes to the source code of the example (the file main.c), simply type make again and the project will rebuild. If you type make after rebuilding, you'll see the following output:

```
$ make
make: `myclient' is up to date.
```

You can then use the make command to test the project:

```
$ make test
```

After you press Enter, the client will run (or perhaps not run). You can then enter your cycle of editing and testing until you're satisfied with the results. You can then use the other entries in your Makefile to install, clean up, and archive the project, by entering command lines such as the following:

```
$ make install
install -g root -o root myclient /usr/local/bin
$ make clean
rm -fr *.o myclient
$ make archive
tar cvzf ../myclient.tgz .
./
./Makefile
./main.c
```

Using imake and xmkmf

The imake client, by Todd Brunhoff, and the xmkmf script, by Jim Fulton, are two legacy software tools used by X11 programmers around the world. Xfree86 includes both utilities, which are designed to aid in the portability and building of X11 clients across different computer platforms.

The imake command can help improve your code's portability because the client uses the local system's X11 configuration files, found under the /usr/X11R6/lib/X11/config directory, in the process of building a `Makefile` for your project. The `imake` command is actually a C preprocessor interface to `make`, and uses the `linux.cf`, `lnxLib.rules`, `lnxLib.tmpl`, `lnxdoc.rules`, and `lnxdoc.tmpl` configuration files when you build a client under X.

During use, the `xmkmf` shell script runs the `imake` command, using a file named `Imakefile` to build your `Makefile`. The `Imakefile` contains directions on where to find specific required elements, such as libraries for your build.

For example, here's a simple `Imakefile` for a sample project:

```
INCLUDES = -I.
SYS_LIBRARIES = XawClientLibs
SRCS= main.c
OBJS= main.o
PROGRAMS = myclient
NormalLibraryObjectRule()
AllTarget(myclient)
NormalProgramTarget(myclient,main.o,NullParameter,NullParameter,NullParameter)
```

This short file details the required X11 libraries (derived from the `XawClientLibs` keyword defined in `/usr/X11R6/lib/X11/config/lnxLib.tmpl`) needed to link into your project. The file also defines the name of your source, object, and target client, `myclient`. Type the `imake` information into a text file using a favorite editor, then save the file with the name `Imakefile` in the same directory as your project code. Next, run the `xmkmf` shell script to create your `Makefile`, as follows:

```
$ xmkmf
imake -DUseInstalled -I/usr/X11R6/lib/X11/config
```

The `imake` command (run by `xmkmf`) reports on its use of your local configuration files and then creates your `Makefile`. You can then enter the `make` command to build your project as follows:

```
# make
rm -f main.o
gcc -c -O3 -fomit-frame-pointer -fno-exceptions -fno-rtti -pipe -s -mpentium -
mcpu=pentium -march=pentium -ffast-math -fexpensive-optimizations   -I. -
I/usr/X11R6/include   -Dlinux -D__i386__ -D_POSIX_C_SOURCE=199309L -D_POSIX_SOURCE
-D_XOPEN_SOURCE=500L -D_BSD_SOURCE -D_SVID_SOURCE   -DFUNCPROTO=15 -DNARROWPROTO
main.c
rm -f myclient
gcc -o myclient -O3 -fomit-frame-pointer -fno-exceptions -fno-rtti -pipe -s -mpen-
tium -mcpu=pentium -march=pentium -ffast-math -fexpensive-optimizations       -
L/usr/X11R6/lib main.o    -lXaw -lXmu -lXt -lSM -lICE -lXext -lX11
```

After you press Enter, the make command generates the commands to build your project. You'll find a number of default keywords defined automatically for your use, such as the following:

- `all` compiles and builds all source and object files
- `myclient` compiles and builds the `myclient` client
- `clean` deletes all temporary files, such as .bak

Using `xmkmf` and `make` can save you a lot of time and effort, even on small projects, as you won't have to type long command lines over and over.

Using autoconf

Another software tool that is becoming increasingly popular is `autoconf`, which automatically generates a `configure` script, which you can then use to quickly configure and build a `Makefile` for a specific computer system. You usually can find documentation for this utility in a GNU `info` file, which you can read by entering the following:

```
# info autoconf
```

The `autoconf` command works by taking an initial ruleset from a file named `configure.in`. This file contains a short list of *macros*, or shortcut definitions that will used to create the larger `configure` script used to test your system for required libraries or `#include` files.

The `configure.in` file is created by the `autoscan` command, which initially creates a file named `configure.scan`. You should then edit or examine `configure.scan` and then rename it as `configure.in` before running `autoconf`. You'll also need to create a file named `Makefile.in`, which is a template that will be used, in turn, when the `configure` script builds the `Makefile` for your project. If these file dependencies sound complicated, it is because `configure` is complex program, and usually used with large, complex software projects involving hundreds of files. Creating the initial files used to build the `Makefile` for a larger project is much easier using `autoconf` than it would be to define manually the command lines and dependencies required for such a project's `Makefile`. However, many Linux and XFree86 programmers use `autoconf` even on smaller projects.

For example, create a short `Makefile.in` for the example project in the project directory:

```
CC =            @CC@
CFLAGS =        @CFLAGS@ @CPPFLAGS@ @DEFS@
LDFLAGS =       @LDFLAGS@ @LIBS@
OBJS =          main.o

all : myclient
```

```
myclient : $(OBJS)
          $(CC) -o $@ $(OBJS) $(LDFLAGS)
```

Note that the structure is very similar to that of the previous Makefile. Next, run the autoscan command as follows:

```
# autoscan
```

This command creates a file named configure.scan in the current directory. The file looks like this:

```
dnl Process this file with autoconf to produce a configure script.
AC_INIT(main.c)


dnl Checks for programs.


dnl Checks for libraries.


dnl Checks for header files.
AC_PATH_X


dnl Checks for typedefs, structures, and compiler characteristics.


dnl Checks for library functions.


AC_OUTPUT()
```

Note that the autoscan command recognized and found the project file, and also determined that X is part of the equation. You should now edit the configure.scan file to look like this:

```
dnl Process this file with autoconf to produce a configure script.
AC_INIT(main.c)


dnl Checks for programs.
AC_PROG_CC


dnl Checks for libraries.
LIBS="-L/usr/X11R6/lib -lX11 -lXt -lXaw -lXext"


dnl Checks for header files.
AC_PATH_X


dnl Checks for typedefs, structures, and compiler characteristics.
```

```
dnl Checks for library functions.
```

```
AC_OUTPUT(Makefile)
```

These changes tell the resulting `configure` script to check for your system's compiler, ensure that the designated libraries are used, and then build your `Makefile`. After you're finished, save the file as `configure.in`, then run the `autoconf` command. The `autoconf` command then creates your `configure` script, which is then run to build your project's `Makefile`, as follows:

```
$ ./configure
creating cache ./config.cache
checking for gcc... gcc
checking whether the C compiler (gcc   ) works... yes
checking whether the C compiler (gcc   ) is a cross-compiler... no
checking whether we are using GNU C... yes
checking whether gcc accepts -g... yes
checking how to run the C preprocessor... gcc -E
checking for X... libraries /usr/X11R6/lib, headers /usr/X11R6/include
updating cache ./config.cache
creating ./config.status
creating Makefile
```

You can then build your project using the `Makefile`. If you'd like to include all the features of the simple `Makefile` discussed earlier, use a `Makefile.in` file that looks like the following:

```
CC =            @CC@
CFLAGS =        @CFLAGS@ @CPPFLAGS@ @DEFS@
LDFLAGS =       @LDFLAGS@ @LIBS@
OBJS =          main.o


all : myclient


myclient : $(OBJS)
        $(CC) -o $@ $(OBJS) $(LDFLAGS)
test :
        ./myclient
install :
        install -g root -o root myclient ${INSTALL}
clean :
        rm -fr *.o myclient
```

```
archive :
        tar cvzf ../myclient.tgz .
```

The configure script will automatically include your additional test, install, clean, and archive commands in the resulting Makefile.

Creating, Building, and Installing a Simple Client

This section introduces a short example program for XFree86 and Linux. The program really doesn't do much, but simply presents a "Hello" message in a movable, resizable window on your desktop. The program leaves it up to you to learn more about programming for XFree86 and Linux. The program shows just the basics and only one way of many to accomplish the same task when programming for X11. Here's the code:

```c
/*
 * main.c - myclient example
 */
#include <X11/Xlib.h>
#include <X11/Xutil.h>
#include <X11/Intrinsic.h>

/* define a short string to display */
char wmsg[]="Hello";

int main(int argc, char ** argv)
{
    Display *myDisplay; /* our display */
    Window myWindow; /* our window */
    GC myGc;
    XSizeHints myHint;
    XWMHints myWmhint;
    XTextProperty wname;
    XEvent event;
    int myScreen;
    unsigned long myForeground, myBackground;

    myDisplay = XOpenDisplay(NULL);
    myScreen = DefaultScreen( myDisplay );

    myBackground = WhitePixel( myDisplay, myScreen );
    myForeground = BlackPixel( myDisplay, myScreen );
```

```
    myHint.x = 0;
    myHint.y = 0;
    myHint.width = 250;
    myHint.height = 30;
    myHint.flags = PPosition | PSize;
    myWmhint.flags = InputHint;
    myWmhint.input = True;

/* create a simple window */
    myWindow = XCreateSimpleWindow( myDisplay,
        DefaultRootWindow( myDisplay ), myHint.x, myHint.y,
        myHint.width, myHint.height, 5, myForeground, myBackground );

/* assign a name to the window titlebar */
    XStringListToTextProperty(&argv[0],1,&wname);
    XSetWMName (myDisplay, myWindow, &wname);
    XSetWMProperties(myDisplay, myWindow, &wname, NULL, NULL, \
0, &myHint, &myWmhint,NULL);

/* set background, foreground color */
    myGc = XCreateGC( myDisplay, myWindow, 0, 0 );
    XSetBackground( myDisplay, myGc, myBackground );
    XSetForeground( myDisplay, myGc, myForeground );

/* set focus to window */
    XSelectInput( myDisplay, myWindow,
                    KeyPressMask | ExposureMask );

    XMapWindow( myDisplay, myWindow );

/* endless loop until window is killed */
    for (;;) {
        XNextEvent(myDisplay,&event);
        if (event.type == Expose && event.xexpose.count == 0) {
            XClearWindow(myDisplay,myWindow);
            XDrawImageString (myDisplay, myWindow, myGc,
                        (myHint.width/10), (myHint.height/2),
                        wmsg, (strlen(wmsg)));
        }
    }
    exit(0);
}
```

The program includes several #include files required by various X11 function calls in the program. Although it is set up to use command-line options, the program includes no code to support X11 Toolkit options. After the initial declarations, the code sets the default display, colors, and sizes. The XcreateSimpleWindow() call creates the client window, and the client's name from the command line provides the basis for the name displayed in the window's titlebar. Finally, in an endless loop, the window is drawn and displayed (using the XdrawImageString function) and is available for dragging, resizing, minimizing, or maximizing. The window contains a simple message: "Hello." The window remains active until the user kills it via the command line or deletes the window's process.

You can build and install the client using any of the Makefile, Imakefile, or auto-conf configuration scripts shown in this chapter. After building the client, you can try running the program as follows:

```
# ./myclient
```

After you press Enter, you'll see a small window, as shown in Figure 18.1.

Figure 18.1 *Building a simple X11 client is easy, but building sophisticated clients with many controls, menus, buttons, or dialog boxes can be a massive challenge.*

Resource Information

http://www.rahul.net/kenton/xsites.html/—Kenton Lee's definitive site of links to X and X-related information.

http://www.x.org—home page for the X Window system and, according to X.org, "...the worldwide consortium empowered with the stewardship and collaborative development of the X Window System technology and standards." This is the site from which to download the "official" X11R6 in source code form; however, when building X for Linux, you should use the X11R6 source provided by the XFree86 Project, Inc., as its source code will build more easily.

ftp://ftp.x.org/contrib—an FTP site for additional software and clients for X, including links to source code included in various books about X.

http://www.hsrl.rutgers.edu/ug/make_help.html—an online tutorial about how to write a Makefile.

http://nis-www.lanl.gov/~rosalia/mydocs/autoconf_tutorial_toc.html—an online tutorial about using the GNU autoconf utility.

comp.windows.x.announce—a Usenet newsgroup that posts announcements about X.

comp.windows.x—a Usenet newsgroup that hosts general discussions about X.

comp.windows.x.apps—a Usenet newsgroup that hosts discussions about X clients.

comp.windows.x.intrinsics—a Usenet newsgroup that hosts discussions about using the X Toolkit.

comp.os.linux.x—a Usenet newsgroup that hosts discussions about using X and XFree86 with Linux.

Chapter 19: X11 Programming Toolkits Overview

Classic toolkits

Popular toolkits

This chapter provides an overview of the various software libraries or toolkits that you can use when programming for X11. You'll learn about some of the classic toolkits that have evolved over the last 10 years, and also get information about some the newest and latest software libraries that you can use when developing clients.

Choosing a toolkit to use for client development can be an important decision for reasons of ease of use, portability, features, and distribution. Nearly all toolkits offer the basics of creating and decorating windows on the X desktop, but some are easier to use than others and may offer additional features. Literally hundreds of special software libraries are available for X programmers. Many provide a base set of convenient functions that you can use to create clients quickly, whereas others provide special functions to aid in handling certain objects or events, such as graphic images, sound, network data, and other objects.

This chapter starts with a basic description of the software libraries included with XFree86. You'll then learn about other libraries and development systems that you can install on your computer to aid you in developing clients that use these special libraries.

Classic Toolkits

This section introduces the classic, low-level toolkits included with XFree86. These toolkits were developed following the start of the 1983 Project Athena, a joint research effort among the Massachusetts Institute of Technology (MIT), IBM, and Digital Equipment Corporation to devise a graphical networking system. That effort has since evolved into X11R6, and is now under the auspices of X.org.

You'll find nearly all X11 software libraries installed under the /usr/X11R6/lib directory.

Xlib

Known as the "assembly language" of X11, the Xlib software libraries contain functions that form the base of X11. As a common base, low-level, and main interface to X, Xlib provides explicit control over created objects such as windows, but also requires more attention to detail regarding events such as keyboard presses and mouse clicks.

The software functions provided by Xlib are contained in the files named libX11.* under the /usr/X11R6/lib directory. Programs requiring Xlib usually start with the following line:

```
#include <X11/Xlib.h>
```

This header file contains definitions, extensions, data structures, and C language interfaces to the library's functions. Extensions to Xlib are contained in the files named libXext* under the /usr/X11R6/lib directory. Miscellaneous routines are contained in files named libXmu*.

Xt Intrinsics

The X Toolkit Instrinsics library, libXt, features additional functions that use Xlib functions to provide enhanced drawing support. You can use this support to draw more complex objects known as *widgets*. In turn, libXt, like libX11, forms the base for creating additional toolkits.

The software functions provided by libXt are contained in the files named libXt* under the /usr/X11R6/lib directory. Programs requiring libXt usually start with the following line:

```
#include <X11/Intrinsic.h>
```

This header file, like Xlib's X11.h, contains definitions, extensions, data structures, and C language interfaces to the library's functions, which provide advanced event, session, error, memory, graphics, and text handling. You can use these functions to build a wide range of widgets, such as buttons or complex dialog boxes with multiple controls. You can usually recognize a libXt function by its name, especially if it begins with Xt*.

Athena

As the base for additional toolkits, libXt is used to build additional widget sets. The best known of these is the Athena widget set, included with XFree86, and Motif (discussed in the next section). The Athena libraries are found under the /usr/X11R6/lib directory. Their filenames start with libXaw*.

Although the Athena toolkit contains the original set of widgets provided for X, its widgets are not as feature-rich as those provided by other toolkits based on libXt, such as Motif. However, using the Athena toolkit makes the job of creating simple widgets easier. For example, you can use the toolkit to create quickly a simple window with a label and quit button:

```
#include  <X11/Intrinsic.h>
#include  <X11/StringDefs.h>
#include  <X11/Shell.h>
#include  <X11/Xaw/Command.h>
#include  <X11/Xaw/Form.h>


void quit_proc () { exit(0); }


int main(int argc, char **argv)
{
    XtAppContext myclient_context;
    Widget toplevel, label, form, quit_button;

    Arg args[10];
    int n;


    XtToolkitInitialize();
    /* create main window */
    toplevel = XtOpenApplication(&myclient_context, "myClient", NULL,
            0, &argc, argv, NULL, applicationShellWidgetClass, NULL, 0);
    n = 0;
    XtSetArg(args[n],XtNheight, 100); n++;
    XtSetArg(args[n],XtNwidth, 200); n++;
    XtSetValues (toplevel, args, (Cardinal)(n));


    form = XtVaCreateManagedWidget ("form", formWidgetClass, toplevel, NULL);


    label = XtVaCreateManagedWidget ("label", labelWidgetClass, form, XtNlabel,
            "Press Quit", XtNborderWidth, 0, NULL);


    quit_button = XtVaCreateManagedWidget ("quit_button", commandWidgetClass,
                        form, XtNlabel, "Quit", XtNfromHoriz, label);


    XtAddCallback(quit_button, XtNcallback, quit_proc, NULL);
    XtRealizeWidget(toplevel);
    XtAppMainLoop(myclient_context);
}
```

You can build the simple client (perhaps named `foo`) like this:

```
# gcc -o foo foo.c -I/usr/X11R6/include -L/usr/X11R6/lib -lX11 -lXaw -lXt
```

You can then run the resulting client named `foo` like this:

```
# ./foo
```

In this example, after you press Enter, a 320×200 pixel window (as shown in Figure 19.1) is created with a label of "Press Quit," and a button labeled "Quit."

Although Athena widgets can look flat and lack decoration, many programmers use this toolkit because of the low overhead, fast execution, and minimal memory demands.

OSF/Motif

Motif is another toolkit based on `libXt`. However, unlike the Athena toolkit, Motif was developed by a consortium of companies under the auspices of X/Open at first, then the Open Software Foundation (OSF), then finally The Open Group, Inc. The toolkit is now known as Open Motif, and the current version is 2.1.30. On May 15,

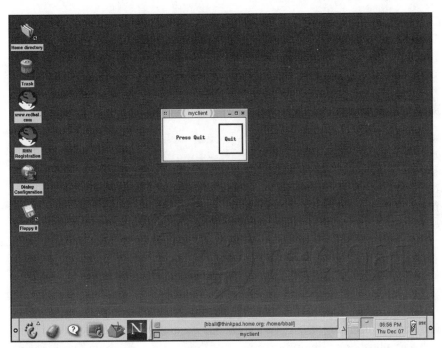

Figure 19.1 *You can construct a simple X11 client by using function calls from the Athena toolkit.*

2000, The Open Group announced that Motif, and its source code, would become available under a "public license." Although this license allows you to download and use Motif, it does not allow you to create binary-only clients for profit; you must still pay a license fee to The Open Group if you wish to sell your client.

Motif libraries provide high-level functions that you can use to build clients quickly. These libraries are pretty much an industry standard between corporate UNIX and X11 developers, and the graphical user interface (GUI) toolkit works on a vast variety of platforms.

Motif widgets support advanced features such as printing and vertical text. Three-dimensional object decorations—such as for window borders, scrollbars, check boxes, and other GUI elements—are supported automatically.

Whereas the Xt Intrinsics library introduced widgets, the Motif toolkit goes a bit further to include widgets known as *gadgets*. Some of these objects include a container, a notebook, a spinbox, a combo box, and a thermometer. Building upon Motif's capabilities, developers can include advanced features such as drag-and-drop and tear-off menus for clients.

Like X11 and XFree86, Motif also includes a window manager. The mwm window manager, when installed with the Motif libraries, may be used for your X sessions and can support clients using Motif features.

Motif has been available for Linux since the first ports of XFree86. Once installed, the Motif library usually resides under the /usr/X11R6/lib directory with filenames such as libXm.* and libMrm.*.

Popular Toolkits

This section introduces some of the more popular toolkits used by Linux and X11 developers today. As the Open Source and free software movements have grown, and the installed Linux user base has proliferated, more and more developers and companies are turning to alternative, noncommercial sources of development libraries. This only makes sense in today's economy, where licensing, royalties, and other monetary caps can hinder or kill small-business software projects altogether.

The Qt Libraries

The Qt libraries from Trolltech AS form the basis and underlying functionality of the K Desktop Environment. First released in 1994 as part of a commercial enterprise with liberal licensing, the libraries quickly became the foundation of KDE. Although initially shunned by programmers wishing to develop only free software clients, the Qt (and KDE) libraries have proven quite capable and appealing to C++ programmers around the world.

Since then, Trolltech has provided a noncommercial version of the libraries, named Qt Free Edition, for use with KDE. However, Trolltech still requires that you obtain and use the commercial versions of Qt, unlike software issued under the GNU General Public and Lesser License, if you want to use the libraries to build proprietary or binary-only software. Nevertheless, KDE developers continue to use Qt Free Edition because the Qt libraries, by agreement between Trolltech and the KDE Free Qt Foundation, will always be available for free for KDE developers and users.

The Qt libraries are generally installed under the `/usr/lib/qt-XXX/lib` directory, where *XXX* is the version of the installed libraries. The current version is 2.2.1, distributed with KDE 2.0.1, and the software libraries have filenames beginning with libqt*. Man pages documenting the available functions and data structures may be located under the `/usr/share/man/man3` directory on your Linux system.

The Qt libraries provide high-level C++ graphical interface function calls for developers. These function calls, also known as *application programming interfaces (APIs)*, provide seamless portability between different operating systems. Although the focus of this book is on Linux and XFree86, you can also easily port clients written using the Qt libraries to Windows 95/98/NT/2000, Solaris, HP-UX, Digital UNIX, Irix, FreeBSD, SCO, and AIX.

The Qt libraries, in concert with KDE's software libraries, provide a way for developers to generate sophisticated clients quickly. For example, the following source for a basic KDE client generated by KDE's KDevelop programming environment consists of less than a dozen lines of source in the `main()` function (see Chapter 21, "Using Qt and KDE" for details on how to quickly build simple clients):

```
#include "hello.h"

int main(int argc, char *argv[])
{
  KApplication app(argc, argv, "hello");

  if (app.isRestored())
  {
    RESTORE(HelloApp);
  }
  else
  {
    HelloApp *hello = new HelloApp();
    hello->show();

    if(argc>1)
    {
```

```
        hello->openDocumentFile(argv[1]);

    }

}


    return app.exec();

}
```

However, when the client is built, the result can be quite astonishing, as shown in Figure 19.2.

The client has a fully resizable window, window controls, a menu bar, a toolbar with icons, four menus with menu items, and a Help menu with active menu items. Much of this work is done through widget definitions in related header files, but even so the result is impressive considering that building the client from scratch takes about 15 seconds on a midrange Pentium computer. As the basis for KDE, these libraries can be used to build indisputably complex and powerful software for X11, as shown in Figure 19.3, which displays KDE's menuing system, the konqueror browser, an .mp3 player, the kworldwatch client, and kpager virtual pager.

GTK +

The GNOME X11 environment has grown steadily more popular since the GNOME Project was first started in 1997. Three years later, on August 15, 2000, a group of GNOME developers and organizations such as Compaq, Eazel, Free Software Foundation, Gnumatic, Helix Code, Henzai, Hewlett-Packard, IBM, Object Management Group, Red Hat, Sun Microsystems, TurboLinux, and VA Linux created the GNOME Foundation.

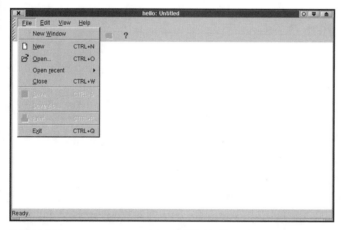

Figure 19.2 *You can construct a simple KDE client from a dozen lines of source code.*

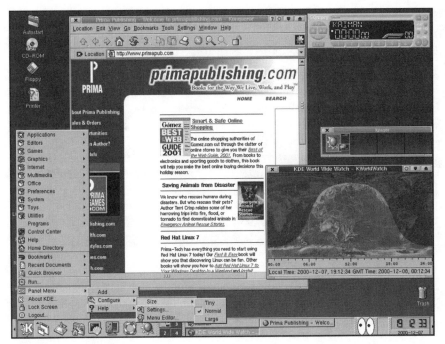

Figure 19.3 *The KDE desktop environment is built upon the Qt software libraries from Trolltech AS.*

The result has been increasing support for a totally free, unencumbered GNU GPL'd X11 development and session environment. GNOME uses the GTK+ toolkit, originally developed to provide a GUI for the premier Linux graphics client, the GIMP. Version 1.0 was released in March 1999, and the current version, 1.2, was released in May 2000. At the time of this writing, version 1.4 was in the works.

Like KDE, GNOME includes a variety of clients that take specific advantage of GNOME's features. One GNOME distribution, named Helix Code, includes a full suite of clients, including a window manager, office suite, and development environment. An example desktop is shown in Figure 19.4.

The GNOME development software consists of several different libraries:

- Glib—Consisting of a base library of "portable" functions, GLib also includes string-handling routines, data structures, and, most important, an event loop.

- GDK—This library is part of GNOME's portability, and is an abstraction layer between using higher-level widgets and creating X windows. Clients use GDK function calls for drawing or screen handling.

- GTK+ Object System—This higher-level toolkit of object-oriented function calls provides signaling, date inheritance, and other sophisticated widgets for such things as event and data handling.

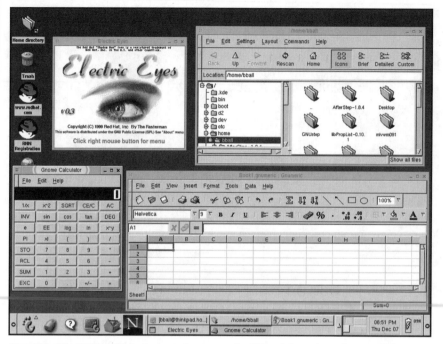

Figure 19.4 *The GNOME desktop environment for XFree86 consists of many different clients, each of which uses a hierarchy of software libraries for a sophisticated graphical interface.*

You'll find GNOME libraries with the names `libgdk*`, `libgnome*`, and `libgnorba*` under the `/usr/lib` directory. Many other libraries are included with a GNOME distribution. These other libraries are used to provide additional features and support for other objects, such as sound, graphics, or 3D objects.

For programmers interested in using automated development tools, GNOME also has a development tool named GLADE that may be of interest. The tool's results are somewhat on a par with those that you can obtain with KDE's KDevelop client, although the GLADE environment is not as sophisticated (at least at this point).

LessTif

The LessTif software libraries and development system, created by a group of developers known as the Hungry Programmers, grew out of a need for a totally free, high-quality, Motif-like toolkit. The LessTif libraries, which are compatible with Motif 1.2, may be used to create Motif-like clients, and offer software developers features similar to Motif.

First released during a time when the cost of acquiring the Motif source code hovered around $12,000, LessTif quickly acquired a legion of users, and scores of clients were built and distributed using the toolkit. The first version of the libraries was released in 1995, and the latest version, 0.91.8, was released August 31, 2000.

You can build LessTif from source code, or install a binary version on your Linux system. The majority of files will be installed under the `/usr/X11R6/LessTif/Motif1.2/lib` and `/usr/X11R6/LessTif/Motif2.0/lib` directories. Symbolic links with the names of the Motif libraries are used under the `/usr/X11R6/lib` directory. As with Motif, these files have names such as `libMrm.*`, `libXm.*`, and `libXlt.*`.

There are several different binary distributions, and the complete distribution consists of four files. The first file, a 1.6MB compressed archive, contains a base set of software libraries and documentation required to run (and develop) LessTif clients:

```
lesstif-0.91.4-1.i386.rpm
```

You can use a small (32KB) distribution of the LessTif `uil` and `xmbind` clients for developing software:

```
lesstif-clients-0.91.4-1.i386.rpm
```

A 350KB compressed package contains `#include` files, an `xmkmf` script, and widget documentation for developing LessTif clients:

```
lesstif-devel-0.91.4-1.i386.rpm
```

A small (90KB) compressed package contains an `mwm`-like window manager:

```
lesstif-mwm-0.91.4-1.i386.rpm
```

Along with `mwm`, one popular client that quickly and easily builds using LessTif, but that formerly required Motif, is the text editor `nedit`. This client, shown in Figure 19.5, is a feature-rich programmer's editor.

According to the Hungry Programmers, a number of Motif 2.0-compatible widgets have been created. However, since The Open Group has dropped Motif 2.0 and has since moved on to Motif 2.1, efforts are now focused on cloning Open Motif 2.1 features.

Open Motif

Open Motif is the source code and binary distribution of OSF/Motif for free operating systems, such as Linux, that use a free kernel. If you are a licensee of The Open Group, you can still distribute the binary form of commercial applications that you build using Open Motif. If you are not a licensee, however, you must provide source code to your client.

Open Motif includes source to the software libraries, window manager, example clients, and documentation (programming, reference, and style guides). You can

Figure 19.5 *You can build the* nedit *client from source code using LessTif or Open Motif.*

download the distribution from The Open Group (see "Resource Information" at the end of this chapter). Several files are available. The following 2.6MB compressed archive contains a ready-to-run copy of the mwm window manager and the basic required software support libraries for Red Hat Linux-based systems:

```
openmotif-2.1.30-linux-i386.tgz
```

The root user must install this runtime file at the base or root (/) directory.

The following 18MB compressed archive contains a directory named motif that includes man pages, documentation, source to the Motif libraries, and demonstration clients:

```
openmotif-2.1.30-src.tgz
```

The following 26MB compressed archive contains prebuilt example clients, necessary #include files, man pages, software development libraries, and documentation:

```
openmotif-devel-2.1.30-linux-i386.tgz
```

You should install this file if you want to develop Open Motif clients on your Linux system.

Resource Information

http://www.x.org/ — home page for the latest version of X11 from X.org, part of The Open Group and stewards of X11R6.

James Gettys and Robert W. Schleifer, *Xlib — C Language Interface* — an introduction to programming Xlib in C. You can find this documentation under the xc/doc/hardcopy/X11 directory of the X11R6's source tree.

Chris D. Peterson, *Athena Widget Set — C Language Interface* — an introduction and tutorial on the Athena toolkit. You can find this documentation under the xc/doc/hardcopy/Xaw directory of X11R6's source tree.

Joel McCormack, Paul Ascente, and Ralph Swick, *X Toolkit Intrinsics — C Language Interface* — a guide to the Xt toolkit. You can find this documentation under the xc/doc/hardcopy/Xt directory of X11R6's source tree.

http://www.opengroup.org/ — home page for The Open Group, Inc., a consortium of 227 companies (at last count) that holds licenses for X and Motif.

http://www.opengroup.org/openmotif/ — browse to this site to download the latest copy of Open Motif.

http://www.trolltech.com — home page for the Troll Tech Qt libraries for KDE.

http://www.kde.org — home page for KDE users.

http://developer.kde.org — home page for KDE developers.

http://www.gnome.org — home page for the GNOME Project, and the place to download GNOME software.

http://developer.gnome.org/ — home page for GNOME developers.

http://primates.helixcode.com/~miguel/gnome-history.html — the history of the GNOME Project.

http://www.lesstif.org — home page for the latest version of LessTif.

http://www.nedit.org — home page of the nedit editor for X11.

http://www-4.ibm.com/software/developer/library/gnome-programming/index.html?dwzone=linux — a development tutorial, hosted by IBM, on building GNOME clients.

http://glade.pn.org — home page for the GNOME GLADE development environment.

http://www.kdevelop.org — home page for the KDevelop client for KDE.

Chapter 20: Using LessTif and Open Motif

Considering licensing issues

Downloading and installing LessTif

Downloading and installing Open Motif

Programming with LessTif/Open Motif

This chapter gives an overview of downloading, installing, and using the LessTif and Open Motif toolkits for XFree86 and Linux. These toolkits provide various X clients and window managers, software libraries, and high-level development libraries that you can use to build sophisticated clients. Although both are free software, only LessTif enables you to develop binary-only clients without worry about royalties or licensing; Open Motif is a free version of the commercial Motif distribution from The Open Group, recently released free for noncommercial use.

These software libraries can help you save time and effort when building portable X11 software. The libraries take advantage of a platform's native environment when you rebuild and compile your software for other target hardware. This means that unless you specifically program your software to have a dependency on a particular computer's hardware, clients that you develop using these toolkits should be extremely portable at the source code level.

This chapter also provides a simple Motif client that shows a sampling of Motif's capabilities.

Considering Licensing Issues

Until recently, licensing was a consideration when using Motif. However, you can now produce clone Motif clients using the LessTif software toolkits. And since The Open Group has released Open Motif, you can now develop Open Source clients using the very latest Motif toolkits. This release can save a Linux developer more than $100, as you previously had to purchase Motif for Linux and XFree86 from a licensed software vendor.

As you learned in Chapter 19, "X11 Programming Toolkits Overview," Motif and its source code became available for free download May 15, 2000. However, remember that you may develop only Open Source clients using this software. Other proprietary avenues still require licensing and perhaps royalties to The Open Group.

Downloading and Installing LessTif

You can download LessTif from the project's home page (see the "Resource Information" section at the end of this chapter). The current version, 0.91.8, was released on August 31, 2000 (and an updated version almost certainly will be released before you read this book). On the home page, you'll find a link to LessTif's download page.

LessTif is available for a variety of computer platforms, operating systems, and Linux distributions. You can download the source code, compressed tarballs of binaries, the binaries in `rpm` format, and binaries in zip format. Binary distributions are available for Red Hat Linux, generic Linux (`libc5`-based), FreeBSD, and OS/2.

Source distributions are available in compressed tarballs in gzip or bzip2 format. The source distribution is available in several packages, but the primary source is contained in a single file, lesstif-0.91.8.tar.bz2, a 2.6MB bzip2 tarball, or lesstif-0.91.8.tar.gz, a 3.5MB tarball. After downloading, decompress the archive like this:

```
# tar xvzf less*gz
lesstif-0.91.8/README
lesstif-0.91.8/release-notes.html
lesstif-0.91.8/AUTHORS
lesstif-0.91.8/BUG-REPORTING
lesstif-0.91.8/COPYING
....
```

In this example, you use the `tar` command to decompress the LessTif source; a directory named `lesstif-0.91.8` is then created. You need nearly 19MB for the directory (and even more for the build). A file named INSTALL immediately under the LessTif directory provides documentation about configuring, building, and installing LessTif. You will need to install on your system a copy of XFree86's development software libraries and header files. To start the process, you can use the included `configure` script.

> See Chapter 18, "Basic X11 Programming," for more information about software development tools such as `make`, `xmkmf`, and `autoconf` for X11 client development.

You can also use this script to specify whether you want to build and install shared or static libraries, debugging symbols in clients, and a production version. You can also specify where to install the distribution. Or you can simply type the following:

```
# ./configure
```

After you press Enter, the script examines your system. If all goes well, after a minute or so the script then creates a top-level file named Makefile (along with many Makefiles in the source tree). You can then use the `make` command to build the distribution, as follows:

```
# make
```

After you press Enter, the build continues. On a 500MHz Intel-based PC, this process takes about six minutes. When finished, you can install the distribution (as root) by again using the make command, as follows:

```
# make install
```

This command copies and installs the software libraries, example programs, man pages, development libraries, and header files onto your system. You can also build an extensive set of test clients if you navigate into the test directory under the LessTif source tree, then type the following command:

```
# make
```

After you press Enter, the build takes nearly as long to complete as it takes to build LessTif itself! To run a client, such as test1 under the lesstif-0.91,8/ test/Xm/filesb directory, you must tell the client where the installed LessTif libraries are located. One way to do this is to create an environment variable named LD_LIBRARY_PATH, like this:

```
$ export LD_LIBRARY_PATH=/usr/local/LessTif/Motif1.2/lib
```

After you press Enter, you can then run the test program, as shown in Figure 20.1.

By default, the LessTif distribution will be installed under the /usr/local/LessTif directory. After installation, you are set up to begin programming using LessTif!

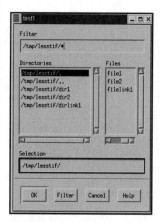

Figure 20.1 *The* test1 *client included with LessTif's Motif clone distribution is one of hundreds of example programs included with the software libraries.*

Downloading and Installing Open Motif

You can download Open Motif from the Open Motif developer's home page (see "Resource Information" at the end of this chapter). First, click the Download Open Motif link. You'll then see another page with links either to download the software or to order the software on CD-ROM (which includes all versions, binaries, documentation, and source).

You need to supply your name and a valid email address. Packages are available in Debian's .deb, rpm's .rpm, and tar's .tgz format. For compressed tarballs and most Linux systems, you can use the following:

- openmotif-2.1.30-linux-i386.tgz, a 26.5MB compressed tarball of binary runtime files for most Linux distributions
- openmotif-2.1.30-src.tgz, an 18MB archive containing the source code to the runtime libraries of Open Motif
- openmotif-devel-2.1.30-linux-i386.tgz, a 26MB file containing the development libraries, header files, and documentation for developing Open Motif clients
- openmotif-2.1.30-2_ICS.src.tgz, a 17MB archive containing the source to Open Motif

The current version is 2.1.30, which was released in December 2000. Like LessTif, Open Motif is available for a variety of computer platforms, operating systems, and Linux distributions. Binary distributions are available for Linux on Compaq Alpha CPUs, ia64 platforms, Intel-based PCs, SPARC workstations, PowerPC platforms, and FreeBSD (Intel only).

Open Motif development requires that you download and install the runtime and development archives. After downloading, decompress the source archive like this:

```
# tar xzvf openmotif-2.1.30-2_ICS.src.tgz
openmotif-2.1.30-icsbuild.patch
openmotif-2.1.30-icsextra.tgz
openmotif-2.1.30-mwm.patch
openmotif-2.1.30-src.tgz
```

The latest release includes some patch files. Next, decompress the source code like this:

```
# tar xzvf openmotif-2.1.30-src.tgz
```

This command creates a directory named `motif`. You should then decompress the "extra" archive (which contains an additional demonstration client and documentation), as follows:

```
# tar xvzf open*extra*tgz
```

After you press Enter, the contents will be saved under the new `motif` directory. Next, you apply both software patches using the `patch` command like this:

```
# patch -p0 < openmotif-2.1.30-icsbuild.patch
...
patching file motif/bindings/Imakefile
patching file motif/config/cf/Imakefile
patching file motif/config/cf/Motif.tmpl
patching file motif/config/cf/host.def
...
# patch -p0 < openmotif-2.1.30-mwm.patch
patching file motif/clients/mwm/WmIconBox.c
```

The changes update the source to Open Motif. Next, use the `chmod` command recursively to ensure write access throughout the source tree:

```
# chmod -R +w motif
```

Next, navigate into the `motif` directory's `config/cf` subdirectory, then create a directory named `OPENGROUP`. Then move everything under the `cf` directory into the new `OPENGROUP` directory, as follows:

```
# cd motif/config/cf
# mkdir OPENGROUP
# mv * OPENGROUP
mv: cannot move `OPENGROUP' to a subdirectory of itself, `OPENGROUP/OPENGROUP'
```

Note that you'll get an error message; proceed anyway, and then create links of the contents of your XFree86's `/usr/X11R6/lib/X11/config` directory by using the `ln` command:

```
# ln -s /usr/X11R6/lib/X11/config/* .
```

Note the trailing period (.) in the preceding command line. Next, delete the links named `Motif.tmpl`, `Motif.rules`, and `host.def`:

```
# rm Motif.tmpl Motif.rules host.def
rm: remove `Motif.tmpl'? y
rm: remove `Motif.rules'? y
rm: remove `host.def'? y
```

Next, move the files `Imakefile`, `Motif.tmp`, `Motif.rules`, and `host.def` from the `OPENGROUP` subdirectory to the `cf` directory, as follows:

```
# mv OPENGROUP/{Imakefile,Motif.tmpl,Motif.rules,host.def} .
```

Again note the trailing period (.). Finally, you can start the build by navigating to the top-level `motif` directory and using the `make` command as follows:

```
# make World >& world.log
```

If you'd like to watch the progress of the `make.log` file, you can use the `tail` command's `-f` option as follows:

```
# tail -f world.log
```

If everything goes well, the build will finish and you can then use the `make` command with the `install` keyword to install the Open Motif libraries and documentation on your system. However, a far easier way to get started is to install the binary distribution for your version of Linux and CPU. For example, Intel-based PC Linux users can download the following binary distributions:

```
openmotif-2.1.30-linux-i386.tgz
openmotif-devel-2.1.30-linux-i386.tgz
```

Root installs these 5MB and 29MB archive files at the base of your Linux system. After downloading the files, copy them to your root directory (/), then use the `tar` command to extract the contents onto your file system, as follows:

```
# tar xvzf openmotif-2.1.30-linux-i386.tgz
...
# tar xvzf openmotif-2.1.30-linux-i386.tgz
...
```

After installation, you're ready to begin developing Open Motif clients!

> You may want to run the `ldconfig` command (as root). After you install the aforementioned archives, a missing link, `libXm.so.2`, may be discovered. You can fix this problem by using the `ldconfig` command (as root). Running `ldconfig` will fix any problems with software library links by creating missing links while scanning your system's libraries.

NOTE

You'll find a number of demonstration clients installed under the `/usr/X11R6/bin` and `/usr/X11R6/xmdemos` directories. For example, you can try the `filemanager` client as follows:

```
# filemanager &
```

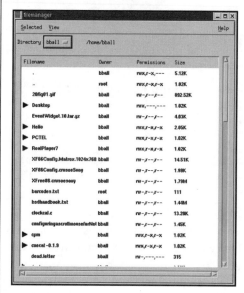

Figure 20.2 *The* `filemanager` *client is just one many different clients installed with Open Motif for XFree86.*

After you press Enter, you'll see the sample client, as shown in Figure 20.2.

Programming with LessTif/Open Motif

To program with the LessTif or Open Motif toolkits, you must understand the variety of function calls and routines included with the software distributions. You can read the individual man pages for each of the documented Open Motif routines by browsing the `/usr/X11R6/man/man3` directory or learn about LesTif by browsing the `/usr/local/LessTif/doc/man/man3` directory. However, one of the best ways to learn about these toolkits is to study the source code of the example clients that are included with the distributions.

You can also peruse various online tutorials available on the Web, check out commercial Motif programming guides from various publishers, or read various FAQs and documentation included with these toolkits. You'll find quite a bit of documentation included with LessTif under its `/usr/local/LessTif/doc` directory. You can find documentation for Open Motif under the `/usr/doc/openmotif-2.1.30` and `/usr/doc/openmotif-devel-2.1.30` directories.

Can't Read the Documentation?

If you find that the gv client included with your Linux distribution cannot read the PostScript files included with Open Motif, don't despair. You can use the GhostScript ps2ps PostScript "distiller" client, which will convert each file to a simpler (and faster) PostScript file. Decompress the files, then run each by entering the following command:

ps2ps *original*.ps *newfile*.ps

You'll then find that you can read the documents if you enlarge them properly.

Creating a Simple Client

This section provides a simple client that you can try with your installed versions of LessTif and Open Motif. This bare-bones client really isn't useful for anything except a demonstration. You'll also get a short Imakefile you can try when building the client, although a simple compiler command line will suffice for this project. Here's the client's code:

```
/* myclient - a simple Motif app */
#include <Xm/RowColumn.h>
#include <Xm/MainW.h>
#include <Xm/CascadeB.h>
#include <Xm/Label.h>
#include <Xm/MessageB.h>
#include <Xm/SeparatoG.h>
#include <Xm/PushBG.h>


Widget myclient;


void myclient_quit_action() { exit(0); }


void myclient_dialog_handler(myclient_dialog)
Widget myclient_dialog;
{
        XtUnmanageChild(myclient_dialog);

}
```

```
void myclient_about_action()
{
    Arg        args[10];
    Widget     about_dialog;
    XmString myclient_aboutstring;

    myclient_aboutstring = \
            XmStringCreateLocalized("Hello! This is About myclient!");
    about_dialog = XmCreateMessageDialog (myclient, "dialog", args, 0);
    XtVaSetValues(about_dialog, XmNmessageString, myclient_aboutstring, \
            NULL, NULL);
    XtAddCallback(about_dialog, XmNokCallback, myclient_dialog_handler, NULL);
    XmStringFree(myclient_aboutstring); XtManageChild(about_dialog);
};

/* main program begins here */
main (argc, argv)
int argc;
char *argv[];
{
    Widget    myclient_window,
              myclient_menubar,
              myclient_filepulldown,
                   NEW,
                   OPEN,
                   CLOSE,
                   SAVE,
                   QUIT,
              myclient_editpulldown,
                   CUT,
                   COPY,
                   PASTE,
              myclient_aboutpulldown,
                   ABOUT,
              myclientlabel;
    XmString  myclient_tempstring;
    XtAppContext myclient_app;
    Pixmap myclient_pixmap;


XtSetLanguageProc (NULL, NULL, NULL);
```

```
myclient = XtVaAppInitialize(&myclient_app, "myclient", NULL, \
        0, &argc, argv, NULL, XmNwidth, 440, XmNheight, 470, NULL);
myclient_window = XtVaCreateManagedWidget("myclient", \
        xmMainWindowWidgetClass, myclient, Xm
NscrollingPolicy, XmAUTOMATIC, NULL);
myclient_menubar = XmCreateMenuBar(myclient_window, \
        "myclient_menubar", NULL, 0);
myclient_filepulldown = XmCreatePulldownMenu (myclient_menubar,
        "File", NULL, 0);
myclient_tempstring = XmStringCreateLocalized ("File");

XtVaCreateManagedWidget ("File", xmCascadeButtonWidgetClass, \
        myclient_menubar, XmNlabelStri
ng, myclient_tempstring, XmNmnemonic, 'F', XmNsubMenuId,\
        myclient_filepulldown, NULL);
XmStringFree(myclient_tempstring);
NEW = XtVaCreateManagedWidget("New", xmPushButtonGadgetClass, \
        myclient_filepulldown, NULL);
OPEN = XtVaCreateManagedWidget("Open", xmPushButtonGadgetClass,\
        myclient_filepulldown, NULL);
XtVaCreateManagedWidget("separator", xmSeparatorGadgetClass, \
        myclient_filepulldown,NULL);
CLOSE = XtVaCreateManagedWidget("Close", xmPushButtonGadgetClass, \
        myclient_filepulldown, NULL);
SAVE = XtVaCreateManagedWidget("Save", xmPushButtonGadgetClass, \
        myclient_filepulldown, NULL);
XtVaCreateManagedWidget("separator", xmSeparatorGadgetClass, \
        myclient_filepulldown,NULL);
QUIT = XtVaCreateManagedWidget("Quit", xmPushButtonGadgetClass, \
        myclient_filepulldown, NULL);
XtAddCallback(QUIT, XmNactivateCallback, myclient_quit_action, NULL);

myclient_editpulldown = XmCreatePulldownMenu(myclient_menubar, \
        "Edit", NULL, 0);
myclient_tempstring = XmStringCreateLocalized ("Edit");
XtVaCreateManagedWidget ("Edit", xmCascadeButtonWidgetClass, \
        myclient_menubar, XmNlabelStri
ng, myclient_tempstring, XmNmnemonic, 'E', XmNsubMenuId, \
        myclient_editpulldown, NULL);
XmStringFree(myclient_tempstring);
```

```
CUT = XtVaCreateManagedWidget("Cut", xmPushButtonGadgetClass, \
        myclient_editpulldown, NULL);
COPY = XtVaCreateManagedWidget("Copy", xmPushButtonGadgetClass, \
        myclient_editpulldown, NULL);
PASTE = XtVaCreateManagedWidget("Paste", xmPushButtonGadgetClass, \
        myclient_editpulldown, NULL);


myclient_aboutpulldown = XmCreatePulldownMenu(myclient_menubar, \
        "About", NULL, 0);
myclient_tempstring = XmStringCreateLocalized ("About");
XtVaCreateManagedWidget ("About", xmCascadeButtonWidgetClass, \
        myclient_menubar, XmNlabelString, myclient_tempstring,\
        XmNmnemonic, 'A', XmNsubMenuId, \
        myclient_aboutpulldown, NULL);
XmStringFree(myclient_tempstring);
XtVaSetValues(myclient_menubar, XmNmenuHelpWidget, \
        XtNameToWidget(myclient_menubar,"About"), NULL);
ABOUT = XtVaCreateManagedWidget ("About", xmPushButtonGadgetClass, \
        myclient_aboutpulldown, NULL);
XtAddCallback(ABOUT, XmNactivateCallback, myclient_about_action, NULL);


myclient_pixmap = XmGetPixmap(XtScreen(myclient),\
        argv[1],BlackPixelOfScreen(XtScreen (myclient)),\
        WhitePixelOfScreen(XtScreen (myclient)));
myclientlabel = XtVaCreateManagedWidget ("myclientlabel", \
        xmLabelWidgetClass,myclient_window, XmNlabelType,\
        XmPIXMAP,XmNlabelPixmap,myclient_pixmap,NULL);
    XtVaSetValues (myclient_window,XmNworkWindow, myclientlabel, NULL);
    XtManageChild(myclient_menubar);
    XtRealizeWidget(myclient);
    XtAppMainLoop (myclient_app);
    return (0);
}
```

This program starts by defining callback routines, or routines that run in response to a menu selection or button press. Next, the main() portion of the client starts by defining a number of widgets such as the main window and menus, later created by the Motif XmCreateMenuBar() and XmCreatePulldownMenu() toolkit functions. After creating the client, menus, and menu items, the program creates a dialog box named ABOUT. Next, the Motif XmGetPixmap() function is used to assign an X11 pixmap, specified on the command line, to display in the main window.

Event handling is even made easier when using Motif, as specifying XmNmnemonic and a shortcut key, or *accelerator*, enables the user to use Alt+*key* to activate a widget. In this case, pressing Alt+F, Alt+E, or Alt+A will activate the File, Edit, or About menus. Using the Motif toolkit functions can make the job of building a graphical interface for your X11 clients a lot easier. However, you can achieve the same result using Xt or even Xlib functions (see the next section, "Building a Simple Client").

Building a Simple Client

You can compile the sample client by using a single command line to instruct the compiler (gcc) where to find the various #include files and using the X11 and Motif toolkit libraries to link into the final client code executable:

```
$ gcc -o myclient myclient.c -I/usr/X11R6/include \
 -L/usr/X11R6/lib -lXp -lXm -lXpm -lXt -lXext -lX11
```

After you press Enter, you can then run the client, specifying a pixmap graphic to display in the root of the window widget, as follows:

```
# ./myclient /home/bball/faces.xpm
```

The client then appears, and should look similar to that shown in Figure 20.3.

Instead of typing the previous command line over and over, you can use this Makefile instead:

```
CC = gcc
INCLUDES = -I/usr/X11R6/include
LIBS= -L/usr/X11R6/lib -lXp -lXm -lXt -lXext -lX11
OBJS = myclient.o
myclient : $(OBJS)
        $(CC) -o myclient $(OBJS) $(INCLUDES) $(LIBS)
```

Enter the text into a file named Makefile. You can then edit and rebuild the client using the make command. If you prefer, you can also craft an Imakefile or use the autoconf command to create a configure script for your project.

To build this client using LessTif, you can use a Makefile like this:

```
CC = gcc
INCLUDES = -I/usr/local/LessTif/Motif1.2/include
LIBS= -L/usr/local/LessTif/Motif1.2/lib -lXm -L/usr/X11R6/lib -lXt -lXext -lX11
OBJS = myclient.o
myclient : $(OBJS)
        $(CC) -o myclient $(OBJS) $(INCLUDES) $(LIBS)
```

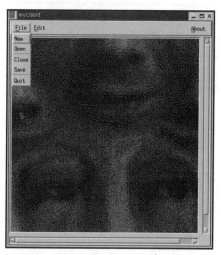

Figure 20.3 *Using Motif can make the job of quickly creating graphical interfaces for your client a lot easier.*

Note that this example specifies the LessTif libXm library instead of Open Motif's libXm. You'll still need to specify XFree86's toolkit libraries in order to link the compiled client properly (and you will still need to add to your environment the path to LessTif's Motif-clone libraries). However, the result will be the same as if you had used Open Motif's toolkit.

Resource Information

http://www.lesstif.org—home page of the Hungry Programmers' LessTif project.

http://www.lesstif.org/download.html—the download page where you can get various versions of LessTif.

ftp://ftp.hungry.com/pub/hungry/lesstif/srcdist/—FTP site for the source to LessTif.

http://www.openmotif.org—home page for Open Motif programming and projects; you'll also find quite a few articles, links to the Open Motif CVS tree (so you can download today's version), along with a link to a bug database.

http://www.motifzone.net—a URL alias for **http://www.openmotif.org**.

http://www.openmotif.org/download—a link from which you can download Open Motif.

ftp://download.motifzone.net/pub/src/—an FTP site for downloading Open Motif.

Chapter 21: Using Qt and KDE

Understanding licensing issues

Downloading and installing Qt and KDE libraries

Programming with Qt and KDE

This chapter provides a short overview of using the Qt and KDE toolkits to build a simple KDE client. You'll learn about licensing considerations, how to download and install the Qt and KDE development libraries, and how to set up and run a graphical development client used for developing complex KDE clients.

Understanding Licensing Issues

As you've already learned, many different software licenses are applied and used in a Linux distribution and for X11 software. Some software is distributed in source code form under the GNU General Public License (GPL), whereas other packages are proprietary, binary-only clients. XFree86 and its fonts, clients, documentation, source code, and graphics are copyrighted by the XFree86 Project, Inc. However, portions are copyrighted and owned by the X Consortium, Inc., and the majority of code is covered by a Berkeley-based copyright. Newer distributions of XFree86 also contain copyrighted material from NVidia, Inc.

Open Source Versus Proprietary Licensing

The spectrum of software licensing ranges from the GNU GPL through Open Source to binary-only, single-user packages. The GNU GPL, along with the Lesser GPL, offers the greatest freedom for software developers. However, the GPL also generally mandates distribution of source code or source code changes to Open Source software. Although the K Desktop Environment and many of its clients are distributed under the GNU GPL, KDE's base set of libraries was built using the Qt Free Edition 2.2.1 toolkit.

This toolkit is distributed under the Q Public License (QPL), which is copyrighted by Trolltech AS. One of the limitations of using this license is that if you use the Qt toolkit to create commercial software, you must purchase a license for Trolltech's Qt Professional Edition of the Qt libraries. This is unlike GNOME and its many clients, which are unencumbered by restrictive licensing. So, although the Qt toolkit technically falls under the category of Open Source software, and its future is certainly protected by the KDE Foundation, you must consider licensing if you desire to create and sell software using this toolkit.

Another consideration is that if you find a problem with a function call in the Qt toolkit and create a fix, you may not distribute the fix with a modified library unless you first contact Trolltech. You will also not get technical support unless you have purchased the Qt Professional Edition.

Breaking News About Qt 2.2.1

The latest release of Qt at the time of this writing is Qt 2.2.1, which is basically a maintenance fix. By the time that you read this book, most commercial Linux distributions will include this toolkit or a newer version. The previous release, version 2.2, was a major upgrade, with compatibility added for other operating systems, graphical user interface (GUI) drawing improvements, and the use of different "modules," or source components, of the toolkit library. The latter change organized the library's widgets into various sets according to function, such as GUI controls, drawing, dialog boxes, and networking.

The previous stable version of Qt was 1.44. At this point, you must use the newer libraries if you want to run clients developed with Qt 2.0 and higher. The Qt 1.44 libraries provide the only support for earlier clients.

Downloading and Installing Qt and KDE Libraries

Although you can download and install Qt and KDE from source, a much easier way to install or upgrade your system is to use software archives used by your system. For example, users of Red Hat Linux–based systems will want to download the requisite set of .rpm packages. A minimal installation of KDE 2.0, along with Qt 2.2.1 and all development files and libraries, requires 27 .rpm archives that will take up more than 63MB hard drive space. Table 21.1 lists these archives and briefly describes their contents.

The library .rpm archives should be installed first, followed by support and utility packages. If you receive any dependency errors, install the required package first. After installation, you'll be able to start KDE 2.0 and begin designing your first clients.

Programming with Qt and KDE

A full overview of programming KDE clients using the Qt toolkit and additional KDE 2.0 development libraries is beyond the scope of this book. However, you can use one or more of the sophisticated development tools included with these distributions to take a few shortcuts on the path to learning more about Qt and KDE. The important thing to remember is that although Qt provides a high-level widget toolkit, you'll also need to use KDE's software toolkit to develop KDE 2.0-compatible clients.

Table 21.1 .rpm Archives Required for a Minimal KDE 2.0 Install

Archive	Description
flex-2.5.4a-13.i386.rpm	Lexical analyzer for KDE documentation
htdig-3.2.0-0..b2.i386.rpm	The ht://Dig Web search engine software
kde1-compat-1.1.2-2.i386.rpm	Compatibility libraries for KDE 1.X users
kde1-compat-devel-1.1.2-2.i386.rpm	Compatibility libraries for developing KDE 1.X clients
kdeadmin-2.0-2.i386.rpm	KDE 2.0 administrative utilities
kdebase-2.0-3.i386.rpm	Base KDE 2.0 clients
kdegames-2.0-2.i386.rpm	KDE 2.0 games distribution
kdegraphics-2.0-2.i386.rpm	KDE 2.0 graphics clients
kdelibs-2.0-7.i386.rpm	KDE 2.0 base libraries
kdelibs-devel-2.0-7.i386.rpm	KDE 2.0 development libraries
kdelibs-sound-2.0-7.i386.rpm	KDE 2.0 sound libraries
kdelibs-sound-devel-2.0-7.i386.rpm	KDE 2.0 sound development libraries
kdemultimedia-2.0-1.i386.rpm	KDE 2.0 multimedia clients
kdenetwork-2.0-4.i386.rpm	KDE 2.0 network clients
kdenetwork-ppp-2.0-4.i386.rpm	KDE 2.0 PPP clients
kdepim-2.0-1.i386.rpm	KDE 2.0 personal information management (PIM) clients
kdesupport-2.0-5.i386.rpm	KDE 2.0 skeleton files, links, and resources
kdesupport-devel-2.0-5.i386.rpm	KDE 2.0 skeleton files, links, and resources
kdetoys-2.0-1.i386.rpm	KDE 2.0 miscellaneous clients
kdeutils-2.0.-1.i386.rpm	KDE 2.0 utilities
koffice-2.0-1.i386.rpm	KDE 2.0's KOffice distribution
libmng-0.9.3-1.i386.rpm	KDE 2.0's JPEG Network Graphics and Multiple-Image Network Graphics (MNG) libraries
qt-2.2.1-6.i386.rpm	The Qt 2.2.1 base libraries
qt-Xt-2.2.1-6.i386.rpm	X11 Xt support for Qt 2.2.1
qt-designer-2.2.1-6.i386.rpm	Qt's GUI development client
qt-devel-2.2.1-6.i386.rpm	Qt development libraries and man pages
qt-static-2.2.1-6.i386.rpm	Libraries to build static Qt clients

You can also develop graphic X11 clients using just the Qt libraries; the applications will be cross-platform–compatible, but won't be able to use KDE 2.0's features. Development for Qt and KDE clients primarily involves the use of the C++ language.

Simple Client Development with Qt Designer

Qt Designer, included with the latest Qt libraries, is a graphical development client for rapidly prototyping applications and generating a *user interface* or .ui file containing a high-level description of your form. You can start this client from the command line of an X terminal window as follows:

```
# designer &
```

After you press Enter, you'll see the client's main window, as shown in Figure 21.1.

The design interface features various widgets that you can apply to a selected layout. To begin your design, click the New menu item from Qt Designer's File menu. You'll then see the New Form dialog box shown in Figure 21.2, from which you can choose a type of *form* or framework for your project.

Figure 21.1 *Qt Designer is a GUI prototyping tool for quickly building the framework of cross-platform applications under XFree86 and Linux.*

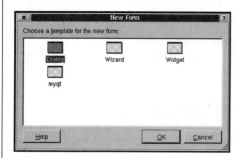

Figure 21.2 *Choose an initial form for your Qt Designer project.*

Click on a form, then click the OK button. The main window changes, and you can add widgets or features, and configure widgets, features, or text labels belonging to your new form. For example, you can create a nearly complete dialog box (named MyForm) for a subsystem of a client, then preview the form (as shown in Figure 21.3) before saving the project to an individual file.

After you are satisfied with the layout and construction of your form, you can then use some of Qt Designer's advanced features to connect messaging between different form elements or elements in your project. To save your project, press Ctrl+s or use the File menu's Save or Save As menu items. The form's project will be saved with a filename ending in .ui. To create a header file and C++ code from your .ui file (perhaps named MyForm), use Qt's user interface compiler, uic, as follows:

```
# uic -o MyForm.h MyForm.ui
```

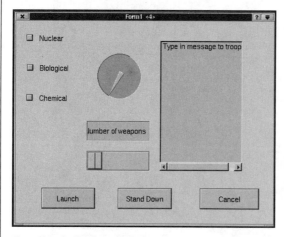

Figure 21.3 *Qt Designer allows you to preview forms prior to saving projects.*

This command creates the header file in C++ format. Next, again use the `uic` command and include your new header file, but this time, specify an output C++ file, as follows:

```
# uic -i MyForm.h -o MyForm.cpp MyForm.ui
```

You can then create a simple client by wrapping the generated code with something like the following:

```
#include <qapplication.h>
#include "MyForm.h"
int main( int argc, char* argv[] );
{
                QApplication app(argc, argv);
                Form1 Form1;
                app.setMainWidget(&Form1);
                Form1.show();
                int ret = app.exec();
                return ret;
}
```

Save the wrapper as `MyFormProtoTest.cpp`. You can then use Qt's Meta Object Compiler, or moc, along with the g++ compiler to build your simple client as follows:

```
# moc -o moc_MyForm.cpp MyForm.h
# g++ -I/opt/kde2 /include MyForm.cpp MyFormProtoTest.cpp  \
moc_MyForm.cpp -L/opt/kde2/lib -lqt
```

In the above example, the g++ compiler is instructed through the `-I` option to look for required #include files under the `/opt/kde2/include` directory. Linking of the compiled program is then accomplished through the library, or `-L` option, followed by a pathname to the Qt software libraries. When the compile and build finishes, you can run the resulting client like this:

```
# ./a.out
```

Simple Client Development with KDevelop

This section provides a short overview of how to use KDevelop version 1.3 to quickly prototype and build a simple KDE client. KDevelop is a complex and capable client with many different features. Version 1.3 is the first version able to create projects aimed at producing KDE 2.0 clients.

To use KDevelop, your system should have an installed base of C and C++ development tools such as g++, GNU make, Perl, autoconf, automake, flex, and, of course, the KDE and Qt development libraries. The current version of KDevelop at the time of this writing, 1.3, also requires the Qt libraries version 1.42 or 1.44 (a newer KDevelop will probably be available by the time that you read this book).

You can start KDevelop from KDE's desktop panel, or through an X terminal window as follows:

```
# kdevelop &
```

You can also specify a project name like this:

```
# kdevelop myproject.kdevprj
```

If you'd like to have KDevelop run through its setup procedure (to check for other installed utilities to enable additional features), use its --setup feature as follows:

```
# kdevelop --setup
```

If you start KDevelop by itself from the command line, you'll see the main window as shown in Figure 21.4.

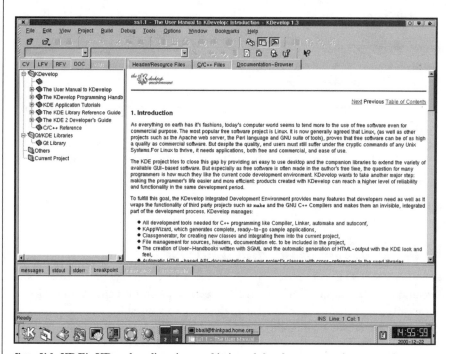

Figure 21.4 *KDE's KDevelop client is a sophisticated development environment for building KDE 2.0 applications.*

Note that the main KDevelop window features a browser-like interface that lists a host of reference materials and documentation, such as the KDE Application Tutorial, the KDE Library Reference Guide, and the KDE Developer's Guide. Although you should read this documentation thoroughly first, you can quickly create your first project by clicking the New menu item under the Project menu. You'll see a six-step KDE Application Wizard, as shown in Figure 21.5.

Note that you can use KDevelop to prototype more than a dozen different types of clients, including a GNOME application. For example, click the Normal application option under the KDE drop-down list in the wizard's scrolling window. When finished, click the Next button. You'll then see the Generate Settings dialog box, as shown in Figure 21.6.

Use the Generate Settings dialog box to select your program's icons, assign a project name, and enter directory, author, and email information. Note that KDevelop automatically generates files, such as the standard GNU install, readme, and copying files. You'll need to add information to these files before distributing your client. When you are finished configuring your project's initial settings, click the Next button to continue. The next dialog box, Version Control System Support (shown in Figure 21.7), enables you to select whether you'd like to use the Concurrent Versions System version control system.

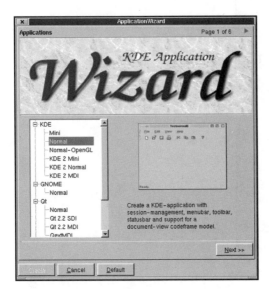

Figure 21.5 *KDevelop features a wizard interface for setting up your project for a variety of systems, including GNOME.*

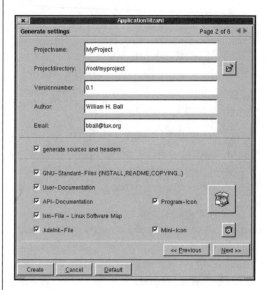

Figure 21.6 *Enter your project name, directory, author, email, and other information when starting a project.*

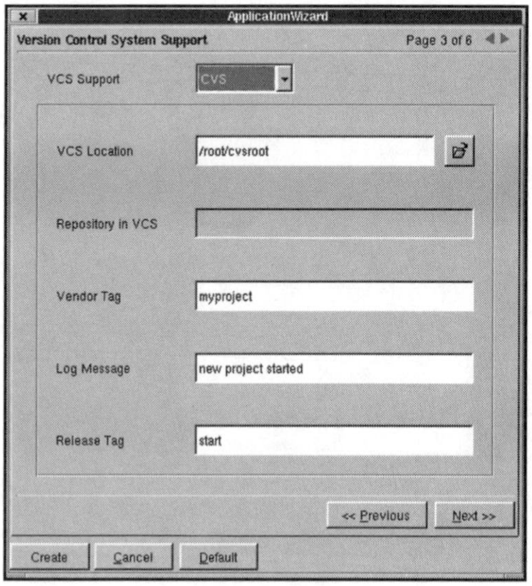

Figure 21.7 *KDevelop can use CVS to control your project.*

Click the Next button to navigate through the next several dialog boxes. These dialog boxes use standard templates for .h and .cpp files. When you are finished, click the Create button. You'll then see the last page of the wizard. Messages scroll by as KDevelop builds your project environment and a skeletal configuration script. Any error messages, such as for missing documentation utilities or other components, appear in the bottom of the dialog box, as shown in Figure 21.8.

If you receive any fatal errors, or if KDevelop is unable to build a project skeleton in your project directory, you may need to reinstall some of the required components listed in Table 21.1. When you are finished, click the Exit button. You should then see the main KDevelop window, as shown in Figure 21.9.

Use the browser on the left side of the main window to click on elements of your client. You can edit or enter changes and additional code using the editor window on the right side of the display. Toolbar buttons along the top of the screen (below KDevelop's menu bar) correspond to menu items. You can use these buttons for file and editing operations, or to compile, make, rebuild, debug, and run your client.

The next step is to use the Build menu's Configure menu item to create a Makefile for your project (see Figure 21.10).

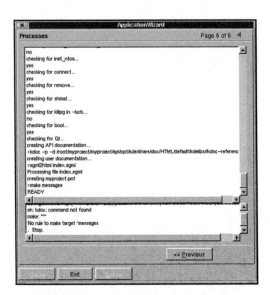

Figure 21.8 *KDevelop automatically checks your build environment when you first create a project.*

Figure 21.9 *Use KDevelop's main window to browse through your project's files and enter working code between program elements.*

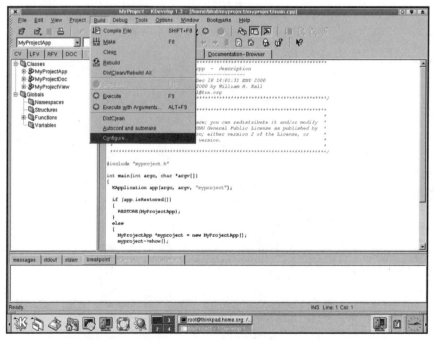

Figure 21.10 *Use KDevelop's Build menu to configure your project before building it.*

A small dialog box prompts you for any arguments to add to the `configure` command line prior to building.

The Build menu contains most of the operations that you would usually accomplish at the command line when using the `make` command, such as the following:

```
# make clean
```

This command line, as well as the Build menu's Clean item, deletes any previously compiled portions of your project, along with any built client. You can also use the Build menu's Configure item to run your created configure script again (a configure script, but no Makefile, is usually found with KDE clients distributed as source code). You'll also use the Build menu's DistClean/Rebuild All menu item prior to packaging your client and distributing it on the Internet or your Web or FTP site.

After creating your Makefile, you can then use KDevelop's Run toolbar item to run your client. After you click the icon (a plain sprocket), your client builds and launches, as shown in Figure 21.11.

Note that KDevelop creates a skeletal client with working dialog boxes, such as the File menu's Open menu item, and the Help menu's Contents and About menu items.

Figure 21.11 *You can use KDevelop to build and launch your project's client during the development cycle.*

Resource Information

http://www.trolltech.com—home page for the Trolltech AS, a Norwegian company distributing Qt Free Edition.

http://www.trolltech.com/qt-snapshots.html—the link to download the very latest (unstable) version of the Qt libraries.

http://www.kde.org—home page for the K Desktop Environment.

http://www.gnu.org—home page for the GNU software distributions, with links to essays, papers, and editorials regarding free software versus Open Source software.

http://www.opensource.org—the starting place to learn more about Open Source software and its definitions.

qt-interest—the first of three mailing lists hosted by Trolltech regarding Qt. You can subscribe by sending a message to **qt-interest-request@trolltech.com**.

qt-announce—the second of three mailing lists hosted by Trolltech regarding Qt. You can subscribe by sending a message to **qt-announce-request@trolltech.com**.

snapshot-users—a forum of discussions, hosted by Trolltech at **http://www.trolltech.com**, regarding the very latest unstable releases of Qt.

http://www.kdevelop.org—home page of the KDevelop client for KDE.

kdevelop—the KDevelop mailing list, available through **kdevelop-request @barney.cs.uni-potsdam.de**.

Chapter 22: Using GTK+

Understanding licensing issues

Downloading and installing GNOME

Programming with GTK+ and GNOME

This chapter provides a short overview of using the GTK+ toolkit and associated GNOME libraries and utilities to build a simple GNOME client. The chapter starts by briefly discussing licensing considerations. You'll then see how to set up and run GNOME's graphical development client GLADE, which you can use for developing GNOME clients. Finally, the chapter presents a short demonstration of using KDE's KDevelop client to build a GNOME client.

Understanding Licensing Issues

How software is distributed can be very important. Software that is distributed in source code form can be very beneficial, especially if you have the tools to build the software from its source. Software that is distributed in binary-only form can also be beneficial, but only if it works well with your operating system and version of software. But even more important than how software is distributed is how the software is licensed.

Software distributed under the GNU General Public License (GPL) will always be free and come with source code. Only one class of software is distributed more freely than GPL software, and that is public domain software. Other than public domain software, any software that is not under the GPL copy-"left" license will have a license with one or more forms of subjective clauses that encumber the possession, use, or distribution of the software. That said, GNOME and its libraries, documentation, and clients are distributed under the GNU GPL. The GNU GPL, along with the Lesser GPL license, offers the greatest freedom to software developers but, in general, also mandates distribution of source code or source code changes to software.

Downloading and Installing GNOME

Although you can download and install GNOME from source, a much easier way to get GNOME is to install a Linux distribution using GNOME or to upgrade your system using native software archives used by your distribution. Most Red Hat Linux–based systems already come with GNOME installed, and you shouldn't have to install additional software libraries unless you chose not to install development software when you first built your system. If you did choose to install the GNU gcc and g++ compiler systems, along with GNOME's development libraries, you'll see them appear in your favorite .rpm archive manager, as shown in Figure 22.1.

If you do not find the GNOME libraries or development tools, you'll need to insert your Linux CD-ROM or download the GNOME distribution over the Internet. To

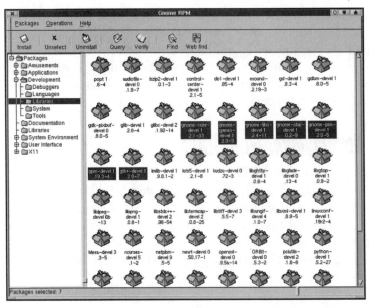

Figure 22.1 *You can use your favorite RPM client, such as* `gnorpm`, *during your X session to check for GNOME's development software.*

use the current version of GNOME's interactive GUI development tools, you'll need the following:

- GTK+ 1.2.0 or greater
- GNOME libraries 1.0.50 or greater
- `automake` 1.4
- `autoconf` 2.13
- The GNU `gettext` package, version 0.10.35

Another way to get GNOME, especially the latest version of Ximian, Inc.'s version of GNOME, is to download an installer and install GNOME via the Internet. If you have broadband access (540Kbps or greater download speed), you can download and install GNOME in less than 20 minutes. Browse to **http://www.ximian.com,** then follow the directions for downloading an installer and a version of GNOME for your system. There are versions of GNOME for nearly any version of XFree86 and Linux, including Linux on the PowerPC CPU.

Programming with GTK+ and GNOME

A full overview of programming GNOME and GNOME clients using the GNOME's development libraries and toolkits is beyond the scope of this book.

However, as discussed in Chapter 21, "Using Qt and KDE," you can use one or more of the sophisticated development tools included with GNOME to develop GNOME-compatible clients. Unlike Qt and KDE development, GNOME client development most commonly requires use of the C language, although you can also use C++. The development clients discussed in this section can help even nonprogrammers get started building clients for GNOME and XFree86.

Simple Client Development with GLADE

GNOME's GLADE, by Damon Chaplin, is a GTK+ user interface builder. Like other development clients, such as Qt Designer or KDevelop, GLADE is a graphical development client for prototyping applications. Unlike Qt Designer, however, GLADE generates a nearly all the source code needed for compiling and building a client, and supports a variety of languages, including C, C++, Ada95, Perl, and Eiffel. You can start GLADE from your desktop's panel menu or the command line of an X terminal window, as follows:

```
# glade &
```

After you press Enter, you'll see GLADE's main window, along with a Properties dialog box and a widget palette, as shown in Figure 22.2.

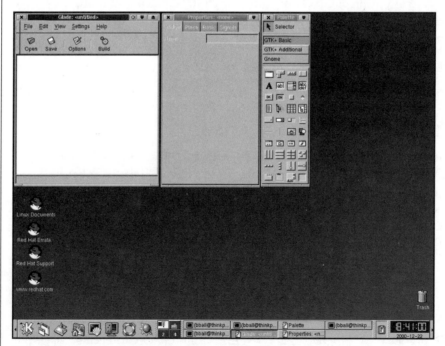

Figure 22.2 *GLADE's initial user interface consists of three separate elements: a main window, a Properties dialog box, and a widget palette.*

The main window is where you control your project. You use the Properties dialog box to fine-tune any created widgets. You can select from three types of widget sets in GLADE's widget palette: GTK+ Basic, GTK+ Additional, and GNOME. To begin your project, click the Save menu item under the File menu. The Project Options dialog box appears (see Figure 22.3). In this dialog box, you specify your project's directory, name, and project file. You can also choose a language and whether or not to include GNOME support. Click the OK button when you finish configuring these settings.

You can also set language options and software library support options. Begin building your project by selecting a portion of your project to create. For example, suppose that you are creating the outline of a simple application. To get the most out of your initial efforts, click the Gnome button on the Palette window. You'll see the palette widget set change. You can then select a client shell to use for your client, named Gnome Application Window (the name will appear as a pop-up message when your pointer hovers over the topmost left icon in the Palette window). Click the icon, and your screen changes as shown in Figure 22.4.

A skeletal GNOME application window appears. Note that the Properties dialog box now lists 16 different resources and settings under the Widget tab that you can apply to your client. For example, you can set the name, titlebar title, default width and height, along with other settings. You can use other tabs to configure other settings; for example, you can use the GK+ Basic tab to add a pop-up tooltip or specific *accelerator* (shortcut) keys.

You can continue to build your client by adding different elements, such as an About dialog box. Click the Palette's GNOME About Dialog icon (the topmost right icon on the Palette), and the About dialog box shown in Figure 22.5 appears.

Figure 22.3 *Use GLADE's Project Options dialog box to configure settings for your project.*

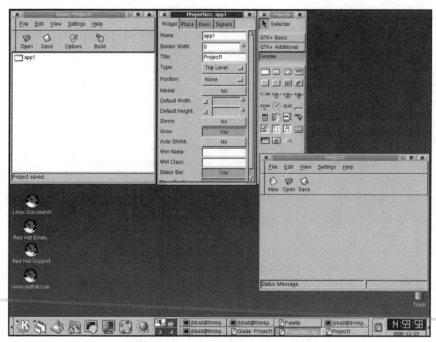

Figure 22.4 *When you use GLADE, building a GNOME client shell is as easy as clicking its icon from the Palette window.*

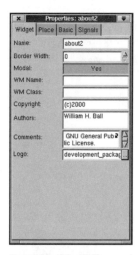

Figure 22.5 *GLADE can also prototype dialog boxes and other elements of your client.*

Click on the Properties dialog box, then enter information for your About dialog box, such as copyright information, author names, and comments. You can also select a logo for the dialog box by clicking the Logo field. When you finished, you can then click the Build toolbar button in the GLADE main window. GLADE will then create an entire source code tree and directory with the name of your project in a subdirectory named `Projects` in your home directory.

The source directory tree contains all the files required to create a `Makefile`, which GLADE then uses to build and assemble your client. The following is an example of such a directory tree:

AUTHORS	NEWS	autogen.sh	pixmaps	CHANGELOG
README	configure.in	po	src	Makefile.in
aconfig.h	macros	project1.glade	stamp-h.in	

To build your client's `Makefile`, navigate into the project directory, then enter the sh command along with the `autogen.sh` shell script as follows:

```
# sh autogen.sh
```

After this script runs, you can then simply use the `make` command to build your client, as follows:

```
# make
```

After you press Enter, you can then navigate into the directory named `src` and run your client by using its name like this:

```
# ./project1
```

After you press Enter, you'll see a dialog box and window, as shown in Figure 22.6.

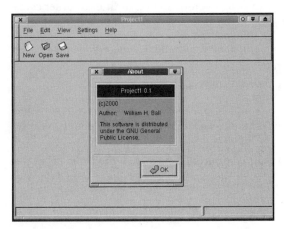

Figure 22.6 *Using GLADE makes creating skeletal clients easy.*

Note, however, that the menus on your client and on the About dialog box do not work at this point. Tying together the actions of menus, accelerator keys, and dialog boxes requires additional work. However, as you can see, using GLADE is one way to get up and running quickly. Although GLADE can save time and effort when designing interfaces for GTK+ and GNOME clients, the hard work is up to you, the programmer.

Simple GNOME Client Development with KDevelop

This section provides a short overview of how to use KDevelop to quickly prototype and build a simple GNOME client. As you learned in Chapter 21, "Using Qt and KDE," KDevelop is a capable development environment with many different features, including the ability to build GNOME clients. You can start KDevelop from KDE's desktop panel, or through an X terminal window as follows:

```
# kdevelop &
```

If you start KDevelop by itself from the command line, you'll see the main window as shown in Figure 21.4. Create your first project by clicking the New menu item under the Project menu. You'll see a six-step KDE Application Wizard, as shown in Figure 21.5.

For example, click the GNOME application under the GNOME drop-down list in the wizard's scrolling window, then click the Next button. You'll then see the Generate Settings dialog box shown in Figure 22.7.

You can also use the subsequent dialog boxes to specify the use of CVS, or to edit the template headers for your project's source code files. When finished, click the Create button. You'll then see the last page of the wizard, as shown in Figure 22.8. Messages scroll by as KDevelop builds your project environment and a skeletal configuration script. Any error messages, such as for missing documentation utilities or other components, appear at the bottom of the dialog box.

If you receive any errors, or if KDevelop is unable to build a project skeleton in your project directory, you may need to reinstall some of the required GNOME components. When you finish configuring your settings, click the Exit button.

In the main KDevelop window, click on the toolbar above the editing window to display various views of your project. For example, KDevelop can display your project by class (object definitions in your source) or simply display the project's source code. Try clicking the LFV button, then click the Sources directory in the browser on the left side of the display. KDevelop then displays your project's source code in the rightmost panel, as shown in Figure 22.9.

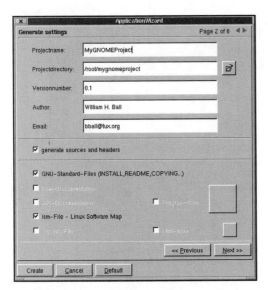

Figure 22.7 *Enter the name of your GNOME project, along with author, email, and other information, when using KDevelop.*

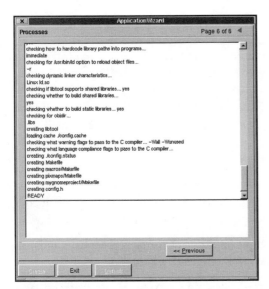

Figure 22.8 *KDevelop automatically checks your build environment when you first create a GNOME project.*

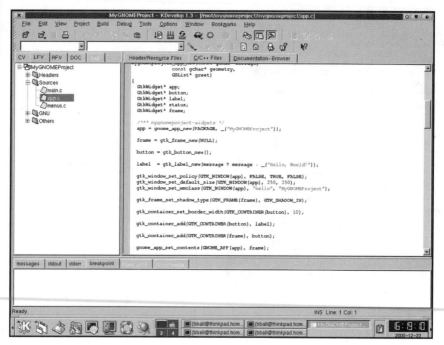

Figure 22.9 *Use KDevelop's main window to browse through your GNOME source code.*

In KDevelop's main editing window, on the right side of the display, you can edit or enter changes and additional code for your GNOME project. Toolbar buttons along the top of the screen (below KDevelop's menu bar) correspond to menu items. The next step is the same as when you use KDevelop to build a KDE client: You use the Build menu's Configure menu item to create a Makefile. If all goes well, you'll see a `*** success ***` message at the bottom of the status window.

The Build menu contains most of the operations that you would normally accomplish from the command line when using the `make` command. You can also use this menu's Make item to build the client using your created `Makefile`. Again, if all goes well, you'll see a `*** success ***` message at the bottom of the status window.

Finally, you can click the Run toolbar button. Your client should launch, and you should see a screen similar to that shown in Figure 22.10.

Note in Figure 22.10 that KDevelop automatically creates your About dialog box and associates it with the skeletal client's Help menu. Thus KDevelop's skeletal build is more advanced than the default GLADE skeletal build. You'll also find that each menu item on the client's menus will also display an associated dialog box, putting you a bit ahead of the game when prototyping clients.

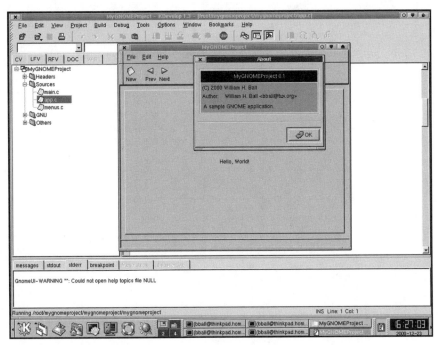

Figure 22.10 *You can also use KDevelop to build and then run your GNOME client.*

Resource Information

http://developer.gnome.org—an online tutorial on programming for GNOME.

http://www-106.ibm.com/developerworks/library/gnome2/?dwzone=linux—IBM's online version of programming for GNOME.

http://www.gnome.org—home page for the GNOME project.

http://glade.pn.org—home page for the GLADE development environment.

http://www.kdevelop.org—home page for the KDevelop KDE development environment.

http://www.lausch.at/gnome/programming/gnome-corba-programming.html—Michael Lausch's online tutorial on programming for GNOME.

http://www2.axian.com/training/linux-gui-gtk-gnome.html—a site offering commercial Linux GUI development training that focuses on GNOME.

http://www.gnu.org—home page for the GNU software distributions, with links to essays, papers, and editorials regarding free software versus Open Source software.

PART V

Connectivity and Resources

23 X11 and Other Operating Systems

Chapter 23: X11 and Other Operating Systems

Using Xvnc

Using Xvnc for MacOS

Using VMware

Using Cygwin

Exploring commercial servers

This chapter provides a short overview of interesting and useful software technologies that you can take advantage of when using XFree86. For example, you'll learn about Xvnc, and how you can use it to control remote desktops,, or to control your own desktop from a remote location. Although you can do this easily if the other computers are using X11, the Xvnc server is cross-platform-independent. This means that you don't have to use X11 on the local or remote server.

You'll also get an introduction on using the VMware emulator, which can help you install and run Linux or other operating systems during your X sessions, or perhaps run XFree86 while using Windows.

Using Xvnc

Xvnc (Virtual Network Computing) is a package of software distributed by AT&T Laboratories in Cambridge, England, and stands for Virtual Network Computing. This amazing software, based on X11R6.3, provides a unique way to run applications across different computer platforms or even on the same computer platform. Distributed under the GNU Public License, Xvnc is available in source code and binary versions are available for a variety of operating systems and computer platforms, including the following:

- DEC Alpha OSF1 3.2
- Java
- Macintosh OS (m68k and PPC)
- Solaris 2.5 (SPARC)
- Win32 (including Windows 9*x* and 2000 as well as Windows NT)
- Windows CE2 2.*x* (for the SH3 and MIPS processors)

Xvnc for Linux

The Xvnc software package for Linux and XFree86 includes a shell script named vnc-server, Xvnc (a modified X server), and a utility client named vncviewer. The package also includes a password client named vncpasswd. You can build the Xvnc software from scratch, but you can get right to work by downloading binary versions for your computer platforms from **http://www.uk.research.att.com/vnc/**. The software should be decompressed and installed. To get started under Linux, first use the vncserver script as follows:

```
# vncserver
```

The script prompts you to enter a password:

```
Password:
```

Type a password used to allow remote access, then press Enter. The program again asks you to verify the password:

```
Verify:
New 'X' desktop is thinkpad.home.org:1

Creating default startup script /root/.vnc/xstartup
Starting applications specified in /root/.vnc/xstartup
Log file is /root/.vnc/thinkpad.home.org:1.log
```

After you type the password again and press Enter, the Xvnc server starts. First, note the $DISPLAY number returned by the server (1 in this example). You'll need to know this number later on if you want to connect remotely. Also note that the server creates a directory named .vnc in your home directory, and copies a file named xstartup to that directory. This file contains directions on the type of virtual X session to run when a remote viewer requests a connection. The file looks like the following:

```
#!/bin/sh

xrdb $HOME/.Xresources
xsetroot -solid grey
xterm -geometry 80x24+10+10 -ls -title "$VNCDESKTOP Desktop" &
twm &
```

As you can see, the default session will use the twm window manager. You can edit this script before starting Xvnc to use a different window manager or to launch various clients before starting twm. The vncserver script also recognizes the X Toolkit -geometry setting, so that you can assign a default size to your sessions. For example, the default session will be 1,024×768, but if you'd prefer to have a remote session at 800×600, use the vncserver client as follows:

```
# vncserver -geometry 800x600
```

Now that you've started the server on your local computer, other remote users can connect and log in, provided they know the password and have an active account.

Xvnc for Windows

To initialize Xvnc on a remote Windows computer, you must download and copy the Windows version of Xvnc onto the computer, then extract its archive with a utility such as WinZip.

You install the Win32 vnc software using the Xvnc SETUP.EXE command, and you can run the Win32 version of Xvnc as a server or as a program. To run Xvnc as a server, first open your desktop's Start menu and click Vnc from the Programs folder, then open the Administrative Tools folder and click the Install Default Registry Settings menu item, as shown in Figure 23.1.

The registry settings will then be updated with information about Xvnc. Click the OK button in the resulting dialog to dismiss the dialog. Next, you can then click the Install WinVNC Service menu item from the Administrative Tools folder. The first time that you run this program, you need to enter a password in the dialog box, then click OK. You can change settings by using the Properties menu item from the Win-Vnc pop-up menu on the Windows taskbar. WinVNC then displays the Current User Properties dialog box shown in Figure 23.2.

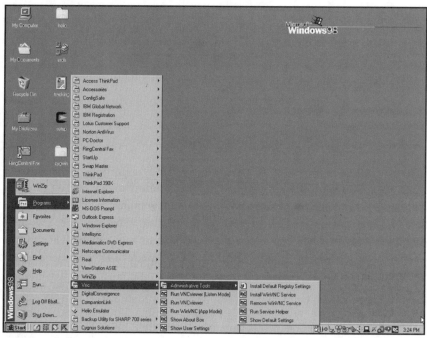

Figure 23.1 *You must first install the Xvnc registry settings under Windows.*

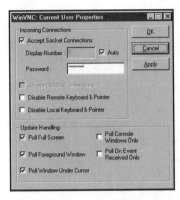

Figure 23.2 *You can modify your password and other settings through the WinVNC Current User Properties dialog box.*

When you finish configuring your settings, click the OK button. You are now ready to view the Windows desktop from a remote Linux computer. To do this, use the vncviewer command on the Linux command line, along with the Windows computer's hostname (or IP address) and server display number (which defaults to 0 for Windows computers):

```
$ vncviewer stinky:0
VNC server supports protocol version 3.3 (viewer 3.3)
Password:
```

When prompted, enter the password. After you press Enter, you'll see the remote desktop.

To view a Linux desktop from a remote Windows computer, launch the Vnc viewer program from the Windows Start menu, as shown in Figure 23.3.

The Connection Details dialog box then appears, as shown in Figure 23.4. Use this dialog box to specify the IP address or hostname of the remote computer (running Linux or another operating system). Also in this dialog box, you specify the $DIS-PLAY number returned when the Xvnc server was started on the remote computer. (Again, this number will always be 0 for any Windows computer, but could be different on remote Linux or UNIX machines.)

When you finish configuring these settings, click the OK button. You then see the remote Linux session, running the twm window manager and a number of X clients, as shown in Figure 23.5.

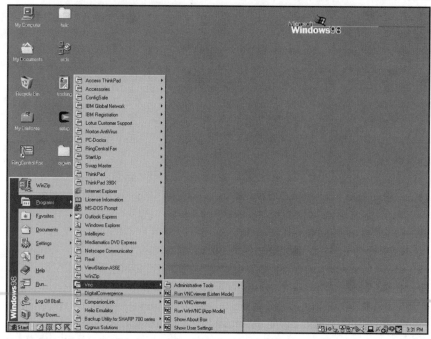

Figure 23.3 *After installing Xvnc, you can begin viewing a remote Linux X session by using the Vnc viewer program.*

Figure 23.4 *Specify the remote IP address or hostname, along with the $DISPLAY- number to connect.*

Using Xvnc for MacOS

Macintosh users don't have to feel left out, because there is a version of Xvnc for the MacOS. To begin, download and install the Mac Xvnc package. Next, select the Vnc Server Control Panel device, as shown in Figure 23.6.

Note that several tabs appear at the top of the dialog box. Click the Display 0 tab, as shown in Figure 23.7, to enter or change your Xvnc MacOS server password.

After you finish configuring your password, click OK or press Cmd+Q to quit the panel device. You can now start the server from the desktop's Apple menu, as shown in Figure 23.8.

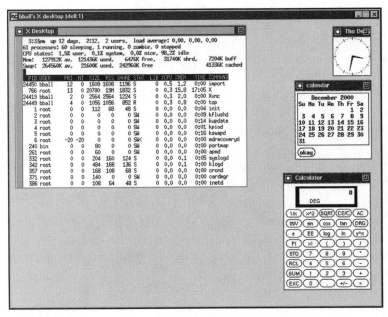

Figure 23.5 *You can view remote Linux sessions when you use Xvnc to run Windows.*

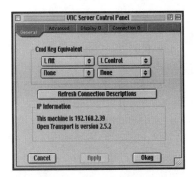

Figure 23.6 *Use the Macintosh Xvnc Server Control Panel under MacOS to verify your IP address.*

Figure 23.7 *Use the Display 0 tab on the Xvnc Control Panel to modify your password.*

You can then connect from a remote computer using the vncviewer client. To view a remote host desktop on your MacOS desktop, launch the VNC Viewer client from the MacOS Apple menu. The New VNC Connection dialog box appears, as shown in Figure 23.9. This dialog box is similar to that which you would see under XFree86 or Windows.

You'll need to specify a hostname or IP address, then a $DISPLAY number. After you click the OK button, the client prompts you for the remote computer's password.

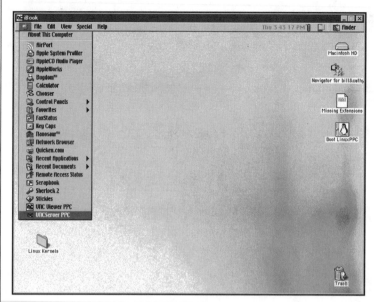

Figure 23.8 *Start Xvnc from the MacOS desktop's Apple menu.*

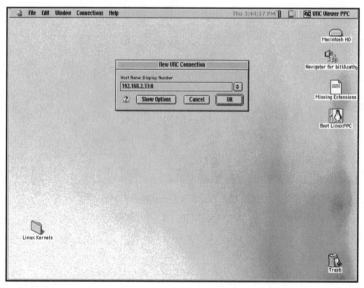

Figure 23.9 *You can view remote Linux sessions while running MacOS by using Xvnc's VNC Viewer and entering a remote IP address, a display number, and then a password.*

Using VMware

Vmware, from VMware, Inc., is an X11 client that can create a virtual host for other operating systems, such as different versions of Linux, DOS, FreeBSD, and the Windows family of operating systems. The client accomplishes this by using a virtual filesystem on your hard drive (somewhat like that used by DOSEMU).

Unlike Xvnc, VMware is a commercial product. You must have a valid license key in order to run this software. To install VMware, download the software (which can be a 6MB compressed tarball or .rpm archive), then install it as root, as in the following example:

```
# tar xvzf VMware-2.0.3-799.tar.gz
# cd vm*
# ./vmware-install.pl
Creating a new installer database using the tar2 format.


Installing the content of the package.


In which directory do you want to install the binary files?
[/usr/bin] /usr/local/bin
In which directory do you want to install the library files?
[/usr/local/lib/vmware]
The path "/usr/local/lib/vmware" does not exist currently. This script is going
to create it, including needed parent directories. Is this what you want?
[yes]
In which directory do you want to install the manual files?
[/usr/local/share/man]
The path "/usr/local/share/man" does not exist currently. This script is going
to create it, including needed parent directories. Is this what you want?
[yes]
In which directory do you want to install the documentation files?
[/usr/local/share/doc/vmware]
The path "/usr/local/share/doc/vmware" does not exist currently. This script is
going to create it, including needed parent directories. Is this what you want?
[yes]
What is the directory under which the init scripts reside (it should contain
init.d/, and from rc0.d/ to rc6.d/)? [/etc/rc.d]
Before running VMware for the first time, you need to configure it for your
running kernel by invoking the following command:
"/usr/local/bin/vmware-config.pl".
Do you want this script to invoke the command for you now? [yes]
```

During the install, the installation script checks your system for compatibility, builds any needed software, and then asks whether you want to enable the virtual host to use networking:

```
Do you want this script to automatically configure your system to allow your
Virtual Machines to access the host filesystem? (yes/no/help)  yes
```

Follow the prompts for networking information and finish the install. After installing your license key, a file named `license` under a folder named `.vmware` in your home directory, you can then start VMware from the command line as follows:

```
$ vmware
```

After you press Enter, the VMware Workstation dialog box appears, as shown in Figure 23.10.

Use VMware's Configuration Wizard to select the type of operating system that you'd like to install, along with other configuration options, such as the size of the virtual host filesystem. You should then use the main window's File menu to save your configuration. If you need to edit the configuration, click the Settings menu, then click Configuration Editor. You'll then see its dialog box shown in Figure 23.11.

You can use this editor to change the drivers, network adapters, or serial and parallel ports, or to alter settings for the mouse, sound, memory, and operating system. After saving your configuration, you can then install the operating system using a floppy disk or CD-ROM. First, click the Power On button in the VMware window. You'll see an initial PC boot screen, complete with BIOS information. Install your operating system (as shown in Figure 23.12), then reboot or restart VMware.

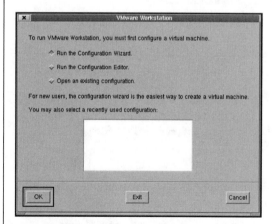

Figure 23.10 *Use the VMware Workstation dialog box to prepare a host filesystem for your operating system install.*

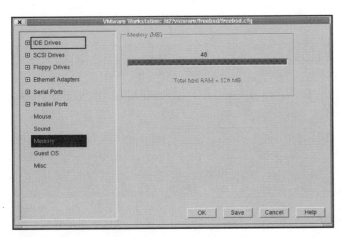

Figure 23.11 *Use the Configuration Editor to make any last-minute changes to your virtual system.*

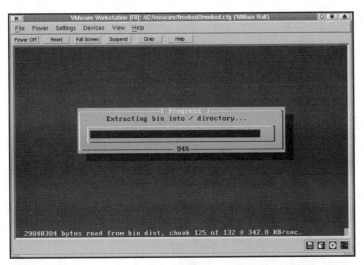

Figure 23.12 *VMware supports the installation and use of a variety of operating systems under Linux and XFree86, such as FreeBSD, shown here.*

The next time that you start VMware, the client asks you to choose a configuration. This feature is handy, as you can have several different operating systems installed on a single hard drive. While VMWare is active, your mouse becomes "attached" (unable to move beyond the confines of the VMWare window) to the operating system's window if you click in the window. Press Ctrl+Alt+Esc in order to "release" your mouse.

Using Cygwin

The Cygwin XFree86 distribution, whose current version is 4.0.1, is for the Win32 platform. This means that if you use Windows 95, 98, NT 4.0, 2000, or Me, you may be able to use XFree86. You'll need to download quite a bit of software and follow numerous steps, but the effort can be worthwhile.

First, download the file SETUP.EXE from the Cygwin site or a mirror (see "Resources Information" at the end of this chapter). Next, run the program and follow the dialog boxes to choose a download directory, connection type, and source for the download. After the download is complete, again run SETUP.EXE to install the Cygwin toolset on your Windows computer. Although the download of 45MB of software can take a while, the initial install takes only a minute or so. After installation, a directory named cygwin, with nearly 370MB of files, will be installed on your C drive. You'll be able to use a bash shell under Windows (as shown in Figure 23.13), and many of your favorite GNU software tools will be available for use.

Windows 9x Users Left Out?

The Cygwin XFree86 project is in flux. Although earlier versions worked with Windows 9x, and despite the information provided at the Cygwin Web site, the current version may work only for Windows 2000 and NT 4.0 and ME. If you're interested in using Cygwin's port of XFree86, check the site **http://www.cygwin.com** regularly for updates, as development on this project is active and new versions are being worked on.

Figure 23.13 *You can use the Cygwin GNU toolset, which includes the* bash *shell,* gcc *compiler, and many other tools under Windows.*

Next, you need to download XFree86 4.0.1 from the Cygwin site, then copy, decompress, and extract the archives in the root Cygwin directory on your Windows hard drive. This download requires an additional 60MB of hard drive space.

According to the Cygwin folks, all you then need to do is to double-click the file named `startxwin.bat` via Windows Explorer, and X will start in full-screen mode. You'll then be able to access other X desktops on your LAN and enjoy the benefits of X.

Exploring Commercial Servers

You can still buy a commercial X server for Intel-based PCs running Linux from at least two sources: Metro Linux, Inc., and Xi Graphics. These servers do offer some advantages in that you may find better support and performance for a particular family of graphics cards, or support for the newest and latest graphics cards. Although most Linux users happily conduct business using XFree86, if you are in a commercial production environment and need that extra bit of performance when using X, you can turn to a commercial server.

If you're a Windows user, you can also check out StarNet's X-Win32 commercial X server for Windows, which includes a terminal application along with a secure-shell solution for X. Other products include Hummingbird's Exceed, XLink's Omni-X, and Pexus System's X-Deep/32 for Windows. In the past, many of these packages were exceedingly expensive, but with the advent of Open Source software and free software from the GNU project, many packages are now reasonably priced and come with technical support and upgrades. But don't be surprised if some are just like XFree86!

Resource Information

http://www.metrolink.com—home page for the commercial Metro-X server for Linux.

http://www.xig.com—home page for the commercial X server from Xi Graphics; there are versions for laptops and desktops.

ftp://ftp.sunsite.utk.edu/pub/cygwin/latest/—one of many mirrors for the Cygwin SETUP.EXE command and related software.

http://cygwin.com/xfree/docs/howto/book1.htm—detailed instructions on downloading and installing Cygwin and XFree86 for Windows.

http://www.uk.research.att.com/vnc/xvnc.html—home page for downloading the latest version of Xvnc.

Jason Compton, *VMware 2 for Linux* (Rocklin, CA: Prima Publishing, 2000)—a fabulous book covering the use of VMware with FreeBSD, DOS, Wine, and Windows 95, 98, 2000, and NT.

http://www.vmware.com—home page for VMware, Inc., from which you can download test or demo versions of VMware for Linux.

http://www.starnet.com/products/—home page for StarNets' X-Win32 X software.

http://www.labtam.fi/why.html—Labtam's Winaxe X server software for Windows.

http://www.hummingbird.com—home page for Hummingbird's Exceed product, which provides X support for Windows.

Appendix: Essential X11 Resources

Popular X11 clients

WWW URLs

Usenet newsgroups

Mailing lists

This appendix provides a short list of essential resources for the X11 and XFree86 user. Although this book has concentrated on XFree86 and Linux running on Intel-based PC platforms, many of the concepts, strategies, and use of X11 will apply to other computer platforms. The appendix is organized into several parts: a section covering popular X clients; a section listing invaluable Web resources; a listing of pertinent Usenet newsgroups; and various mailing lists that may help provide answers or an avenue for questions.

If you're looking for definitive technical information regarding X11, download the source to X11R6.5 from **http://www.X.org**. The source archives contain technical papers by the authors and X programming, generally in compressed PostScript form.

Popular X11 Clients

Table A.1 lists just a few common X11 clients, along with a concise description (the table was derived from output of the `apropos` command). You can generally learn more about a command by reading its man page, and you may find documentation under the `/usr/doc/`, `/usr/share/doc`, or `/usr/info` directories. If you're looking for a specific client or game for X11, use your favorite search engine (such as **http://google.com**) or Linux link (**http://freshmeat.net**)—you're sure to find what you're looking for!

Table A.1 X Clients and Descriptions

Client	Description
animate	Displays image sequences
bitmap	Provides a simple X bitmap editor
bmtoa	Converts an X bitmap to ASCII
bounce	Displays an X screensaver
display	Views and edits ImageMagick images
editres	Edits X11 resources
flsfonts	Lists X fonts
fly8	Simulates an X11 flight
fsinfo	Provides an X font server utility
gears	Displays an X screensaver
gedit	Provides a simple GNOME text editor
gphoto	Downloads a digital camera and edits images
gv	Views and prints PostScript files

Table A.1 X Clients and Descriptions *(continued)*

Client	Description
ico	Displays an X graphic demonstration
import	Captures a local or remote X display
kmahjongg	Offers a KDE Mah-Jongg game
kscd	Launches a KDE CD player
lxdoom	Provides a port of DOOM for X
maze	Launches an X11 demonstration that creates and solves a random maze
mcam	Provides an X11 front-end for the Zora Web cam
mcookie	Generates magic cookies for xauth
mkfontdir	Builds an index of X font files in a directory
oclock	Displays a round X clock
pbmtoxbm	Converts a portable bitmap into an X11 bitmap
ppmtopuzz	Converts a portable pixmap into an X11 "puzzle" file
ppmtoxpm	Converts a portable pixmap into an X11 pixmap
rclock	Displays an X11 clock with appointments and alarms
showfont	Provides an X11 font dump utility
showrgb	Displays an X color table (rgb.txt)
startx	Starts an X session with optional arguments
viewres	Provides a graphical class browser for X
x11perf	Tests the performance of X11 servers
x11perfcomp	Compares the performance of X11 servers
xaumix	Launches an aumix audio mixer wrapper for X
xauth	Provides an X authority file utility
xbiff	Launches a mailbox flag client for X
xbmtopbm	Converts an X11 or X10 bitmap into a portable bitmap
xboing	Provides the classic X Breakout game
xcalc	Displays a scientific calculator for X
xcam	Launches the graphical camera front-end for SANE
xclipboard	Provides an X clipboard client
xclock	Displays an analog or digital clock for X
xcmap	Displays a default colormap on X11 displays
xconsole	Provides a system monitor for console messages with X
xcutsel	Provides an interchange between cut buffer and selection
xditview	Displays ditroff output
xdm	Launches the X display manager
xdpyinfo	Displays an information utility for X
xearth	Displays a rotating image of the earth in color in the root window

Table A.1 X Clients and Descriptions *(continued)*

Client	Description
xedit	Launches a simple text editor for X
xev	Shows the contents of X events
xeyes	Displays an unnerving follow-the-mouse X demonstration
xf86cfg	Provides a graphical configuration tool for XFree86 4.0
xf86config	Generates XF86Config files
xfd	Shows all the characters in an X font
xfindproxy	Locates the proxy services utility
xflame	Draws animated flames
xfontsel	Enables point-and-click selection of X11 font names
xfs	Launches the X font server
xfwp	Provides the X firewall proxy
xgalaga	Launches an X arcade game
xgamma	Alters a monitor's gamma correction for XFree86
xgc	Displays an X drawing demonstration
xhost	Provides the server access control program for X
xieperf	Launches the XIE server extension test and demo program
xinit	Initializes the X Window system
xjack	Displays an "all work and no play" screensaver
xjewel	Provides a classic falling-blocks X game
xkbcomp	Compiles an XKB keyboard description
xkbevd	Runs an XKB event daemon
xkbprint	Prints an XKB keyboard description
xkill	Kills a client by its X resource
xkobo	Launches a video-oriented game for X
xli	Loads images into an X11 window or onto the root window
xlincity	Launches the LinCity simulator for X
xload	Displays the system load average for X
xlock	Locks the password for the local X display
xlogo	Displays the X Window system logo
xlsclients	Lists client applications running on a display
xlsfonts	Displays the server font list for X
xmag	Magnifies parts of the screen
xmahjongg	Launches a classic Mah-Jongg game for X
xman	Displays manual pages
xmatrix	Provides an X screensaver that simulates computer displays
xmessage	Displays a message client

Table A.1 X Clients and Descriptions *(continued)*

Client	Description
xmh	Launches a mail transport utility with an X interface to Message Handler
xmixer	Provides a simple audio mixer client for X
xmkmf	Generates a Makefile from an Imakefile
xmodmap	Modifies keymaps and pointer button mappings in X
xon	Starts an X program on a remote machine
xosview	Launches a graphic system load client
xpat2	Provides a solitaire patience card game for X11
xplaycd	Launches a simple X audio CD player
xpmtoppm	Converts an X11 pixmap into a portable pixmap
xprop	Displays X properties
xrdb	Provides the X server resource database utility
xrefresh	Refreshes all or part of an X screen
xroger	Displays an X logo screensaver
xsane	Launches the scanner front-end for SANE
xscanimage	Scans X11 images
xset	Enables the user to configure preferences for X
xsetmode	Sets the mode for an X input device
xsetpointer	Sets an X Input device as the main pointer
xsetroot	Sets root window parameters for X
xsm	Manages X sessions
xstdcmap	Displays the standard X colormap
xsublim	Displays an X screensaver
xteevee	Displays a screensaver that simulates various TV problems
xterm	Launches the terminal emulator for X
xv	Views, converts, and edits an X11 image
xvidtune	Tunes video modes for XFree86
xvminitoppm	Converts an XV "thumbnail" picture to the PPM format
xvpictoppm	Converts XV 'thumbnail' files to the standard PPM format
xwd	Captures an X11 display
xwdtopnm	Converts an X11 or X10 window dump file into a portable anymap
xwininfo	Displays window information for X
xwud	Displays an xwd capture

WWW URLs

This section presents a short list of essential Web sites with information about X and XFree86. Many hundreds of Web sites are devoted to X, XFree86, X11 programming, and X clients, but these pages provide a good starting place for more information:

http://www.xfree86.org—the definitive home page for XFree86.

http://www.X.org—home page for the custodians of X, X.org.

http://www.openmotif.org—also known as the MotifZone, this site is the best place for the latest information about OpenMotif.

http://www.rahul.net/kenton/xsites.framed.html—without a doubt the "Mother Lode" of X and Motif information. Kenton Lee has put together the best place to start if you want to learn about X, Motif, or X programming, or read about X.

http://www.cs.utexas.edu/users/kharker/linux-laptop/—the first place that you should check regarding using X on a laptop. This site lists hundreds of laptop models, with links to owners' pages filled with solutions and answers to getting X up and running on a laptop.

http://www.gnome.org—the definitive starting place for GNOME users.

http://www.koffice.org—home page for the K Office suite.

http://www.konqueror.org—development page for the KDE konqueror Web browser and file manager.

http://www.kdevelop.org—KDE's GUI developer client's home page.

http://devel-home.kde.org—home page for a number of KDE clients.

http://developer.kde.org—home page for KDE developers.

http://lists.kde.org—a page of KDE mailing lists.

http://artist.kde.org—a page for KDE icon/graphic artists.

http://bugs.kde.org—report your KDE bugs to this site.

http://i18n.kde.org—KDE internationalization and translation utility development.

http://kde.themes.org—home page for various KDE themes.

http://dot.kde.org—KDE news.

http://webcvs.kde.org—CVS access to KDE sources.

http://multimedia.kde.org—KDE multimedia client pages.

http://games.kde.org—home page for various KDE games.

Finally, if you're a registered user of a commercial Linux distribution, always check the company's Web site for support issues, bug fixes, or updates. If you have a problem getting a particular graphics card to work with XFree86, check the card's manufacturer for possible Open Source drivers or other support—and ask the manufacturer to provide support for Linux!

Usenet Newsgroups

This section lists some Usenet newsgroups with discussions focused on X11 and specific computer platforms. If you have a question regarding a problem with X, XFree86, or Linux, make sure that you follow these guidelines:

- Always post your question in the correct newsgroup.
- Don't post across many groups.
- Always use a clear subject line in your post.
- Don't rant and rave or use obscene language; you'll be ignored.
- Include as much technical information about the problem as possible, such as the type of graphics card, Linux kernel, XFree86 distribution version, and so on.

Here then are the Usenet groups:

comp.os.linux.x—discussion about Linux and X.

comp.unix.aux—discussions about Apple's defunct AU/X.

comp.unix.bsd.freebsd—discussions about FreeBSD.

comp.unix.bsd.netbsd—discussions about NetBSD.

comp.unix.bsd.openbsd.misc—discussions about OpenBSD.

comp.unix.cde—discussions about Common Desktop Environment.

comp.unix.machten—discussions about Tenon's BSD for MacOS.

comp.unix.osf.osf1—discussions about OSF/1.

comp.unix.programmer—discussions about programming under UNIX.

comp.unix.tru64—Tru64 UNIX discussions.

comp.windows.x.announce—announcements about X.

comp.windows.x.apps—discussions about X-based applications.

comp.windows.x.i386unix—discussions about X for UNIX PCs.

comp.windows.x.intrinsics—X Toolkit library discussions.

comp.windows.x.kde—KDE and X discussions.

comp.windows.x.motif—all about Motif.

comp.windows.x—discussions about X in general.

Mailing Lists

This section provides a short list of mailing lists that you may find useful. Note that each list may have different ways to subscribe and unsubscribe. You can usually get help with a mailing list by using a built-in help facility. Carefully note any preliminary messages received from a mail-list server and save the messages for future reference.

> **http://www.geocrawler.com/lists/3/**—although not a mailing list, this Web page provides links to Linux and X-related archives of mailing lists.

> **win32-x11 (win32-x11@sources.redhat.com)**—a general discussion about using X11 under Windows 32 platforms.

> **linux-x11 (majordomo@vger.rutgers.edu)**—a mailing list about Linux and using X11.

> **mklinux-x (mklinux-x-request@mklinux.apple.com)**—a (possibly) defunct mailing list about using Linux and X on Macintosh platforms

Table A.2 lists some GNOME-oriented mailing lists, as listed at **http://mail.gnome.org/mailman/listinfo**. You can quickly subscribe to any of these lists by clicking on a list's name. You'll also find direct links to many other GNOME lists at **http://www.gnome.org/resources/mailing-lists.html**.

Table A.2 GNOME Mailing Lists

Mailing List	Description
foundation-announce	Official GNOME Foundation announcements
gnome-1.4-list	Release coordination for GNOME 1.4
gnome-announce-list	GNOME announcements only
gnome-db-list	GNOME-DB discussions
gnome-debugger-list	Debugging tools for GNOME
gnome-devel-list	GNOME development
gnome-devtools	Discussion of GNOME development tools
gnome-doc-list	GNOME documentation issues
gnome-gui-list	GNOME GUI standards
gnome-kde-list	GNOME/KDE interoperability
gnome-list	General discussions
gnome-office-list	Discussion of the GNOME office suite
gnome-pilot-list	Tools for GNOME and hand-held pilots
GNOME-sound-list	GNOME sounds

Table A.2 GNOME Mailing Lists *(continued)*

Mailing List	Description
gnome-themes-list	GNOME and GTK+ themes
Gnome-ui-hackers	The GNOME User Interface team administrative mailing list
gnome-workshop-list	GNOME office suite
gnomecc-list	GNOME Control Center
gnumeric-list	GNOME spreadsheet
gtk-app-devel-list	Information on writing applications with GTK+
gtk-devel-list	Development of GTK+
gtk-doc-list	Coordination of GTK+ documentation
gtk-list	General discussion of GTK+
orbit-list	ORBit CORBA implementation use and development

Table A.3 lists some KDE-oriented mailing lists, as listed and archived at **http://lists.kde.org**. You can peruse the contents of any of these lists by clicking on a list's name.

Table A.3 KDE Mailing Lists

List	Description
kde	General discussions about KDE
kde-announce	KDE announcements
kde-artists	KDE artist issues
kde-bugs-dist	Discussions and announcements of bugs
kde-core-devel	Information for developers
kde-cvs	Discussions of using KDE's CVS
kde-devel	Information for developers
kde-freeqt	Discussions about the FreeQt toolkit
kde-i18n	Discussions about internationalization
kde-i18n-doc	Discussions about translations and internationalization
kde-java	Discussions about KDE and Java
kde-kdoc	KDE documentation
kde-kimageshop	KDE graphics client discussion
kde-krn-devel	Newsreader use and development
kde-licensing	KDE licensing issues

Table A.3 KDE Mailing Lists *(continued)*

List	Description
kde-multimedia	KDE multimedia client issues
kde-pim	KDE personal information manager (PIM) issues
kde-user	Discussion about using KDE
kde2-porting	KDE client porting issues
kdevelop	Discussions about using and developing with KDevelop
kdevelop-bugs	Bug discussions
kfm-devel	`kfm` development (may soon be obsolete)
klyx	Discussions about using the `klyx` editor
kmail	Mail client discussions
koffice	Discussions about using KOffice clients
koffice-devel	Developers' issues with KOffice

Finally, don't overlook information included with the Linux HOWTOs or FAQs. A number of these concise guides cover X11 topics, such as using fonts or remote terminals. You'll find links to these documents through **http://www.linuxdoc.org**. Table A.4 lists a few HOWTOs that may be of interest to you.

Table A.4 Linux HOWTOs

HOWTO	Description
LBX-mini-HOWTO	Using low-bandwidth X
NCD-X-Terminal-mini-HOWTO	Using an NCD X terminal
Netscape+Proxy-mini-HOWTO	Setting up a proxy server for Netscape
Remote-X-Apps-mini-HOWTO	Running remote X clients
X-Big-Cursor-mini-HOWTO	Enlarging your X pointer
XFree86-HOWTO	Installing, configuring, and using XFree86
XFree86-Touch-Screen-HOWTO	Using touch screens
Xinerama-HOWTO	Setting up dual-head displays
Xterm-Title-mini-HOWTO	Using titles in `xterm` titlebars
XWindow-User-HOWTO	General X11 user advice